50 Ways to Close the Achievement Gap

THIRD EDITION

Institute for Learning Partnership
University of Wisconsin-Green Bay
2420 Nicolet Dr, WH 424
Green Bay, WI 54311-7001

50 Ways to Close the Achievement Gap

THIRD EDITION

Carolyn J. Downey
Betty E. Steffy
William K. Poston, Jr.
Fenwick W. English

CORWIN PRESS
A SAGE Company

For information:

Corwin Press
A SAGE Company
2455 Teller Road
Thousand Oaks, California 91320
www.corwinpress.com

SAGE Ltd.
1 Oliver's Yard
55 City Road
London EC1Y 1SP
United Kingdom

SAGE India Pvt. Ltd.
B 1/I 1 Mohan Cooperative
   Industrial Area
Mathura Road, New Delhi 110 044
India

SAGE Asia-Pacific Pte. Ltd.
33 Pekin Street #02-01
Far East Square
Singapore 048763

Printed in the United States of America.

Library of Congress Cataloging-in-Publication Data

50 ways to close the achievement gap/Carolyn J. Downey . . . [et al.]. — 3rd ed.
    p. cm.
Includes bibliographical references and index.
ISBN 978-1-4129-5897-4 (cloth)
ISBN 978-1-4129-5898-1 (pbk.)
    1. Academic achievement. 2. School improvement programs. I. Downey, Carolyn J. II. Title: Fifty ways to close the achievement gap.

LB1062.6.A15 2009
379.1′58—dc22   2008017913

This book is printed on acid-free paper.

08   09   10   11   12   10   9   8   7   6   5   4   3   2

Acquisitions Editor:	Hudson Perigo
Editorial Assistant:	Lesley Blake
Production Editor:	Libby Larson
Copy Editor:	Kathy Anne Savadel
Typesetter:	C&M Digitals (P) Ltd.
Proofreader:	Theresa Kay
Indexer:	Molly Hall
Cover Designer:	Lisa Miller
Graphic Designer:	Karine Hovsepian

Contents

Preface

Creating High Performing Schools: It Isn't Just About the Curriculum!

There is no mystery to developing high-performing schools. The major problem is how educators, schooling critics, and many within the public think about them. The term *low-performing schools* typically conjures up images of poor teaching; lazy or unmotivated faculty; incompetent administrators; overcrowded classrooms; outdated textbooks; or tragically stupid, hostile, or unmotivated students. A low-performing school is considered "bad," and the traditional remedies run the gamut from doing more work ("better" planning, staff development, class size reduction, technology, curriculum change, some new off-the-shelf remedy) to doing something different (extending the school day, parent tutors, community involvement, uniforms, block scheduling, peer collaboration) to doing away with them (academic bankruptcy, probation, intervention, takeover, privatization, vouchers, etc.).

None of these approaches address the true nature of the problem. Instead of jumping to a solution designed to solve the problem of low student performance (low-performing schools), the strategies recommended in these pages begin at the end and work back. The end is how low-performing schools are identified through an evaluation instrument of some sort—usually by one or more tests. Thus, the solution to the problem begins by separating out the evaluation instrument and trying to determine the following:

- How the instruments in use define learning and teaching, both implicitly and explicitly
- How the assessment selects exactly which learnings will be measured
- How measured learnings and sublearnings can be tracked back to specific materials provided to teachers to teach (normally called a *curriculum*)
- Which learnings and sublearnings that are included in the curriculum are also included on the test, and which of those learnings are not on the test

- Which learnings and sublearnings not included in the curriculum are on the test, at least to the point of test mastery (developing a supplementary curriculum)

In short, *it is the test or assessment instrument that defines what performances are to be expected*. It is the testing norms that define acceptable levels of performance. These are not established by the curriculum. Curriculum standards are independent of test specifications. In many cases, the curriculum framework is so nebulous that a test actually represents a further delineation of the curriculum instead of a congruent measurement of it. That is why working from an inadequate curriculum framework will not improve test scores unless one is unusually lucky.

The educator who understands the problem must begin by understanding that a low-performing school has been identified by a test of student learning and that assessment is but a sample of all the learning going on in any school. Understanding the nature of sampling, knowing what and where school learning will be sampled, and ensuring that tested learning will be adequately taught to students represents the means to remove a school from the category of low-performing, and that's all it means. It doesn't necessarily mean that the school suddenly becomes "good." All it means is that the performance that the test is sampling looks better within the boundaries of the test. There are a lot of good schools whose test scores are low.

In short, performance is always defined by the instrument measuring and defining it, not by the curriculum that included it or the teacher who taught it. The test is the final arbiter of performance. And we all know that tests aren't perfect. That is why it is even more critical to know something about the dynamics of raising student test scores by starting with the test instead of ending with its administration.

The bottom line is pretty simple: *Don't surprise the kids!* Tests that surprise children translate into a measurement of that which they were not taught and did not learn. A second corollary is *don't surprise the teachers!* Chances are that if teachers are surprised, students will also be surprised. We advocate in this publication the doctrine of *no surprises for teachers and children*.

Tests of accountability are not primarily diagnostic. They are designed to establish, or result in the establishment of, a foundation for legal and often-punitive actions on the part of state agencies and authorities against administrators, teachers, students, and certain school communities. These communities are often those most in need of help: children of the poor and of color. The well-documented correlation among socioeconomic status, gender, and race has run through the testing literature for at least 3 decades, and that's no accident. Avoiding serious interrogation of the tests at the end of the sequence simply perpetuates the status quo. In fact, for schools serving the poor, there is no way off the bottom of an imposed bell curve without paying strict attention to the parameters, content, and testing protocols embodied on the instrument that identifies low-performing schools.

This book is about how to unmask the variables and practices that account for low-performing schools and turn them into high-performing schools. It is about how to put an end to the self-fulfilling and false prophecies that poverty or certain gender and race automatically translate into low test performance. It is about opportunity. It is about equity. It is about fairness. It begins with knowing where to start. Whatever defines performance and the norms regarding low, middle, and high performance, *it isn't just the curriculum!*

Acknowledgments

A book is always a node in a much larger network of people and ideas. This one is no exception. Indeed, *50 Ways* began as a conversation around schools in great need of change. Carolyn J. Downey, one of the senior authors, remarked that there were *at least* "50 ways" to bring about that change. That led to creating some kind of framework in which to position the "50 ways" and to more forms of staff development around them.

This book is an extension of many of the precepts and standards in the curriculum management audit that was unveiled by Fenwick W. English in 1979 in Columbus, Ohio. From the audit came the Downey "walk-through" model, deep alignment methods, curriculum-driven budgeting, and many more derivations, including "50 ways."

We acknowledge the work of many, many colleagues and collaborators over the past 20 years who have contributed to the rich tapestry that is woven throughout this book: Roger Anton, Joe Bazenas, Judy Birmingham, Virginia Boris, Bruce Burpee, Curtis Cain, Laura Canciamilla, Mary Cannie, Charles Chernosky, Elizabeth Clark, Randall Clegg, Laverne Daniels, Patricia Dickson, Robert Douglas, Beverly Freedman, Penny Gray, Audrey Hains, Jan Jacob, Gene Johnson, Holly Jean Kemp, Daniel King, Penny Kowal, David Lutkemeir, Olive McArdle-Kulas, Jackie Mitchell, Margret Montgomery, John Murdoch, Beverly Nichols, Carlos Pagan, Ricki Price-Baugh, Eve Profitt, Cole Pugh, Joanne Rice, Carolyn Ross, John Rouse, James Scott, Josephine Scott, Sue Shidaker, Keven Singer, William Streshly, Rosanne Stripling, Eustace Thompson, Nancy Timmons, Joy Torgerson, Susan Townsend, Jeff Tuneberg, Susan Van Hoozer, John Van Pelt, and Patricia Williams. A special thanks to Holly Kaptain for her suggestions and commentary.

Finally, we want to pay tribute to two of our original senior cadre who tragically passed on during the culmination of so much of what is contained in these pages: Larry E. Frase and Raymond G. (Jerry) Melton. We miss you guys more than we can express. We are sustained by the many wonderful memories of hard work and good times together all over the world.

To our readers, we transmit our work and ideas to your minds and hands in the cause of improved public education in America and the world. This book is testimony to the wisdom of the practitioners who toil daily in the vineyards of our schools and classrooms and who have created a kind of gritty common sense and "can-do" outlook that permeates their work and this book. For this gift we are extremely grateful, and we hope that you will find our ideas and advice worthy of your continued dedication and professionalism.

Carolyn J. Downey, San Diego, CA
Betty E. Steffy, Chapel Hill, NC
William K. Poston, Jr. , Johnston, IA
Fenwick W. English, Chapel Hill, NC

About the Authors

Carolyn J. Downey is president of Palo Verde Associates, an educational consultant firm. She is also Professor Emeritus in the Educational Leadership Department, College of Education, at San Diego State University. She formerly was the Superintendent for the Kyrene School District, Tempe, Arizona, and served over 30 years as an administrator in K–12 systems. Dr. Downey has written several books and numerous articles. Her book and multimedia kit—*The Three-Minute Classroom Walk-Through,* by Corwin Press—is a bestseller. Dr. Downey has conducted many curriculum management audits of school systems and was the major architect of the Curriculum Management Systems, Inc.'s Individual School Audit for Low-Performing Schools. Dr. Downey is an international consultant in several areas, including quality leadership, systems thinking, organizational development and motivation, planning and the change process, working with low-performing schools and districts, instructional supervision, curriculum development, staff development, program evaluation, site-based management, and program budgeting. She received her MS from the University of Southern California and her PhD from Arizona State University.

Betty E. Steffy is a former superintendent of schools in New Jersey and Dean of the College of Education at a regional campus of Purdue University in Fort Wayne, Indiana. She has been a classroom teacher and director of curriculum in the Pittsburgh, Pennsylvania, area and an assistant superintendent in the Lynbrook Public Schools, Long Island, New York. Prior to Dr. Steffy's transition to higher education she served as the Deputy Superintendent of Instruction in the Kentucky Department of Education, after which she wrote the definitive history of that period in a book entitled *The Kentucky Education Reform Act: Lessons for America.* She is also the originator of the concept of career stages for classroom teachers, which became a touchstone of national work and publications for Kappa Delta Pi, 1997–2006. She is known nationally for being a coauthor of the Corwin Press best-seller *The Three-Minute Classroom Walk-Through*. She earned her BA, MAT, and EdD from the University of Pittsburgh.

William K. Poston, Jr., is a professor emeritus of educational leadership at Iowa State University, where he taught courses in leadership and business practices for school administrators. He is nationally known for his work in curriculum-centered budgeting and for leading more than 70 curriculum audits in the United States and internationally. Dr. Poston served as a superintendent of schools for 15 years in Arizona and Montana, and he holds the record for being the youngest elected president of Phi Delta Kappa in its history. He is the author or coauthor of several books on curriculum auditing and school board governance and more than 30 journal articles. He has presented symposium papers to the University Council for Educational Administration in the areas of accountability and financial management practices, and for many years he was the director of the Iowa School Business Academy. He continues to be active nationally in Phi Delta Kappa and to serve as a consultant to major U.S. school systems. He earned his BA from the University of Northern Iowa and his EdD from Arizona State University.

Fenwick W. English is the R. Wendell Eaves Senior Distinguished Professor of Educational Leadership in the School of Education at the University of North Carolina at Chapel Hill. He has been both a practitioner and a professor and has served in leadership positions in K–12 education and higher education since 1961. He is the author or coauthor of more than 25 books in education, including the 2008 *The Art of Educational Leadership: Balancing Performance and Accountability* released by Sage and the 2008 *Anatomy of Professional Practice: Promising Research Perspectives on Educational Leadership* released by Rowman and Littlefield. Dr. English has been a member of the University Council for Educational Administration Executive Committee since 2001 and was elected President of the University Council for Educational Administration for 2006–2007. He earned his BS and MS from the University of Southern California and his PhD from Arizona State University.

Introduction

50 Ways to Achieve High-Performing Schools

Abandoning Simplistic Mindsets

The achievement gap problem, the most complex and compelling educational dilemma facing schools in the twenty-first century, has no universal solution; instead, there are "solutions" in combinations, because the problem is multicausal, historical, and multidimensional. This fact is not easily understood, because educators, legislators, foundations, think tank pundits, and policy wonks often frame the problem as unidimensional. When problems are so framed, their solution is similarly framed. But the fact that no single solution has shown itself to be viable anywhere over an extended time period suggests that something is missing. The most important piece that is missing is how the problem is conceptualized or framed.

The first important step to take in confronting the achievement gap problem is to abandon the idea that one single thing, or even a few things in combination, will crack this apparently baffling educational conundrum. And the very first factor to confront is that there is no single "achievement gap" but many kinds of gaps. Using a national educational longitudinal data set, Carpenter, Ramirez, and Severn (2006) found "not one but multiple achievement gaps, within and between groups" (p. 120) and "gaps between races may not be the most serious of them" (p. 123). Data from such research as this should provide convincing evidence that there are no silver bullets, flashy new curricula, technologies, computer programs, textbooks, programs, administrative arrangements, or salary incentives that will solely be able to deliver an effective response.

Instead, the way to think about the achievement gap(s) issue is to conceptualize all of the possible causes of the gap(s), group them in some intelligible manner, and systematically begin to eliminate them as causes. When this is done, educators can begin to see that although perhaps most situations in which the gap(s) becomes manifest contain some common elements, others are about combinations of elements whereby arrangements are contingent on context, that is, "it all depends" on the interaction of teachers and students, actions and reactions to teaching, curriculum and curriculum surrogates (textbooks), and various types of assessments in use. Understanding what "it all depends" means is what this chapter is about.

THE PLAYERS AND THE CHALLENGES

Leaving aside for the moment the sociopolitical role of schools in perpetuating or changing a given social structure (a theme to which we will return), schools as specific kinds of human work structures define, divide, and allocate work tasks to a variety of actors within them to fulfill their societal mission. Within a democratic society, and particularly within American society, where authority is dispersed and diffused among at least three major governmental levels and where the values behind schooling differ rather widely and sharply on some issues, the perspective on the achievement gap and its causes is controversial because it is contested (see Fuller & Rasiah, 2005).

Many parents of children of low-income groups see schools as inhospitable to their children's success. They see school staff as indifferent at best, hostile at worst (see Sleeter, 2005). They often see their children in broken-down schools in need of great repair and their children not having access to the latest technology or a rich curriculum. The stark contrast whereby children of the suburbs attend bright and modern schools with greatly expanded curricular offerings and crammed with technology reminds them that they are not considered as important as the "rich white folks" on the other side of the city or county line (see Monahan, 2005).

Teachers find themselves under escalating pressure to improve test scores and to pay attention to centralized curricula. These curricula often are indifferent to teachers' insights and that have embedded in them reforms to which teachers are expected to be compliant implementers (see Brooks, 2006), even when they see the disparities in the assumptions of the tests and find the constraints working against their best efforts to lift achievement as a whole outside of the narrow confines of the multiple-choice, lowest contract bidder award for mass-produced assessments. Teachers who at one time found teaching intrinsically rewarding in helping children learn and grow find an increasingly repugnant test preparation industry embedded in accountability legislation that is limiting their professionalism and destroying their joy in continuing to be teachers (Bushnell, 2003).

Politicians and legislators continue to bring to the equation their own set of biases. If they are from the private sector, they generally see the achievement gap question as one of the lack of motivation on the part of administrators and/or teachers believing that they have no incentives for improving schooling. Believing that the issue is simply a lack of willpower, they pass legislation that increase rewards and punishments, that install merit pay plans based on improved test scores, trying to get the attention of personnel within the schools to focus on "results," and their definition of *results* is primarily improved test scores (Emery & Ohanian, 2004). Finding that schools are resistant to the changes they sometimes propose, they then move to create "alternative schools": "end run" agencies designed to bypass the laggards. They subscribe to the idea that the public schools have no incentives to improve because they are a monopoly, a perspective advanced by the late Milton Friedman (1962).

This bias on the part of the for-profit sector believes that competition is the lever for school improvement. They see the issue as a run for money in a fluid marketplace where profits come to those who find a way to maximize return and lower costs. In fact, a recent report released by the U.S. Chamber of Commerce rated the respective states on educational reform with an index regarding "return on investment" (see J. Archer, 2007).

Bottery (2004) commented that transforming an educational problem into one framed by a supplier–consumer relationship built on the profit motive "is likely to subordinate and transfer values as goodwill, sincerity, fairness, as they are primarily used as instrumental values to service a commercial relationship" (p. 70). The transformation of these values within a for-profit mentality are oblivious to the concept of a public agency designed for the commonweal instead of a group of stockholders who want to make money (see Houston, 2006).

Caught in this maelstrom are school administrators. First charged with the maintenance of the institution, their stabilizing role is often maligned, because without stability there would be no organization to change, only one to bury. Balancing stability and change is no easy administrative task. A huge amount of energy is invested in making sure the school ship does not roll over or sink. Students have to be educated even under the most trying of circumstances and even when programs may be weak and the institution itself financially strapped.

The context of schooling, especially in urban settings where students are often most at odds with the middle-class culture and prevalent school routines, where school staff are often the least prepared to deal with the alienation of the communities in which they work, is the ground zero of public education (see Lucas, 1999). Poverty and social alienation, despair, anomie, violence of all kinds, drugs, domestic abuse, and gang cultures overlay school routines and practices. Administrators working in this environment are very hard pressed to envision or lead the kind of internal transformation required to close the achievement gap. And often, these school settings are the ones most fractious politically, where school boards are representative of the larger community divisions and controversies, where members are the least schooled in the art of compromise, and personal and political agendas are pushed with strident urgency.

The clamor for "instant fixes" far exceeds the capacity of the schools to comply even when the desire is present and the complexity of the tasks somewhat clear. Too often, the demand for such fixes takes on the most egregious forms of micromanagement of the school administration imaginable. Added to this volatile mix is the inevitable cult of the personality of either the superintendent or individual board members. The cult of personality is the temptation to see the achievement gap as an issue that is responsive to the charisma of the leadership as opposed to the kind of internal, transformed work patterns that is the real nexus of the problem. It is to this issue that we now turn.

THE BASIC CONCEPTUAL STRUCTURE THAT FRAMES THE PROBLEM

The basic conceptual frame upon which all of the six standards and the 50 strategies are elaborated in this book is shown in Figure 0.1. This frame was first enumerated by English (1978) and later expanded (1987, 1988; also see English & Larson, 1996).

Schools and school systems are an example of one kind of human work organization. As such, schools are created not to turn a profit but to render an important social/cultural function of reproducing the most important values of any given society. Originally in the Western world formal schooling was reserved for the social elites, but with the creation of mass democracies and

Figure 0.1   The Three Elements of Quality Control

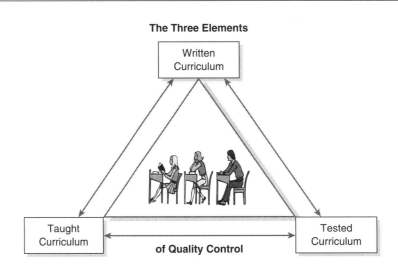

expanded voting franchise to nearly everyone, the function of the schools has been to prepare students to live and work in them. As the nature of work has changed, social alternatives for those who were ill prepared in schools has decreased, forcing the schools to keep students longer and to focus on enabling them to be more economically viable in a changing marketplace (see Labaree, 1988).

Today, the rhetoric about maintaining an international competitive edge in a global market place dominates much of the criticism from the commercial sector, even as it is recognized by some that the lack of a competitive "edge" is not an educational problem but a business problem (see Cuban, 2004). We see the achievement gap problem not fundamentally as a commercial problem with indexes of return on investment but as a moral one, and we believe that resolving the achievement gap issue is fundamentally about realizing the promise of public education as a ladder to the good life for all children, even as the evidence suggests the schools have never served the poor at any time very well in U.S. history (see Bowles & Gintis, 1976; Brantlinger, 2003; Katz, 1973; C. Marshall & Oliva, 2006; Parenti, 1978; Tyack, 1974).

Within schools, the *written curriculum* consists not only of curriculum guides, curricular frameworks, and courses of study but also of a wide range of *curricular surrogates*. In most schools, a plethora of documents may be in use. Collectively, we call this group of documents *the curriculum in use*, but it is rarely a solitary document. Linking the curriculum in use to the extant teaching and the *tests in use* so that there is a focused linkage among all three is the definition of *quality control*. In this case, the measure of quality is how each of three components provides the basis for the definition of assessment results or outcomes. There is clearly a danger here, which is if the *tests in use* are cheap, one dimensional, culturally biased, and low-level indicators of the educational process, then looking good on them is counterproductive to providing quality education. We say much more about this later in the book, because we do not assume that a simple curriculum–test congruence is all that is necessary. We like very much John Dewey's (1964) distinction written over a half century ago on this matter:

> If you want schools to perpetuate the present order, with at most the elimination of waste and with such additions as enable it to do better what it is already doing, then one type of intellectual method . . . is indicated. But if one conceives that a social order different in quality and direction from the present is desirable and that schools should strive to educate with social change in view by providing individuals not complacent about what already exists, and equipped with desires and abilities in transforming it, quite a different method and content is indicated. (pp. 174–175)

With this caveat in mind, the six standards by which the 50 strategies are grouped in this book are shown in Figure 0.2. The key linkages to the other elements of quality control shown in Figure 0.1 are also described in Figure 0.2.

Figure 0.2   Quality Control, Six Standards, and Linkages to Close the Achievement Gap

Quality Control in Schools and School Systems		
Curriculum In Use	*Teaching*	*Assessment(s) in Use*
Standard 1: Establish a Well-Crafted, Focused, Valid, and Clear Curriculum to Direct Teaching	Standard 4: Use a Mastery Learning Approach and Effective Teaching Strategies	Standard 2: Provide Assessments Aligned With the Curriculum
Standard 3: Align Program and Instructional Resources With the Curriculum and Provide Student Equality and Equity	Linkage here to Standard 3 with alignment of resources for the classroom in the delivery of the curriculum	Linkage here to Standard 3 because assessment is usually the means to judge student equality and equity
Standard 5: Establish Curriculum Expectations, Monitoring, and Accountability	Linkage here to Standard 5 because it pertains to monitoring and accountability	Linkage here to Standard 5 because it pertains to accountability
Standard 6: Institute Effective District and School Planning, Staff Development, and Resource Allocation, and Provide a Quality Learning Environment	Linkage here to Standard 6 because it pertains to a quality learning environment	Linkage here to Standard 6 because it pertains to the effectiveness of resource allocation

ADVANTAGES OF FRAMING THE PROBLEM THIS WAY

The advantages of framing the achievement gap from this perspective are as follows.

1. The Problem Is Clearly a Complex and Systemic One That Defies Simplistic Antidotes

The basic problem in confronting the achievement gap concerns transforming the way educators and support staff conceptualize the work they do. So, in the beginning it is not about doing any one thing differently; instead, it is about changing *how we think* about the problem. Because there is no one thing that causes the achievement gap, but many things operating collectively in situated contexts, we have to think about approaching a complex, multifaceted problem in a diagnostic mode that tries to capture the variables and the key interactions and then eliminating the major causative components one by one. Also, we have to envision this work as progressive and steady, informed by the understanding that it will be a combination of our actions that attains the results and that, furthermore, gains will not necessarily be uniform from year to year; instead, we should see steady gains year to year and expect some years to be more fruitful than others. We look for multiyear progress because organizations define the work to be done in a variety of ways, and one characteristic of organizations is stability. We see stability as a strength instead of a barrier, because once we alter the patterns of work it is reasonable to expect them to remain in place.

2. The Blame Game Becomes Unnecessary, Because Everyone Is Part of the Problem and Part of the Solution

Another key feature of conceptualizing the achievement gap in the manner described is that because everyone is part of the problem, everyone is then part of the solution. Also, because everyone is part of the problem, it makes no sense to engage in finger pointing or second-guessing. It just is not productive, and it clearly doesn't help. The idea should be to fix the problem and not fix the blame.

3. It Shifts the Focus From Fads to Foundational Issues

Once the achievement gap problem is seen as a matter of redefining the work and the work structures within school systems (see Snipes, Doolittle, & Herlihy, 2002), unproductive ways of defining and attacking the problem can be avoided. There are no quick fixes to shifting the definition of work and altering work structures and patterns in schools, so one can avoid spending time buying new technologies, new textbooks, programs that substitute for an effective curriculum, funding alternative schools, passing laws that up the ante for more rewards or punishments on the basis of test results, and finding new ways to re-fix the blame for the lack of progress based on who the students are or who their parents may be. The blame-the-victim game is totally unproductive and unethical, but it still goes on.

4. A New Sense of Realism and Hope Is Established

Not to be overlooked in framing the achievement gap problem in the manner we have chosen is that by grasping the complex and situated nature of its source and how to attack it we no longer have to bear the inevitable disappointments over the last promise made for the quick fix we thought might work. Instead, the problem is laid out in its complex form, we approach it more logically and more realistically, and we have a renewed sense of hope based on that realism. Our constituents no longer expect miracles and will begin to see that we are seeking a long-term strategy to remove the gap and that both practice and research support our choices.

SUMMARY

The achievement gap has been a long-standing issue in American public education (see Carpenter et al., 2006; Jencks, 1972; Jencks & Phillips, 1998; Ream, 2003). To date, no programs or approaches have erased it, although some actions in school systems have shown promise (see Snipes et al., 2002). In this chapter, we have set forth the basic conceptual frame to conceptualize the multidimensional nature of the gap issue and help define the means by which educators can begin to scope out a program of work and change to attack it successfully.

Six Standards for High-Performing Schools

Creating and Implementing Constancy of Purpose

Perhaps the best overall guide for discussing the six standards for high-performing schools is W. Edward Deming's (1986) concept of *constancy of purpose*. These three words embody the essence of how to create a high-performing school.

Implicit in Deming's (1986) idea is that a successful organization requires a purpose, that is, a clear sense of direction, a unified and strategic focus. In schools, this purpose must relate to goals and objectives regarding student learning. Such objectives must be valid, clear, and compelling. They must embody significant national and international standards. They must be understood by everyone involved in teaching children and by those monitoring the delivery of the instructional program. In curriculum auditing, the notion of purpose is embedded in the idea of *curriculum design* (English & Poston, 1999).

The second part of quality is contained in the word *constancy*. Constancy comprises staying power under duress. It pertains to consistency in orientation when one is examining related problems in schools even if that institutional capacity has undergone change. Implicit in the idea of institutional capacity building is installing quality control as a part of the infrastructure in which the written, taught, and tested curricula are connected, integrated, and interactive. It means when one of these three elements changes or is changed, the others will and should also change. Constancy involves grounding the day-to-day operations of schools in teaching, administering, assessment, motivating, linking, modifying, and working for improved gains. Although it is largely concerned with curriculum delivery, constancy—this "hanging in there" attitude—is established through curriculum design.

Let's examine these six critical standards for high-performing schools one by one.

STANDARD ONE: ESTABLISH A WELL-CRAFTED, FOCUSED, VALID, AND CLEAR CURRICULUM TO DIRECT TEACHING

Curriculum is the fundamental work plan for what goes on in schools. It not only embodies organizational philosophy, but it also incorporates the legal and operational requirements within which schools function. In the past, *curriculum* has meant just about anything that could be conceived within schools. It not only represented aspirations and lofty social goals, but it also embodied challenging the social order with objectives that were radically opposed to the existing class structure.

Although curriculum may be regarded as incorporating revolutionary content and the intellectual agenda of either the political left or right, in the model of high-performing schools it is primarily focused on attaining the goals and objectives explicit and implicit in the program of testing and assessment. This is not a politically naive decision on the part of curriculum workers. Instead, if schools do not demonstrate their capacity to attain even a modest range of general mainstream purposes, the trend is already unmistakably clear. Such low-performing schools are dealt with harshly and punitively, perhaps even put out of business by a kind of fiduciary slow death, or even abolished in the name of academic bankruptcy.

In addition to valid and clear curriculum content, the curriculum of the high-performing school has to be modest, not grandiose. Achieving constancy of purpose requires that teachers and administrators have a reasonable number of goals and objectives to attain. Such goals and objectives should be capable of being achieved and not overwhelming. The easiest way to accomplish this is to limit the goals and objectives to be pursued, at least initially, to those tested.

This tenet usually brings howls and protests not only from teachers who fear a loss of control over curriculum content, but also from curriculum developers who understand that tests are just samples of the whole curriculum, as well as from assessment directors who also understand the limitations of the types of learning their tests embody. We find these arguments ill conceived, even illogical. If it is performance as defined by any test that results in the imposition of sanctions or rewards, then the content embodied in the measuring tool should trigger those same positive and/or negative responses. Informing teachers and administrators that they should not be too concerned, or that they should dump other things in the curriculum to spend time solely or exclusively on the tested curriculum, is to confess the following:

- that the test is not all that important and may not be assessing the most important learning that could be taught (why, then, is it attached to rewards and/or sanctions?); and/or
- that the attainment of high performance by any group on any test requires a concentration of resources and less attention to that which will not result in success. Failing to emphasize actions that lead to a concentration of resources on priority targets undermines organizational effectiveness and detracts from the capacity of the school to improve student achievement.

Finally, we note that the current popular notion of assessment-driven instruction is a clear message that teaching should be and must be connected to tests in use. Reformers see tests being used as the device to ratchet up learning.

It should be clear that, at least for curriculum development, the concept of high performance is reductionistic; that is, because performance is defined and bordered, it both promotes concentration of resources and discourages resources from being expended on content not included within the boundaries of performance. Teachers and administrators who fail to grasp the clear implication of becoming a high-performance school usually do not understand the meaning of *constancy*. Not everything has the same priority in a high-performance school; some things are much more important than others. The final arbiter of the matter of importance is the tested curriculum.

Another aspect of constancy within this standard is that curriculum should be easy to use, or "user friendly." High-performing schools have teachers and administrators who are not afraid to try different formats for curriculum materials. They understand that connecting the written, taught, and tested curricula can take a variety of forms as long as the essential connectivity and clarity are not compromised. They are also not fooled into thinking that superficial uniformity or standardization is not an important matter and will not promote constancy if it is not functional. There are differences in the ways various curricular content areas are conceptualized and set into a work plan. Essential skills tend to require a different shaping than essential content. There will be differences between elementary and secondary curriculum guides.

STANDARD TWO: PROVIDE ASSESSMENTS ALIGNED WITH THE CURRICULUM

Curriculum provides focus and connectivity from the work of classroom teachers and how that effort fits into an overall structure of defined performance. All of this can take place in the absence of specific assessment strategies or tools. However, with the advent of high-stakes testing that essentially defines the nature of performance itself, curriculum development must include alignment with the tests in use. This ensures that the energy of teachers and administrators will result in improved student performance on the instrument that has defined the nature of improvement and that will also become the triggering device for rewards and sanctions.

Alignment means not only matching tested content to curriculum content but also engaging in *deep parallelism,* which ensures congruence between the tested and written curriculum. We have learned that since alignment has become popularized, nearly every school or district claims that it is aligned. A close inspection, however, demonstrates that the matching that has occurred is often superficial. "Drill and kill" worksheets have proliferated in schools located in states where high-stakes tests are in use. Such responses will not result in sustained student gains and will also produce classrooms of incredible boredom and mindlessness.

Learning in such places has been tragically dumbed down. Responses to high-stakes testing in the superficial vein amounts to lobotomizing teachers and students. Schools and the curriculum have been debased.

Engaging in deep alignment results in instruction that extends far beyond the test. It means that teachers anticipate the directions in which the test may be moving. It also means that teachers focus on the underlying principles and processes involved in truly comprehending and mastering the multiple learnings that are a part of every single test item included on any given test. In short, the practice of deep alignment is *teaching to the test that is not yet created*, and although it begins with current assessment it runs far more broadly and deeply than with just the tests in use. It is necessary to understand current test logic, protocols, norms, objectives, format, item construction, content domain sampling, weighting and frequency of questions within the test, and overall content coverage, but even this is clearly not enough. This is where high-performing schools start, but it is not where they end. High-performing schools are in an *anticipatory mode* as it pertains to any test in use. Schools that are not high performing are in a *reactionary mode*. They are playing constant catch-up; they are always behind the curve.

STANDARD THREE: ALIGN PROGRAM AND INSTRUCTIONAL RESOURCES WITH THE CURRICULUM AND PROVIDE STUDENT EQUALITY AND EQUITY

The major resource in schools is *teacher quality time* with students. We define *teacher quality time* as teaching students to be creatively responsive in a deeply aligned curriculum with plenty of opportunities for pedagogical parallelism from the classroom to beyond the tests in use.

In addition, the resources of the school and district must be prioritized to similarly reflect a commitment to improving tested learning, and they must be adjusted so that more resources are diverted to students and programs with greater educational needs than others. School system formulae that level resources to ratios are not effective. They undermine the concept of constancy by shortchanging some children and overspending on others. The idea of *economy of scale* is relative to the needs of the children being considered. What is economical is not a simple arithmetic calculation; it is, rather, needs centered. The idea of adjusting resources to identified needs is that of *equity*.

STANDARD FOUR: USE A MASTERY LEARNING APPROACH AND EFFECTIVE TEACHING STRATEGIES

Mastery learning includes the idea of linking the written and tested curricula with the taught curriculum. It also means that individual learning plans are developed for students who are underachieving. Mastery learning includes instruction at the right level of difficulty for a student. This means that diagnostic assessments are given regularly to ascertain where a student is in his or her learning.

Moreover, there are many well-researched, effective teaching practices that, when used, increase the likelihood of student achievement. It is our expectation that teachers are cognizant of these techniques and use them routinely.

STANDARD FIVE: ESTABLISH CURRICULUM EXPECTATIONS, MONITORING, AND ACCOUNTABILITY

This standard relates to the expression of high curriculum standards by administrators but also includes administrative competence in actually monitoring curriculum design and delivery in school classrooms. It means that the principal feels comfortable in working with teachers to disaggregate test data and then use those data to make classroom decisions. Furthermore, it means that district-level officers recognize that their main mission is higher student achievement and that they must also monitor to see whether the curriculum is being implemented. Their role in the supervision of principals is essential.

STANDARD SIX: INSTITUTE EFFECTIVE DISTRICT AND SCHOOL PLANNING, STAFF DEVELOPMENT, AND RESOURCE ALLOCATION, AND PROVIDE A QUALITY LEARNING ENVIRONMENT

School planning is essential to establish the means for specifying purpose and relating the structure required to attain constancy. Planning must include multi-year goals and determine the requisite change strategies to be employed. On the other hand, plans must retain flexibility and adaptability so that the planning process does not promote organizational rigor mortis.

Staff development must be related to the goals contained within school plans. Staff development is not an end unto itself; instead, it is a means toward enhancing the human element required to attain organizational ends. As staff become more proficient, the school becomes increasingly capable of improving its performance levels.

The school budget is configured by how it is related to curricular priorities. It promotes equity, and it supports learning priorities that are established on the basis of need.

Personnel in the school are qualified and motivated. Marginal teachers are brought up to satisfactory standards or encouraged to leave. Crime is minimal, and fear is not present. School facilities are adequate, clean, and safe, and they promote a wide variety of learning and teaching variations in shaping and reshaping an instructional program.

Many school staff members across the United States are floundering in trying to achieve high student success based on student achievement measures. Tremendous amounts of money are spent every year purchasing program after program in an attempt to raise test scores. Many of these efforts prove to be fruitless. Staff members are becoming discouraged and frustrated as they put energy into these programs to no avail. It is time for us to focus our efforts on powerful strategies that research has proven will make a difference.

That is what this book is about. Review the six standards and 50 strategies presented in this book in a diagnostic way, with a view to determining your district's and/or school's present status. At the end of each strategy is a space for you to record your analysis, either for private speculation or for use as a collaborative tool with colleagues or other stakeholders. This book is ultimately meant to serve as both a yardstick and a game plan to assist schools in achieving the highest level of performance possible.

1

Standard One

Establish a Well-Crafted, Focused, Valid, and Clear Curriculum to Direct Teaching

A standards-based curriculum has become the norm for districts across the United States. The objective of this movement is to see that standards become the target for instructional planning, that schools ensure that all students are working toward the same goals, that teachers understand what they are accountable for, and that students are provided with a learning environment that enables them to achieve the standards (Perna & Davis, 2007). However, in the fervor to develop standards by learned organizations and state departments of education, there has been a proliferation of standards to the point where it would be impossible for teachers to achieve mastery of all the standards identified for the respective content areas. A review by Kendall and Marzano in 1998 revealed that content standard documents available at that time included 200 separate standards and addressed 3,093 topics or benchmarks. They concluded that a student would have to master 1.5 standards per day for 13 years in order to achieve mastery of all of the standards (p. 6).

It is also becoming clear that the quality of standards differs from one state to another (Kowalski, Lasley, & Mahoney, 2008). Comparisons between state standards and standards for the National Assessment of Educational Progress (NAEP) reveal a wide range of disparities. All of this makes it critical for local school districts to become actively engaged in the development of documents that detail curriculum standards that are appropriate for a specific district. This standard focuses on the development of these documents.

The following are nine highly powerful strategies related to curriculum that can be used to achieve higher student achievement.

1. **Strategy 1: Embed External Assessment Target Objectives in the Written Content Standards and Link Them to State Standards.** There is a written set of district curriculum content standards that embed all external assessments administered to students and that are linked to state standards/ expectations for every grade/instructional level and course offered.

2. **Strategy 2: Have Clear and Precise District Curriculum Objectives— Content, Context, and Cognitive Type.** The district curriculum objectives, aligned to the external assessment objectives, provide clearly specified content (skills, knowledge, concepts, processes, attitudes, etc.) to be learned; the context in which the learning must be demonstrated, including the test format; the appropriate cognitive type to be mastered; and the standard of performance—that is, the degree of mastery required.

3. **Strategy 3: Deeply Align Objectives From External Assessments.** Objectives based on external assessments are placed (embedded) in the curriculum in a deeply aligned manner (content, context, and cognitive type).

4. **Strategy 4: Sequence Objectives for Mastery Well Before They Are Tested.** Objectives are placed in the sequence of learning at least 6 months to 1 year before the student must first demonstrate mastery on the external test.

5. **Strategy 5: Provide a Feasible Number of Objectives to Be Taught.** There are a feasible number of objectives to be learned so that students can master them. A time range for each is noted. District time allocations for all subject areas/courses are in place from which to compare feasibility.

6. **Strategy 6: Identify Specific Objectives as Benchmark Standards.** Some of the objectives have been identified as district benchmark standards to be used as feedback for learning progress, program value, curriculum redesign, promotion, and so on.

7. **Strategy 7: Place Objectives in a Teaching Sequence.** The objectives are developed in a teaching sequence rather than in the order of state standard/ framework strands and are presented to teachers in the same manner.

8. **Strategy 8: Provide Access to Written Curriculum Documents and Direct the Objectives to Be Taught.** The school-based administrators and teachers have in their possession current curriculum and instructional documents (e.g., scope and sequence charts, courses of study, guides) for all curricular areas. Policy directs teachers to teach to the objectives and administrators to monitor their implementation.

9. **Strategy 9: Conduct Staff Development in Curriculum and Its Delivery.** School-based staff members receive quality training in the curriculum scope and sequence and in the use of curriculum documents.

STRATEGY 1

Embed External Assessment Target Objectives in the Written Content Standards and Link Them to State Standards

There is a written set of district curriculum content standards that embed all external assessments administered to students and that are linked to state standards/expectations for every grade/instructional level and course offered.

STRATEGY 1: WHAT

Locally developed written curriculum documents that clearly state the goals and objectives for each grade level and content area provide the basis for instructional planning, materials acquisition, and locally development assessments. Unfortunately, it is common practice today for districts to rely solely on state frameworks as the district curriculum. Depending on the content area, these state frameworks are often vague, repeat the same objectives for several grade levels, may not be available for all content areas, and typically contain more objectives than is possible to master at a grade level.

Today, we live in a world where the knowledge base is rapidly expanding, and access to that knowledge is readily available through technology. There is a need to continually review and revise curriculum documents to ensure that students are being taught that which is most valuable to learn and understand (Armstrong, Henson, & Savage, 2005). It is not unusual for state departments of education to revise content standards every few years to reflect this knowledge explosion. State accountability assessments undergo frequent revisions as well. Other forms of assessment, such as the NAEP, Advanced Placement tests, the SAT, and the International Baccalaureate tests, are also revised over time. This growing knowledge base and refinement of assessments makes it doubly important for districts to maintain control over the district written curriculum. Still, it is difficult to implement change in schools (Armstrong, 2003). The pressure to make curricular changes will only mount in the future. So, where do we begin?

First and foremost, we must teach that which is assessed. We should embed the tested objectives in the written curriculum goals and objectives. Then, when teachers use these objectives to direct their teaching, there is a high probability students will score as well on external tests as they do on teacher-made and district assessments.

The mission of the district is defined by the curriculum. A written curriculum is essential to meet the aim of the mission. The mission of a school system is to prepare students to function as effective citizens in our country, to live personally satisfying lives, and to contribute to and improve society. The tested curriculum is an important part of the mission and thus must be an essential part of the written curriculum.

A well-written curriculum provides the content standards (goals) and objectives to be taught.

- *District content standards* describe the core knowledge, strategies, and skills for schools to teach and for students to acquire and be able to demonstrate in each subject area. They describe what students should know and be able to do, as well as the attitudes they will hold after completing an entire program of study.
- *District objectives* (at the course or instructional level) describe behaviors in specific terms as to what students will master by the end of a year, semester, or level in a particular area of study.

Content standards need to be linked to state expectations but, most important, objectives derived from all external assessments need to form the initial base of the curriculum.

District content standards and objectives need not be directly aligned with the state or national standards; such standards are often too broad and vague to direct teaching, or there are far too many objectives to realistically teach. It is important to select only the most essential and significant objectives to teach. Begin by selecting the tested objectives, taking into consideration all of the assessments deemed important to the district. Such efforts begin the journey toward a connected and coordinated curriculum delivery.

STRATEGY 1: WHY

If the curriculum fails to include objectives that are ultimately tested, students often will not fare well on the tests. Tests are used to collect data about what students know. They are a subset of assessment (Neukrug & Fawcett, 2006). Research is quite clear that students who are heavily dependent on the schools for their learning, such as those who come from lower socioeconomic milieus, will typically fail to demonstrate success on the tests unless we teach to them. Surprise, surprise! Students from affluent cultures tend to have extracurricular experiences that are reflected in testing. They will often do well on the tests in spite of what is taught in school.

It has been shown that schools with strong instructional program coherence produce higher student achievement than schools without instructional program coherence (Newmann, Smith, Allensworth, & Bryk, 2001). *Instructional coherence* has been defined as "a set of interrelated programs for students and staff that are guided by a common framework for curriculum, instruction, assessment, and learning climate that is pursued over a sustained period" (Newmann et al., 2001, p. 297). When it is evident, three major conditions exist:

1. A common instructional framework guides curriculum, teaching, assessment, and learning climate.

2. Staff working conditions support implementation of the framework.

3. The school allocates resources, such as funding, materials, time, and staff assignments, to advance the common instructional framework and to avoid diffuse, scattered improvement efforts. (Newmann et al., 2001, pp. 299–300)

This concept of instructional coherence embraces many of the individual strategies outlined in this book and is grounded on the premise that there is a district curriculum framework that is tightly aligned to both external and internal assessments. To begin the construction of this type of a framework, we recommend that you start by identifying the goals and objectives assessed on external tests.

In the past, teachers have taught what they thought was most important for students to learn, whether it matched the state standards or not. Students learned, but they often did not learn that which was assessed on external accountability tests. If students do not have access to information that is tested, then we cannot expect them to demonstrate knowledge of the learnings. If a teacher is directed by the textbook curriculum or other instructional resource, then it is doubtful that many of the ideas presented in these resources will be tested.

Although textbook publishers typically state that they include in the textbooks all of the state standards and all areas tested, the match is often superficial at best.

STRATEGY 1: HOW

Try the following steps to achieve Strategy 1:

1. Decide which external assessments will be used to begin to identify district goals and objectives, for example, state accountability assessment, Advanced Placement examinations, or NAEP assessments.

2. Review each test item, if available, on the external tests and derive the objectives by deconstructing the test items. *Deconstructing* a test item means identifying what is being taught (the content) and how it is being tested (item format; e.g., multiple choice, bubble in). You may not have access to the actual test items if states are keeping the tests secured, but many states provide sample items for practice tests. If your state does not provide items,

go to Web pages from several states and review the test items they use. Although the format may vary from that used in your state, the content and testing objectives covered will likely be close enough for the requirements of your state framework.

3. Obtain a different form of the test and deconstruct the test items (if the tests are norm-referenced standardized tests).

4. Determine the grade level at which the test item is first tested. Often, on both state criterion-referenced tests and norm-referenced tests, similar test items will be used at different grades. Analyze the items across grade levels.

5. Identify the frequency with which a given objective is tested and note the level of difficulty. Norm-referenced test companies frequently provide such information. Be sure to reflect such frequency and difficulty on your practice tests.

6. Place the objectives in content standards. You might want to use the state content standard/framework areas as a tool.

7. Develop a correlation matrix of the tested objectives in relation to the state and/or national standards/frameworks. Be generous in your correlation. Often, state officials will want evidence that you are teaching the state standards. Be sure the matrix is readily available if requested.

8. Begin the design of the curriculum content standards at each grade level and for each course for the tested subject areas.

STRATEGY 2

Have Clear and Precise District Curriculum Objectives—Content, Context, and Cognitive Type

The district curriculum objectives, aligned to the external assessment objectives, provide clearly specified content (skills, knowledge, attitude, etc.) to be learned; the context in which the learning must be demonstrated, including the test format; the appropriate cognitive type to be mastered; and the standard of performance—that is, the degree of mastery required.

STRATEGY 2: WHAT

Design the curriculum so that you teach what is tested (Strategy 1), and then add to that design the *way* it is tested. From a curriculum point of view, this means that the district curriculum needs to be so clear that any teacher will know what to teach and how to practice the learning, as well as how to assess it. As stated earlier, state and national content standards/frameworks are often broad in nature and duplicative across grade levels. A district's curriculum needs to be written to the precise objective level so that there is no question about what will be taught and when.

As mentioned in the discussion of Strategy 1, objectives for a course, grade, or instructional level describe in specific behavioral terms what students will be able to do at the end of a year/semester/level in a particular area. Objectives need to be clearly written to minimally include the content to be learned (skill, knowledge, concept, process, attitude, etc.), the type of cognition required, and the context in which the learning is to be demonstrated.

An objective needs four components to precisely guide teaching:

- **Content:** The topic, concept, process, skill, knowledge, or attitude to be learned
- **Context:** The performance conditions under which the student will demonstrate the content
- **Cognitive Type:** The level of thought process required, typically using Bloom's taxonomy (knowledge, comprehension, application, analysis, synthesis, evaluation; Bloom, Englehart, Furst, Hill, & Krathwohl, 1956)
- **Standard of Performance:** The degree to which the students need to show they have mastered the learning

Most objectives are written with just a vague idea of content and a verb that might indicate the cognitive type of the objective, for example: "Classify objects as acid or alkaline." Just how would one teach to this objective, and how would one know when students have mastered this learning? The content of the objective needs to be more precise, for example: "Classify objects as acid or alkaline substances according to their molecular structure."

Furthermore, the missing piece that really affects the teacher's planning is the context in which the student is to show he or she knows the content. *Context* means the conditions or situations in which the student is to demonstrate the learning. There are least three context dimensions:

- Instructional or environmental conditions (what the teacher says; what the directions state; vocabulary needed to learn; level of reading ability required; use of graphs, visuals, and other materials, etc.). These are often called *givens*.
- The operation performed or the learner's task requirements (classify, supply information, recall, and develop a product).
- Student behavior mode or the physical characteristics of the learner's behavior or product (writing, oral presentation, pointing, circling, filling in an answer, bubbling in a response).

Here is a better example of a written objective: "The student will demonstrate knowledge (cognitive type) of acid and alkali substances as well as their complex molecular structure (content) by writing (context—student mode of response) in order of molecular structure (context—task specifications) 10 chemical substances (context—environmental conditions) correctly on at least three assessments over a 5-month period (standard of performance)."

Because this is difficult to read, sometimes the objective is written this way:

Content: Acid and alkali substances as well as their complex molecular structure

Cognitive Type: Knowledge

Context: Given 10 chemical substances

Put in order of molecular structure

Student will write down the order

Standard of Performance: Correctly on at least three assessments over a 5-month period

Also presented in the preceding objective is the standard of performance. Standards of performance are used to judge student achievement at a minimum level of performance. They answer the question "How well must a student perform the behavior to demonstrate mastery?" The performance standard can be quantitative or qualitative in nature. The way the preceding objective is written is an example of typical practice items in a textbook.

When developing a precise curriculum that ensures sample items from external assessments are backloaded into the curriculum, a "given" of the contexts will have the item format, as exemplified thus:

Context:

- Given four chemical substances in four different sequences placed in an (a), (b), (c), (d) format and (e) as "none of the above"
- Student will identify the correct sequence, if presented
- Student will bubble in response

When a district wishes to write a curriculum that moves beyond the external assessments, then multiple contexts will be written. For example, educators will use the tested context just presented, the textbook context (e.g., write the answer), and, we would hope, a real world context such as the following:

Context:

- Given 20 chemical substances that are household substances
- Place in order of molecular structure
- Write a page for a household guide using secondary writing rubrics

For educators who are not willing to have the external assessments comprise the totality of the curriculum, we can then develop contexts that require higher level thought processes needed in real world situations. The way we do this is by changing the cognitive type and the context of the objective.

However, start your curriculum development with the external assessments to get what we call *topological alignment*: a one-to-one match of the test item's content, context, and cognitive type requirements (English & Steffy, 2000).

STRATEGY 2: WHY

When the content standards lack precision, teachers often end up teaching the same or similar student learnings across grades and courses. Such duplication takes valuable instructional time away from new, essential learnings.

Providing various contexts in which the teacher has students practice the content of the objective increases the likelihood that the students will be able to transfer their learning to the various contexts. We know from studies on the transfer of learning (Thorndike, 1924) that when the pedagogy of the classroom mirrors the situation in which we want the student to demonstrate the content, the student has higher success. One context to which we want students to transfer their learning is the external assessment situation. We must teach what is tested (Strategy 1) in the way it is tested and in the context in which it is tested (Strategy 2). When this occurs, we achieve higher measured student achievement on the tests. To attain higher student achievement in multiple situations we must provide practice and ongoing assessments in many contexts.

STRATEGY 2: HOW

Try the following steps to achieve Strategy 2:

1. Complete the steps for Strategy 1.

2. Review each test item from the external assessments, if available, and derive the content and context of the tested objective (by deconstructing the test item). Then determine the cognitive type of the test item (topological alignment). If the tests are norm-referenced standardized tests, obtain a different form of the test and deconstruct the test items.

3. Place these objectives under the derived content standards from Strategy 1.

4. Note common patterns in the context of how questions are stated when reviewing a set of questions, such as "What is the *best* response?" or "Which graphic *best* depicts the reported situation?"

5. Note the number of questions in a particular content set; for example, language arts comprehension assessments typically start with a short passage and then ask students to respond to 15 to 18 multiple-choice questions. This information is important to teachers as they plan how to provide students with practice not only with the content of the assessment but also with the context.

6. Note whether the assessments include different types of assessment contexts, such as short response, extended response, and multiple choice.

7. If the assessments include a variety of types of questions, determine the weighting of the types in determining the final scores.

8. Determine the standard of performance for each objective.

9. Add other contexts as desired, for example, a textbook/instructional resource approach, application, or higher cognitive type in a real world context.

STRATEGY 3

Deeply Align Objectives From External Assessments

Objectives based on external assessments are placed (embedded) in the curriculum in a deeply aligned manner (content, context, and cognitive type).

STRATEGY 3: WHAT

The first two strategies are used to design the curriculum so that you teach what is tested (content) and teach it the way it is tested (context). The third strategy is to design the curriculum in a deeply aligned way so that when the objectives are taught students can transfer that learning to a wide variety of situations. Deeply aligned objectives are those that include a broad range of content and contexts. Whether the objective is backloaded from an external assessment or designed in a frontloaded way, it is an essential process to help students score well on a test and use the learning in life.

If your district has schools with low scores on state tests, it is absolutely imperative that you deeply backload from the external test. Developing a curriculum for deeper alignment has two major steps. The initial step is to deconstruct the test item and develop curriculum objectives that mirror directly the content, context, and cognitive type of the test item. This is called a *surface alignment*. A teacher, when reading the objective, will know exactly what the test item will look like.

The first type of alignment is called *topological (surface) alignment*—a one-to-one match of the following:

- Content (topic, subject to be learned)
- Context (test situation—conditions under which the students will demonstrate the content)
- Cognitive level required

For example, the following is a fifth-grade mathematics practice test item used by the State of Florida. This test item uses a gridded response question in which students must arrive at a numeric answer independently, then write the answer and bubble in the grid.

Florida Sunshine Example—Gridded Response Question

The gymnastics class stood in rows to have their team picture taken. The photographer told 2 people to stand in the first row, 4 people to stand in the second row, and 6 people to stand in the third row.

The photographer continued the pattern. How many people did he tell to stand in the sixth row?

⓪	⓪	⓪	⓪
①	①	①	①
②	②	②	②
③	③	③	③
④	④	④	④
⑤	⑤	⑤	⑤
⑥	⑥	⑥	⑥
⑦	⑦	⑦	⑦
⑧	⑧	⑧	⑧
⑨	⑨	⑨	⑨

Here is what the objective would look like for topological alignment when you deconstruct the test item:

Objective That Has Been Topologically Aligned to the Fifth-Grade Test Item

Content: Specify the number in a repeated number pattern that requires a skip in the pattern using the simple operations of addition and/or multiplication

Context:

- Given a word problem that is split by a visual depiction of the word problem
- Given a visual depiction that is only part of the problem
- Vocabulary specific to learning that includes ordinal and cardinal numbers, row, continued, pattern
- Student writes answer and then bubbles answer into a number grid

Cognitive Type: Knowledge

Some student gains will be accomplished using topological alignment, but they are minimal, and they do not ensure that the student understands the concept being tested. Furthermore, a classroom situation that focuses only on topological alignment can become boring, almost meaningless, unless a teacher understands that this is only one way the learning should be practiced.

However, if you deeply align the objectives in their design from the test item, you begin to provide a curriculum that not only brings meaning to the learning but also provides for high achievement on state and national tests. The process for deep alignment involves the following:

- Broadens the content to a reasonable range of learning
- Expands alternative ways of assessing the content
- Moves the type of cognition to higher levels

The more you move one or more of these three areas, the deeper the alignment. In this type of curriculum design you identify the situations (including various types of test formats) in which you are preparing students to transfer the content learning. This is done so that when teachers teach the content learning, it will be practiced in various contexts and at several cognitive levels. Such practice increases the probability that students will transfer this learning to multiple situations.

The following is an example of how you would take the topologically aligned objective from the Florida fifth-grade test item shown earlier and write it in a deeply aligned way. Italics indicate the changes that move the objective from topological to deep alignment. Note also the additional contexts.

Objective That Is Deeply Aligned to the Fifth-Grade Test Item

Content: Specify the number, *letter,* or *visual symbol* in a repeated number, *letter, or visual symbol* pattern that requires a *next in line* and a skip in the pattern using the simple operations of addition and/or multiplication, *subtraction, or division.*

Context 1: *(Gridded response)*

- Given a word problem that is split by a visual depiction of the word problem
- Given a visual depiction that is only part of the problem
- Vocabulary that includes ordinal and cardinal numbers, words such as *gymnastics, photographer, row, continued, pattern*
- Student writes answer and then bubbles answer into a number grid

Cognitive Type: Knowledge

Context 2: *(Multiple-choice test)*

- Given a word problem that is split by a visual depiction of the word problem
- Given a visual depiction that is only part of the problem
- Vocabulary that includes ordinal and cardinal numbers and words such as *gymnastics, photographer, row, continued, pattern*
- Student *selects answer from four possible answers with distracters, most frequent errors, and a "none of the above" answer*
- *Student bubbles correct answer on Scantron-type separate answer sheets*

Cognitive Type: Knowledge

Context 3: *(Multiple-choice test)*

- *Given symbolic pattern*
- *Student selects answer from four possible answers with distracters, most frequent errors, and a "none of the above" answer*
- *Student bubbles correct answer on Scantron-type separate answer sheet*

Cognitive Type: Knowledge

Context 4: *(Typical textbook approach)*

- *Given symbolic pattern, student writes in answer and explains the answer*

Cognitive Type: *Comprehension*

Context 5: *(Real world pattern simulation, requiring student to show reasoning, per writing objective)*

- Given a word problem depicting a real world situation
- Given a direction to determine a pattern
- Student writes the pattern and a descriptive paragraph explaining the reasoning behind the correct answer
- Paragraph must meet fifth-grade writing rubric

Cognitive Type: *Application*

STRATEGY 3: WHY

Deep alignment provides for a maximization of design and, subsequently, classroom delivery parallelism and, therefore, learning. Educators should maximize the pedagogical and environmental congruence between teaching and the various testing situations a student might experience as well as provide the real use of the learning.

Deep alignment is based on Thorndike's (1924) concept of *transfer*. Transfer is enhanced when the situational contexts are similar. Thorndike called his idea "the identical element theory" of the transfer of learning. When students practice and learn a skill, knowledge, concept, or process in a certain way, they should be able to transfer the learning to a similar situation. Because there are many ways students will be challenged to use the learning in school and out, they should practice it in as many of those contexts as possible.

A deeply aligned curriculum and its delivery provide exceptionally high gains in student achievement. This is simply common sense, when you think about it. If you practice a learning to mastery in many different ways, you increase the probability that you can successfully use the learning in many ways. When a deeply aligned curriculum is delivered, such learnings take on more meaning for students as well. One thing we have often noticed in our classroom observations is that much learning is not being taught in a real world way. We strongly advocate and emphasize that one of the contexts to which you transfer learning be a real world situation.

STRATEGY 3: HOW

After accomplishing the steps in Strategies 1 and 2, try the following steps to achieve Strategy 3:

1. Use a deconstructed objective (content, context, cognitive level) and a test item from Strategy 2 to develop a revised objective by broadening the content, by writing various real world contexts, and by changing the cognitive level as desired.

2. Add more contexts to reflect the way you want the learning tested within the district; include contexts that will allow for higher cognitive levels and more authentic assessments.

We highly recommend that no objective be written without the contexts, or without writing at least one district sample test item for each of the contexts identified (see Strategy 10).

STRATEGY 4

Sequence Objectives for Mastery Well Before They Are Tested

Objectives are placed in the sequence of learning at least 6 months to 1 year before the student must first demonstrate mastery on the external test.

STRATEGY 4: WHAT

It is important that students have the opportunity to learn well that which is tested. To *learn well* means that a student has mastered the learning or can go beyond mere recall with the learned facts or concepts and apply them in a variety of contexts and at challenging cognitive levels. Many times, student learning does not progress beyond the simple memorization of facts, figures, or concepts, and the application of the same in limited contexts. We want our instructional practice to move past surface learning; students' knowledge is useless if it cannot be quickly and efficiently recalled to be used in classroom and real life situations. This strategy deals with changing instructional practice to better facilitate the learning of skills, facts, and concepts and to then provide students with enough time to apply that learning in new and challenging situations (contexts). The application of the content needs to take place over time—ideally, a full 6 months to 1 year before the content is tested—while the students are given intermittent reinforcement.

Strategy 4 is accomplished in two ways: (1) sequencing the learning objectives so they are mastered well in advance of being tested and (2) including the standard of performance within an objective. One of the reasons for including the standard of performance in an objective is to provide teachers with an idea of what constitutes "mastering the content." This involves the point at which a student not only has committed the learning to memory but also can recall and use the information in many different situations, including a testing situation. For instance, in the example dealing with acid and alkaline provided earlier, the following was the standard of performance: "[Student performs this task] correctly on at least three assessments over a 7-month period."

STRATEGY 4: WHY

When a student is held accountable on a test for a particular learning, it is only fair that that student has had the opportunity to master that learning in advance of the testing situation and has had adequate time in which to apply that learning in various contexts (practice). When designing the curriculum, many district staff members place an objective into the curriculum the same year it is tested externally; however, objectives need to be placed in the curriculum earlier, so students have adequate time to demonstrate mastery. The standard of performance is the gauge by which teachers can determine whether mastery has been reached.

Students across the country, good students, "cram" for a test, yet 1 year later they remember little of what they learned, because the practice of that learning occurred during a few long study sessions. This is referred to as *massed practice*. In contrast, when students are given more time to learn material and additional opportunities to practice that material (distributed practice), they are more likely to retain their learning and use it in future situations, including testing situations (Woolfolk, 1987).

Our premise here is that we must decide on the important learnings and provide students with adequate opportunities to acquire the learnings and apply them in multiple situations and problems. Furthermore, if these learnings are tested in advance, teachers and students will have the time and practice necessary to master the test situation and question formats.

One of the nice side effects of placing objectives in a teaching sequence well before the objectives are tested is that the curriculum becomes more challenging.

However, one has to be careful to make sure that the instructional resources and textbooks used are aligned with the curriculum (see Strategy 22).

STRATEGY 4: HOW

Try the following steps to achieve Strategy 4:

1. Review the tested objectives and then locate that objective in the curriculum at least 6 months to 1 year earlier in the scope and sequence of learning.

2. Examine norm-referenced test planning documents to determine where the objective is first tested. Most objectives are tested over more than a 2- to 3-year span.

3. Sequence the objectives in the scope in such a way that teachers have plenty of time to move students to mastery.

4. Create a scope matrix across grades so teachers can see when the student is to learn (master) the objective and when it is tested.

5. Create a matrix showing where in each grade/level/course each objective is to be mastered.

6. Choose not to use a scope matrix with the terms *introduce*, *develop*, and *master*. Such words have little meaning for teachers and provide an avenue for them to not be held accountable for student learning in an area.

STRATEGY 5

Provide a Feasible Number of Objectives to Be Taught

There are a feasible number of objectives to be learned so that students can master them. A time range for each is noted. District time allocations for all subject areas/ courses are in place from which to compare feasibility.

STRATEGY 5: WHAT

"Less is more," as the saying goes. Fewer objectives taught in depth have a higher probability of being remembered. It is important that a district curriculum, in its design, has a feasible number of objectives that can be taught to mastery. A district needs to identify the most essential skills to be taught to students and that students are expected to master. When we estimate the time needed to not only acquire the learning (short-term memory) but also to master the learning (long-term memory), we must limit the number of objectives taught.

Identifying the most essential skills is easy to mandate but difficult to do. What students should learn is based on opinion. We have the opinions of national experts, state committees, and test makers as to what are the most important things to learn. Certainly you need to include as essential those learnings for which a student will be held accountable through assessments. Also, if we could influence you, we would include real world learnings such as those shown in the 1991 report by the Secretary's Commission on Achieving Necessary Skills.

When teaching to mastery, provide numerous practice opportunities over several months to help students retain the learning. The range of time needed to master an objective varies greatly depending on the complexity and meaning of the learning. For example, learning one's ABCs requires only rote memorization, whereas learning how to write an expository paragraph with certain elements requires a synthesis of ideas, and, therefore, greater time to master.

Curriculum designers need to give objectives a best estimate of time—not only time for a typical student to acquire the learning but also the time needed to retain the learning. For example, if we have a 10- to 15-hour range of time per objective and have 150 hours available in a year for the learning, it is easy to see that we could work with no more than 10 to 15 objectives per year in a given subject area.

Design a curriculum around the typical learner and ensure that there are not too many objectives to be taught. Consider developing the curriculum around instructional levels rather than grade levels. This will allow each student to advance to the next level of objectives when ready and stay with his or her age-mates. This concept is known as *continuous progress*, and it works in conjunction with the differentiation of instruction described in Strategy 30. Each student is moved along the continuum of learning objectives at a challenging and appropriate learning pace.

STRATEGY 5: WHY

It is time to be reasonable. We hand a teacher 100+ objectives to teach in a 150-hour period of time and then wonder why the students have not mastered the objectives. It is no wonder voluminous curriculum guides with hundreds of objectives sit on shelves, and teachers, when receiving the state standards, sigh. It's wrong! It's ridiculous! Why does such nonsense persist? It is very understandable why teachers turn to their textbooks and start with page 1. However, textbooks have far too many objectives as well, and their alignment with the tested objectives is usually very poor (see Strategy 22).

Some people call this "March Madness," but this madness happens any time teachers begin to realize that there is no way that they can cover all the objectives they have been told to teach by the end of the year. Some teachers, under pressure, begin to skim even more quickly over some objectives, with the result that students lose opportunities to remember the learnings of the objectives. The same thing happens if teaching is textbook driven. This is illogical.

Although the number of curriculum objectives in the United States is growing, countries whose students are obtaining the highest scores on international tests are teaching fewer objectives but with greater depth. How could it be that fewer objectives are taught, but students remember more? It comes back to the concept of practice as discussed in Strategy 3, teaching for a deeper understanding of content versus rote memorization.

A feasible number of objectives means we have a higher probability that the students will learn what we want them to learn. This strategy works hand in hand with Strategy 4: Design curriculum so that teachers teach the learning well in advance of it being tested. When you have a doable number of objectives and students are learning the skills to mastery, you have a high probability not only that the students will do well on tests but also that they will also remember the knowledge, skill, concept, or process for use in life.

One of the complaints we often hear from teachers is that their students do not have the prerequisite skills expected. In most cases, this is attributed to the fact that students are not learning to master the knowledge or skills taught in the previous grade. When there are too many objectives to be taught, the teachers just move from one objective to the next without allowing for the practice opportunities needed to obtain retention of the learning.

Because students of low-performing schools are often at a disadvantage with respect to the areas taught, limiting the objectives gives them an equal opportunity to score well on external assessments. Why is it that test scores float on demographics? It is not because students from certain demographics are smarter than other students. One contributing factor is the major difference in experiences students bring to the testing situation, experiences that occur outside of the school setting. Giving students access to the learnings for which they are going to be held accountable on tests means we have to be smart about the number of objectives we are going to place in the curriculum for teachers to teach.

Furthermore, we need to make sure that the learnings for which students will be held accountable are in the curriculum. In no way would this limit the teaching of other objectives once the externally tested objectives are mastered.

STRATEGY 5: HOW

Try the following steps to achieve Strategy 5:

1. Identify the tested objectives and embed them in the curriculum.

2. Specify the content, context, and cognitive level of each objective.

3. Broaden the range of the content, context, and cognitive level of each objective.

4. Place the objectives early in the learning sequence before testing externally.

5. Establish curriculum time allocation guidelines.

The steps in establishing these guidelines are as follows:

a. Establish *curriculum time allocations*—the amount of instructional time to be devoted to each subject area/course for every grade level. For example:

Grade level	Subject area	Time allocation daily
2	Language arts (including SSR)	150 minutes (15 minutes)
	Mathematics	90 minutes
	Social studies	90 minutes 3 times a week
	Science	90 minutes 2 times a week
	Physical education/health	50 minutes 2 times every 6 days
	Music	50 minutes 2 times every 6 days
	Art	50 minutes 2 times every 6 days

b. Determine a probable range of time for each objective for a typical student to learn it to mastery; estimate the amount of acquisition time and practice time needed for retention of the learning.

c. Total up the number of hours for a subject area/course in a given semester or year.

d. Compare the number of hours to teach the objectives you want to teach with the number of available instructional hours. You have too many, right? Now that you have found that you do not have enough time, eliminate some of the objectives. (This is the hard part.) Eliminate last those areas tested most frequently.

e. Work across grade levels as this project is accomplished, because more time may be found at other grade levels. Remember to place an objective where it is first tested, not in every grade in which it is tested.

f. Publish the content standards and objectives for teachers, parents, and students.

Learning can and does take place in an integrated way in school. A student learns more about reading in social studies and uses more math skills in science. Our approach to determining the number of objectives is linear, yet we expect integrated teaching. However, we have found that when you complete Strategy 5 in a subject-specific way, you get closer to a feasible number of objectives. If teachers find they have more time to teach more objectives than required, they should move along the continuum of objectives.

STRATEGY 6

Identify Specific Objectives as Benchmark Standards

Some of the objectives have been identified as district benchmark standards to be used as feedback for learning progress, program value, curriculum redesign, promotion, and so on.

STRATEGY 6: WHAT

A *benchmark* is a milestone you are trying to reach. Benchmark standards serve as milestones for a particular level of learning—a goal to be attained. Benchmarks should be a sampling of the curriculum objectives that could be used to ascertain accomplishment of learnings in a group of grades, a program, or a curriculum.

These district benchmarks typically are for grade spans, such as at the end of Grades 3, 6, 9, and 11. They often are set a year in advance of any state benchmark testing. Because we suggest that any objective tested be placed early in the sequence of learning (see Strategy 4), it makes sense that the district benchmarks would be a year earlier than the state benchmark assessments.

Some districts are beginning to develop benchmark standards for every year because of annual high-stakes testing. Whatever you do must in part be determined by the consequences of students not performing well on state and national assessments. Recently, benchmark standards have been required by states as a means to determine retention of students in a grade. This makes placement of learnings early in the curriculum even more critical to ensure that no student is retained.

The frequency with which benchmarks are assessed will depend on how you plan to use the information. We hope that it will not be for retention of students in grades but rather to ensure promotion to the next grade of all students and for program and curriculum decision making. In the latter situation, only a random sampling of students need be assessed.

There are two types of benchmark standards: (1) benchmark content/objective standards and (2) benchmark performance standards. They go hand in hand. The first is what we want students to learn; the second is how that learning is measured. The following definitions explain them better:

Benchmark content standards and objectives are selected student objectives that will serve as a summative point at certain times in the schooling of a student. They describe what students will know or be able to do, or attitudes they will hold after completing an entire program of study or groups of years/courses.

Benchmark performance standards state the evidence required to document attainment of the benchmark content standard and/or objective and the quality of student performance deemed acceptable (e.g., mastered, or a rubric of advanced, proficient, basic, and fail levels).

For more information on performance benchmark standards, see Strategy 11.

STRATEGY 6: WHY

This strategy is difficult to discuss, because much of the public debate surrounding benchmarks centers on the belief that students should be retained in a grade if they have not mastered a certain set of learnings. Research is quite clear about the negative impact of retaining students: Retention damages self-concept, retention creates a negative attitude toward school, retained students are more likely to drop out of school, and the learning problems that lead to retention are rarely addressed (Owings & Magliaro, 1998).

Students should not be penalized because they have not been taught successfully. Benchmarks need to be used to assist us in helping students, not punishing them. The century's worth of research in this area is irrefutable. You will need to be principled about your beliefs in this arena. Furthermore, you will need to set up both a design and delivery of curriculum that will increase the likelihood that students who might not reach the benchmarks are identified early, so that an intensive approach to student promotion is in place. In some ways, the focus on retention in so many states moves us to do the work we should have been doing anyway—providing high success for all students in their achievement.

Our approach to benchmarks in this strategy is not for the purpose of retaining students in school; instead, it is to underscore that educators should have expectations of learning, goals to be accomplished. These benchmarks may be used to determine the effectiveness of our programs, our curriculum, and our educators.

If we use benchmarks in a data-gathering approach to help us improve, they will help us determine when we need to revise the curriculum or make it more challenging. Benchmarks can be used to set school improvement goals, faculty goals, and personal student achievement goals.

STRATEGY 6: HOW

Try the following steps to implement this strategy after accomplishing the steps for Strategies 1 through 5:

1. Peruse the objectives to determine which of all of the objectives you will use as benchmark standards.

2. Use the state and national high-stakes assessed objectives that are most frequently tested and that typically should have been mastered prior to a specific grade level.

3. Establish retention benchmark standards that are mainly from the previous grade. This prevents one from unfairly penalizing a student. However, expect the grade-level benchmarks for assessing educator success.

4. Revise the benchmarks as students learn.

5. Publish the benchmark objectives for teachers, parents, and students.

STRATEGY 7

Place Objectives in a Teaching Sequence

The objectives are developed in a teaching sequence rather than in the order of state standard/framework strands and are presented to teachers in the same manner.

STRATEGY 7: WHAT

Once the objectives have been identified, it is important to put them in some logical sequence: the order in which the objectives are to be taught. For years, curriculum designers thought there were a tremendous number of dependencies from one learning to another. Through testing this belief it has been established that most learnings have few *dependencies*, that is, one learning required before another. For example, for many years it was thought that addition and subtraction needed to be taught before multiplication and division. We have now found that this is not the case; these basic mathematical operations can be taught in a variety of sequences.

However, it is still important to put the objectives in some sort of acquisition and maintenance sequence for teachers. The first sequencing of objectives needs to be tied to state and national tests and when curriculum designers want mastery to be achieved (see Strategy 4). After that, a logical approach can be used.

We suggest educators follow the typical sequence in a textbook; however, do not suggest the teacher tackle all the objectives in a textbook or other instructional resource; this would far exceed what is feasible (see Strategy 5). If, however, it is feasible, then there is less skipping around.

In addition to sequencing the learning early, it is important to sequence the objectives across grade or instructional levels. Such sequencing provides not only for connectivity from one type of objective to another but also for the increasing complexity of a concept through a spiraling type of approach.

STRATEGY 7: WHY

Most state standards or frameworks are built around strands, for example, number sense. One should not teach an entire strand of a subject area and then move on to another strand. Instead, teach multiple strands at the same time. If curriculum documents do not provide the sequence of objectives, then this decision is left to teachers. Such a decision can increase the probability of a disjointed and fragmented delivery of the objectives. Furthermore, it would not provide for the integration of objectives across disciplines when students have multiple teachers.

Sequencing the objectives in the order in which they tend to show up in a textbook helps teachers become aware that they are not to teach everything in the textbook. We could gradually move teachers away from being textbook driven by such an approach. We could also increase the possibility of connectivity from one teacher to another in the same grade and the consistency in teaching the same course throughout a district.

Coordination means that the student has access to the same curriculum when in the same course or grade/instructional level, regardless of the school or teacher. For instance, in one school district there were 11 teachers of U.S. history. The course catalog across the high schools had the same course title and course description. However, when the objectives were examined, 11 electives were found. The objectives were not the same; there was minimal coordination in place.

Moreover, the sequence of objectives needs to be designed in an articulated way from one grade to another. This vertical alignment is known as *articulation*, and it provides a flow or sequence from one objective to the next. Providing this articulation increases the likelihood of coordination or horizontal alignment as the curriculum is delivered. You need to decide how much vertical articulation and horizontal coordination you are going to have.

STRATEGY 7: HOW

Try the following steps to achieve Strategy 7:

1. Place the objectives in a logical teaching sequence once they have been decided on.

2. Build into the sequence both acquisition and mastery practice expectations. Some educators describe this as a type of curriculum mapping, although the formal term *curriculum mapping* has a much greater meaning in educational literature, as a type of gap analysis between what is being taught and what is supposed to be taught.

3. Sequence all objectives across grade or instructional levels and across courses.

4. Place the results in a matrix and indicate a probable timetable based on the estimated time needed to master the objective based on the typical student (see Strategy 5).

STRATEGY 8

Provide Access to Written Curriculum Documents and Direct the Objectives to Be Taught

The school-based administrators and teachers have in their possession current curriculum and instructional documents (e.g., scope and sequence charts, courses of studies, guides) for all curricular areas. Policy directs teachers to teach to the objectives and administrators to monitor their implementation.

STRATEGY 8: WHAT

A simple step not often taken in school districts is ensuring that all the users of the curriculum have access to it. This means not only that teachers and other educators should have access to the curriculum but also that the principals and other site-based administrators should have access. All teachers must have the scope and sequences of objectives for every subject and every grade; these need to be located in each written curriculum document.

However, staff members also need copies of matrixes of aligned resources and assessments for areas they do not teach. Each school and district office should have a professional library so teachers have access to the curriculum taught by other staff members. As curriculum is placed online, access becomes even easier.

Documents need to be available for students and parents as well. The scope and sequence of learning objectives needs to be on the district Web page and on the school Web page.

A second point in Strategy 8 is to determine and direct curriculum, assessment, and instructional expectations. It is essential that staff understand that the curriculum is the mission of the school. The curriculum is the very work plan of the organization. Assessments must be aligned with the curriculum, and teachers are to teach the curriculum.

To ensure the alignment of the curriculum, teaching, and assessment, the following directive statements should appear in either district board policy or administrative regulations:

- An aligned written, tested, and taught curriculum
- Board adoption of the curriculum
- Accountability through roles and responsibilities
- Written curriculum for all subject/learning areas
- Periodic review of the curriculum
- Textbook/resource alignment to curriculum and assessment
- Program integration and alignment with curriculum
- Vertical articulation and horizontal coordination
- Training for staff in the delivery of the curriculum

- Delivery of the curriculum by teachers
- Monitoring of the delivery of the curriculum by principals
- Equitable student access to the curriculum
- A student and program assessment plan
- Use of data from assessment to determine program and curriculum effectiveness
- Resource allocation tied to curriculum priorities
- Data-driven decisions for the purpose of increasing student learning

Moreover, it needs to be clear which curriculum design decisions should be system based at the district level and which should be school based. District-level curriculum design decisions are ones that are considered *tightly held*, meaning that everyone in the district is required to abide by them. These are usually board approved and deal with the mission of the district, standards, goals and priorities, student objectives, and districtwide student assessment. Curricular delivery decisions are often made at the classroom level, and these are considered *loosely held*. These include decisions about the means teachers will use to enable students to reach mastery. They include instructional strategies, groupings, staffing, resources, and textbooks.

The curriculum—what we want students to learn—and its assessment are district responsibilities. These can be decided collaboratively, but they are non-negotiable once determined. How the curriculum is delivered could be the decision of a school, grade, department, or even teacher. Before a district moves to this division of responsibility, however, a focused, precise set of learning objectives must be in place along with locally aligned assessments (see Strategies 10, 11, and 12).

In addition, the roles and responsibilities of staff regarding the design and delivery of the curriculum need to be in place. These directives should be obvious through job descriptions, appraisal processes, and student progress reports.

A third critical point in this strategy is to develop a format of the curriculum that is easy for users to understand. Provide a menu of ways users could access the information based on their preferences. Some teachers, for instance, will want only the scope and sequence of objectives. Other staff members will want example assessment items and time frames. Some staff members may want all of these plus information regarding aligned resources (see Strategy 22).

STRATEGY 8: WHY

Staff members typically will have access to the curriculum when it is initially rolled out. As the curriculum evolves, however, the revisions are not provided in a systematic way to staff. Furthermore, new staff coming on board in later years are sometimes not given the documents. It is amazing how many school districts have not provided teachers with copies of the district's curriculum documents. Teachers often report that they requested these documents several times and then gave up.

Our own observations are that principals and other school-based administrators rarely have complete copies of the curriculum in their offices. Furthermore, most school-based administrators have little or no knowledge of the curriculum. It is essential that the individuals who are supervising the work *know* the work. Most senior officers do not expect this requirement of their administrative core.

In examining board policy and administrative regulations, we came across volumes of directives, but few focused on the mission of the organization. Seldom do we come across directives requiring a written curriculum. Furthermore, policies are weak on aligned assessment expectations. Most policies do not require teachers to teach the curriculum. Policies or administrative regulations need to clearly spell out the responsibilities of curriculum, assessment, and instruction.

Job descriptions are often weak in setting up job functions regarding curriculum and its implementation. Teacher appraisal systems often fail to include the expectation that teachers are to teach the curriculum. Principal evaluation systems infrequently include the responsibility of monitoring the curriculum. (For more ideas, see Strategy 39.)

Student progress reports and grade reports rarely include the student objectives to be learned; instead, they call for a vague report on a few areas and for a grade.

Last, it is important to provide the curriculum and supporting information to teachers in a form that they will use. "One size fits all" is not a rational approach. Discussions with the users of the curriculum will tell you what they want.

STRATEGY 8: HOW

Try the following steps to achieve Strategy 8:

1. Write and adopt polices and/or approve administrative regulations that direct the design of the written curriculum, philosophical design parameters, assessment expectations, and the expectation that teachers teach the curriculum and principals monitor its use.

2. Review job descriptions of all educators to ascertain whether critical competencies regarding the curriculum and its implementation are included. Revise the job descriptions as needed.

3. Examine the teacher and principal appraisal systems to ensure that there are expectations regarding the teaching and monitoring of the curriculum.

4. Design student progress reports around the curriculum objectives as well as a specified grade.

5. Set up a process to ensure that every instructional staff member has access to a complete and current set of curriculum documents.

6. Develop a menu of ways the curriculum can be packaged to assist users in its implementation.

STRATEGY 9

Conduct Staff Development in Curriculum and Its Delivery

School-based staff members receive quality training in the curriculum scope and sequence and in the use of curriculum documents.

STRATEGY 9: WHAT

This is a commonsense strategy. Unfortunately, most districts do not even come close to providing the training necessary to prepare teachers and other staff to understand the need for a curriculum, its design, and the expectations and strategies for its implementation.

Here are some initial ideas for minimal training you need to consider:

- If you embark on a curriculum development effort, the individuals selected for this design task must have the skills needed to perform this function.
- Designers need to understand the various audiences that will use the curriculum and the various ways of packaging the curriculum, including an online curriculum for parent, student, teacher, and community member use.
- Attitudinal training is needed to ensure that teachers have a commitment to teaching the curriculum.
- Training in how the curriculum was designed and the philosophical underpinnings of its design, including alignment, is essential.
- Once the curriculum is designed, teachers, administrators, instructional aides, and other educators need to know how to enter the curriculum and how to review and use the various curriculum documents available.
- Decision-making strategies for how to implement the curriculum are absolutely imperative for teachers in ensuring the curriculum is taught.

It is critical that the curriculum design trainers recognize approaches to adult learning and establish a learning community environment. The Curriculum Management Improvement Model Criteria are as follows:

- Provides for organizational, unit, and individual development in a systemic manner
- Is based on a careful analysis of data and is data driven
- Focuses on proven research-based approaches that increase productivity
- Provides for three phases of the change process: (1) initiation, (2) implementation, and (3) institutionalization
- Is based on human learning and development as well as adult learning
- Uses a variety of staff development approaches

- Provides the follow-up and on-the-job application necessary to ensure improvement
- Requires an evaluation process that is ongoing, includes multiple sources of information, focuses on all levels of the organization, and is based on actual cases of changed behavior

STRATEGY 9: WHY

Most curriculum is designed in a hurried way over the summer, by well-meaning people who, with little or no training, attempt to design a complex curriculum in a short period of time. The result is, in almost all cases, a curriculum that is typically

- Misaligned to state and national testing scenarios
- Poorly written (goals and objectives have little precision)
- Fragmented and often duplicative
- Haphazardly articulated across grades and courses
- Overstuffed with too many objectives to be addressed within the time frame available

To write a clear, valid, and aligned curriculum requires technical curriculum-writing skills. It is imperative that the curriculum designers either have the skills or are trained in the skills to carry out the task. At a minimum, the individuals need to be analytical people with a broad understanding of the learnings across grades and disciplines. The ability to write objectives, spiral these objectives across the grades, and write aligned assessments are basic skill requirements.

Curriculum designers need to consider the various audiences who will be using the curriculum and design user-friendly documents for them. What will parents want to know? How will students use the knowledge of what they are to learn? How will teachers understand the relationship between what they are accountable to teach in relation to what other teachers are teaching? Establishing these essential questions is a first step in this process.

We have found that in most of the schools we have visited across the country, staff members are seldom committed to teaching the district curriculum; instead, staff members are textbook committed. This is in part because educators have not focused on the need for a curriculum and required that it be followed. Training in the "why" of the curriculum, its philosophical framework, and the need to follow it must take place before it is ever put into the hands of staff members.

We do not want doorstop curriculum; instead, we want a living and dynamic curriculum. There are so many reasons for teachers to use the curriculum that it would take several pages to present them, but three of the most pressing reasons are the need to

- Focus teaching on the most essential learnings, including those tested by the state or other external agencies, so that students have the opportunity to thoroughly learn ideas that will be tested.

- Connect learnings to provide a smooth flow for students across multiple teachers and to ensure students have the prerequisite learnings needed from grade to grade.
- Provide equal access to the same continuum of learning objectives even though these may be delivered in different ways. It is the right of the student to have equal access to as well as equal success with individualized strategies.

Unfortunately, and for a variety of reasons, many staff members do not have this commitment. Teaching staff are for the most part good people who work hard every day. We need to provide them with the training opportunities to achieve the expectation that faculty are not individual entrepreneurs but rather employees of the system expected to deliver the planned curriculum. K–12 public schools should not be a place where academic freedom prevails.

After the curriculum is designed and staff members have a commitment to teach it, provide training in its use. Training staff members in how to house and manage the curriculum documents—whether online, on a computer disk, or via hard copy—is critical; after this, train teachers in the various ways they can use the documents to direct their teaching.

STRATEGY 9: HOW

Try the following steps to achieve Strategy 9:

1. List all the various audiences who will need training in the curriculum and the purposes of the training.

2. Specify the competencies needed for the various audiences and purposes.

3. Establish ways to diagnose the various competencies to differentiate the staff members' development opportunities.

4. Design evaluation processes to provide feedback on the improvements of the training design as well as to assess individual proficiencies after training.

5. Develop the training opportunities around the National Staff Development Council (2001) standards.

6. Set up the timing of the training to provide staff members a minimum of six months to prepare before they are to use the curriculum.

7. Implement the training and evaluate it.

ANALYSIS OF STANDARD ONE

Now it is time for you to evaluate the status of your school or school district on *Standard One: Establish a Well-Crafted, Focused, Valid, and Clear Curriculum to Direct*

Teaching. For each strategy, think about the current status of your situation with regard to these strategies and whether the status is adequate. Then determine what changes are needed to meet the criteria of Standard One. Use the spaces below to record your observations.

Strategy	*Current status*	*Changes needed*
1. Embed external assessment target objectives in the written content standards and link them to state standards.	❐ Adequate ❐ Not adequate	
2. Have clear and precise district curriculum objectives—content, context, and cognitive type.	❐ Adequate ❐ Not adequate	
3. Deeply align objectives from external assessments.	❐ Adequate ❐ Not adequate	
4. Sequence objectives for mastery well before they are tested.	❐ Adequate ❐ Not adequate	
5. Provide a feasible number of objectives to be taught.	❐ Adequate ❐ Not adequate	
6. Identify specific objectives as benchmark standards.	❐ Adequate ❐ Not adequate	
7. Place objectives in a teaching sequence.	❐ Adequate ❐ Not adequate	
8. Provide access to written curriculum documents and direct the objectives to be taught.	❐ Adequate ❐ Not adequate	
9. Conduct staff development in curriculum and its delivery.	❐ Adequate ❐ Not adequate	

2

Standard Two

Provide Assessments Aligned With the Curriculum

Τhis chapter deals with strategies to align the district assessment practices with the district-developed curriculum. These strategies are not related just to the state accountability test but include other national and district assessments as well. Certainly, the impact of the No Child Left Behind Act (NCLB) is evident in these strategies, because that legislation has so dramatically affected what teachers teach and how school and district effectiveness are reported publicly. Criteria and cutoff scores for meeting annual yearly progress is set by states, and those criteria differ state by state. It is interesting to note that when the state definitions of proficiency are compared state by state with the National Assessment of Educational Progress (NAEP) definition, some states exceed the proficiency standard set for the NAEP, and some states fail to meet that standard. A recent article in *Education Week* compared these data (Cavanagh, 2007). While acknowledging that the study was comparing two different kinds of tests, the article pointed out that the definitions of proficiency are not consistent among state tests; neither are the state definitions of proficiency consistent with NAEP's definition. Of the 36 states that took part in the eighth-grade math test, only 3 state tests had a cutoff score that exceeded the NAEP's. Eight states had a cutoff score that was lower than the basic cutoff on the NAEP. Missouri's cutoff was the highest, and Tennessee's was the lowest. The bottom line is that state test score comparisons of annual yearly progress are based on state tests that vary in their level of difficulty.

It is assumed here that districts have taken this information under consideration when they developed their local district written curriculum and adjusted the level of difficulty of that curriculum to reflect a variety of assessments, including the addition of local district assessments as a measure of district accountability. In addition, curriculum and assessment of students proceed logically from one grade level to another, and there is an increasing level of difficulty in subject matter and application as students proceed through grades.

The impact on local district assessment practices under NCLB has been extensive. In 2006, the Center on Education Policy released results of a 4-year study about the effects of NCLB (Jennings & Rentner, 2006). These included the following:

- Scores on state tests in reading and mathematics that are used for NCLB purposes are going up, according to nearly three fourths of the states and school districts, and achievement gaps on these same tests are generally narrowing or staying the same;
- Schools are spending more time on reading and math, sometimes at the expense of subjects not tested;
- Schools are paying much more attention to the alignment of curriculum and instruction and are analyzing test score data much more closely;
- Low-performing schools are undergoing make-overs rather than the most radical kinds of restructuring;
- Schools and teachers have made considerable progress in demonstrating that teachers meet the law's academic qualifications—but many educators are skeptical this will really improve the quality of teaching;
- Students are taking a lot more tests;
- Schools are paying much more attention to achievement gaps and the learning needs of particular groups of students;
- The percentage of schools on state "needs improvement" lists has been steady but is not growing. Schools so designated are subject to NCLB sanctions, such as being required to offer students public school choice or tutoring services;
- The federal government is playing a bigger role in education; and
- NCLB requirements have meant that state governments and school districts also have expanded roles in school operations, but often without adequate federal funds to carry out their duties. (Jennings & Rentner, 2006, pp. 110–113)

When creating a local district assessment system, a good starting point is to review the state's assessment system and to go beyond it to match the district's assessment system with the district curriculum. The strategies recommended here apply to that expanded assessment system. The following are nine powerful strategies regarding the assessment process that can be used to achieve high student achievement:

1. **Strategy 10: Develop Aligned District Pre–Post Criterion-Referenced Assessments.** For each objective, there are criterion-referenced assessment items aligned by content, context, and type of cognition. From these items the district has secure, district-level, pre–post assessments aligned with each district objective and external assessment. Practice assessments are also available. All assessment items for each objective are equivalent/parallel. These tests will be given to students at the appropriate instructional level.

2. **Strategy 11: Have a Pool of Unsecured Test Items by Objective.** The district staff provide multiple, equivalent (unsecured) criterion-referenced assessments for each objective. These are provided to teachers for use in diagnosing prerequisite skills acquisition and mastery of objectives.

3. **Strategy 12: Establish Secured Performance Benchmark Assessments.** The district staff provide secured performance benchmark tests that assess some of the objectives for each grade level/course. These are administered as pre–post tests at the beginning of and near the end of the school year or at the end of each grading period.

4. **Strategy 13: Conduct Assessment Training.** The district staff provide adequate training in classroom use of aligned assessments for directing classroom teaching.

5. **Strategy 14: Use Assessments Diagnostically.** Teachers use the assessments to gain diagnostic data regarding student learning of the objectives (prerequisite skills acquisition and mastery), for program assessment, and to direct instruction.

6. **Strategy 15: Teach Students to Be "Test Wise."** Teachers teach students test-taking skills that are aligned with the type of high-stakes tests being administered at the national, state, and district levels.

7. **Strategy 16: Establish a Reasonable Testing Schedule and Environment.** The district staff and school staff provide a reasonable schedule of testing as well as a proper physical setting for all assessment situations.

8. **Strategy 17: Disaggregate Assessment Data.** District assessments, as well as external assessments, are disaggregated by student, teacher, course/class/grade level, gender, race, socioeconomic level, and primary language and are used in making program and classroom decisions.

9. **Strategy 18: Maintain Student Progress Reports.** Teachers maintain individual student progress reports by district objectives; students and parents are knowledgeable about the student's progress on such objectives.

STRATEGY 10

Develop Aligned District Pre–Post Criterion-Referenced Assessments

For each objective, there are criterion-referenced assessment items aligned by content, context, and type of cognition. From these items the district has secure, district-level, pre–post assessments aligned to each district objective and external assessment. Practice assessments are also available. All assessment items for each objective are equivalent/parallel. These tests will be given to students at the appropriate instructional level.

STRATEGY 10: WHAT

Student assessment has always been an integral part of the classroom teaching process. Teachers regularly assess students to determine what they have learned. These assessments generally take place at the end of a unit, chapter, or semester. They provide teachers with valuable information that informs their instructional planning for the next sequence.

With this strategy we are suggesting that a key component of the assessment process is the notion of both pretesting and posttesting students so that instruction can be planned that takes into consideration the skills and knowledge students bring to the learning situation. The key beginning point here is the pretesting. In order for teachers to develop a pretest, they must have a clear understanding of the objectives that are going to be included in a teaching sequence. Yeh (2006) went so far as to suggest that rapid assessment can enable teachers to use test results to deliver more balanced instruction. Rapid assessment involves the use of frequent, short assessments to provide teachers with information about what students have learned after a few days of instruction. The data are used to help create future instructional planning; they provide teachers with "rapid diagnostic information about student progress, and support more effective, efficient, individualized instruction that keeps more students at grade level with less effort" (Yeh, 2006, p. 93). This practice ultimately helps teachers reduce the need for "drill and kill" teaching and results in increased instructional time to focus on higher order skills and a balanced curriculum.

As discussed earlier, by reviewing test results teachers know which students are mastering the objectives and which students need more practice. With this information, subsequent instruction can be designed to remediate the areas of deficiency and bring all students up to a level of proficiency deemed necessary by the teacher.

The sequence of planning, teaching, testing, and reviewing results needs to be applied beyond the classroom to the broader context of district, state, and national accountability assessment. Moreover, it is important that we not look at the model as a teach-and-test approach but as a pretest, plan, teach, test, reteach, and extend approach as well. This is elaborated in Strategy 28 (Implement a Mastery Learning Model).

STRATEGY 10: WHY

There is an old adage that says, "Students do better on tests if you teach them what you test than if you don't." It is common sense to be sure that students are taught the material on which they are tested. This is just as true for state and national accountability assessments as it is for classroom assessments.

These assessments must include both content and context alignment. *Content alignment* refers to the subject matter being assessed. If students are to be tested on two-digit multiplication, then they should be taught two-digit multiplication. Most published state and national frameworks describe the content goals and objectives that are to be assessed on the state examination. *Context alignment* refers to the format of the assessment. Typical classroom assessments include true–false, completion, and short essay responses. Students become familiar with these types of assessments and are not surprised when faced with them. On the other hand, students may not be familiar with multiple-choice assessments or open-ended response items. If the first time a student sees this type of assessment is on the state test, the lack of familiarity may prevent the student from answering correctly and not allow the student to display the knowledge he or she possesses.

Teachers should think of the state and other external assessment systems as graphic organizers for their teaching. For example, the state curriculum framework becomes the content taught (similar to a teaching unit), the state assessment becomes the measure of how well students learned the content (similar to the end-of-unit test), and the lessons teachers plan enable students to learn the material. The process entails taking what is already common practice in classrooms and expanding it to a broader arena.

By constructing a pre- and posttest assessment system that is aligned with the state framework and assessment system, classroom teachers are simply following the good pedagogy they currently understand and use. These pre- and posttest assessments allow teachers to gain knowledge about how well students are performing and allow them to construct lesson plans that specifically address gaining the assessed skills.

In most states, accountability assessment does not occur for all content areas, but it should occur for all content areas at the district level. This means that the district should have developed curriculum objectives for all content areas and grade levels so that curriculum teachers can prepare pre- and posttests. Moreover, it is important that for every objective there are pre–post measures available. This will serve a diagnostic purpose as well as provide for mastery assessment of the curriculum objectives. We need to know what students know *before* we begin to teach them (pretest), and we need to know what the students have learned (posttest). If something is important enough to teach, then it is important enough to evaluate.

STRATEGY 10: HOW

Try the following steps to achieve Strategy 10:

1. Identify state accountability benchmark assessments and other external assessments. These include not only tests that are currently in use but also future tests that are in the planning stage. Most states are moving away from standardized, norm-referenced tests to a combination of criterion-referenced tests and short- and extended-response items.

2. Disaggregate released test items to identify areas for content and context alignment. Identify the vocabulary, knowledge, and skills assessed. This can be done in a teacher in-service session. It provides teachers with a greater understanding of exactly what skills and knowledge students need to be successful on state tests. Do this in conjunction with Strategy 3.

3. Backload developmental skills into earlier grade levels to identify where mastery should take place. All tests assess cumulative knowledge. The level at which a skill is tested is not necessarily the level at which that skill is mastered. By disaggregating test items and determining where mastery of subskills takes place, teachers are better able to understand which skills students need at each grade level. Do this in conjunction with Strategy 4.

4. Construct pre–post tests to assess student mastery of necessary vocabulary, knowledge, and skills. If the state test is the first time a student encounters a particular test item format, the student is not likely to perform as well as if she or he had practice with the format during regular instruction.

5. Utilize assessment data to teach and reteach until mastery is achieved.

6. Require teachers to teach to mastery so that they will be able to determine when mastery has been achieved. Merely "covering" the material is not sufficient (see also Strategy 28).

7. Develop data entry and tracking systems for students, classes, grades, and schools. This will undoubtedly require the use of computer management systems to enable the teacher to continuously update student achievement data. Many such systems are currently available.

8. Treat this sequence as the formative assessment portion of both the curriculum design and its delivery (e.g., classroom instruction and teacher-made tests should be considered part of the formative assessment system). This system enables teachers to provide extensions, remediation, and enrichment. As the saying goes, "All students do not learn in the same way on the same day." The era when it was acceptable for teachers to feel satisfied if they merely taught the material is over. It is no longer acceptable for teachers to blame society, the economy, the student, or parents for lack of student achievement. Although all of these areas do influence student achievement, they do not relieve the teacher from accountability for student achievement.

STRATEGY 11

Have a Pool of Unsecured Test Items by Objective

The district staff provide multiple, equivalent (unsecured) criterion-referenced assessments for each objective. These are provided to teachers for use in diagnosing prerequisite skills acquisition and mastery of objectives.

STRATEGY 11: WHAT

In order for teachers to use ongoing assessments for diagnostic, acquisition, and mastery purposes throughout the instructional process, they need access to a pool of unsecured test items for each curricular objective. This is traditionally accomplished by deconstructing released test items from various external assessments, assessing and identifying the objectives assessed, and backloading them into appropriate grade levels and content areas.

These test items should be easily available to all teachers on computers in their classrooms. Furthermore, teachers should be able to access multiple items simply by placing a request into the system by objective. Such a system can be developed at the district level, or one can be secured from a private vendor. Textbook publishers routinely develop banks of test items in a variety of contexts that are linked to the content of textbooks. Although textbook publishers will almost always assure districts that the content objectives in the text match the content objectives assessed on the state accountability assessment, these materials need to be reviewed to ensure that the match includes not only the content objective but also the type of cognition and the context of the state test. If the district has broadened its written curriculum to include content objectives that go beyond the state framework, then additional test items must be developed locally that can be used for pre- and posttesting.

Teachers are always interested in how well students are doing in their acquisition of needed skills. However, their time is limited, and this time should be spent primarily on designing individualized instruction instead of on test item development. Students, too, need to be trained to seek feedback about how well they are doing. Easy access to test items can enable students to prepare their own preassessments before requesting competency assessment from the teacher.

Good assessment is good instruction. The two should not be seen as separate activities; instead, assessment should reinforce teaching and be considered part of instruction.

In far too many classrooms, assessment is not considered instruction. When teachers and students become adept at utilizing the pool of backloaded assessment items matched to the district curriculum, improved achievement is almost assured.

This process facilitates the utilization of on-demand assessment by students; that is, when a student feels she or he has achieved the skills to be assessed, she or he requests a posttest from the teacher and takes it. These tests are usually given in class while students are working on a variety of activities. There is little test anxiety, because the teacher does not ask the student to take the assessment before determining whether the student is ready to display the necessary skills.

STRATEGY 11: WHY

Many problems related to improving student achievement are related not so much to the inability of students to learn but to providing an instructional environment in which there is a tight relationship among the written, taught, and tested curriculum—in other words, where there is alignment.

The more familiar students are with the content and context of the assessment, the greater the parallelism, or transfer of the learning. For example, if the state accountability assessment at the fourth-grade level requires a student to write a paragraph with a beginning, middle, and end, then a student who has practiced writing many paragraphs with a beginning, middle, and end will perform much better than a student who has practiced only writing topic sentences or completing workbook sheets on grammar.

Access to a pool of unsecured test items helps inform teachers about what is tested and what form the test will take. This availability also helps inform students and enables them to take more responsibility for their own learning.

Most important of all is the teacher's ability to differentiate instruction so that the objectives being taught are at the right level of difficulty for each student. Without ongoing assessments, teachers often prepare and deliver total class instruction that does not take into account whether students have the appropriate prerequisite skills or whether they have already mastered the objectives and can demonstrate this mastery in multiple-assessment scenarios.

STRATEGY 11: HOW

Try the following steps to achieve Strategy 11:

1. Obtain lists of district curriculum objectives assessed by content area and grade level.

2. Identify sources of test items in the same format as the state, national, and international accountability assessments. Many companies advertise the availability of parallel test items for almost every state assessment. Buyers beware! First, note any constraints by the state regarding access to such items. In the past, some states have included using past editions of tests as a violation of the state's code of ethics for testing. Be sure to check this out for your state. Second, if the district is considering buying such materials,

they should be analyzed carefully to ensure there is content, type of cognition, and context alignment. It is important to understand that sometimes these items are overused to "drill and kill" student interest and motivation. In this scenario, students may become proficient at doing similar problems without gaining any understanding of the skills necessary for dealing with more difficult problems. These materials can be useful, but they should not be the only source of skill application for students.

3. Conduct a cost–benefit analysis. Is it more costly to buy test items, or would it be better to commission curriculum developers or teachers within the district to develop the alternate test items? The development of these alternate test items can be a useful staff development activity.

4. Pilot test the test items.

5. Train teachers to deconstruct test items and develop parallel items to match daily lesson plans.

6. Consider using test items as "starters" for students to complete at the beginning of class. This practice not only would give students more opportunity to become proficient with the context of test items but also could reinforce previously taught skills and content.

STRATEGY 12

Establish Secured Performance Benchmark Assessments

The district staff provide secured performance benchmark tests that assess some of the objectives for each grade level/course. These are administered as pre–post tests at the beginning of and near the end of the school year or at the end of each grading period.

STRATEGY 12: WHAT

Just as there is a need for formative assessment measures to determine how effective teacher instruction has been, there is also a need for periodic, benchmark assessment of a summative nature. Summative evaluation enables educators to know whether they have met their target. To hit the target, all students must show mastery of standards and objectives in the written district curriculum. Benchmarks are different than *benchmarking*: "Benchmarks are outcomes, numbers, metrics, standards. Benchmarks tell you where you can improve" (Grayson, 2007, p. 44).

It is recommended that districts develop summative assessment measures that parallel not only the state's accountability assessment but also the district curriculum objectives. These assessments supplement the more frequently given pre–post test assessments developed by teachers.

Summative assessments are referred to as *performance benchmark tests*. These tests are secured and administered following the same procedures used to administer the state and national assessments, and they are common across the school district. Although the pre–post test assessments may be included as part of a testing bank available to all teachers in the system, the performance benchmark tests are not.

If the district is large enough, and has the expertise necessary to develop reliable and valid parallel assessments, these performance benchmark tests can be constructed internally within the system. Most large public school systems now develop their own benchmark assessments. These are typically given at the end of a grading period and enable the district to determine the extent to which students have mastered the knowledge and skills that will be part of formalized accountability assessments typically administered near the end of the school year. If the district is small and lacks this area of specialization, it may be necessary to secure these assessments from an outside source. In some states, these benchmark assessments are provided by the state for a nominal charge. In addition, many companies offer test construction services, including the construction of benchmark assessments, to districts.

Today, most districts have developed what they call *pacing guides*. These guides identify the goals and objectives to be taught during a grading period. They are intended to produce more uniformity across a district in the pacing of instruction. The good thing about pacing guides is that they help provide uniformity of instruction among schools so that, for example, when a third-grader moves to a new section of town and enrolls in a new elementary school, the new school is teaching approximately the same objectives as the previously attended school. The bad thing about pacing guides is that teachers tend to feel they must keep up with the objectives listed for each grading period regardless of whether students have mastered the skills. Often these guides do not allow enough time for reteaching unmastered skills. Without adequate time for reteaching to attain mastery, these pacing guides can actually become a deterrent to mastery (see Standard Four).

There may be a need for differentiated benchmarking. Admittedly, with the exception of modifications for students identified for special services, state and national accountability assessments are not differentiated; however, there may be merit in developing benchmark assessments to more closely match the curriculum objectives for students in different programs. State accountability assessments are written, and cutoff scores determined, with the understanding that almost all students will be taking the same test. More useful data may be gathered by differentiating the benchmark assessments for students in Advanced Placement (AP) classes versus students in classes designed to enable them to meet the minimum standards of the state accountability assessments. A benchmark assessment for students enrolled in the International Baccalaureate program would be more useful to the teachers and students in that program if the benchmark assessment were more closely linked to the assessments for that program than for the state accountability assessment. Few districts are approaching benchmark assessment in this way.

Another consideration is the timely scoring of benchmark assessments. Results of these assessments must include information at the student level and by groups in the same way as the state and national accountability assessments. This means that data are provided by gender; ethnicity; and special designation, such as eligibility for free and reduced lunch and special education. These data can inform the need for modification in the district curriculum, instructional materials, and teaching strategies. All of this points to the need for more local district customization in benchmark assessment.

STRATEGY 12: WHY

By constructing this internal system of assessment, the district can be assured that all teachers are focusing instruction on the curriculum assessed by the state and expected by the district. It also enables districts to track the achievement of students enrolled in programs that exceed state standards.

At present, most classroom teachers use the textbook as their major resource for instructional planning. As stated earlier, this practice is ineffective in producing the type of content, context, and type of cognition alignment required for various groups of students. Without district performance assessment there is insufficient assurance of coordination across grades and schools as well as articulation from one level of the system to the next (e.g., elementary school to middle school to high school).

Results from benchmark assessment measures enable teachers and administrators to determine the extent to which students are achieving across the system, school by school, class by class, and program by program. Without this information, educators cannot take the necessary steps to refocus instruction on areas of deficiency.

STRATEGY 12: HOW

Try the following steps to achieve Strategy 12:

1. Treat differentiated performance benchmark assessments as summative assessments for students. A summative assessment is used to determine whether students have met the standard of student achievement required. It is a periodic line drawn in the sand to determine how well we are doing as a school or a system in achieving stated benchmarks for students. These summative assessments can be presented within a grading period or after a level of instruction, such as elementary school or high school. They can be developed to measure multiyear achievement in basic skill development. Most typically, these assessments are given in the areas of mathematics, science, reading, and writing; however, the district eventually needs to design them for all subject areas and levels of instruction.

2. Be sure goals and objectives assessed are understood by the faculty. This mandate should apply to all teachers in all grades and all content areas. The physical education teachers should be just as aware of the writing assessment as the art teacher and the reading teacher. Because the school typically is the unit of accountability today, all teachers in the school are often judged by the public on very narrow areas of the curriculum. All teachers must accept accountability for all areas of content assessment.

3. Classroom instruction/assessment should mirror content/context performance benchmark tests. State testing should not be a time when teachers stop doing what they normally do in classrooms to provide different instruction for test taking. Whatever format is used for the test should sometimes be incorporated into regular classroom instruction through practice exercises and in the classroom testing situations.

4. Arrange for timely scoring. It is not uncommon for results of state assessment measures given in the spring to arrive back in the district in August. States are working hard to shorten this time frame so that teachers have access to the data before the school year ends. This access enables teachers to analyze these results and determine how they need to modify and adjust their instructional strategies to increase the achievement level of their students. Unfortunately, this is not always possible. School and district leaders should apply whatever pressure they can to ensure that results are returned to the school in a timely manner, and certainly the district measures should be returned in a timely manner.

5. Identify a school contact person. Each school needs to have an official assessment contact person so that parents, students, and faculty can get a quick response to questions regarding assessment. Most districts have one central office person with this designation. Because assessment accountability has become so important to public education, it is time to provide such a contact at the school level.

6. Report results to teachers at all grades, not just the grades tested (see also Strategy 38). Teachers in grade levels not assessed are equally in need of the results so that they can be sure that students at their grade level have achieved mastery of the subskills necessary for subsequent learning.

7. Ensure that teachers in all content areas are preparing students to achieve at high levels on these tests. If reading scores are low, all teachers in all content areas can be held accountable for providing students with opportunities to read, comprehend, and think critically about what they are learning. These are fundamental skills and not reserved solely for reading class.

8. Link school improvement plans to improved student achievement (see also Strategy 42). Far too often, school improvement plans address enabling activities as opposed to student achievement activities. For instance, it is common to see school improvement plans that call for the development of new programs, such as after-school child care. Too often,

the initiation of these programs becomes an end in itself, and they may not be linked to improved student achievement. Supplementary programs not linked to improved student achievement should be reviewed to determine their benefits.

9. Require that data from these benchmark assessments be utilized in the school improvement process. This means that specific student results will be reflected in the school improvement plans and targets for improvement will be set. The meeting of these requirements is linked to the development or continuation of school site programs. There is an expectation that schools will improve each year.

STRATEGY 13

Conduct Assessment Training

The district staff provide adequate training in classroom use of aligned assessments for directing classroom teaching.

STRATEGY 13: WHAT

Teachers and building administrators need to be trained in the proper and ethical use of assessments (Neukrug & Fawcett, 2006). Many teachers employed in schools today were trained at a time when there were no state accountability systems in place. Norm-referenced tests were commonly used as a sorting mechanism, and teachers rarely saw test results unless they specifically asked for them. There was a general belief that teachers knew best what students should learn and accomplish, and test results were rarely used to make a determination as to whether schools were effective. All of that has changed with the accountability movement.

What we have learned, rather painfully, is not that teachers are doing a poor job in the classroom but rather that there has been little focus and connectivity within school systems regarding what students should know and be able to do.

Because attitudes about assessment are firmly linked to a teacher's fundamental belief system, it is critically important to provide teachers with the necessary assessment training to ensure that they understand accountability assessment; adopt the dispositions necessary to support accountability assessment; and change their instructional planning to ensure congruence among the written, taught, and tested curriculum.

The Code of Fair Testing Practices was developed by the Joint Committee on Testing Practices (2004). This code covers the following topics:

1. Developing and Selecting Appropriate Tests

2. Administering and Scoring Tests

3. Reporting and Interpreting Test Results

4. Informing Test Takers

The Joint Committee includes representation from a variety of professional organizations, including the American Educational Research Association, American Psychological Association, and the National Council on Measurement in Education, in addition to others.

A few of the practices recommended for use include the following:

- Define the purpose for testing, the content and skills to be tested, and the intended test takers. Select and use the most appropriate test based on a thorough review of the available information.
- Evaluate evidence of the technical quality of the test provided by the test developers and any independent reviewers.
- Review the procedures for setting performance standards or passing scores. Avoid using stigmatizing labels.
- Encourage test users to base decisions about test takers on multiple sources of appropriate information, not on a single test score. (Joint Committee on Testing Practices, 2004, pp. 259–262)

See the full report for additional information about recommended practices for test developers and test users.

STRATEGY 13: WHY

Most classroom teachers today remember when it was necessary to sign a document attesting to adherence to a testing code of ethics. These documents were prepared by state departments of education to ensure that teachers were not testing students with the exact items that would appear on a state accountability test. To do so was (and still is) considered a breach of ethics that merited severe penalties, sometimes even loss of one's teaching license.

For some teachers, adhering to a testing code of ethics has been mistakenly interpreted to mean that teaching the skills assessed on the state accountability test is a violation of the code. Fortunately, the number of teachers who believe this today is small.

What is also unclear to teachers is the degree to which it is ethical to teach to the test learnings. This is especially troublesome in states that continue to use a norm-referenced test as their measure of accountability.

The vast majority of states are moving to a state accountability system that is more transparent and provides teachers with examples of test item content, context, and type of cognition. In these states, the objectives students are to learn are stated, made available to teachers, and form the basis for the development of the state test. These states routinely make sample test items available to teachers so that teachers can develop instruction aligned to the state assessment.

Regardless of the type of state assessment used, all teachers need a clear understanding of the assessments in use. As the district builds the item pool, pre–post tests, and benchmark performance assessments, teachers need to understand the system and how to use it in order to maximize student achievement.

What teachers need to know about assessment has expanded greatly in this age of accountability. Topics appropriate for staff development include the following:

- Choosing assessment procedures based on test worthiness
- Ensuring competence in the use of tests
- Disaggregating test scores and using data to inform instructional planning
- Keeping information confidential
- Attending to cross-cultural issues
- Obtaining informed consent when required
- Releasing information properly and carefully
- Ensuring the integrity of test content and test security
- Promptly scoring and interpreting test scores

STRATEGY 13: HOW

Try the following steps to achieve Strategy 13:

1. Identify the most common traditional and authentic assessment instruments used to assess student achievement. All teachers in the system must be aware of these assessments and understand how these assessments are used to make accountability decisions within the school. This information should not be confined simply to the content areas assessed, such as mathematics and reading; instead, all teachers at all grade levels should understand the accountability assessments used within the system. They should also understand that they are accountable for ensuring that students perform well on these assessments.

2. Focus initial training on types of instruments used for accountability assessment. Although initial training should focus on state-mandated accountability assessments, additional training should be provided for all districtwide assessments used within the system.

3. Identify assessment trainers/coaches. Because teachers vary considerably in their knowledge and understanding of assessment, it is worthwhile to appoint school assessment trainers/coaches and pay them the same stipend paid to athletic trainers/coaches.

4. Develop training modules over time for use over time with teachers of varying levels of expertise/competence:
   - Novice—For newly hired teachers
     Provide an overview of the accountability instruments. These teachers are generally nontenured, inexperienced teachers working in their first job.

What they know about assessment is usually confined to what they learned in their preservice training. The reality of accountability assessment is often foreign to them, and they often need help in understanding how these assessments affect their instructional planning.

- Professional—For experienced teachers
  Provide information about a wide variety of traditional and authentic assessments. Professional teachers have usually been in the system for some time. Their skills in the area of assessment can be expanded to include a wider variety of assessments, including more authentic assessment techniques.

  Train professional teachers to serve as assessment coaches for a novice teacher, a role they often enjoy. By serving in this role, professional teachers gain additional competence and self-esteem and continue to move toward the role of expert teacher.

- Expert—For teachers wanting to keep abreast of the latest developments in assessment
  Provide opportunities for study groups, outside-district training, and stipends for teaching in-service sessions to district staff. Teachers at this level can serve as the district's cutting-edge experts. They enjoy following the latest research on effective assessment strategies and can be influential in bringing this information back to the district.

5. Develop examples of quality anchor assessments suitable for use at a variety of grade levels and content areas. Anchor assessments enable teachers to see actual examples of quality work at each grade level. These assessments can also be used as examples of exemplary work and shared with students.

6. Train staff in the utilization of assessment technology programs. A large number of companies are developing assessment technology programs to enable teachers to construct individualized tests for students. All districts should be investigating these programs and investing in appropriate technology and software so that those teachers can construct on-demand tests for students.

7. Provide focus group opportunities for teachers to talk about their attitudes regarding the utilization of assessment items. With the large proportion of teachers who still have negative feelings about teaching to tests, these focus groups offer an opportunity for discussion about these issues.

8. Create a professional assessment library. Every school should have a large inventory of professional development materials in the area of assessment. These can include videotapes, books, journal articles, and research studies.

STRATEGY 14

Use Assessments Diagnostically

Teachers use the assessments to gain diagnostic data regarding student learning of the objectives (prerequisite skills acquisition and mastery), for program assessment, and to direct instruction.

STRATEGY 14: WHAT

Using assessment data diagnostically should take place at the classroom, school, and district levels. Data from this type of assessment can be used to assess student readiness, differentiate instruction, design new program initiatives, plan and conduct instruction, place students, provide feedback, and track the progress of various groups of students. In the course of a given day, a teacher may use diagnostic data to make a multitude of decisions, such as the following:

- Move a student from one group to another
- Reteach a skill
- Discontinue a planned lesson in order to review a key skill
- Group certain students together
- Assign grades
- Decide to spend additional time for students to review their portfolios
- Assign homework in one subject and not another
- Develop a scoring rubric with students to assess their writing
- Review last year's assessment data

The list could go on and on. In making most of these decisions, teachers are utilizing assessment data and using them diagnostically. Airasian (2000) defined *assessment* as "the process of collecting, synthesizing and interpreting information to aid in decision-making." Teachers generally utilize three types of assessments: (1) official, (2) instructional, and (3) sizing-up assessments (Airasian, 1997). Official assessments are often standardized at the district, state, or national level and often rely on paper-and-pencil techniques such as short- and extended-response items and selected response items. The NAEP, the SAT, and AP tests are all examples of official assessments; however, teachers rely on a multitude of non-standardized assessments to make diagnostic decisions. These nonstandardized assessments may include observations, oral questioning, teacher-made tests, and performance assessments.

Data from both standardized and nonstandardized diagnostic assessments can be disaggregated in many ways, such as by student, gender, ethnicity, and socioeconomic level (see also Strategy 17 and Strategy 38). Diagnostic assessment data can be used to identify trends and track these patterns over time.

Diagnostic assessment involves making judgments about how students are performing against a predetermined set of criteria. For instance, it is common practice for diagnostic tests to be given to children entering kindergarten to assess their readiness for school. "Readiness tests measure what a person has learned and then use this information to discern whether he or she is ready to enter the next educational level" (Neukrug & Fawcett, 2006, p. 115).

To be most effective, diagnostic assessment should be build into the curriculum and not seen as an add-on. It must be linked to predetermined learning objectives and provide teachers with information about the learning needs of students at a level of specificity that will enable the teacher to design instruction at the right level of difficulty. Students can also be involved in the review of diagnostic assessments so that they better understand where they are relative to the stated objectives. This analysis should enable students and teachers to identify the appropriate next steps in the learning process.

Diagnostic assessment can be approached in both an informal and a formal way. Informal diagnostic assessment can occur by giving individual students short assessments on an ad hoc basis as teachers see a need for more information about an individual student's mastery of a particular skill. These informal assessments can be given to individual students, small groups, or the whole class. Regular student assignments can be reviewed with an eye for identification of particular skills on which students need to work. Formal diagnostic assessments are currently available for assessing individuals or large groups of students. The Key Math—Revised assessment has been described as one of the best diagnostic instruments for assessing a student's understanding of basic math concepts (Wollack, 2001). Many diagnostic assessments have been developed since the passage of Public Law 94-142 in 1975. These assessments initially were used to identify students with learning disabilities. Today, formal diagnostic assessments are used for a multitude of purposes, from assessing a student's language proficiency to his or her overall achievement.

Classroom teachers should review assessment data to determine where students are achieving and where additional instruction is needed. Teachers should be able to identify subgroups in the classroom that need extra support and provide for that support in the regular classroom. If outside support is offered, there should be clear communication between the classroom teacher and the support teacher in order to maximize improved results.

At the building and district levels, school administrators should routinely analyze test data to determine current overall levels of student achievement and to project realistic yearly goals. These data should become the basic needs assessment for school improvement plans, and they should be shared with interested stakeholders in the community via newsletters, press releases, and presentations. It should be understood that the school and staff operate from a data-driven culture. When new programs are designed, they should be data based, with a clear link between program objectives and improved student achievement (see also Strategy 19).

STRATEGY 14: WHY

The volume of things to teach is limitless, but the time to teach them is finite. Instructional time is probably our most valuable resource; we cannot afford to use it unwisely. By using data, diagnostic assessment, and disaggregation techniques, teachers and school principals can maximize the use of instructional time.

When a data-driven culture is created in classrooms and schools, a new synergy arises because teachers and students can see, track, and celebrate their success. There is a greater sense of relevance among teachers about the value of assessment and how the knowledge gained can actually lead to expanding the amount of instructional time by eliminating time spent on skills students have already mastered and focusing instruction on students' areas of need. These practices lead to a renewed sense of ownership among teachers in managing learning.

It is important to keep in mind that in using assessment data our primary objective is to help each student achieve his or her potential. In doing this we should be mindful to respect a student's desire to pursue learning in a variety of ways, not just the one prescribed by the teacher; not place students in situations where they will be embarrassed or treated unkindly; and not exclude students or deny benefits from participation or grant some students an advantage over others.

STRATEGY 14: HOW

Try the following steps to achieve Strategy 14:

1. Ensure that teachers are using the pool of assessment items on a regular basis in the classroom to diagnose where each student is in his or her learning and to use these data to differentiate the instruction (see also Strategy 30).

2. Use the "Pareto Principle" (according to which a few account for the many) to determine instructional priorities on the basis of the analysis of assessment results. Raising an average score is accomplished by dealing with the largest group of students in a common area (e.g., by quartile) and improving their scores. The greater the gain by those nearest the bottom, the more impact there is on raising average scores (greater than by raising the scores of those at the top). This is true if the number of students in the bottom quartile is greater than the number of students near the top, which is typically the case.

3. At the beginning of the school year, provide classroom teachers with student achievement results for the new class (based on previous assessments) as well as for last year's class. This enables the teacher to understand the skill deficiencies of the present class and determine deficiencies experienced the year prior. Conduct an item-by-item analysis of class results. This item analysis reveals the specific areas of skill deficiency both

of students entering the class at the beginning of the year and students who were in the teacher's class last year.

4. Determine skill areas on which to focus from the item analysis. More instructional time will need to be devoted to the areas of deficiency for the students entering the class at the beginning of the year. In addition, the teacher will have to develop alternative instructional strategies for the areas of deficiency of students who were in the teacher's class the year prior.

5. Develop parallel test items to assess the prerequisite skills that students should have mastered coming into the course/class. These pretests will help the teacher identify specific skill deficiencies.

6. Identify students who require development support. Not all students in the class will need additional instruction and time for guided practice, but those who do must be targeted, or their future learning will not be successful.

7. Determine the type of support needed. By pinpointing the area of difficulty, teachers can provides students with focused instruction and coaching to overcome the deficiency.

8. Current instructional materials must be reviewed to determine whether they provide for content and context alignment. If they do not, additional support materials will need to be acquired or developed by the teacher.

9. Make needed adjustments to maximize alignment.

10. Develop deeply aligned test items. Deeply aligned test items not only ask the student to apply skills assessed on parallel test items but also demand more sophisticated transfer. For instance, if an item calls for interpretation of a single bar graph, a deeply aligned item may require interpretation of a multiple-bar graph.

STRATEGY 15

Teach Students to Be "Test Wise"

Teachers teach students test-taking skills that are aligned with the type of high-stakes tests being administered at the national, state, and district levels.

STRATEGY 15: WHAT

To be "test wise" is to understand how tests are formatted and how to properly respond and record answers. Without this knowledge, students do not perform as well as they could. They may know the information, but they lack knowledge of the testing approach. Students should not fear the testing situation. Fear usually comes from the unknown. When students learn about the nature of tests, practice successfully completing them, and think about how they accomplished what they did, the fear of the testing situation is dissipated.

The public preoccupation with test scores can be traced back to the 1980s and the publication of *A Nation at Risk* (National Commission on Excellence in Education, 1983). With the passage of NCLB, the United States moved into an unprecedented era of high-stakes assessment. This began with the general public's growing discontent about the effectiveness of U.S. schools. As the movement gained force, there was more pressure to use norm-referenced test results as an indicator for how well students were learning. By the early 1990s, many states were requiring that students be tested by a common state test at the elementary level, middle school level, and high school level, and the results of these assessments were made public. Tests were often administered in Grades 4, 8, and 10. The tests were usually norm referenced and multiple choice in format. Now, NCLB regulations require assessment in Grades 3 through 8 in math and reading. Many states have added writing assessments, and the tests have become criterion-referenced tests. Some states have expended the content areas assessed to include science, technology, and other subjects. High school graduation tests are frequently used, and more states are adding end-of-course assessments to the state battery of required evaluations (Gewertz, 2007).

As time passed, these high-stakes, legislatively mandated tests became increasingly important, because actions were taken by states on the basis of the results. For students, results were often linked to high school graduation. For districts, the public tended to make a judgment about the quality of a school district based on the percentage of students who reached a particular cutoff score that brought with it a certain designation. In the 1990s, these designations were applied to districts and schools. With the passage of NCLB, the level of data disaggregation includes analysis by gender, ethnicity, socioeconomic status, and language proficiency, among other variables.

During this time, questions about ethical testing practices were raised. Articles began to appear detailing incidents where teacher and administrators engaged in unethical test preparation practices to affect test results. In 1995, James Pophan wrote a book entitled *Classroom Assessment: What Teachers Need to Know*. The intent of this book was to provide teachers with information about how they should make assessment decisions that would impact student learning in a positive way. Pophan identified two overarching standards that classroom assessment practices should meet. One standard dealt with professional ethics, and the other dealt with educational defensibility. Pophan took the position that both standards must be met:

- Professional Ethics: No test-preparation practice should violate the ethical norms of the education profession.
- Educational Defensibility: No test-preparation practice should increase students' test scores without simultaneously increasing students' mastery of the assessment domain tested. (pp. 233–235)

Pophan (1995) further outlined five test-preparation practices and discussed whether he felt they met the two standards:

- Previous-form preparation
- Current-form preparation
- Generalized test-taking preparation
- Same format preparation
- Varied format preparation (pp. 236–238)

Only two of these practices met both of Pophan's (1995) standards: (1) generalized test-taking practices and (2) varied format practices. He argued against the use of previous forms and the current form of the test and felt that using the same format, though ethical, did not meet the standard of educational defensibility. Of course, we would all agree that using test items from the current assessment in test preparation is unethical and probably criminal. Because state assessments only sample a knowledge domain, then if the test-preparation activities focus primarily on taking previously released tests, students are not prepared for the entire knowledge domain. However, we believe that if prior assessments are used to disaggregate the skills students need in order to understand how to approach a particular test item format, and these skills are built into the district's instructional program, then that practice meets both criteria. We would describe that as *topological alignment* (see Strategy 3). Our position is that topological alignment is a place to start. We then advocate *deep alignment*, which involves going beyond the current state assessment system and using a variety of assessments to deepen the students' knowledge of the content domain, using many different types of cognition.

STRATEGY 15: WHY

Once again, this is the doctrine of "no surprises." By preparing students to anticipate what may be on the test and providing them with the skills necessary to approach the testing situation, students are empowered. These students tend not to be hampered by test phobia. They know they have been successful in all kinds of testing situations, so they go into a new testing situation confident that they will be successful. When students are test wise, it is their knowledge that is tested instead of their ability to take a particular type of test.

STRATEGY 15: HOW

Try the following steps to achieve Strategy 15:

1. Practice the doctrine of "no surprises." Be sure that students have had ample opportunity to practice both the content and context of the various assessments they may encounter.

2. Utilize accountability test context during regular, ongoing instruction. Accountability assessment can take many forms, including multiple-choice items, true–false, matching, completion, open-ended response items, interpretative essays, and others. Teachers should be familiar with the format of the accountability testing and use this format often in class as part of practice activities and/or classroom assessments.

3. Develop test-taking rubrics and teach them to students. Students like to use scoring rubrics. Test-taking rubrics enable students to have a predetermined method for approaching a problem. For example, a test-taking rubric for responding to a multiple-choice test item might include the following:

   • Look for vague words, such as *some* or *often*. These are typically used in correct responses.
   • Watch for long and precisely stated responses. These are often the correct ones.
   • If the words used do not make sense or do not read smoothly with the stem, the response is probably not correct.
   • Choices with grammatical or spelling errors are probably not correct.

4. Have students engage in self-assessment and peer assessment using the rubrics. No student should read a question without having some idea of how to respond. If there is an open-ended response item on a test, such as one that asks students to identify the advantages and disadvantages of some course of action, there should have been many opportunities for students to encounter parallel items during part of the regular classroom instruction.

5. Construct metacognition lessons dealing with test-taking strategies. Teach lessons in which students describe how they would respond to common types of questions (e.g., predict an outcome, cause and effect) or take a position and defend it. Have students discuss how they approach these responses and provide suggestions for how they should proceed.

6. Provide good instructions for the testing situation. If students do not understand the test directions, the chances are they will not do well.

7. Review key concepts and objectives that will appear on the test; do this periodically throughout the year and again prior to the accountability assessment. The type of review enables students to revisit material previously mastered, provides an opportunity for students to practice, and enables them to ask questions to clarify any points that are not well understood.

STRATEGY 16

Establish a Reasonable
Testing Schedule and Environment

The district staff and school staff provide a reasonable schedule of testing as well as a proper physical setting for all assessment situations.

STRATEGY 16: WHAT

Every effort should be made to ensure that students and staff are as comfortable as possible with the testing schedule and environment. The testing schedule should be planned far in advance and incorporated into the district's yearly calendar. Every effort should be made to avoid conflicts. Scheduling assessments the week before or after a vacation is not a good idea. The week before breaks is often filled with activity related to what will happen on the break. Also, students and staff need some time after a vacation to become reoriented to the school routine and to refocus their attention.

The testing environment should parallel the teaching environment as much as possible. Tests should be administered in the classroom where instruction takes place, if at all possible. Students generally do better if they take the mathematics assessment in the room where they have their math class, and with their math teacher present. This environment enables students to better visualize solutions to problems. It also helps reduce the anxiety commonly associated with the testing situation. If the ideas we suggest have been put into place, chances are that the students will feel fairly comfortable.

If possible, students should be able to have outlets for their anxiety. The addition of squeezable rubber balls or other kinesthetic stress relievers, munchies, and access to water are all factors designed to reduce stress.

If students have been properly prepared for the test, this should be an opportunity for them to show what they can do, and they should be encouraged to approach the task with that point of view.

The Washington Educational Research Association (2001) developed a white paper that outlined guidelines for test preparation and administration of teachers and principals. These guidelines are summarized as follows.

The teacher's role:

- Understand the expectations for test administration.
- Share the assessment calendar with students and parents and explain how the results will be used.
- Integrate the context and process skills used in the assessments throughout the year.

- Determine which students will need special accommodation for different assessments and work with the administration to be sure these accommodations are provided.
- Develop a procedure for accommodating students who need to make up tests and share this with students and parents prior to the official test.
- Talk to students about the implications of student performance on the tests. Point out to them how instructional strategies used over the year have helped prepare them for the test. Students should enter the testing situation feeling confident of their abilities to perform well.
- Organize for the tests so that the process moves smoothly.
- Organize the classroom for the test is such a way to support student privacy and eliminate unnecessary distraction that might interfere with the student's ability to concentrate on the task.
- Make accommodations for students who complete the test so they will not distract students still concentrating on the task.

The principal's role:

- Inform students and parents at the beginning of the year about the test schedule. Be sure to provide information about each test, its importance, and how it will impact students and the school.
- Remind parents in advance about when a test is being given.
- Arrange for teachers to have the help they need with test preparation professional development, monitoring the test delivery, and conducting necessary test follow-up responsibilities.
- Develop a process to monitor test makeup procedures to ensure that all students are accounted for.
- Help develop a testing environment free from interruptions.
- Share test results with staff and provide guidance in the utilization of results to improve instruction.

STRATEGY 16: WHY

In our discussion of this strategy we are talking primarily about the district's formalized assessment system. This includes state accountability assessments, national assessments, and districtwide assessments. These assessments normally are scheduled to be given at specific times with the expectation that there will be uniformity across the system. With a district-developed assessment system it is common that not all students will be involved in the same assessments. For example, students taking AP assessments would be taking those assessments at a time designated for specific AP tests. This is also true for International Baccalaureate assessments. NAEP assessments may be given to a sampling of students. These assessments are not given at all grade levels. State accountability assessment schedules are normally set by the state department of education.

Given all of this, it is incumbent on the district to develop a testing schedule that includes information about all of the district, state, and national assessments to be given in a school year and that this information is shared with all teachers and administrators in the system prior to the beginning of the academic year.

STRATEGY 16: HOW

Try the following steps to achieve Strategy 16:

1. Teach the skills assessed to the mastery level throughout the year, not just before the test is given.

2. Communicate to all stakeholders, students, parents, and the public what the district assessment system does and how the results will be used.

3. Schedule and provide an appropriate amount of time before the test, for the test, and after the test to ensure that administrators and teachers understand the expectation for test administration, conduct themselves ethically during the administration of the test, and have sufficient time after the test to handle all necessary administration responsibilities.

4. Build into the testing schedule an appropriate amount of time to administer makeup tests.

5. Develop procedures to ensure the security of tests prior to and following the administration of the test(s).

6. Match the testing schedule to what we know about student attention span. The attention span of an elementary school child can range from 15 to 30 minutes. Placing students in testing situations where they have to remain focused for several hours at a time is not conducive to producing the best results.

7. Assess students in regular classrooms. Familiar surroundings enable the students to relax.

8. Provide for various learning modalities. If possible, the testing situation should accommodate students who need to get up and move around for short periods of time as well as students who work best in private areas, such as learning carrels. It should be possible to accommodate a variety of different testing situations in the same classroom.

9. Make sure parents are aware of the testing schedule. Parents should be encouraged to talk with their children about the importance of the tests. Parents should be made aware of the format of the tests and should be encouraged to help their children become familiar with this format.

10. Schedule tests for mornings on Tuesday through Thursday. Avoid Monday and Friday.

11. Consider allocating one proctor for every 20 students if more than 30 students are being assessed, and actively proctor students while the test is being administered.

12. Consider the level of difficulty of the test when making a decision about whether to schedule one or more tests for a single day.

The following activities are to be avoided:

1. Using test preparation materials that promise to raise test scores. Most of these are simply items from previous assessments that may or may not represent the breadth of the content area domain.
2. "Cramming" a short period of time before the test.
3. Revealing verbally, copying, or developing alternate items for any part of the secure test.
4. Giving special help or coaching any student.
5. Excluding students who should rightly take the test.
6. Changing student responses.
7. Misleading students or parents regarding the results of the assessments.

Test scheduling and the creation of a supportive testing environment are major responsibilities of every teacher and administrator.

STRATEGY 17

Disaggregate Assessment Data

District assessments, as well as external assessments, are disaggregated by student, teacher, course/class/grade level, gender, race, socioeconomic level, and primary language and are used in making program and classroom decisions.

STRATEGY 17: WHAT

The term *data disaggregation* refers to "taking apart" tests results to a level of specificity to enable central office administrators, principals, and classroom teachers to see the skills that are being assessed and what can be done to improve test results. Data can be used in many ways to improve schools. Johnson (2002, pp. 36–37) identified the following uses of data:

- Improving the quality of criteria used in problem solving and decision making
- Describing institutional processes, practices, and progress in schools and districts

- Examining institutional belief systems, underlying assumptions, and behaviors
- Mobilizing the school or district community for action
- Monitoring implementation of reforms
- Accountability

With the passage of NCLB, the accountability function of data disaggregation has become a primary concern for all districts. Data disaggregation is essential for improving student achievement results. The level of data disaggregation should go beyond the analysis of test scores; it should enable professionals within the system to make decisions regarding what to teach and reteach, what materials to use, and what teaching strategies to employ.

Data disaggregation should bring the level of analysis to the classroom. With these data, teachers should be able to determine which students have mastered specific skills. Current data disaggregation requirements enable analysis by student, teacher, course/class/grade level, gender, race, socioeconomic level, and primary language, where appropriate.

In order to disaggregate achievement results, it is necessary that the district/school have a written curriculum that is clearly aligned to the assessment system in regard to content and context alignment. Such a written curriculum will enable staff to determine where the breakdown in student mastery has occurred. It may be at the grade level where the test is administered, or it may be at preceding grade levels.

Outcome data may be disaggregated a multitude of ways, including outcome data from standardized and criterion-referenced tests, student grades, tests for the college bound, student progress in college preparatory courses, graduation rates, and college-going rates, to name a few. It is important to determine just what information is wanted, why, and how this information will be used by various roles within the system. These data may be collected by district, K–12 feeder patterns, school levels, grade level, programs and tracks, classroom teacher, and student. It can be aggregated by quartile, cohorts, content clusters, or over time.

When examining these data it is important to look for patterns over time. Do the data suggest that things are getting better, worse, or staying the same? In looking at trends over time, some districts have begun to look at whether the improvements in test scores are sufficient to reduce the achievement gap between groups over time. This is sometimes referred to as "years to parity," meaning "If we keep making the same progress we are making now, how many years will it take to eliminate the achievement gap among groups?" These data can be very revealing. In some cases it could take 5 or 6 years to eliminate the achievement gap, and in other cases the gains are so small that if they continue at the present rate it may take 20 or more years to close the gap (Curriculum Management Systems, Inc. [2007] Level I Audit Training).

Often, numbers alone cannot reveal the total picture. Student scores on a vocabulary section of an achievement test do not reveal how many questions were asked, how the questions were weighted, or how the subskills were assessed. Test publishers and state departments of education can provide these data.

STRATEGY 17: WHY

Without accurate, current disaggregated data, administrators and classroom teachers do not have enough information to focus and connect their work and ultimately improve student achievement.

State departments of education are increasing accountability practices by passing legislation that mandates district and school accountability for all children learning at high levels. Nationally, NCLB has brought data disaggregation to a new level. Currently, most of this legislation is directed toward documenting student achievement in the areas of mathematics, science, reading, and writing, but more and more states are expanding the areas of accountability to include technology, fine arts, vocational education, and social studies.

Under the federal legislation, state departments of education are responsible for selecting the state accountability assessments. As described earlier in this chapter, there is variation among states in the level of difficulty of these tests. There is also variability among the states in the format or context of the assessments. Some states still rely on multiple-choice assessments, whereas others include short essays, open-ended responses, and multistep questions. With all of these assessments students are being asked to use types of cognition that require analysis and application. A typical multiple-choice question may ask a student to select the "best" from a list of correct responses, or predict an outcome using the student's knowledge base on a topic. State departments of education are also expanding the types of assessment they are mandating. Most states are periodically upgrading the tests and making them more difficult. Texas and Florida are examples of states actively engaged in using the state assessment system as a mechanism for increasing expectations of what students should know and be able to do.

No school or district administration can afford to ignore state accountability measures. Even schools with traditionally high achievement levels must now be concerned with the achievement levels of all subgroups within the system. In the past, schools serving large percentages of students from high socioeconomic levels were content to report average achievement data for all students. Because NCLB requires that achievement data be reported by gender, ethnicity, and socioeconomic class (i.e., the percentage of students who qualify for free and reduced-price lunch), this reporting mechanism makes visible the discrepancy between these groups and highlights the fact that, in general, students who qualify for free and reduced-price lunch, African American males, and students of Hispanic origin score lower on state-mandated tests than other students do.

We grant that the American system of public education has not met the needs of all of the children of all of the people. Now, high test scores have become the political agenda of almost every presidential candidate, governor, and many legislators across the country. Given the public visibility of the student achievement data, this has led to the proliferation of legislation that has placed significantly higher demands on public school educators.

The student ultimately pays the price for failing to achieve these expectations. Students are placed, labeled, and sorted by the scores they achieve on these assessments. It is becoming more popular to label administrators and teachers on the basis of these scores. All of this requires that everyone in the system, including the students and parents, understand the concept of alignment, how it impacts student achievement, and what that means for improving the accountability measures of the system.

All of this applies equally well to the district's assessment system. If a district has a unified assessment system, then data must be disaggregated by the same categories: gender, ethnicity, and socioeconomic level. As a caveat, some systems claim they are "better" than the results of the state accountability system would indicate. The general public does not understand that this idea is only sometimes true. It could be true that the district assessment system assesses much higher order skills than the state assessment system does. If this is the case, the district needs to report the results of these assessments in the same way that the state requires, and even then, the public has difficulty accepting the notion that students can perform poorly on state-mandated tests and still be learning at high levels.

Professional educators no longer ignore district and school results on mandated tests. The trick is to develop a district assessment system and procedures for disaggregating the results so that hard data are available to document improvement at all levels and with all groups over time.

STRATEGY 17: HOW

The following steps are recommended for achieving Strategy 17:

1. The improvement of student achievement becomes one of the central goals of the organization and is included as a measure of performance for teachers, school administrators, and central office staff.

2. All teachers and administrators within the system accept their responsibility to be held accountable for improving student achievement.

3. When the district receives achievement data, the data are synthesized by student, teacher, and school and reported to school administrators.

4. These data include an item analysis by student and class configuration so that a given teacher can analyze these data by the current and preceding class.

5. Teachers are expected to be able to interpret these data and relate them to instructional planning.

6. Teachers are expected to design instructional strategies to remediate deficiencies that lead to student mastery of essential skills.

7. All educators in the system are expected to understand the concepts of content and context alignment.

8. Teachers are expected to analyze present instructional materials and determine the content and context alignment with the assessment system.

9. Teachers are expected to modify, expand, and adjust the present instructional materials to bring them in better alignment with the assessments.

10. Written curriculum documents should be aligned with the state and district assessment systems.

11. Building administrators are expected to monitor the implementation of the district curriculum.

12. The district is expected to have developed a formative student achievement assessment system that will enable teachers to receive data regarding student mastery, all in sufficient time to remediate deficiencies so that students will achieve mastery before the summative evaluation.

13. District personnel should provide parents and the public with appropriate information regarding the concept of alignment and what it means for student achievement.

14. Parent groups need to work actively within the system to mentor parents who traditionally do not support the schools to ensure that there is positive parental support for students who perform well on the state and district assessments.

15. Provide the board with periodic updates regarding strategies to improve student achievement.

16. Include in these reports the trend data over time for all of the subgroups within the system.

17. Continue to hold everyone in the system accountable for sustaining improvement of student achievement over time.

STRATEGY 18

Maintain Student Progress Reports

Teachers maintain individual student progress reports by district objectives; students and parents are knowledgeable about the student's progress on such objectives.

STRATEGY 18: WHAT

Teachers make decisions about student progress every day. In general, these decisions are made individually, teacher by teacher, and they are used to inform instructional planning and provide teachers with information about the effectiveness of their teaching. Students receive information about how well they are doing through informal comments made by teachers and by grades on quizzes and homework and periodic unit tests.

Over time, reporting student progress becomes more formalized, and the audience receiving information broadens. The reporting mechanism typically expands to include quarterly report cards with letter grades at the intermediate and secondary levels and with some variation of "satisfactory," "unsatisfactory," and "outstanding" at the primary level. Often there is no consistent definition for the meaning of letter grades across content areas, teachers, or schools. Two teachers may teach Algebra I in the same high school, and both teachers usually maintain their own grading system; consequently, a B in one class may or may not denote the same level of learning as a B in another class.

What we mean by *reporting student progress* refers to the mechanism a school or district has in place to provide students, teachers, parents, and district administrators with clear, consistent feedback about how well students are achieving the mastery-level skills, content, and knowledge included in the district's core curriculum. Again, note that the skills designated in the district core curriculum are those that students must be able to demonstrate at the mastery level. This requires that the mastery level has been defined in terms specific enough to enable a teacher to make a judgment about whether one student has mastered the objectives and another has not. This requires a totally different level of specificity from the one currently in use with our present grading system.

Students, teachers, and parents are all interested in assessment results at the instructional level. Stiggins (1994) identified the type of information needed and the uses of this information by these three users. Students want to track their own success, identify needs, connect what they do to results, and use assessment data to make future educational plans. To do this, they need ongoing and continuous assessment of mastery of required material and assessment of outcomes that are prerequisites for future learning goals. Teachers use assessments to identify the needs of groups, the class as a whole, and individual students as well as to determine grades, evaluate instruction, and evaluate their effectiveness. To accomplish this, they need access to assessment results for individual students, subgroups of students, and summaries of results over time. Parents use assessments to track children's success, identify needs, and evaluate teachers and the school. To do this, they need information about student mastery of specific objectives and periodic comparison of school performance with other schools.

To meet these assessment goals, student progress reports must include a wide variety of information. This type of reporting system requires that the strategies addressed in Standards One and Two are in place.

The design of a student progress assessment system should address the following questions:

- Are the important outcomes assessed?
- Are the assessment procedures appropriate for the nature of the outcomes?
- Are there sufficient samples of behavior to allow for a fair judgment?
- Do the measurement tools meet adequate technical standards?
- Is the assessment appropriate for the developmental level of the learners?

- Are the assessment procedures free of bias?
- How are the results of the assessment interpreted and used? (Armstrong, Henson, & Savage, 2005, pp. 267–268)

STRATEGY 18: WHY

In order for students, teachers, and parents to understand that student achievement on district and state tests is important, everyone must understand why these tests are given and the value of receiving information about how well students are performing. If the district's stance is that these assessments are not important, then teachers and students are more likely not to take them too seriously. By making clear to everyone that these assessments are regarded as a serious accountability measure for the system, and by providing the necessary information to inform everyone about how well individual students, schools, and the district are doing, it is possible to change the attitude of those receiving information about these assessments.

For example, everyone who takes driver's training knows that the training is designed to enable the participant to successfully drive a car, have knowledge of the state statutes regarding motor vehicle safety, and display that knowledge and skill by passing a multiple-choice test and a driver's test. Successfully driving the car is a performance event designed to ensure that the candidate not only has content knowledge but also can apply that knowledge in a real world setting. Mastery-level expectations are clearly specified. The format of the performance event and the multiple-choice test are known. There seems to be no difficulty in maintaining student motivation or in explaining to parents why these courses are offered. Even the use of driving simulators is not questioned—it is understood that they are used to assist students in understanding their skill level and helping them improve.

Providing students with formative and summative feedback is common practice in most of our vocational education courses, fine and performing arts courses, physical education courses and, more recently, technology applications. Understanding the relationship between formative feedback and how it relates to summative assessment is not a concept foreign to educators. The relationship between formative assessment on mandated district and state accountability assessments needs to be made clearer so that it is well understood by everyone in the system.

STRATEGY 18: HOW

Try the following steps to achieve Strategy 18:

1. Work with teachers to develop common criteria for evaluating student work.

2. Monitor the application of these criteria to ensure consistency across grade levels and among schools.

3. Meet with parents to explain these criteria so that parents understand the meaning of the grades given to students.

4. Expand the assessment system to include such things as running records and portfolios as well as formalized tests.

5. Identify all district, state, and federally mandated assessments.

6. Review the content, type of cognition, and context embedded in each assessment.

7. Develop a testing schedule and distribute it to teachers, parents, and administrators.

8. Develop a plan to provide teachers and students with formative assessment information at timely intervals throughout the year prior to the summative assessment point. These procedures should include information of a formative nature for teachers instructing the grades prior to the assessment grade. For instance, if the state assessments are given in Grades 3 through 8 and Grade 11, then the formative measures should provide teachers instructing in kindergarten through second grade with information about student mastery of the enabling skills students must have in order to demonstrate mastery on the summative test given in third grade.

9. Select or develop additional assessments for the skill and content areas not assessed as part of the state system.

10. Supplement or modify the current grading system and report cards to provide students and parents with information about student mastery of core curriculum competencies.

11. Provide the necessary information to parents and students to help them understand why these assessments are given and how information about student mastery will be provided.

ANALYSIS OF STANDARD TWO

Now it is time for you to evaluate the status of your school or school district on *Standard Two: Provide Assessments Aligned With the Curriculum*. For each strategy, think about what the current status of your situation is regarding these strategies and the changes you feel are needed. Write your responses in the spaces provided.

Strategy	Current status	Changes needed
10. Develop aligned district pre–post criterion-referenced assessments.	❏ Adequate ❏ Not adequate	
11. Have a pool of unsecured test items by objective.	❏ Adequate ❏ Not adequate	
12. Establish secured performance benchmark assessments.	❏ Adequate ❏ Not adequate	
13. Conduct assessment training.	❏ Adequate ❏ Not adequate	
14. Use assessments diagnostically.	❏ Adequate ❏ Not adequate	
15. Teach students to be "test wise."	❏ Adequate ❏ Not adequate	
16. Establish a reasonable testing schedule and environment.	❏ Adequate ❏ Not adequate	
17. Disaggregate assessment data.	❏ Adequate ❏ Not adequate	
18. Maintain student progress reports.	❏ Adequate ❏ Not adequate	

3

Standard Three

Align Program and Instructional Resources With the Curriculum and Provide Student Equality and Equity

I n Standard One and Standard Two, the strategies were related to questions of curricular design. In Standard Three, the focus is on ensuring that programs, textbooks, and other instructional resources are aligned with support of the district written and assessed curriculum.

Teachers, administrators, and students need to be assured that district programs support the implementation of the district curriculum. This requires an alignment that goes beyond a superficial review and gets to the specificity of making these choices on the basis of careful analysis of congruity between the content, context, and type of cognition supported by a program or instructional material and the content, context, and type of cognition reflected in the district curriculum.

Schools have historically been less than rational in selecting program interventions to improve student achievement. The selection process has been characterized by idiosyncratic perspectives, without documentation of needs and a priori determinations of program efficacy. Given shortcomings in student achievement, schools need a systematic method for identifying system needs and addressing them to continuously improve their capacity to meet the needs of their students and achieve their goals.

When program interventions are called for, schools need to use documentation and data from research to determine specific actions to improve student performances or experiences. With that careful scrutiny of options, program interventions contribute to improved productivity.

For the school efforts to be worthwhile, the program intervention design must impact student achievement and address planning, implementation, and evaluation. An intervention that has a positive impact on improving teacher and student performance is connected to district needs, well planned and well funded, and fully implemented.

Intervention selections that follow a rational process will have the capability of addressing district needs, priorities, and goals as well as how to sustain productivity. Implementation of program interventions is a complex process that must be carefully managed if desired results are to be realized.

Educational programs, practices, and activities need to be evaluated to determine the quality they provide and to provide the information needed to drive their improvement. Without evaluation information, educational leaders may be uninformed about a program's true nature, characteristics, or accomplishments. Any program worth doing is worth doing properly and well, but unless substantive evaluation data are available, decisions may easily be weakened or thwarted.

This standard addresses nine essential strategies to achieve program and instructional resource alignment.

1. **Strategy 19: Align Programs With the Curriculum to Ensure Congruity**. All formal and informal programs are investigated for their alignment with the district curriculum objectives, and modifications are made to ensure close alignment.

2. **Strategy 20: Use Research and Data That Document Results to Drive Program Selection, and Validate the Implementation of Programs With Action Research**. Programs selected for use are research and data driven. Furthermore, the school staff members collect their own action research on the programs selected.

3. **Strategy 21: Evaluate Programs to Determine Their Effectiveness in Strengthening Student Achievement of Curriculum Objectives**. Programs are evaluated to determine their effectiveness in facilitating student achievement on the curricular objectives.

4. **Strategy 22: Align Textbooks and Instructional Resources With the District Curriculum Objectives and Assessments in Both Content and Context Dimensions**. The district staff have a process to ensure that textbooks and instructional resources are aligned with district objectives and assessments as well as other external assessments. Analysis includes deep alignment both at the content and context levels.

5. **Strategy 23: Use Technology in Design or Selection Procedures to Ensure Strong Connections to System Learning Expectations and Feedback**. Technology software is designed or selected on the basis of strong alignment

with the content, context, and cognitive type of the district objectives and assessments and its potential to enhance the quality of instruction and learning.

6. **Strategy 24: Provide Training in the Use of Instructional Resources and Their Alignment With System Curriculum Objectives—Content, Context, and Cognitive Type**. Staff members have been provided quality training on the use of instructional resources in alignment with district objectives, with a focus on the content, context, and cognitive type of the objectives (or external assessments).

7. **Strategy 25: Select or Modify Instructional Resources for Lessons to Ensure Full Alignment With System Objectives and Tested Learning**. Teachers select or modify instructional resources for lessons to ensure 100% alignment with the content and context of the district objectives and assessments, including external assessments.

8. **Strategy 26: Place Students in Programs and Activities in an Equitable Manner and With Equal Access to the Curriculum**. Students are placed in programs/activities in an equitable manner with equal access to the curriculum.

9. **Strategy 27: Implement Effective Programs and Strategies With English Language Learners**. Effective programs and strategies for working with students whose primary language is not English are in place to focus on vocabulary development and reading comprehension approaches.

STRATEGY 19

Align Programs With the Curriculum to Ensure Congruity

All formal and informal programs are investigated for their alignment with the district curriculum objectives, and modifications are made to ensure close alignment.

STRATEGY 19: WHAT

At the core of any effective and productive school system is a set of well-defined values and beliefs that guide the structure, goals and purposes, and activities required to achieve the defined intentions and purposes of the organization. If the system is optimized, all members of the organization work in concert toward common goals and objectives. This strategy calls for school leaders to organize all work components, programs, and services in a congruent framework so the system is more likely to be successful in accomplishing its purposes. Schools, subunits within a larger system, need to align their programs and actions with the system's core beliefs, expectations, and desired ends, which builds connectivity within the system.

A concrete foundation for implementing programs and services is needed in order to ensure that the system has *organizational integrity*. Organizational integrity throughout the system equates with compatible and mutually supportive work by the members of the school system staff and faculty. When programs are selected, consideration needs to be given to each program's congruity with the total system's purposes and goals.

STRATEGY 19: WHY

Fragmentation of effort and activities at odds with the greater organization result in suboptimization, or an undermining of effectiveness and success. Given that organizations generally have a purpose and an intention to accomplish something, efforts and energies need to be structured and mobilized to address those aims and purposes. This commonality of purpose usually results in a *work plan*, or a carefully delineated scope of work to accomplish the stated goals and objectives of the organization. So, if any subunit (school) of the organization (district or system) has the discretion to select specific courses of action or programmatic initiatives to implement within the organization, it makes sense for those subunits to serve as allies to the greater organization's goals and purposes. Organizational integrity and effectiveness are more probable results accordingly.

If, for example, a system identifies specific shortcomings in the results obtained from its work and effort, it may identify a broad goal to address those shortcomings. If the shortcomings are in an area of curriculum evidenced by less than desirable achievement—say, mathematics—it makes sense for all units within the system to rally together and work in concert to address those problems. A school's selection of specific interventions or programmatic initiatives needs to flow from the system's assessment of need and deficiencies. Selecting a program or service in another direction would serve to divide and undermine the system's intentions and aspirations.

Attainment of a specific goal is not unlike climbing a mountain. Choosing a route that leads elsewhere will subvert accomplishment, as will spending too much time thinking and planning about the route. Picking equipment that breaks down and fails halfway up the mountain also will subvert accomplishment. Hopping on one foot, though helpful to physical conditioning, may subvert reaching the peak as well. It is easy to see how many activities, sometimes even those that are fun to do, can get in the way of attaining an objective. This often holds true for schools.

For decades, what teachers were to do in the classrooms or the programs that were selected for use in a given school depended on the vicissitudes of individual or school choices. Such choices were often based on the popularity of some programs (due to the vagaries of trends) or on the intrinsic nature of the activities instead of on demonstrated evidence of results relative to assessment. However, with underperforming schools, only those learnings germane to the measure of the assessment system are worth selecting or maintaining within the system. Popular or favorite programs must stand scrutiny against desired results, but often such connections are not made.

Unless strong connections are established that ensure parallelism between program content, contexts, resource use, and demonstrated results and system objectives, the school has little or no control over its fate or achievement. Investigating and verifying that program characteristics and features are consonant with system ends helps surmount one of the key factors often undermining achievement: the fragmentation and inconsistency of organizational effort. Building consistency and harmony between deeds and intended results will maximize achievement performance.

Overall, programs used in schools need to be checked for alignment to system objectives and affirmed, modified, or terminated to assure consequential congruity. This ensures that the school system is reducing fragmentation, contradiction, and rudderless activity within the organization. Sound curriculum management takes steps to eliminate activities that are unrelated, irrelevant, or unnecessary in terms of accomplishing the system's defined learner objectives. Given little or no congruity of programs with the system's learning objectives, the system will be less than effective in accomplishing its purposes. Specific steps might include the following:

- Once the system defines what it expects students to learn (know, think, do, feel, or be like), it is essential that it take specific steps to secure programs and to deliver services designed to accomplish its expectations. Unfortunately, program or strategic choices are often less focused on an organization's purposes than on its ways of doing things. For example, many programs address specific teaching skills but overlook what content is taught, in which context it is taught, and the cognitive type with which it is taught. Good teaching helps, of course, but good teaching has to teach something relevant to the system's expectations or the assessment criterion in place.

- Every program selected for use in a school system needs to have its objectives scrutinized for how it fits with the system's purposes and needs. Ask the following questions: "What are the factors and attributes that characterize this potential program's intended outcomes or effects?" "What is its stated purpose, and how does that match our system's needs and intentions?"

- It also helps when potential programs are evaluated and measured for the level of instructional efficacy they have demonstrated in actual use and application in other places. Ask "What evidence is there that this program works, affects achievement, and lines up with our system's aspirations, needs, and aims?" The intended outcomes and expectations of any program must be carefully considered and examined against the system objectives. If there is a good fit between what the program intends to deliver and what the system wants, then the program may be worth implementing on a trial basis.

- Curriculum management requires the principal or educational administrator to connect various components of organizational structure together in a way that not only produces harmony with the system but also shows concrete connectivity with the system's product (learning). Some of these components include program activities, teaching strategies, and formal or informal organizational conduct with what learners are expected to learn. This connection and the flow of activity of some of the major components in organizational integrity and congruity are illustrated in Figure 3.1.

Figure 3.1   Connectivity of Programs and System Objectives

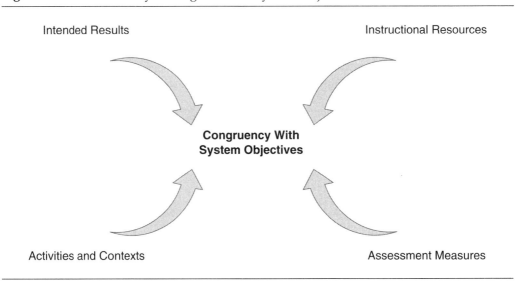

Intended Results

Instructional Resources

**Congruency With
System Objectives**

Activities and Contexts

Assessment Measures

What do the elements in Figure 3.1 indicate? There are four categories or elements that influence system congruence and organizational integrity, focused on accomplishing the objectives and aims of the system. Each element is important in ensuring quality control in achieving the aims and purposes of the school system as interpreted by the assessment framework.

- **Intended Results.** A well-connected curriculum demonstrates high levels of congruity between the intended results of programs selected for use in the system and the intended results of the system, most often system objectives. The intended results for the system need to predict the actual configuration of work; selection of programs; implementation of work; and the nature of initiatives, interventions, and innovation.
- **Instructional Resources.** School staff frequently report that goals are set, and work is delineated, but the resources to accomplish the work are less than adequate, weakening the efforts of the system. Leaders need to make sure that instructional resources, including the use of time available for instruction, also demonstrate cohesion with the system's objectives for learners in the system. Time available for teaching and learning is precious, and it must be carefully budgeted. If time is wasted or inefficiently used, the system's ability to achieve its purposes may be suboptimized or undermined. In addition to time,

adequate materiel (equipment, supplies, facilities, etc.) is needed. Without the "stuff" needed to accomplish a task, improvisation may fall short of assuring goal accomplishment and achievement of aims. (For other resource alignment issues, see Strategy 22.)

- **Activities and Contexts.** Activities and contexts must match or align with system objectives for learners. The connection students make between assessment item contexts and classroom contexts must be unconstrained and clearly evident. If a concept is measured by the assessment in a certain context, students without prior experience in that context (i.e., word problems in math, inquiry-type questions requiring inductive thinking in science, etc.) will be disadvantaged, and performance success will be diminished. The type of instructional activity needs to be predicted from the types of measurable goals and/or assessment determinants. Simply stated, that which is measured, and how it is measured, must be reflected in what and how it is taught. This caveat is often described as *pedagogical parallelism.*

- **Assessment Measures.** Assessment measures used on a day-to-day basis must also reflect the intended learner outcomes or achievement expectations implied by the system's mission and statement of objectives. For example, if a program is evaluated only on the basis of student, parent, or teacher perceptions, but the system objectives specify a particular cognitive skill result, then the evaluation may be positive and encouraging regardless of actual performance or results in achievement of the intended skill. Matching assessment to curriculum expectations is referred to as *frontloading*; matching the curriculum delivered to what is measured or assessed is referred to as *backloading*. (See Standard One, Strategy 3, for more information on this topic.)

There is no substitute for program coherence, that is, diverse efforts within a system working in harmony. The proficient principal, curriculum manager, or superintendent needs to check and verify that any selected program's intentions, resources used, types of activities selected, and assessment measures utilized at the classroom level align and demonstrate high congruency with the system's defined objectives and assessment modes. With these elements working in concert, organizational success has a better chance.

STRATEGY 19: HOW

The following steps are suggested to implement this strategy:

1. Conduct an inventory of all programs currently implemented within a school or school system. List each program by name, identify the nature of its objectives, locate and fix its grade-level boundaries, delineate its strategies and methods, and determine how each program is measured for success.

2. After deconstruction of the measured achievement instrument (see Strategy 1), identify system objectives and learner expectations with as much specificity as possible for each grade level.

3. Investigate or check actual program results against system objectives, if possible. For example, locate any specific assessment items that measure the program's intended results, and identify levels of success in terms of student mastery of the expectation.

4. Match program intentions or results with system objectives or desired results, item by item. Map out the matches, overlaps, gaps, and discrepancies between program results or expectations and system objectives. Determine the level of the match in terms of percentage, for example, "The program addresses X% of the system objectives."

5. If the program effectively addresses 50% or more of the system objectives, it is worthy of modification and improvement efforts to increase its efficacy. If the program effectively addresses 70% or more of the objectives of the system, it is adequate. A match of less than 50% indicates that the program needs to be considered for termination.

6. Require that all future and new program requests or proposals demonstrate a match between system objectives and the program's intentions. In addition, all new programs that appear congruent with system objectives need to be pilot tested for actual results within the system. A small-scale implementation with careful monitoring of results (see Strategy 17) should demonstrate at least 70% congruence with the system's desired results before it is implemented across the system.

If one pays careful attention to aligning programs with system objectives, then an underperforming school can avoid and overcome historical patterns of incongruity between the plethora of programs available to system mission and objectives. In the words of one sage school administrator, "We need to stop jumping on our horse and riding off in all directions." When programs are selected in accordance with system objectives and are measured with system assessment processes that align with organizational aims and purposes, the congruity between programs and the system's needs are enhanced. When these are aligned, organizational integrity, constancy of purpose, and focus on measured performance are amplified, and organizational excellence is advanced.

STRATEGY 20

Use Research and Data That Document Results to Drive Program Selection, and Validate the Implementation of Programs With Action Research

Programs selected for use are research and data driven. Furthermore, the school staff members collect their own action research on the programs selected.

STRATEGY 20: WHAT

When school systems identify problem areas in student achievement, organizational operations, or other areas of possible concern, a natural response has been to seek a specific set of actions or activities to address the problem area of concern. Frequently, the response seeks and procures a program, but all too often there is scarce information about the efficacy of the program available to use. Choosing programs is not an easy task. For the school practitioner, it is difficult, and often impossible, to know ahead of time whether a program proposal is based on research or is simply a current fad that has gained substantial momentum. Without research, it is safe to say that programs vary in nature and type, and they widely differ in efficacy and results.

School improvement calls for the implementation of practices in a school that enable all students to learn at the highest levels possible. Research at hand on educational strategies and methods helps practitioners identify the best practices to bolster student achievement. Before implementing any intervention, innovation, or program, schools must consider the research evidence available regarding the choice they wish to use to accomplish school improvement.

It is understood that educational leaders must pick educational strategies that have been shown to work and address the specific needs of the school. Any of hundreds of learning, teaching, and school management programs need to demonstrate their effectiveness. This is even stated as a requirement in federal legislation, as defined in section 9101 (37) of the No Child Left Behind Act. That section calls for scientific "research that involves the application of rigorous, systematic, and objective procedures to obtain reliable and valid knowledge relevant to education activities and programs." In the event that such scientific research is not available, schools need to consider other convincing empirical evidence.

Discernment in selecting programs is called for in the effective curriculum leader, and such discernment needs to be based largely on documented evidence of results and on research validation. There are criteria one can use to discern whether a program is successful or worthwhile, and such criteria require substantiation through careful and systematic research in educational institutions.

Given good foundations of research for program selection, the school curriculum leader can be assured that using research will prevent unsuitable selection of program alternatives. Strategies to assist school administrators in determining program efficacy are available, but in studies conducted by curriculum auditors over the past decade, rational research findings seldom have been used in choosing programs for implementation in schools.

Even after adopting and implementing programs, too seldom does the educational institution conduct its own research to determine whether the program is meeting the need it was designated to address. Pilot testing a program in a selected sample environment can provide home-grown, locally developed knowledge about a program's efficacy. Without empirical evidence, program selection and/or implementation encounters significant risk that results may impair achievement and thwart system accomplishment of its aims and purposes. With empirical evidence, decisions regarding program selection and implementation are more likely to reflect assurance that results will be in keeping with design.

The school's process for change usually begins with the gathering and analysis of data about the school. Once this process is completed, needs are identified and prioritized, and goals are established. Once completed, the school follows a step-by-step process to select and implement a program intervention.

The following steps to implement this strategy are recommended:

Step 1	School stakeholders analyze data to determine and prioritize needs and build shared commitment to change.
Step 2	Schools evaluate potential strategies (see "Strategy 20: How" section) for efficacy and applicability to the school.
Step 3	The school explores the research base of potential strategies for validity, reliability, and demonstrated effect or evidence of the effects of each program or practice on student achievement.
Step 4	If the program intervention study shows relevance to the identified needs of the school, the program intervention needs to be examined in greater detail. See the U.S. Department of Education questions to consider.
Step 5	The program intervention's research base must be of high quality, with strong evidence that this practice, program, or intervention will improve student achievement.

Validating evidence of effects on student achievement is important, but schools are advised to approach any program intervention from three perspectives: (1) the theoretical base of the program intervention, (2) implementation and reproducibility information, and (3) evidence of effects on student achievement.

The U.S. Department of Education has offered some questions designed to help schools address these perspectives (Comprehensive School Reform Program Office, 2002):

Question 1: Is there a theoretical base for the practice or program being considered?

Questions	Judging quality
What are the ideas behind this practice or program? What are its guiding principles? How does it work? Why does it work?	1. Is there a clear, nontechnical description of the central idea and goals of the practice or program? 2. Is there a clear description of the instructional activities that are central to this program or practice? 3. Is the practice clearly tied to an established learning theory, for example, child development or language acquisition?

Question 2: Is there evidence that this practice or program (intervention) has been successfully implemented and has produced positive outcomes in a variety of situations? Has it been successful in a context similar to that of the school considering this practice?

Questions	Judging quality
Has this program or practice been widely used? Where is this reform likely to work? Under what circumstances is it most effective?	1. How many schools have used this practice or program? 2. Did the schools using it fully implement the practice or program? 3. In what settings has it been implemented? 4. Has improved student achievement been convincingly demonstrated in a variety of settings?

Question 3: Is there evidence that this practice or program has a significant positive effect on student achievement?

	Judging quality	
Questions	Scientifically based research	Developing toward scientifically based research
Is there evidence based on rigorous research showing that this practice and/or program improves student achievement?	For each practice or program identified: 1. Are there studies looking at the impact on students of that practice or program? 2. Are those studies of high quality? (See Guidelines for Judging Quality of Study, pp. 7–10.) 3. Are there at least 5 high-quality studies? 4. Do 4 of the 5 high-quality studies show that the practice improves student achievement?	For each practice or program identified: 1. Are there studies looking at the impact on students of that practice or program? 2. Are those studies of reasonable quality? (See Guidelines for Judging Quality of Study, pp. 7–10). 3. Are there at least 5 studies of high or reasonable quality? 4. Do 4 of the 5 reasonable-quality studies show that the practice improves student achievement?

(Continued)

(Continued)

Questions	Judging quality	
	Scientifically based research	*Developing toward scientifically based research*
	5. If yes, are the findings significant in 3 of those 4 studies? (See p. 11.)	5. If yes, are the findings significant in 3 of those 4 studies? (See p. 11.)
	If the answer to all of these questions is yes, there is scientifically based research regarding this practice or program.	If the answer to all of these questions is yes, there is strong evidence regarding this practice or program, even though the research on which it is based did not meet all the requirements of scientifically based research as defined in the law.
	The "Gold" Standard	The "Silver" Standard

The preceding questions provide a basis for clearly identifying program interventions' likelihood of helping schools select sound and appropriate actions and activities to improve student achievement.

Once a program intervention is selected and implemented, assessment does not stop. Continuous evaluation of program effects and results is critical to assure the school that its actions are meaningfully productive and cost-effective.

Schools are much more likely to successfully make a positive impact on student achievement when they implement program interventions that are grounded in solid and valid research.

STRATEGY 20: WHY

There are two main issues or concerns among educators in terms of program selection and implementation. On the one hand, "agents at all levels wonder how to get more and more programs institutionalized, but their teachers think that it's the same promoters of change who need to be institutionalized, not the programs" (Fullan, 2001). On the other hand, the nature of the program selection and implementation process has been found to be less than rational. The need for change has been often blunted by "innovation overload" or undermined by ineptitude in deciding on what intervention to buy or develop and put into operation. Schools may try to do too much, and what they do is not supported by research.

It is surprising to learn that most schools have not made well-informed decisions about program choices, even though opportunities to gather information were available. In an alarming study conducted with multiple schools, informed choice occurred in only one school (and even there the staff did not consider multiple options seriously) and partially occurred in only a couple of others. Educators in most schools operated in ways that were questionable by considering only a small number of programs or interventions (in some cases only one or two). Moreover, the educators in the study stopped gathering information when they found a tolerable course of action. Many times, those choices, in the eyes of many school educators, were those that were compatible with current practices. This kind of selection process did not produce any dramatic change or improvement.

Ease of implementation seemed to be the most compelling selection criterion, making it unusual to change the status quo in schools. This is called *symbolic change*. Even more absurd was the predilection of some schools to mimic another school's program, often because of uncertainty about which program to choose.

There are actions educational leaders can take to overcome these deficiencies. For example, having evidence of program effectiveness ahead of time provides administrators greater precision in selecting and implementing programmatic options and alternatives to deliver organizational aims and purposes. Given good information about previous research on a specific program option or alternative, educational leaders can make better decisions relative to choosing, keeping, or dropping programs. Better decisions are characterized as resulting in greater organizational effectiveness, less wasted effort and resources, and greater satisfaction of the learning needs of clientele.

A plethora of program options has been tried in many schools without research justification. For example, consider the following list of program options that was implemented in one large midwestern school system.

Types of Supplemental Programs Operating in a Midwestern School District (65 elementary schools)

• AARP Tutors	• Grandparents Tutors	• Proficiency Tutoring
• Accelerated Reader	• HOSTS—Help One Student to Succeed	• Reading/Math After School Tutoring
• Adopt-A-School	• I Know I Can—Peer Mediation	• RIF—Reading Is Fundamental
• After School tutoring	• IBM Tutors	• Rolling Readers
• AME Zion Reading	• Mt. Carmel Adapters Tutoring	• Science/Math Workshop
• America Reads	• ODE (Ohio Department of Education) Phonics Grants	• SFA—Success for All

(Continued)

(Continued)

• Attendance Partners	• Ohio Wesleyan Tutors	• SMART—Self-Monitoring Analysis and Reporting Technology
• Curriculum Alignment	• OSU Tutoring	• South High Mentors
• Direct Reading Instruction	• Parent Tutors	• Sylvan School
• Early Literacy	• Parent Volunteer Reading	• Target Teach
• Early Reading Workshop	• Peaceful Schools	• Title I Pullout Reading
• East High Mentors	• Peer Counseling	• Title I Math
• East of High Street Tutoring	• Peer Mediation	• UHC—Urban Health Collaborative Proficiency Tutoring
• Expanded Learning Opportunity	• Peer Tutoring	• USI—University of Southern Indiana
• Family Focus Centers	• Proficiency Intervention	• Work Study Tutors
• Gladden Tutoring	• Proficiency Saturday Tutoring	

In this one district alone, 47 different program options were being tried in the elementary schools. This confirms what Michael Fullan (2001) described as "innovation overload." It is ironic that when staff members were asked for data on the performance or success of these programs, only three of the programs had such information. In this case, the school system was implementing many programmatic options, but the system was not determining whether the programs were valid, appropriate, or producing desired results. This "blind" approach, laden with happenstance, provides no assurance to the school that its money, time, and staff are being well used.

The enormity of problems resulting from such haphazard or aimless program selection and implementation compels the conjecture that, under such circumstances, it might come as no surprise that the "shotgun" approach would fail. Better approaches for meaningful change are needed.

STRATEGY 20: HOW

Selecting a program intervention is a difficult process of clearly identifying the school's needs, examining the broad range of programs available, and finding one that has promising and sound evidence in its support, one that is congruent with the school's needs. Any adopted program needs to build on the specific school's strengths and needs to address its weaknesses. The individuals who evaluate program intervention options first need to sift through the available information and ask the following crucial questions:

- What is the program intervention's documented positive impact on student achievement?
- Does the program intervention clearly demonstrate a connection to research on "what works" and the nature of the school's specific needs?
- How can the program intervention's promoters help schools to successfully implement the program?
- How will the school determine whether the program intervention is cost-effective?

Once these questions are answered and a consensus is reached about moving ahead with program interventions, or change, the following actions need to take place:

1. Document the current situation within the given school or system (use appropriate assessment information).

2. Identify the problems or needs that are evident and delineate them.

3. Identify options and alternatives (programs or services) that address the problems and needs identified.

4. Develop a formal framework with goals and measurable objectives to address the problems or needs. (What will it take to solve this problem or to meet the need? What will resolution of the issues look like?)

5. Select the program alternatives that seem to address the problem or need.

6. Request from the program intervention source (or proposing individual or group) the results produced by this program option.

7. Review and analyze the information provided. (N.B.: If none is provided, conduct a search for evidence and/or empirical information about use of this program.)

8. Profile research findings against system objectives using the data gathered through the evaluation.

9. Determine the level and efficacy of relevance of the research and documented results; if the evidence indicates a strong result, from the program's implementation, it may be considered for adoption.

10. After implementing the program intervention, continue to conduct research on the program's efficacy in meeting the needs of the organization.

Programs that have not been scrutinized in this process often do not address district needs, priorities, and goals, and they do not sustain productivity. Implementation of programs is a complex process that must be carefully managed and based on sound research if desired results are to be realized successfully.

STRATEGY 21

Evaluate Programs to Determine Their Effectiveness in Strengthening Student Achievement of Curriculum Objectives

Programs are evaluated to determine their effectiveness in facilitating student achievement on the curricular objectives.

STRATEGY 21: WHAT

Programs are often adopted by schools (see Strategy 20), which may or may not be a beneficial thing. For example, it is noteworthy to acknowledge that student achievement is usually measured by some type of test, and that tests measure the level of attainment of curriculum objectives, but a program is not a curriculum—it is a strategy, approach, or technique (or sets of these). There is no question that any program needs to be evaluated to see how well it delivers a curriculum. This connection may or may not be clear in schools. What needs to be clear is that any program needs to be conscientiously evaluated for efficacy.

A successful leader needs to meet two essential requirements for organizational effectiveness. First, he or she must know what the purposes of the organization are: What is the organization trying to accomplish? Second, he or she must be able to determine how well the organization is achieving its purposes (Deming, 1986). It is the leader's responsibility to clarify and disseminate the organization's purpose, vision, and mission in order to build organizational unity and constancy of purpose. Just as important is that the leader needs to know how well the organization is meeting its purpose. Without feedback on performance, results, and success, leaders are operating in the dark when making operational and organizational decisions.

It helps to be clear about what a program is and is not. A program is a planned, developed, or adopted set of procedures intended to deliver mastery of concepts, knowledge, skills, attitudes, or behaviors for students. To know whether a program is useful, it must be evaluated to see if does what it is intended to do effectively and whether it is worth its cost, time, effort, and support.

To begin, recognize that program evaluation involves collecting information about the aims and purposes of a program, how it works, what it takes to function, and what ends are attained. Program evaluation can include any or a variety of at least 35 different types of evaluation, such as for needs assessments; accreditation; cost–benefit analysis; evaluations of effectiveness and efficiency; and formative, summative, goal-based, process, and outcomes evaluations (McNamara, 2002).

School leaders need primarily to ascertain the specific impact of a program on learners and decide whether the program is worth keeping or modifying, or whether it should be terminated. Of course, any actions taken by an organizational leader need to be informed actions. The leader needs to know specifically what the objectives are, how well the system is performing against those objectives, and what is and is not working. It is critical that performance shortcomings be identified by the organization so the needs of the organization and its appropriate responses can be developed and determined.

Evaluation of programs requires objective measures to analyze how well a program is working in terms of reaching its intended ends. A meaningful and carefully designed evaluation will provide important information about why a program did or did not succeed, and several research approaches can help determine whether there is a causal connection between program approaches and student achievement outcomes. It is helpful if the program's contributions to success can be isolated and identified separately from a plethora of other potential influences.

Program evaluation will help the school leader determine the following:

- What is and what is not working in the program
- Whether the program benefits students in important ways
- Weaknesses and strengths in the program, which may be useful for later modifications

Despite these important benefits, program managers often are reluctant to evaluate their programs. This reluctance usually is due to concerns stemming from a lack of understanding about the evaluation process (Administration for Children and Families, 2007).

Given the leader's resolve to overcome resistance to seeking solid evaluation data on programs, he or she is enabled to make sound, data-driven decisions. Solid evaluation data are usually objective, empirical, and replicable. Perceptual data often are of little value. Opinions may be influenced by a plethora of factors, but data speak for themselves. Perceptions are often skewed because of a number of factors, so clinical methods of testing assumptions about programs are necessary. Unless a program stands the test of scrutiny and evaluation of its performance, the leader will be less than sure of the program's worth or value.

STRATEGY 21: WHY

Schools often gather data. Less often, data are scrutinized for meaning by school personnel and used in guiding action. In curriculum management audits conducted by affiliates of Curriculum Management Systems, Inc., across the United States, school systems were frequently found to have had inadequate data and information about programs and program performance. Moreover, school systems were frequently found to have misused or not used information they had in hand.

One example of a system's use of data shows how data on program interventions can be often overlooked. In a southeastern school district (Poston, 1991a), a program had been instituted for Title I students (previously called *Chapter I students*—funded by the U.S. Department of Education). The special program was for the so-called underachieving students, as measured by the California Achievement Test. The program, after 5 years, was evaluated as to its impact on student reading scores. The program's treatment involved separate grouping for the Title I students, with reduced class sizes. The perceptions of staff and others familiar with the program indicated support for the program, and the program was considered helpful to the low-achieving students.

The exhibit that follows, which documents evaluation data from the special program, shows that the program was indicating diminishing achievement of the group of students. Over the 5-year period, the students fell further and further behind the expected rate of achievement gain in terms of reading on a nationally standardized test. The recommendation of the curriculum auditing team was to terminate the program because of its dysfunctionality.

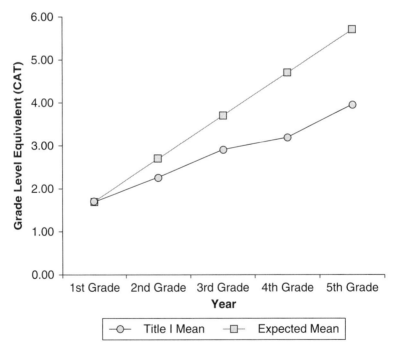

California Achievement Test (CAT) Reading Scores, First Through Fifth Grades, Southeastern School System Cohort Group.

The curriculum audit that revealed this information noted that the school system had these data but had not disaggregated and used the data to determine whether the school's program for this select group was succeeding. It appears that the program was not succeeding, but prior to the curriculum audit the program was perceived to be successful. The point is that sometimes perceptions can be mistakenly drawn without sound and useful evidence of actual performance of programs. Regrettably, the select group of students was not experiencing success as hoped for in the special program.

Although this is an isolated instance, findings such as these are helpful in informing administrators of what actions to consider; what programs to keep, modify, or terminate; and what student needs to address. It is easy to see how the power of evaluative data can be a very useful tool for school administrators to guide and direct decision making, organizational improvement, and constructive action.

Evaluation is a simple form of accountability. If a program is purported to accomplish a specific purpose (i.e., deliver achievement of learner objectives), it is essential to determine whether the program is successful against its expected results. Deficiencies in accomplishing program objectives call for administrative action and curriculum leadership.

A sample program evaluation plan is provided on the following page. The plan was adapted from a U.S. Department of Health and Human Services agency (Administration for Children and Families, 2007). The plan (checklist of questions) is useful for educational leaders to organize an effective approach to determining the level of success of specific programs, interventions, or innovations.

In this era of high-stakes testing, ignorance is not bliss when one is trying to reform underperforming schools, and disregarding data about program performance and success is imprudent at best and potentially harmful to the system's clientele at worst. Competent and visionary leaders gladly welcome the opportunity to connect measurement of results (in terms of reaching intentions) to determine how to better serve the organization's clientele and meet the learning needs of its students.

Sample Outline for Evaluation Plan (Administration for Children and Families, 2007)

I. Evaluation framework

   A. What is going to be evaluated

      1. Program model (assumptions about target population, interventions, immediate outcomes, intermediate outcomes, and final outcomes)

      2. Program implementation objectives (stated in general and then measurable terms)

        a. What will be done and how

        b. Who will do it

        c. Student population and recruitment strategies

      3. Student outcome objectives (stated in general and measurable terms)

(Continued)

(Continued)

Sample Outline for Evaluation Plan (Administration for Children and Families, 2007)

B. Questions to be addressed in the evaluation

   1. Are implementation objectives being attained? If not, why (that is, what barriers or problems have been encountered)? What kinds of things facilitated or hindered implementation?

   2. Are student outcome objectives being attained? If not, what barriers or problems have been encountered? What kinds of things facilitated attainment of student outcomes?

      a. Do student outcomes vary as a function of program features or aspects of the program—what characteristics are most predictive of expected outcomes?

      b. Do student outcomes vary as a function of characteristics of the student groups or staff?

C. Timeframe for the evaluation

   1. When will data collection begin and end

   2. How and why timeframe was selected

II. Evaluating program implementation objectives—procedures and methods

   A. Are program implementation objectives being attained, and if not, why not?

      1. Objective 1 (state objective in measurable terms)

         a. Type of information needed to determine if Objective 1 is being attained and to assess barriers and facilitators

         b. Sources of information (that is, where you plan to get the information including staff, students, program documents). Be sure to include your plans for maintaining confidentiality of the information obtained during the evaluation

         c. How sources of information were selected

         d. Time frame for collecting information

         e. Methods for collecting the information (such as interviews, paper and pencil instruments, observations, records reviews)

         f. Methods for analyzing the information to determine whether the objective was attained (that is, tabulation of frequencies, assessment of relationships between or among variables)

   B. Repeat this information for each implementation objective being assessed in the evaluation

III. Evaluating Student outcome objectives—procedures and methods
(question 2: Are student outcome objectives being attained and if not, why not?)

A. Evaluation design—describe fully, paying attention to consideration of effect upon achievement

B. Student Objective(s) (state each outcome objective in measurable terms)

1. Types of information needed to determine if each objective is being attained (that is, what evidence will you use to demonstrate the change?)

2. Methods of collecting that information (for example, questionnaires, observations, surveys, interviews) and plans for pilot-testing information collection methods

3. Sources of information (such as students, program staff, district staff, program managers, etc.) and sampling plan, if relevant

4. Timeframe for collecting information

5. Methods for analyzing the information to determine whether each objective was attained (i.e., tabulation of frequencies, assessment of relationships between or among variables using statistical tests)

C. Repeat this information for each student outcome objective being assessed in the evaluation

IV. Procedures for managing and monitoring the evaluation

A. Procedures for training staff to collect evaluation-related information

B. Procedures for conducting quality control checks of the information collection process

C. Timelines for collecting, analyzing, and reporting information, including procedures for providing evaluation-related feedback to program managers and staff

SOURCE: This material was taken from *The Program Manager's Guide to Evaluation*, 1997, issued by the Department of Health and Human Services, Office of Head Start, Washington, DC 20447.

The following steps are suggested to determine the strategy's relevance and to inaugurate its implementation:

1. It is best to first identify what programs are currently in existence. A list of current programs should indicate grade levels, content areas, and specific schools where those programs are being implemented.

2. Each program needs to have information obtained or developed to identify the following:
   a. The nature of the goals and purposes of the program
   b. A description of the needs or problems that were to be satisfied or solved by the program
   c. The type of evaluation process in place and the type of information provided for decision making

3. Once the inventory is completed, an evaluation plan can be developed to fill in the gaps for current programs and establish an evaluation framework for new programs.

    a. The program evaluation standards (see above) need to be addressed in the evaluation planning.

    b. Specific targets for action with timelines need to be established and followed closely to maximize program effectiveness.

STRATEGY 21: HOW

Carrying out program evaluation to guide decisions relative to pupil achievement requires a number of specific steps and procedural activities. Specific procedural steps to follow in planning for a program's evaluation include the following:

1. Identify and clarify what is to be measured. What significant learning objectives are being addressed in the program? What is the program supposed to accomplish, and how can that be measured?

2. Develop and design evaluation strategies with a focus on feedback and improvement of student achievement against the program objectives (include all assessment items and instruments that parallel the program objectives).

3. Seek to develop and implement a pre–post, criterion-referenced assessment procedure that documents, records, and reports student achievement against specific program objectives. Cohort groups are preferable, including use of control groups (evaluated nonparticipants in the program under study) if at all possible.

4. Disaggregate and analyze feedback information to evaluate differences related to gender, ethnicity, and economically disadvantaged status.

5. Note discrepancies between groups, and compare gains of all students to expectations set forth in the program objectives. Identify the scope and nature of objective achievement.

6. Communicate results to stakeholders, teachers, and others for consideration of program options, alternatives, and courses of action for improvement.

7. Use programmatic feedback data in administrative decision-making support or modify effective programs and terminate ineffective programs.

Another tool of importance to the school leader is the work completed by the Joint Committee on Standards for Educational Evaluation. The standards were developed to guide the design, employment, and critique of evaluations of educational programs, projects, and materials (Sanders, 1994).

The standards include four areas for consideration by program evaluators: (1) utility standards, (2) feasibility standards, (3) proprietary standards, and (4) accuracy standards.

Utility Standards

The utility standards are intended to ensure that an evaluation will serve the information needs of intended users.

U1 Stakeholder Identification: Persons involved in or affected by the evaluation should be identified, so that their needs can be addressed.

U2 Evaluator Credibility: The persons conducting the evaluation should be both trustworthy and competent to perform the evaluation, so that the evaluation findings achieve maximum credibility and acceptance.

U3 Information Scope and Selection: Information collected should be broadly selected to address pertinent questions about the program and be responsive to the needs and interests of clients and other specified stakeholders.

U4 Values Identification: The perspectives, procedures, and rationale used to interpret the findings should be carefully described, so that the bases for value judgments are clear.

U5 Report Clarity: Evaluation reports should clearly describe the program being evaluated, including its context and the purposes, procedures, and findings of the evaluation, so that essential information is provided and easily understood.

U6 Report Timeliness and Dissemination: Significant interim findings and evaluation reports should be disseminated to intended users, so that they can be used in a timely fashion.

U7 Evaluation Impact: Evaluations should be planned, conducted, and reported in ways that encourage follow-through by stakeholders, so that the likelihood that the evaluation will be used is increased.

Feasibility Standards

The feasibility standards are intended to ensure that an evaluation will be realistic, prudent, diplomatic, and frugal.

F1 Practical Procedures: The evaluation procedures should be practical, to keep disruption to a minimum while needed information is obtained.

F2 Political Viability: The evaluation should be planned and conducted with anticipation of the different positions of various interest groups, so that their cooperation may be obtained and so that possible attempts by any of these groups to curtail evaluation operations or to bias or misapply the results can be averted or counteracted.

F3 Cost-Effectiveness: The evaluation should be efficient and produce information of sufficient value, so that the resources expended can be justified.

Propriety Standards

The propriety standards are intended to ensure that an evaluation will be conducted legally, ethically, and with due regard for the welfare of those involved in the evaluation as well as those affected by its results.

P1 Service Orientation: Evaluations should be designed to help organizations address and effectively serve the needs of the full range of targeted participants.

P2 Formal Agreements: Obligations of the formal parties to an evaluation (what is to be done, how, by whom, when) should be agreed to in writing, so that these parties are obligated to adhere to all conditions of the agreement or formally to renegotiate it.

P3 Rights of Human Subjects: Evaluations should be designed and conducted to respect and protect the rights and welfare of human subjects.

P4 Human Interactions: Evaluators should respect human dignity and worth in their interactions with other persons associated with an evaluation, so that participants are not threatened or harmed.

P5 Complete and Fair Assessment: The evaluation should be complete and fair in its examination and recording of strengths and weaknesses of the program being evaluated, so that strengths can be built upon and problem areas addressed.

P6 Disclosure of Findings: The formal parties to an evaluation should ensure that the full set of evaluation findings along with pertinent limitations are made accessible to the persons affected by the evaluation and any other persons with expressed legal rights to receive the results.

P7 Conflict of Interest: Conflict of interest should be dealt with openly and honestly so that it does not compromise the evaluation processes and results.

P8 Fiscal Responsibility: The evaluator's allocation and expenditure of resources should reflect sound accountability procedures and otherwise be prudent and ethically responsible, so that expenditures are accounted for and appropriate.

Accuracy Standards

The accuracy standards are intended to ensure that an evaluation will reveal and convey technically adequate information about the features that determine worth or merit of the program being evaluated.

A1 Program Documentation: The program being evaluated should be described and documented clearly and accurately, so that it is clearly identified.

A2 Context Analysis: The context in which the program exists should be examined in enough detail so that its likely influences on the program can be identified.

A3 Described Purposes and Procedures: The purposes and procedures of the evaluation should be monitored and described in enough detail so that they can be identified and assessed.

A4 Defensible Information Sources: The sources of information used in a program evaluation should be described in enough detail so that the adequacy of the information can be assessed.

A5 Valid Information: The information-gathering procedures should be chosen or developed and then implemented so that they will ensure that the interpretation arrived at is valid for intended use.

A6 Reliable Information: The information-gathering procedures should be chosen or developed and then implemented so that they will ensure that the information obtained is sufficiently reliable for the intended use.

A7 Systematic Information: The information collected, processed, and reported in an evaluation should be systematically reviewed, and any errors found should be corrected.

A8 Analysis of Quantitative Information: Quantitative information in an evaluation should be appropriately and systematically analyzed so that evaluation questions are effectively answered.

A9 Analysis of Qualitative Information: Qualitative information in an evaluation should be appropriately and systematically analyzed so that evaluation questions are effectively answered.

A10 Justified Conclusions: The conclusions reached in an evaluation should be explicitly justified, so that stakeholders can assess them.

A11 Impartial Reporting: Reporting procedures should guard against distortion caused by personal feelings and biases of any party to the evaluation, so that evaluation reports fairly reflect the evaluation findings.

A12 Meta-Evaluation: The evaluation itself should be formatively and summatively evaluated against these and other pertinent standards, so that its conduct is appropriately guided and, on completion, stakeholders can closely examine its strengths and weaknesses.

Given educational leadership's use of the preceding standards, program evaluation can have a high likelihood of success and have a higher level of probity and usefulness in finding, developing, and implementing high-quality programs helpful to improvement of student achievement.

STRATEGY 22

Align Textbooks and Instructional Resources With the District Curriculum Objectives and Assessments in Both Content and Context Dimensions

The district staff have a process to ensure that textbooks and instructional resources are aligned with district objectives and assessments as well as other external assessments. Analysis includes deep alignment both at the content and context levels.

STRATEGY 22: WHAT

It is ironic that although schools for the most part are public institutions, curricular materials are largely produced by private, commercial publishers; consequently, obtaining textbooks that are well aligned with a school system's curriculum is a difficult undertaking. Imagine a situation in which students were expected to learn certain things, but the textbook used in instruction was unrelated to the topics expected. The objective would call for one thing, but the textbook would deal with another. Of course, that would cause considerable concern, as it should, but it is often the case in schools.

Research studies have shown that "when highly structured textbooks are used as a basis for a curriculum, teachers commonly make independent and idiosyncratic decisions regarding what should be covered and to what extent, creating huge holes in the continuum of content" (Marzano, 2003, p. 23).

Unfortunately, textbooks have not been shown to be well connected in content or context to standardized tests commonly used in the United States, whether they are norm- or criterion-referenced assessments. Some textbooks provide less than a 20% match with major national instruments used to test learning. It is often advisable to be skeptical of what publishers say about alignment. What textbooks generally do is a surface job of alignment. The type of alignment called for in this book is a substantive type of match—in content, context, and cognitive type (English & Steffy, 2001). Only when all three of these factors are incorporated into the selection of curricular materials can the school system achieve greater assurance that their instructional materials choices are appropriate.

Instructional resources may, in and of themselves, be powerful and exciting tools to use, but unless there is a connection with (1) what actual learning is desired and (2) what is measured, achievement will fall short of the system's intentions. It will usually take multiple resources to align with an entire course of study.

STRATEGY 22: WHY

Some states set statewide curricula, and some select and approve textbooks for use within that state. However, the development and implementation of most curriculum materials are usually the responsibility of the local school district and, in some states, the local schools. When schools use a textbook as the sole mode of instructional delivery, they may inadvertently create a situation in which the tested objectives are not taught adequately. To ensure maximum alignment with the criterion of success (tested learning), it is critical that educational leaders select and selectively use textbooks and other instructional materials that parallel and match that criterion. In effect, the leader is ensuring continuity among objectives (what is desired), and teaching (what and how they are taught), and what constitutes the measure of success (what is tested). Quality control demands alignment of the written and tested curriculum with the taught curriculum, including textbooks and instructional resources.

Studies of test scores in reading and mathematics for students in Grades 4 through 6 in several school districts that practiced alignment have shown substantial improvement in nearly all cases. One of the studies, conducted in Ohio, indicated that the system purposely selected textbooks that were aligned with the standards of the state at each grade level, among several other alignment strategies. Alignment of instructional resources, although not the sole factor, was identified as one of the actions that contributed to the overall success in improving student achievement (Blanchard & Gorin, 2004).

High-performing schools anticipate what students are expected to know, think, do, feel, or be like, and they teach to that set of expectations. However, the methods and modes of measurement need to be manifested and incorporated within the curriculum taught. For example, if a textbook presents a particular concept (i.e., the concept of "perimeter") in a specific manner, then that manner of presentation must resemble or parallel how "perimeter" is measured in the assessment system. If there is no match or parallelism, the learners will not successfully transfer what they have encountered in the textbook to the test (English & Steffy, 2001).

In addition, if the textbook leaves out the particular concept or does not treat it similarly, the learners will be greatly disadvantaged when the concept is tested later. These issues would not be problematic if textbooks were better aligned, or if teachers did not depend so heavily on textbooks for activities, content, and contexts. However, recent curriculum management audits have indicated that teachers often do depend heavily on textbooks for instructional use (Stripling, 2007).

For example, one recent curriculum audit pointed out a lack of consistency in the selection of resources, which has led to self-selected or textbook-driven curriculum decisions by some teachers. Faulty alignment of resources in this case impeded consistent implementation of the intended curriculum across all schools. The lack of internal consistency impedes the delivery of curriculum based on the state's standards in some instances and likely will leave students only partially ready to demonstrate the expected skills and knowledge when tested on high-stakes assessments.

The same audit pointed out that textbooks often do not align with the cognitive complexity inherent in high-stakes testing questions. An analysis based on cognitive complexity revealed numerous examples of high dependence on simpler types of thinking skills—*knowledge* and *comprehension*—particularly in instructional strategies and student work samples. The skills of *analysis*, *synthesis*, and *evaluation* were noticeably limited in number in most of the materials and classroom activities (Stripling, 2007).

In other curriculum evaluations educators have found that tested concepts were omitted largely in textbooks, some concepts were superficially treated, and some concepts were unnecessarily taught repeatedly. Moreover, the Council of Chief State Schools Officers (2000) reported that schools do not yet have access to top-quality curriculum materials aligned with the states' standards.

In another study, not one of the widely used science textbooks for middle schools was found to be considered satisfactory. The study found that not a single one of the books met even the minimum requirements for effectively teaching science (Budiansky, 2001).

Achievement is lessened when instruction includes textbooks and instructional resources that do not anticipate or match content, contexts, and cognitive types of underlying objectives in instruments for measuring (or testing) learning.

STRATEGY 22: HOW

The leaders of high-performing schools take steps to ensure that instructional materials selected and used in their schools are adequately aligned with learner expectations, system objectives, and tested learning. To accomplish this task, the following steps are suggested:

1. Identify specifically what students are expected to learn. System objectives, measurement circumstances, structured factors, and learner expectations need to be included in the identified body of learning. This process may need to include backloading from instruments used to test learning (see Strategy 12).

2. Deconstruct released test items to identify the underlying objectives of the measurement instrumentation.

3. Once the objectives, or expected learnings, are identified, they need to be organized by content area and grade level.

4. Selecting a content area and one grade level, the specific learner expectations are listed in table form down the first column on a large chart (see Textbook Content Treatment Chart).

5. Procure available textbooks for the selected grade level and content area (publishers are willing to provide copies for examination).

6. Create a column for each textbook (see Textbook Content Treatment Chart).

7. Tear out the section of each textbook and paste its treatment of the particular expectation in its column and in the row for that expectation. Repeat until all learner concepts have corresponding textbook sections pasted in a row.

8. Compare each textbook's treatment of the learning concept. Select the textbook section that best matches the expectation for learners, and circle it in red. Repeat this step for all learner concepts and expectations.

9. Tabulate all responses, and identify the textbook that best matches the set of learner expectations for the content area and grade level selected. Also note the areas that are not addressed in the textbook. Those expectations will require other instructional materials.

10. Use the textbook that has the greatest number of matches with curriculum expectations.

Textbook Content/Treatment Comparisons Chart (Use for Each Grade Level and Subject Matter Area)

Learner Concepts	Textbook A	Textbook B	Textbook C
(Example:) "Measure and accurately determine the perimeter of a multisided building."	No treatment of concept	Cut out and paste treatment of concept here	Cut out and paste treatment of concept here
			Select best match

(N.B.: It is also possible to do the textbook or instructional material matching with computer technology. Textbook sections can be scanned into a computer, catalogued, and labeled for pasting into an electronic chart. Projecting the chart onto a wall screen facilitates group comparisons.)

Of course, there are several ways to compare textbook treatments of learner expectations and concepts (Muther, 1990). The important thing is that the instructional leader needs to make sure that materials used in instruction are appropriate and that they match and align with the specific learner concepts and expectations. Without the alignment of instructional materials, student achievement will diminish in terms of tested learning.

In summary, alignment of instructional resources is a powerful determinant of students' access to learning that is imbedded in high-stakes testing. When instructional resources such as textbooks, software, and other materials are selected on the basis of their alignment with the curriculum objectives, tested objectives, and curriculum priorities of the system, levels of student achievement increase.

STRATEGY 23

Use Technology in Design or Selection Procedures to Ensure Strong Connections to System Learning Expectations and Feedback

Technology is designed or selected on the basis of strong alignment with the content, context, and cognitive type of the district objectives and assessments and its potential to enhance the quality of instruction and learning.

STRATEGY 23: WHAT

In the past two decades, computer-based instructional media have grown in popularity across the United States, and computer companies have sold millions of hardware and software systems to schools for use in the classroom and in school offices. Very ambitious claims have been made on behalf of these technology programs, and new evidence has been provided to justify their use in an instructional system.

For example, schools in West Virginia introduced some carefully selected software in their curriculum, provided adequate hardware and training for teachers, and found that student achievement scores on national tests improved (Mann, Shakeshaft, Becker, & Kottkamp, 1999).

Moreover, despite deep discrepancies in educational opportunities across school systems, technology offers promise in leveling the playing field for all learners. On this point, the National Academy of Sciences emphasized the importance of technology in promoting educational opportunities for all students:

> Technology deployed in education can help remove inequities between the schools of the inner city and the suburbs, between cities and rural districts. . . . Technology can become the force that equalizes the educational opportunities of all children regardless of location and social and economic circumstance. (National Academy of Sciences & National Academy of Engineering, 1995)

Schools began to use modern electronic technology in the beginning to augment the course offerings within the school, sometimes in mathematics, business, industrial education, and vocational education. However, in latter days, modern hardware and software programs are providing broad learning opportunities for students, complete with incorporation into state standards of assessment.

The dilemma facing many educational leaders is that technology-based instructional programs may or may not be congruent with what students are expected to learn within a given school system. Moreover, some of the technology systems offer tempting options and alternatives for schools. Some of these newer options include the following:

- There is software that "teaches" and that requires little time of a teacher. For example, one program provides short video lessons on concepts in algebra taught by a "cybernetic teacher" via a desktop computer located in the classroom or at home. Students access their lessons individually at a computer screen and get the instruction from the computer. No teacher is required.
- Information on student performance is available for teacher diagnoses. The computer combines classroom, school, district, and state data to give teachers real-time information designed to benefit students immediately. Teachers use test scores to diagnose weaknesses or locate areas of the curriculum that have not been mastered and address them before the school year ends.
- Teachers without formal software programming can use problem-based scenarios. For example, one problem set for a science class might state that "A dead fish washes up on shore and the students must find the source of the pollution that killed the fish, using the computer as their research tool." As students work on the problems in small groups, specially designed mapping software keeps track of the steps students take in attempting to solve each problem. The teacher can review the process students use to solve the problems, with different patterns revealing the depth of the students' grasp of the subject matter. Timely access to the mapping information lets teachers quickly adjust strategies for struggling students.
- Educators can also use computerized achievement testing to measure how students are mastering state and local curriculum standards. Combining advances in measurement theory and technology, computerized adaptive testing provides information about the actual level of a student's achievement. It also has the ability to customize a test to a student's achievement level. Such tests begin by asking a question at the average level. If the question is answered correctly, the computer increases the level of difficulty on the next question. When a question is answered incorrectly, the next question presented will be at or below the level of the previous question. Students at different levels of achievement in the same classroom can take different versions of the same test, versions targeted to their own achievement level.

The major issue regarding technology is not whether its spectacular claims are true, although this can be debated; the major issue is whether it is the right tool, at the right time, in the right place.

STRATEGY 23: WHY

Every day, students navigate through the voluminous and overwhelming information that today permeates the world around them. If students are to thrive in a world enabled by information technology, skills are needed to help them handle the tidal wave of information—and the sooner, the better.

When one thinks of technology, the natural inclination is to think of computers and surfing the Internet. Today, that's just the tip of the iceberg. Consider the following technologies now available to students:

- Desktop, notebook, and pocket computers
- Digital cameras and image manipulation software
- Digital microscopes and scientific analytical equipment
- Web-based video equipment and high-definition television
- Hand-held computers, graphing calculators
- Global positioning equipment and weather tracking devices
- Telephonic messaging and voice interactions

The items on this list are mostly just tools for users. There are more categories of technology influencing society and schools (Trinity Church of England School, 1996), as enumerated in the following:

Classes of Technology:

1. **Technology as Objects:**

   Tools, machines, instruments, weapons, appliances—the physical devices of technical performance

2. **Technology as Knowledge:**

   The know-how behind technological innovation

3. **Technology as Activities:**

   What people do—their skills, methods, procedures, routines

4. **Technology as a Process:**

   Begins with a need and ends with a solution

5. **Technology as a Sociotechnical System:**

   The manufacture and use of objects involving people and other objects in combination

There is no question that students of today need to become responsible, savvy users and purveyors of information and the tools and processes provided by technology. With access to the world at their fingertips, students need to know how to collaborate successfully across miles and cultures.

There is little doubt that technology affords great and extraordinary processes and content to learners. Unfortunately, much of the time spent using technology may be on topics, content, or material that are less than optimally relevant to the learning the school system expects its students to acquire. Unless there is a strong connection between the technology and the school's needs, use of technology may undermine the aims and purposes of the system under the guise of provocative and tantalizing activities and devices.

It is a responsibility of instructional leaders to ensure that technological hardware and software used in school classrooms are appropriate in both function and consequence. Much of the cutting-edge technology observed in schools has demonstrated insufficient connections to desired learning for students. As an example, a recent curriculum audit found, in a large-district sample of 1,105 classrooms and computer laboratories in 80 schools, that the sampled classrooms contained approximately 6,019 computers; however, at the time of the auditors' visits, only 1,432 (24%) of the computers were being used (English, 2007).

In addition, students may spend hours on the computer and enjoy it to the fullest, but in the end they acquire either inadequate amounts of learning or inappropriate types of learning. The key question for instructional leaders in addressing software and hardware considerations is "SO WHAT?" WHAT is the result, effect, or impact of using a particular type of technology? WHAT difference does it make? WHAT does it add to, or how does it enhance, the quality of learning measured by system assessment instruments? Unfortunately, answers to such questions are not altogether absent.

Many studies published in the last decade have documented the benefits of technology (Chaika, 2005):

- Researchers found that students studying language arts in a multimedia environment gained more auditory, language, decoding-in-context, and story composition skills than did students in a control group who did not use computers.
- Another study documented quicker student solutions of multistep word problems in Grade 5 and up when using computer software products.
- High school students were found to retain math skills longer after using commercially available software, while also showing less math anxiety.
- A study of elementary school students found that students who used multimedia computer software in math more frequently perceived math as relevant to everyday life than students in a control group did.
- A national study discovered that math teachers who used computers could significantly boost fourth- and eighth-grade students' standardized test scores. Students were also found to have improved attitudes, motivation, and behaviors when they used computers in school.

Given these data, the case for using technology in schools and classrooms continues to grow and become more credible.

STRATEGY 23: HOW

Scrutiny of technology, including devices and processes (hardware and software), requires assertive action on the part of the instructional leader. Perhaps the biggest compelling factor in such action is in obtaining sufficient funds to acquire needed technology. The National Education Association (NEA) has taken a position to address funding, as well as several other positions on technology in schools, which may be instructive to educational leaders. The NEA positions include the following points, which bear consideration in technology planning (NEA, 2007):

NEA Positions on Technology and Education

- More funding is needed at all levels to better integrate technology into schools and classrooms.
- The technology available to educators and students should be compatible with, and at least on the same level as, technology in general use outside of schools.
- Education technology budgets should reflect the importance of professional development. At least one third of all technology budgets should be reserved for school staff to become proficient in using and integrating technology into their classrooms.
- Educators themselves should be involved in decisions on planning, purchasing, and deploying education technology.
- Teacher education programs need to embrace educational technology and help prospective teachers use it effectively in the classroom.
- Technology should be deployed and applied equitably among all students and educators, regardless of geography or demographics.
- Students should also be taught the appropriate and safe use of technology.

The following steps are offered as suggestions on how to avoid wasting precious resources and to ensure connectivity to demonstration of learning desired by the system:

1. Determine what type of technology, system, or application is under consideration. What does it purport to offer? Unless the hardware or software manifests a strong connection between what it does and what the school system needs, it should be disregarded. If the proposed device or process appears to connect with documented system needs, then further consideration may be carried out.

Technology Factors to Consider:

- *Type of device or application (Does it fit?)*
- *Validation of results (Does it work?)*
- *Match with expectations (Is it congruent?)*
- *Documentation within system (Pilot test?)*
- *Content, context, cognitive level (What's the nature?)*
- *Cost–benefit (What worth or value?)*

---

2. Clearly identify validation that confirms that the technology in fact delivers what it promises. What studies are offered to confirm the technology's capabilities and results (and how good were they)? Without validation

information, technology may be promising something it cannot and will not deliver. Of course, the school leader needs to discern validity and reliability of research. For example, note that if the manufacturer is using its own research to demonstrate the value of the technology, such information is less valuable than external, third party, independent research.

3. Proceed to determine the match between the technology and the school system's desired learning expectations for students. Is the technology a process, or does it deliver a product? The leader must determine whether the process is congruent with system procedures and policies and confirm that the product delivered is congruent with what the school system expects its clientele to acquire. Without such congruence or confirmation, the technology may disjoin the instructional integrity of the system.

4. Document the content and context of the technology as to how and where it fits within the system's curriculum. What tested learning does it purport to deliver? Review processes, such as pilot studies, must experimentally validate such expectations. The educational leader must provide assurance that the technology does in fact deliver curriculum content or context consistent with system expectations.

5. Determine the cognitive level of the content and context of the technology applications or apparatus. Given use of the technology, what level of thinking is addressed when students use it? Some technology software has been found to be very simplistic and fundamental in its cognitive level. The instructional leader must prevent adverse consequences resulting from the use of low-level activities or devices and ensure that the technology promulgates complex, high-order thinking and problem-solving levels congruent with system requirements.

6. The instructional leader must determine whether the technology is worth its cost. How much does it cost, and is it a good use of system funds? Much technology is very expensive, and the benefits are often less than clear. It is critical for the costs to be tabulated and then evaluated against system priorities and needs to determine whether the expenditure is appropriate or justified. In most cases, school systems may find that the consumption of scarce system financial resources in acquiring and maintaining technology is not worth it. Determining ahead of time what benefits accrue to the system, and how those benefits meet the needs of the system, will help in deciding whether to support and expend the cost amount.

Technology offers much for schools; however, it does not guarantee learning. What the system needs, requires, desires, and seeks should drive all decisions for acquisition of material of all types. Equally crucial are data that confirm that the choices are congruent with indicators of improved achievement for students; otherwise, scarce resources may not be used to best advantage in fostering achievement for students in the system.

STRATEGY 24

Provide Training in the Use of Instructional Resources and Their Alignment With System Curriculum Objectives—Content, Context, and Cognitive Type

Staff members have been provided quality training on the use of instructional resources in alignment with district objectives, with a focus on the content, context, and cognitive type of the objectives (or external assessments).

STRATEGY 24: WHAT

It is one thing to have organizational purposes; it is quite another to carry out those purposes. Faculty and staff often need training on the nature and purpose of organizational goals as well as training on how to accomplish these goals. Without strategies, methods, or approaches—without training—personnel will flounder in their efforts to initiate improvement. They may even cease to progress at all.

Assumptions about the readiness of personnel to undertake any change or process in order to reach an organization's goals are often mistaken. Change requires considerable time, planning, and training for its initiation, and the educational leader is responsible for meeting the needs of personnel during this process.

There are hundreds, if not thousands, of things and activities used in classrooms for learners, such as books, supplemental materials, films, videos, Internet Web sites, artifacts or handouts, field trips, electronic devices (computers, calculators, messaging equipment), special guest speakers, experiments, dramatic productions, and so on. Whatever activity or material is selected, the impact or influence on learning must be known, so the precious time available for classroom activities (little more than 1,000 hours/year) can be efficiently used. Aligning resources used to objectives or goals maximizes the potency of the strategy employed.

A characterization of this phenomenon is illustrated in Figure 3.2 (Marino, 2006).

Depicting resources and activities within the educational organization as arrows moving in a certain direction shows how, without alignment, the arrows (activities and resources, if you will) may or may not hit the organizational goal (or target). Getting all activities and objects in harmony with the goal is a major step toward greater student achievement.

In overcoming factors that contribute to underperforming schools, training in the area of alignment is essential. Instructional resources used by teachers in the classroom must be congruent with the goals and objectives addressed, and all resources must be equivalent in content, context, and cognitive type in order to be used effectively. For example, learning how to read and use a map to find your way to a previously unknown destination is a difficult cognitive objective. Memorizing the capitals of the states shown on state maps (a simpler cognitive

Figure 3.2   Quality in Education: The Power of Alignment

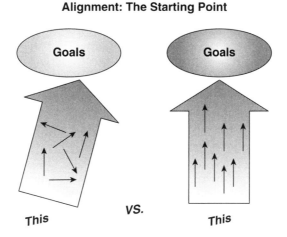

skill) would be incongruent with the former objective and not connected to the learning expectation.

Teachers need to be able to discern the specific skills dealt with in instructional materials and determine whether the skills are equivalent in content, context, and cognitive type to the system's learner expectations. Such discernment and determinations require training and development.

STRATEGY 24: WHY

High-performing schools need to focus on all dimensions of their operations—time, materials, activities, sequencing, and so on—while always keeping the mission and expected results of the system's curriculum in mind. Focusing on all dimensions creates greater harmony in the organizational effort and ensures a greater degree of success. This harmonizing process is referred to as "optimization in organizational quality improvement." With all forces and actions headed in the same direction, the organization has an opportunity to gain momentum and accomplishment from its efforts.

Studies have demonstrated this relationship to be highly viable and powerfully determinative in delivering student achievement. One study examined the connections between teachers' resource selections and achievement among several other factors and found that schools need to "use data to identify deficiencies and to drive instructional decisions . . . (in the choice of) . . . resources present in schools" (Billig, Jaime, Abrams, Fitzpatrick, & Kendrick, 2005).

The study also called for strong professional development and administrative support.

In teaching, many factors collide with learning. Use of time can affect the level of learning, the specificity of content presented can impact the quality of learning, and parallel contextual frames can improve the nature of learning. However, curriculum audits have found that some of the classroom activity observed is largely undirected, unfocused, and unplanned in implementation. To overcome such ineffectiveness, and to obtain greater organizational focus, training of personnel is required.

Reasons for Aligning Resources to Instructional Goals (Downey & English, 2004):

- The level of difficulty of resources one might use in planning lessons needs to match the level of difficulty of the goal or objective.
- Fidelity to the system or state curriculum requires congruity of support operations and functions to avoid fragmentation and discrepancies between what is expected and what is delivered.
- Claims about published materials are occasionally less than accurate, requiring rigorous local effort to examine and select such materials.
- Differentiating resources to better meet student needs helps all students advance in mastering the approved and authorized curriculum.

As in any effective staff development activity, training in aligning instructional resources is necessary for creating capacity and skill levels in professional personnel and their work. Training in alignment is for improved student achievement and is not intended to establish an individual inspection system for individual feedback to a teacher. Teachers simply need to learn how to analyze materials and activities and how to apply them congruently to learner expectations.

STRATEGY 24: HOW

Instructional leaders create the conditions for effective staff development and training. Several principles need to be considered for efficacious training.

1. The school leader needs to foster an expectation of professional growth. Much of this is accomplished through his or her own self-directed professional growth and development. In effect, the leader models good professional growth.

2. All training for personnel needs to be based on a careful analysis of data and must be data driven. Training for individual teachers needs to be different and in accordance with individual needs. No "shotgun" or one-size-fits-all approach should be used. Careful diagnosis of needs and provision of matching training should be commonplace.

3. Training efforts must be extrapolated from district goals and instructional priorities (policy, plans, etc.) and focus on proven research-based approaches that have been shown to increase productivity.

4. To be successful, training must be based on valid theories of human learning and development and adult learning, use a variety of staff development approaches, and be matched with the individual's diagnosed needs.

5. The system's curriculum expectations need to be organized by grade level and content area to inform teachers what is to be taught at each juncture. Content, context, and cognitive type are to be included. A chart that illustrates this characterization is shown below.

Matrix of Learner Objectives and Grade Levels: Sample Reading and Language Arts Objectives

Grade level	Content	Context	Cognitive type
K	(Sample) Recognize letters of the alphabet and demonstrate the correct sound for each letter	Nomenclature of alphabet letters	Comprehension
1	(Sample) Decode and explain the meaning of short passages with simple words	Interpretation of meaning (sequenced with individual reading)	Application
2	(Sample) Read and identify the main characters of a short youth adventure book	Character interpretation	Analysis and application
Etc. ⇩	Etc. ⇩	Etc. ⇩	Etc. ⇩

6. Finally, training needs to include feedback from assessment to identify how well the specific learning expectations are being met by the system.

Appropriate training in alignment frees up the educational leader's time by giving each member of the instructional team the skills to implement alignment of the curriculum expectations and content, context, and cognitive levels accordingly. Delegation of the skill to the classroom level produces great dividends in that it ensures better adherence to what the system requires in terms of learning.

Training Outcomes and Objectives

The process for training teachers in the alignment of instructional resources to objectives needs to incorporate the following learner outcomes for faculty and staff (Downey & English, 2005a, pp. 1.8–1.13).

The teacher needs to be able to do the following:

1. Deconstruct educational materials and "calibrate" the materials for specific content outcomes, context conditions and nature, and cognitive type. (Low-performing schools are often below level in their objectives and activities.)

2. Examine classroom artifacts and identify the subject and grade level suitable for use, without taking descriptive labels for granted.

3. Analyze and specify student objectives for precise content with the student action required.

4. Using an identified and specified objective, categorize the objective in the state and/or local curriculum. Calibrate objectives to the lowest level found.

5. Identify and define the context of the objective, in terms of the situation or conditions imposed, what information is given to the student and the nature of its format, and the expected observable student's response.

6. Categorize the context of objectives as real world like, test like, or classroom like. The types of contexts used need to be used in lesson planning for acquisition and mastery of learning objectives.

7. Examine and classify objectives by cognitive type and compare instructional materials to identify and use matching types.

Principals and other administrators seeking to provide professional development and training in aligning instructional resources might review training modules suited for this purpose. One example is *Examining Student Work for Standards Alignment and Real World/Test Formats: Connecting Resources to the Curriculum* (Downey & English, 2005a). Another example is found in the training program *Aligning Lessons* (Dickson, 2006). Both are available for administrators to use in training personnel in the art and science of aligning resources with curriculum objectives.

Regardless of the resources that are used, it is essential that the decision to use them is based on a careful analysis and determination of the connectivity among the resources; the intended outcome of the learning activity; and the content, context, and cognitive type of the objective. Training for the purposes of maintaining the commitment to congruence of the system will go a long way toward enhancing the quality and robustness of the instructional process within any school.

STRATEGY 25

Select or Modify Instructional Resources for Lessons to Ensure Full Alignment With System Objectives and Tested Learning

Teachers select or modify instructional resources for lessons to ensure 100% alignment with the content and context of the district objectives and assessments, including external assessments.

STRATEGY 25: WHAT

Many instructional materials are commercially produced, but most of the commercial products do not fit easily into local educational environments or suit the learner expectations of a given system. Resources used in the classroom are often locally developed or modified to fit the needs of a local community's clientele and curriculum.

Teachers are expected to do a great many things, but the central focus of their role is quality instruction. They must teach what is assessed, and they must teach according to the established objectives. To do this, materials and instructional resources may have to be modified or created to provide suitable instructional support for the unique curriculum.

Some of the key tasks teachers need to demonstrate in providing alignment in lessons include the following (Wuersten, 2005):

- Teaches to the essential learnings or measured learnings in their state
- Implements research-based best teaching practices
- Reflects on and monitors his or her own effectiveness during and after instruction
- Uses summative classroom data to make instructional decisions
- Uses action research to ensure effective delivery of student learning
- Uses technology to assess, record, and report on student progress
- Participates in collaborations that develop better teaching practices

What teachers need to do to "select and modify" instructional resources is not unlike *action research*, which comprises research and action simultaneously or sequentially in close proximity. The teacher engages in lesson planning that is based on a clear understanding of student needs (prediagnosis), followed by implementation of the plan (action), and then examination of the results of the lesson (research). Using this process, teachers can channel their work in the needed direction, modify lesson plans and resources used, and appraise the efficacy of their decisions and actions to improve teaching and learning.

Tools used by teachers in delivering instruction must fit the need. Unfortunately, many needed tools are not available off the shelf, compelling teachers to develop their own resources or to modify available resources.

STRATEGY 25: WHY

With high-stakes testing firmly embedded in nearly all states, whether the factors that have improved student achievement in the past must be attended to is no longer optional. The test is the instrument of accountability, and the test needs to drive *what* and *how* knowledge and skills are imparted to students. It is important for lessons implemented by teachers to minimize student surprises when they encounter high-stakes assessments. That statement is based on the venerable Thorndike theory of transfer of knowledge from nearly 100 years ago (De Corte,

1999). Thorndike's transfer theory predicts that knowledge is most likely to occur when situations are parallel. In this case, the classroom experience and the testing situation need to be parallel. *Pedagogical parallelism* is what happens when teachers create similar and parallel situations so that students are learning what they will need when they are tested and learn even beyond that which is measured (English & Steffy, 2001).

High-stakes tests are designed to collect evidence that students have learned the knowledge and skills called for in the state's standards. To provide adequate evidence and acceptable student performance, classroom activities and the nature of the test need to be synchronized and well connected to attain the best results in performance from all students.

If instructional resources are not germane to the system's curriculum expectations and do not match the content, context, and cognitive levels, then students will not perform well on the assessment. Commercial materials are designed to address a very wide audience and often claim to meet the needs of all school systems.

However, research has indicated that school improvement is definitely achieved when teachers engage in "frequent, continuous and increasingly concrete and precise talk about teaching practices . . . capable of distinguishing one practice and its virtues from another" (Little, 2003, p. 186).

School systems are unique and distinctive, particularly in terms of the varying needs of each system's clientele. Instructional resources and materials need to be modified to match the nature of the system's clientele, to support instruction related to student performance on assessments, and to give teachers appropriate tools for use in the classroom.

STRATEGY 25: HOW

The following steps are recommended to achieve this strategy:

1. First, identify the nature of individual learner expectations in all grade levels and in all content areas. This might be accomplished by backloading from the assessment process used by the system.

2. Next, review student results against those expectations and ask teachers to review the areas that demonstrate inadequate achievement or student success.

3. Recommend that teachers problem-solve possible reasons for inadequate performance, and identify likely options and alternatives for improvement. Separate out all those areas that are due to improper or impotent instructional resources.

4. With the list generated from Step 3, recommend that teachers be provided with time and materials to develop instructional resources to close the gaps and that they be requested to develop appropriate materials or modify existing resources. Teachers may need support to get this task completed and at some time other than during the school year.

5. Resources developed or modified by teachers must be inventoried, reproduced, and maintained by the system. Modified or developed resources
   need to be shared with all teachers in comparable content areas and grade
   levels.

The bottom line is that one must create a level playing field so all students will
have access to instructional resources that meet their needs. Adapting resources to
the specific needs of students helps ensure that the gaps in their prior learning and
experiences are addressed. Although we recognize that the textbook is the primary resource of choice for many teachers, it is important to recognize that the
power of textbooks is limited in terms of their delivery of the measured or tested
learning. Some precepts worthy of note when aligning instructional resources
with teaching and learning objectives include the following (Dickson & McArdle-
Kulas, 2006b):

- From a teaching perspective, consistency of instruction and more equitable
  access to the curriculum are accomplished when instructional materials
  provide teachers with ideas and strategies that are aligned with content and
  cognitive type of the tested standards.
  o Insufficient alignment may call for teacher augmentation of resources or
    abandonment of unaligned resources.
  o Resources need to be analyzed from the perspective of the teacher and
    from the perspective of the student.

- Clarity and practicality in strategies should produce explanations, modeling, and demonstrations of the learning for students and include different
  learning needs of clientele.
  o Students need rich experiences of new information during acquisition of
    learning, but they also need quality opportunities for expanded practice
    and application.
  o Opportunities need to be provided for guided practice and extended
    practice for learning mastery and retention.

- Instructional strategies to teach an objective may call for teachers to design
  and select the most appropriate strategies to teach the content and skills and
  to address a particular group of students.
  o Learning may be presented in a variety of modes: inductive, deductive,
    and direct instruction; conceptual formation; modalities of learning styles
    (visual, auditory, written, tactile, or kinesthetic).

Opportunities to adapt instructional resources to local system needs and curriculum expectations will enhance alignment of resources with the tested curriculum and contribute dramatically to student achievement improvement.

STRATEGY 26

Place Students in Programs and Activities in an Equitable Manner and With Equal Access to the Curriculum

Students are placed in programs/activities in an equitable manner with equal access to the curriculum.

STRATEGY 26: WHAT

A well-managed school system reflects a strong commitment to both consistency and equity. *Equity* is defined as the state, action, or principle of treating people in accordance with differentiated needs. This contrasts with the notion of *equality,* which is the quality, or condition, of being exactly the same as something else. Equity and fairness to all students are expected in all areas, including student placement, course access, program opportunities, and so on.

Equity is an elusive concept, and it is difficult to achieve. Its roots are found in the material, social, and cultural resources provided in homes and schools (Marks, Cresswell, & Ainley, 2006). With these differences, a high-performing school system takes steps to adjust its instructional responses to the needs of different students and provides different educational treatments to meet those individual needs. Comparing equity and equality may help clarify the difference. Note the chart that compares the two.

Equality	Equity
• Access	• Need
• Comparability	• Differences
• Opportunities	• Disparities (requisite)
• Averages	• Ranges
• Formulaic allocations based on enrollment or numbers of clientele	• Differential allocations based on antecedent characteristics and divergence among clientele

The differences between equality and equity comprise a slippery slope, making it difficult to consistently distinguish between them (Poston, 1991b). Former President John F. Kennedy has been quoted as saying "There is nothing so unequal as equal treatment of unequals." Although this might be apocryphal, it is tautological, or self-evident. Treating clientele the same without consideration of differences in need may be equal, but unfair. In general, what needs to be equal is the accomplishment of goals for all clientele.

For example, it is natural for most parents of two or more children to know that each individual child may need treatment, support, or resources different from those of their siblings. If one child has appendicitis, no parent would hesitate to provide medical attention to that child while withholding similar treatment for another child who does not have that affliction. Nevertheless, schools frequently allocate resources and support to schools in a one-size-fits-all framework, whereby numbers of students rather than individual student needs are used as the basis for resource allocation.

Curriculum audits of school districts in the United States have historically shown that most school systems, including low-performing ones, allocate resources and assign educational responses generally on the basis of student enrollment counts rather than on measured needs. Such systems ineffectively regard the measured needs of students (Curriculum Management Systems, Inc., 2007).

STRATEGY 26: WHY

Different needs require different treatments. Treating students the same when their characteristics and needs are different is often unfair and inappropriate. If one child has not learned to read adequately by the third grade, that child may need different instruction than the other students. Greater intensification, extension, or specialized instructional support or settings may be called for in such cases. Failing to acknowledge and differentiate instruction according to needs will prevent opportunities for students to overcome their circumstances.

Instances in which student achievement differences were not considered in resource allocation have been frequently found in curriculum management auditing. The chart below was extrapolated from a midwestern school system's curriculum audit report (Poston, Mitchell, Sweeney, Rice, & Willis, 1991) and serves as an example of how equity applies to schools. Achievement across schools was obviously different. That would be no surprise, because some variation is normal. However, students were achieving success in uneven ways related to socioeconomic differences, and that would not be normally expected.

In the chart, it is evident that School G and School H were underperforming schools. That was no surprise—nearly every school system of any size has a few schools that do not perform up to the levels of others. The surprise was that the two schools were treated identically to the other schools in terms of resources and personnel assignments. They received the same per-pupil allocation of funding, the same number of students per teacher, the same materials and textbooks, and the same instructional support as other schools on a per-pupil basis. Such a condition was equal, albeit inequitable, because no differentiation in resource allocation was made in response to different student needs.

Without accommodation of different needs, underperforming schools would have little likelihood of closing the gap with other schools. In the preceding case, the school system took measures to overcome the gaps and the discrepancies in achievement between the schools. The two underperforming schools received an

Third-Grade Reading Achievement Differences by School: Midwestern School District. ITBS = Iowa Test of Basic Skills; NCE = norm curve equivalent.

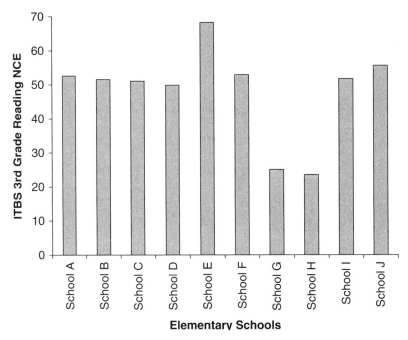

additional $100,000 each (all schools were about the same size) for reading program augmentation.

Special teachers were obtained to deal with the reading deficits, and their duties included the following:

- Diagnose individual student reading achievement against system learner objectives and provide specific information on individual students on a daily basis to teachers for use in prescribing different reading activities for students with low achievement.
- Prepare and maintain an extensive collection of special instructional resources for use in classrooms with underperforming students that were designed to enhance reading achievement.
- Disaggregate assessment information about achievement against system reading objectives for use in identifying curriculum areas not being adequately taught.
- Provide staff development to teachers on how to address the critical needs in reading of underperforming students better.
- Individually tutor chronically underperforming students in reading by use of a program in which external volunteers assist classroom teachers.

Given this differential treatment of students with different needs, there was good news: The two underperforming schools began to show achievement gains immediately, and after 3 years the achievement gap between schools had diminished substantially.

The point is a simple one: Different needs require different responses and treatments in instruction. Treating all students with equal resources and equal treatments when the students are unequal in terms of learning is inequitable and unjust. No society can afford to resign itself to such a large incidence of failure among its school clientele.

STRATEGY 26: HOW

School organizations tend to be very conscious of promoting equality and of being seen as agents of equality, particularly in the area of resource allocation. Equal allocations in organizations responding to diverse needs, however, do not promote equity. School districts that are committed to overcoming the ill effects of inequity devise and implement strategies that create a climate of high expectations for all students regardless of race, gender, or home background. Instructional leaders monitor instruction to ensure that the delivery of instruction reflects a clear understanding of how different children learn.

The National Coalition for Equity in Education has a diagnostic tool comprised of questions that help identify equity issues. Diagnosing the conditions in one's own school district involves using and documenting answers to questions such as the following (National Coalition for Equity in Education, 2007):

- Are ELLs receiving adequate support for learning academic subjects, or is the emphasis on increasing reading scores impeding their learning of other subjects?
- How do people explain the disproportionate failure/success by students of color, language-minority students, and students from low economic classes?
- Does the decontextualization of subjects (subjects being taught outside of a meaningful context and/or not connected to students' culture or experience) affect students' success?
- Are high-level math and science classes taught bilingually or with sheltered methods?
- Do the most experienced and better qualified teachers teach classes with a disproportionately high number of white or affluent students?
- How are resources allocated to different schools within the district? Do schools with the most needy students also have the least experienced teachers and worst equipment?
- Does the district and school leadership emphasize equity and practice what they preach? Are administrators providing both intellectual and emotional support to teachers for changing unequal success rates? Do teachers of color report having difficulty with one or more administrators?
- Do administrators and school boards support teachers' attempts to implement new curriculum or pedagogical approaches that provide access to the curriculum for more students?

Given data gathered with this instrument, school districts may determine whether their system has equity issues.

Another approach is to use an *equity audit* approach to identify, analyze, and evaluate a school district's practices in student placement, promotion, and retention decision making; teacher experience and expertise distribution; and curricular offerings for all students for fairness and equal access (J. Mitchell & Poston, 1992).

The following are some suggestions to overcome learning deficits for students with diverse needs in underperforming schools:

1. The governing body needs to support the school sites in their efforts to meet the needs of different students. Allocation of resources needs to follow the needs of individual schools and, within a school, in accordance with different needs of pupils. The governing body needs to select, adopt, and allocate instructional and human resources across schools to help schools in a consistent and equitable manner *based on need*.

2. Staff development and parental education needs to be geared toward enhancing the community's beliefs in the difference of needs and skills and toward a commitment to reach and achieve success with all students.

3. After diagnosing the needs of different student groups, undertake a comprehensive effort to modify or terminate programs that are creating major issues affecting ethnicity and gender.

4. Modify course offerings and improve access to courses to enhance consistency and equity.

5. Develop procedures and monitor the implementation of processes that foster comparability across school sites and grade levels.

6. Develop and implement a research-based program of instruction supported by staff development that capitalizes on the strengths of all students.

7. Develop a 5-year comprehensive staff development plan that focuses on the delivery of the curriculum to all students. Monitor the use of strategies with periodic assessment of the effectiveness of the staff development in increasing student learning.

8. Devise assessment strategies that not only consider the analytical skills of students but also support and encourage the creative, practical, and social skills of all students.

9. Take assertive action to disaggregate assessment data to pinpoint specific learning skill deficits, and realign instruction to better address those differential needs in the classroom. Monitor results on a weekly basis against the system's learning objectives.

Doing the same things for all students and expecting different results is impractical and futile. To overcome differences among learners, different approaches, greater amounts of time, variable strategies, and intensified efforts are necessary, particularly in ensuring alignment of instruction with feedback from assessment instruments. Gaps among learners are simply the result of individual differences, and gaps can be overcome given appropriate action and confidence in differentiated educational remedies.

STRATEGY 27

Implement Effective Programs and Strategies With English Language Learners

Effective programs and strategies for working with students whose primary language is not English are in place to focus on vocabulary development and reading comprehension approaches.

STRATEGY 27: WHAT

Given the growth of immigration in many states and provinces in recent years, many schools have found themselves with a considerable number of students whose first language is not English. These schools are faced not only with a challenge to provide instruction in desirable knowledge and skills but also the task of helping students build literacy in English—the language of the national culture. Such programs have many different names, including *English as a second language* (ESL), *limited English learners* (LELs), *limited English proficient* (LEP), *English language learners* (ELLs), *structured English immersion* (SEI), and so on. Whatever the appellation, the need to be met is the same: Non–English-speaking students need to learn English in order to be successful in the mainstream culture.

The need to provide for non–English-speaking students is not always welcomed with eagerness. Some states have passed referendums to require teaching non–English-speaking children in English-only approach, which has generated some controversy among educators. For example, in June 1998, California's voters replaced the country's most extensive bilingual education program for limited–English-proficient students with an SEI program. California's policy is to permit only 1 year of SEI before mainstreaming the students in regular classrooms (K. Baker, 1998).

It goes without saying that schools need to use effective programs and strategies for working with students whose primary language is not English, and they need to select learning activities that focus on vocabulary development and reading comprehension approaches.

STRATEGY 27: WHY

It goes without saying that children of all cultures have differential social, cognitive, physical, emotional, and language needs. The complex assortment of issues related to placing ELL students must not be overlooked in placement decisions.

Integration and/or immersion may force students to compromise their total education just to acquire minimal skills. Once intermediate skills are acquired, students may more fully participate in classroom activities in English.

It is no surprise that students fail in school for a variety of reasons, but in some situations the failures may be directly attributed to limited English capabilities because students do not have access to effective ESL instruction (Ortiz, 1997).

Language diversity in many schools has reached substantive levels unprecedented in schools in recent years. For example, large school systems, such as the Toronto School Board in Ontario, Canada, have literally dozens of languages among their student clientele. To meet the needs of these students, a systematic, comprehensive approach is required. It can be a part of a bilingual program (using two languages of instruction in the student's schooling), but this is not the only possibility.

School systems may choose from a variety of programs for students, including immersion (all or part day), pullout programs, summer extension, extended day, and so on. ELL students may be offered any or all of the program options available. In ESL, a systematic approach following specific methodologies for learning English is used. Sheltered English programs provide instruction for non-native speakers in a way adapted to the students' English proficiency levels. Immersion programs place students in a totally English-speaking environment, without any use of their native language. Students learn from constant and perpetual exposure to the English language via visual, aural, oral, and tactile means. Many programs are time-extending programs that give students additional time to acquire the English language.

There are many other things teachers and principals can do to help non–English-speaking students (Kaptain, 2006). First, it is important to recognize and accept that placement with peers is desirable for many reasons, but it is unrealistic to assume that students new to English can learn it fast enough to keep up with their peers for the first year or two. Prior learning in the student's native language is a major factor. If the student's proficiency includes facility with an alphabet and Latin/European characters, it will be easier for him or her to learn English.

Other demographic factors play a part in student success as well, just as they do with English-speaking children; these include parents' educational level, living conditions, parental relationships, supportive personal affirmation, and so on. Two critical factors are the attitude and response of the host society (the child's home school) in regard to the student's language and needs.

Teachers and classroom situations must be fully ready for the cultural diversity and learning challenge that non–English-speaking students present. The more the teachers are trained, the better. The more other students readily accept and help ELL students, the better. The more the school reaches out to parents and the child's home, the better. Teachers need to understand that a child's diminished ability to work in English may not reflect the child's intellectual capacities. Teachers who have high expectations, competence in classroom instruction for ELL students, and sensitivity to children's needs make a big difference in the success of ELL students.

Bilingual education avoids the "sink or swim" approach, which can be very successful, but only if students are being instructed increasingly in English, and

only if adequate attention is given to their native language to maintain proficiency. The goal is proficiency in both languages and for skills to transfer from one
language to the next. However, when bilingual programs are not viable, the best
alternative is to provide students with comprehensive, specially designed instruction in English (Alexandrowicz, 2000).

STRATEGY 27: HOW

Ideally, students are permitted to add a second language to their native language
in speaking, reading, and writing (Alexandrowicz, 2000). The aim is for students
to become literate in two languages and to move from instruction in their own
tongue until they are proficient enough to transfer to regular classrooms. By the
time students reach middle school age they need to be proficient enough to be
taught exclusively in English, except, of course, for a language arts component
used to strengthen their own language. Administrators need to know that acquisition of skills and knowledge in one language obviates the necessity for learning
those things again in another language.

Some advocates of mainstreaming accept the simplistic view that the consistent exposure to English provides the best (and only legitimate) avenue for
students to acquire English language skills; however, unless mainstream teachers
understand second language acquisition and are sensitive to the complex issues
facing ESL students, success is jeopardized. Moreover, teachers must have specialized skills to work effectively with ESL students; otherwise, mainstreaming is
not a viable solution (Young, 1996).

In "English-only" situations (where bilingual education is not allowed), the
educational community needs to continue to identify individual student needs as
well as the available alternatives and courses of action and how to best meet those
needs. Collaborative involvement of the home and community in such decision
making is helpful.

Instruction for ELL students calls for special staff development for faculty
and staff. Faculty need to have training in the area of second language acquisition; cultural diversity engagement and interactions; and classroom management
in classrooms with a wide spectrum of intellectual, academic, and language backgrounds. Well-trained teachers exemplify the highest levels of competency in lesson delivery. Directions and explanations need to be carefully delivered so as to
meet the needs of second language learners. Use of graphics, pictures, and other
nonverbal clues are helpful. In addition, careful planning in the use of vocabulary and instructions must include repetition and paraphrasing to help the
student gain an understanding of what is expected. Teachers need to focus on
critical thinking and hold realistic expectations for academic interactions with
ELL students. Lowering expectations is detrimental to ELL students just as it is
for any student.

Effective strategies and approaches for ELL students extrapolated from
research and experience are delineated next as guidance for teachers and principals (Kaptain, 2005).

Effective ELL Strategies and Approaches

Underlying Principles:

- Translating lessons into the student's native language undermines the acquisition of English/Spanish.
- Bilingualism and biliteracy are an asset to the student and the classroom and should be encouraged and supported whenever possible.
- All instruction should be delivered within a context that supports comprehension so that translation is not necessary for the student's understanding.

Strategies to Support the ELL Student's Learning:

1. Expect and allow a "silent period" from ELL/LEP students. The length of this period depends on personality, level of comfort with the school environment, familiarity with the language, and age. Forcing a student's verbal participation may be detrimental during this phase; instead, creating a safe, supportive, and encouraging environment will make the student feel more comfortable taking risks and in volunteering to participate. This period is similar to a toddler's early years when he or she observes speech patterns before forming complete sentences. The student will participate once he or she feels ready.

2. Modify speech. Always speak clearly and with good enunciation, without compromising the content of the message. Use multiple synonyms for all words critical to understanding the lesson—in other words, present or explain things in multiple ways, using simpler language to explain more complex words or concepts. Use objects and pictures to assist comprehension (see Strategy 3). Resist translating into the student's native language or allowing another student to do the same. This should occur only as a last resort and/or only during the student's initial days at school.

3. Use nonlinguistic representations and concrete referents whenever possible. Concepts, knowledge, skills, and vocabulary being taught are more readily understood by the ELL student when they are accompanied by pictures or manipulatives. The focus is on providing the student with concrete representations for the important words, concepts, or processes, particularly those that are more abstract. Hands-on activities support comprehension as well (see Strategy 5).

4. Provide older, literate ELL students with lists of key words prior to beginning a new lesson or unit. The list would give definitions for the words with pictures or simple English explanations and would support the student's comprehension throughout the lesson or unit. For literate elementary-age students, provide a list of key school-based words, including "playground words," such as *ball*, *jump rope*, *swing*, *slide*, and so on.

5. Provide ample opportunities for hands-on, peer-interactive learning (particularly in lieu of lecturing or worksheets). Students learn from peers (if

they are not translating) and are usually more comfortable participating in a pair or cooperative group setting. Hands-on activities (e.g., experiments, math problem solving with manipulatives) give students the concrete referents they need to support comprehension.

6. Structure certain learning activities to ensure a degree of success for the ELL/LEP student, and provide recognition and sincere praise whenever possible. Remember that concepts transfer from one language to another, so if a student has mastered addition in his or her own language, that skill transfers to English, and he or she can be just as successful at it in the classroom.

7. Encourage and allow students to contribute to lessons and discussions from their unique cultural perspective whenever possible. For example, invite a family member to come in and prepare a special dish with the students for a nutrition unit; encourage a student to share the kind of housing typical in his or her home country (if he or she is old enough to remember) during a city/communities unit, or share a family tradition during a holidays/customs unit. These kinds of participatory activities are important for ELL students of every age and encourage a greater sense of worth and belonging, important factors in facilitating academic success.

8. Take steps to make the ELL students feel included within the classroom. Lack of English proficiency can make a student feel isolated and even inferior; it is important to make them feel as much a part of the class and the school routine as possible. Assigning a "buddy" from among their classmates to show them familiar routines, accompany them around the building, and include them on the playground (or during extracurricular activities) can be a big step to helping ELL students feel a part of the group. Part of this also involves recognizing the difference between being "slow" and lacking adequate language proficiency. It is easy to think ELL students are slow, because for a long time their level of speech resembles that of a small child. It is important for both the teacher and classmates to remember that intelligence cannot be equated with a student's ability to express himself or herself verbally.

The preceding strategies and approaches speak to classroom practice; however, there are many other considerations for teachers to use and administrators to observe and coach. Included in these considerations are the following (Kaptain, 2006).

Effective Instructional Delivery Practices in the ESL/ELL Classroom (For Use in Staff Development and Instructional Coaching)

1. Translation is consciously and studiously avoided. Languages are kept separate, particularly with spoken language.

2. Multiple, effective strategies are used to ensure student comprehension of lessons, concepts, and objectives. These strategies include the following:

Verbal Strategies

- The teacher uses short, simple sentences with ample repetition.
- The teacher rephrases or paraphrases statements, using synonyms when possible.
- The teacher uses a somewhat slower rate of speech (with beginning level students), with clear pronunciation and controlled vocabulary. The teacher's mouth is visible to the student.
- The teacher "thinks aloud," explaining everything he or she is doing to the students (e.g., "I'm looking for my pen. I can't find my pen. Here it is!").
- The teacher provides verbal examples for ideas and concepts presented, building on words and concepts with which students are already familiar.
- The teacher interprets and expands on verbal contributions students make in class (focus is always on the message, not just on the language structure or grammar. Error correction is made within a positive, encouraging context that shows appreciation for the student's contribution).
- The teacher always builds review and repetition into every lesson.

Nonverbal Strategies

- The teacher uses gestures, modeling, pantomime, or Total Physical Response to clarify meaning.
- The teacher uses clear and focused visuals to aid in comprehension. These visuals include the following:
  - Photographs
  - Illustrations
  - Props and realia
  - Graphic organizers
  - Multiple examples
  - Body language
  - Facial expressions

3. Contextual support for students' comprehension is evident in many ways. These include the teacher's use of the following:

Concrete Experiences

- Realia
- Manipulatives
- Hands-on activities and experiments
- Gouin series

Classroom Organization

- Use of established routines
  - Morning routines
  - Routines for lining up
  - Routines for attendance/lunch count, and so on
  - Lesson routines (lessons follow a predictable sequence)

- Use and teaching of functional chunks (phrases necessary for life—these are sometimes posted for student use)
  - "I need to use the bathroom."
  - "I can't find my . . ."
  - "I don't understand."
  - "Please stop that."
  - "Could you repeat that, please." (etc.)

- Prevalence of environmental print (newspapers, magazines, books, signs, etc.)
- Labels on all classroom objects and over doors to different rooms/areas of the school (library, music room, office, etc.)
- Use of word walls (think creatively here—this can be very interactive and culturally relevant!)

4. The teacher makes use of effective questioning, sequencing questions in response to students' verbal ability and comfort level (answers progress from one-word to full sentences)
   - Name ("Who is the attendance monitor today?")
   - Yes/no
   - Either/or ("Is it cloudy or sunny today?")
   - *What, when, where,* and *who* questions that require single- or two-word answers
   - Open-ended questions: Answer requires entire sentence or action ("What did you do this weekend?")
   - Open dialogues
   - Interviews (no yes/no questions—extended response)

5. The teacher designs classroom activities that facilitate and encourage students' verbal interactions, such as partner activities, cooperative learning groups, and so on.

6. Language is explicitly and continuously taught while teaching regular classroom content, before, during, and after regular lessons.
   - Preteaching key vocabulary for a story that will be read aloud.
   - Emphasizing new words and phrases related to a concept as they arise throughout the lesson (making them available in written form to every student, posting them on a word wall, etc.)
   - Drawing attention to specific grammatical structures/language constructs as they come up in a reading selection that pertains to a previous language lesson.

- New vocabulary and phrases are expected to appear in student work and writing samples, or in everyday classroom conversation.

7. The students' native languages and cultures are respected and valued, and every effort is made to establish and maintain positive relationships and communication with the students' parents.

8. The teacher exhibits a positive, encouraging demeanor toward all students at all times, even when communication is proving difficult. The teacher is sensitive to and guards against exhibiting frustration or dissatisfaction with a student's progress—not all students progress verbally at the same rate, and progress is rarely constant.

9. The differences in cultures, heritages, and language are openly acknowledged and discussed, from a perspective of excitement and enthusiasm to learn more about one another and enrich each other by sharing personal experiences and perspectives.

The preceding instructional delivery variables contribute to successful and effective learning of ESL. Not unlike any successful English language arts classroom, ESL classrooms need to have an environment in which ESL students are successfully integrated with native speakers of English, a high amount of interaction is encouraged between and among students in heterogeneous small groups, and a print-rich classroom environment is provided where student work is celebrated and displayed. In such classrooms there is an emphasis on exploration, creation, and presentation of ideas, and confidence is developed in interpretation and analysis through peer and teacher interactive strategies (Cook, 1996).

Other organizational variables also may be worthy of note, including the environment for learning (see Standard Six, Strategy 49).

In searching for environments that are conducive to successful language learning, some variables appeared to be significant. However, a common problem is the instructional constraints imposed by large classes. An optimal setting for learning a second language is one that allows for extensive dialogue between teacher and learner, which is not viable in classes with more than eight students. Drastic reductions in class size may be the most productive step that could be taken to improve the instruction of LEP students (Ramirez & Baker, 1997).

In summary, the responsibility for successful ELL programs rests heavily on the individual school and the individual classroom. The principal must model the highest commitment to building a community in which ELL students, teachers, parents, students, and others work together harmoniously and where respect permeates all activity. Classrooms need to mirror best practice in teaching ELL students. Given effective approaches and commitment, any child—ELL or otherwise—can succeed in school.

ANALYSIS OF STANDARD THREE

Now it is time for you to evaluate the status of your school or school district on *Standard Three: Align Program and Instructional Resources With the Curriculum and Provide Student Equality and Equity.* What is the status of your situation regarding these strategies and what changes are needed? Write your responses in the spaces provided.

Strategy	Current status	Changes needed
19. Align programs with the curriculum to ensure congruity.	❐ Adequate ❐ Not adequate	
20. Use research and data that document results to drive program selection, and validate the implementation of programs with action research.	❐ Adequate ❐ Not adequate	
21. Evaluate programs to determine their effectiveness in strengthening student achievement of curriculum objectives.	❐ Adequate ❐ Not adequate	
22. Align textbooks and instructional resources with the district curriculum objectives and assessments in both content and context dimensions.	❐ Adequate ❐ Not adequate	
23. Use technology in design or selection procedures to ensure strong connections to system learning expectations and feedback.	❐ Adequate ❐ Not adequate	
24. Provide training in the use of instructional resources and their alignment with system curriculum objectives—content, context, and cognitive type.	❐ Adequate ❐ Not adequate	

(Continued)

(Continued)

Strategy	Current status	Changes needed
25. Select or modify instructional resources for lessons to ensure full alignment with system objectives and tested learning.	❒ Adequate ❒ Not adequate	
26. Place students in programs and activities in an equitable manner and with equal access to the curriculum.	❒ Adequate ❒ Not adequate	
27. Implement effective programs and strategies with English language learners.	❒ Adequate ❒ Not adequate	

4

Standard Four

Use a Mastery Learning Approach and Effective Teaching Strategies

Raising student achievement scores can be accomplished using a conceptually simple formula. Teach what you test, teach it the way you test it some of the time, and vary teaching methodology accordingly so that mastery is assured. Putting this formula on paper is easy, but we all know how difficult it can be to implement this type of process in both a consistent and persistent manner. The "Teach what you test" and "Teach it the way you test it" sections have been covered in other portions of this book. This segment focuses on the last part of the formula: "Vary teaching methodologies accordingly so that mastery is assured."

We propose the use of a *mastery learning model* as the focus of the teaching methodologies used. This is our best research instructional model; it has been around for more than 40 years. During this time, the approach has gone through many adaptations, and it is now quite refined. However, mastery learning is sporadically used in most schools across the United States. Mastery learning is a way for teachers to provide higher quality and more appropriate instruction for their students (Guskey, 1997). Davis and Sorrell (1995) stated that mastery learning is "based on the concept that all students can learn when provided with conditions appropriate to their situation."

The installation and institutionalization of a mastery learning model are crucial to creating a learning environment in which students experience the opportunity to be successful on that which we wish them to learn. The learning of students and their continuous progress toward district standards and objectives are the central foci of an instructional model. This does not mean dictating the exact strategies a teacher is to use to teach a specific objective; instead, it means to direct the instructional structure for the overall delivery of instruction.

Within the context of the mastery learning approach the full implementation of well-researched instructional practices takes on more power, because the instruction is at the right level of difficulty for each student. First and foremost is the alignment of the teaching to the curriculum (English, 1993). Next is the differentiation of the learning objective for each student. Differentiation is based on a philosophy that recognizes and expects student differences in learning and believes that teaching should be adjusted to these differences. It is not a "one-size-fits-all" approach, which is less effective than a mastery learning approach when it comes to student achievement, especially when we are trying to close the achievement gap. When students fall behind in their learning and we fail to use a differentiated approach to our teaching, then we exacerbate the gap, not close it.

After alignment and differentiation attributes of teaching are in place, then the numerous effective instructional practices are to be used. There is so much research in this area that the practices are extensive. In this chapter, we focus on just a few of the more noted instructional researched practices.

The following are seven highly powerful strategies regarding the instructional teaching process:

1. **Strategy 28: Implement a Mastery Learning Model.** School-based administrators and all instructional staff have been trained in the mastery learning model and use it.

2. **Strategy 29: Align Teaching With the Curriculum.** Teachers and other instructional staff align their teaching with the content and cognitive type and in the context specified by the district curriculum objectives and/or other external assessments, especially if the district objectives do not have this type of precision.

3. **Strategy 30: Provide Differentiated Curriculum and Instruction as Well as Differentiated Time to Learn.** Teachers and other instructional staff modify their instruction to provide objectives at the right level of difficulty for each student based on ongoing diagnostic assessment, provide differentiated instruction based on student learning needs, and teach prerequisite knowledge as needed. Teachers and other instructional staff provide differentiated time for students to master the objectives, recognizing that students learn at different rates.

4. **Strategy 31: Provide Practice to Master the Curriculum.** Teachers and other instructional staff teach to individual student mastery of the objectives, providing ample practice opportunities over time for both short- and long-term mastery.

5. **Strategy 32: Use Effective Instructional Practices.** Teachers have high engagement rates for all students and use a variety of effective instructional practices, such as smooth, efficient classroom routines; clear and focused instruction; brisk instructional pace and smooth transitions between activities; effective questioning techniques; feedback and reinforcement regarding their learning progress; practices that promote student success in classroom interaction; comparing, contrasting, classifying; using analogies and metaphors; using nonlinguistic representations; providing for active engagement of students; high but realistic expectations for student learning and their own instructional practices; and so on.

6. **Strategy 33: Use Powerful Vocabulary Development Strategies.** Teachers and other instructional staff purposefully incorporate powerful vocabulary development strategies throughout their teaching.

7. **Strategy 34: Establish Individual Learning Plans for Low-Achieving Students.** Individual learning plans are developed for students who test data indicate are underachieving. Low-quartile students or "bubble" students are provided intensive assistance to remediate deficiencies.

STRATEGY 28

Implement a Mastery Learning Model

School-based administrators and all instructional staff have been trained in the mastery learning model and use it.

STRATEGY 28: WHAT

The term *mastery learning* is attributed mainly to Benjamin S. Bloom (1968, 1974), who extended the ideas of John B. Carroll's (1963) *model for school learning*, which challenged the idea that aptitude was the predictor of student success. Carroll argued that all students had the potential to learn quite well but that they differ in the amount of time needed to learn a particular learning. Berliner (2007b) stated that "He made academic/intellectual aptitude a simple time variable" and that Carroll illustrated how the "well-established relationship between aptitude and achievement could be altered if the schools were to leave the time allocations that they had made for instruction open-ended" (Berliner, 2007a). Carroll expressed this in the following equation, with f representing the function of time spent on learning relative to the time the student needs to spend to learn (Guskey, 1997):

$$\text{Degree of learning} = f \text{ (time spent/time needed)}$$

Bloom's mastery learning initially included the components of instruction, formative assessment, feedback with correctives, and a second formative assessment.

Later, the idea of enrichment activities was added to the model for students who demonstrated mastery in the first formative assessment while corrective actions were taken for those who had not (Guskey, 1997). Guskey (1997) indicated that the feedback, correctives, and enrichment part of the approach must provide information that is

> both diagnostic and prescriptive; that is the information or feedback students regularly receive should: (1) reinforce precisely what was most important for them to learn in each unit of instruction, (2) recognize what students learned well, and (3) identify the specific concepts on which students need to spend more time. To be effective, this feedback also must be appropriate for students' level of learning. (p. 11)

In 1980, Denham and Lieberman wrote a document titled *Time to Learn,* in which they presented the *academic learning time model.* This model included the assessment of student prerequisite and entry-level skills to assist in determining the correct level of difficulty for a given student. From this preassessment, prescriptions would be made to determine instructional goals/objectives, activities, grouping, and scheduling for each student, while recognizing that many of the students will be ready for the same learning. Another evolution of the mastery learning model is illustrated in Figure 4.1.

Figure 4.1   Instructional Functions in the Academic Learning Time Model of Classroom Instruction

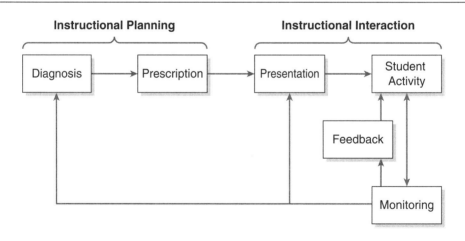

In the mastery learning model, students identified as not having the prerequisite learnings for the new objectives would receive "just-in-time" learning prior to the new unit of study or as a part of that unit's lesson delivery.

Over the next decades, the mastery learning approach evolved as more research was conducted, especially about the use of formative assessments. A mastery learning approach that is used in the Curriculum Management Systems, Inc.'s (CMSi's) seminar "Raising Test Scores: A Baker's Dozen" (Downey & English, 2005b) is presented in Figure 4.2.

Figure 4.2 Curriculum Management Systems, Inc.'s Mastery Learning Instructional Model

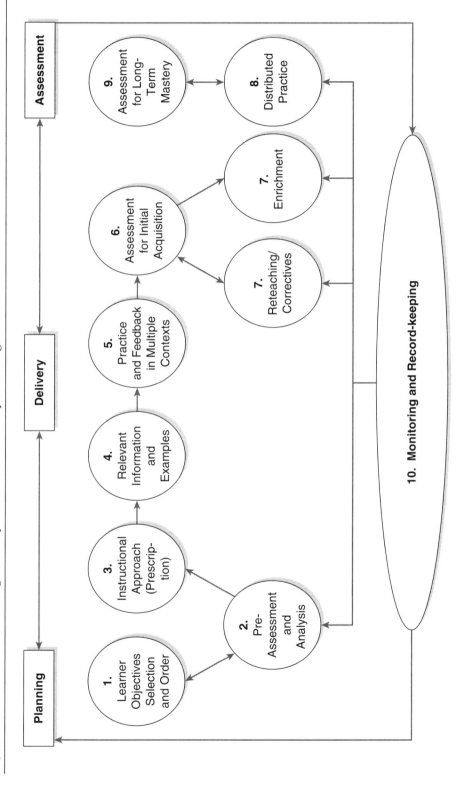

Downey, English, Poston, and Steffy (2007), as part of CMSi's "Maximizing Student Achievement" seminars, enhanced the mastery learning model to also incorporate both mass and distributed practice and ongoing assessments needed to teach not only to initial acquisition of learning but also long-term learning—retention of the learning. This model is depicted in Figure 4.3.

The following is a brief explanation of each component as described in *Maximizing Student Achievement: Curriculum and Assessment* (CMSi,* Downey et al., 2007).

Instructional Planning

1. Specify and order the learner objectives and their prerequisite learnings. The first function in instructional planning is to identify the learner objectives in terms of what each student will know and be able to do after instruction. This is really a product of curriculum design, so it is expected that teachers will select and order the lesson objectives from the expected district standards and objectives to ensure alignment of the written and taught curriculum. Prerequisite learnings to the specific lesson objectives also need to be identified to assess whether students have the necessary entry skills.

2. Assess and analyze student learning on the proposed objectives as well as the necessary prerequisite learnings. Here diagnostic assessments are used to determine each student's status in relationship to the identified objectives selected in Step 1 as well as the prerequisite learnings needed to bring students forward for high success with the new learnings. This includes, for each student, assessment and analysis of the following:

- Student's interests and prior learning and experiences
- Student's quality of current skills and understandings
- Conditions under which successful learning have occurred previously
- Student's motivation in being a partner in his or her own learning

3. Design and/or select instructional approach (prescription). Next, the teacher plans the student interactions on the specified curricular objectives. This is based on the teacher's assessment of each student's needs and the instructional strategies that are likely to lead to durable learning in the most effective manner. This is often called *lesson design*. Decisions are made regarding appropriate modes of the following:

- Objectives for each student and which students need prerequisite teaching
- Resources and materials aligned in the content, context, and cognition desired
- Activities and experiences using a variety of contexts for transfer purposes, including testlike scenarios
- Grouping, scheduling, and projected time to learn

---

*Permission was granted to reproduce this section from the Participant's Manual of the document *Maximizing Student Achievement: Curriculum and Assessment* (2007), Curriculum Management Systems, Inc., Johnston, Iowa.

Figure 4.3 Curriculum Management Systems, Inc.'s Mastery Learning and Teaching Mastery Instructional Model

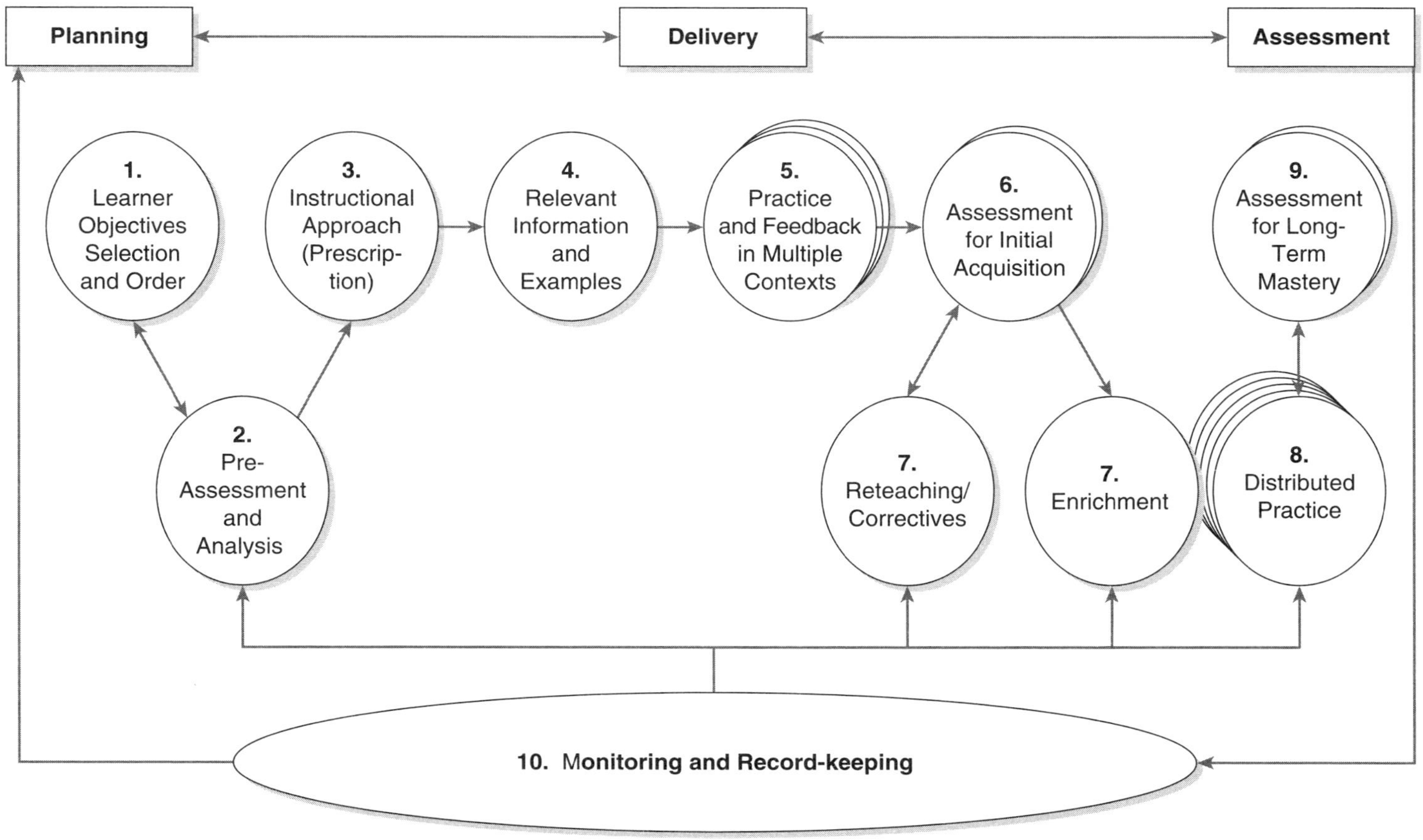

145

- Assessment tools and student products
- Delivery approach and effective teaching practices to use
- Possible reteach and enrichment approaches one might use

Instructional Delivery

4. Provide or generate information and examples that directly correspond to the specified learning objective. The information and examples may be conveyed in numerous ways. The mastery learning process does not dictate teaching delivery strategies; these need to be determined by the teacher to fit his or her own teaching style. The key is whether the students have the relevant information they need to master the specific objective. This information may be conveyed through a number of means, some of which are the following:

- Explicit statements of critical attributes of the learning (deductive, direct)
- Inductive and discovery approaches to determine the critical attributes
- Demonstration
- Modeling using a metacognitive approach
- Use of examples and nonexamples
- Questions designed to call attention to critical attributes, procedural routines, rules and facts, and so on

5 & 8. Provide practice for acquisition and mastery of the learning objective. How a student responds to initial instruction influences the teacher's selection of practice opportunities. Practice opportunities vary by amount, duration, distribution, and meaningfulness. They need to be built into the teaching act both for initial acquisition of learning using massed practice and then distributed practice over time to move the student to mastery. A student's progress shapes decisions that a teacher makes regarding the variables of practice that need to be emphasized. Practice activities need to be structured to match the learning status of each student.

Furnish feedback to students on their status on each objective. The purpose of feedback is to alert the student to both the accuracy and completeness of his or her response. Feedback is a teacher action that allows analysis of information gathered during the monitoring. The timing of feedback is limited to student needs and may occur any time during the learning.

7. Reteach using correctives or provide enrichment activities as needed. Guided by the information obtained during continuous monitoring and the analysis of this information, the teacher determines whether to begin teaching a new learning, reteach the current learning objective using correctives, or provide an enrichment opportunity for each student. If a student's responses indicate that reteaching is needed, the teacher reviews the initial teaching plan and adjusts and/or changes delivery strategies, if the need for a different approach is indicated.

Assessment

6 & 9. Assess student learning throughout the instructional process. Assessment involves comparison of the student's status with the desired objective. The day-to-day formative assessments of students' responses to the delivery of instruction provide the data to determine whether a student has initially acquired the learning as well as mastered the learning. Assessment should guide selection of new learning for the student and the design of future instructional strategies.

Monitoring and Record-keeping

10. Monitor and keep records of student learning on the objectives. This component occurs throughout teaching events. Monitoring of data-gathering strategies includes examining student participation and products. Effective monitoring is continuous, guiding future teacher planning and shaping immediate teacher responses for each student.

There are many misconceptions of the Bloom mastery learning approach. Guskey (1997) identified several, such as confusing it with individualized instruction (e.g., personalized systems of instruction); performance-based or results-based education, which are philosophically similar but focus on the curriculum and its assessment, not the instructional planning and delivery approach; and simple low-level learning skills. He pointed out that the model is neutral regarding the curriculum learnings.

Gentile and Lalley (2003) identified a common misunderstanding in the use of assessments. Thinking that because a student has passed a mastery test (benchmark) in the initial stages of learning (we would call this *initial acquisition of learning*) means that that student has mastered the learning is a mistake. Passing a mastery test is not an endpoint; instead, it is information about the initial stage of learning/memory process. We would propose that such tests be called not *benchmark tests* but *acquisition tests*. Benchmark tests could be reserved for cumulative tests to be administered when a teacher has provided ample practice over time and believes the student has mastered the learning.

Another misunderstanding Gentile and Lalley (2003) identified is embedding a mastery testing approach into an overall grading scheme, which they indicated is often a leftover norm-referenced and competitive scheme. Such an approach contradicts the goal of achieving mastery by all (a criterion-referenced purpose).

STRATEGY 28: WHY

Many studies have pointed out the power of the mastery learning model (Block & Burns, 1976; Bloom, 1974, 1999; Burns, 1986; Guskey & Gates, 1986; Guskey & Pigott, 1988, 1997; Kulik, Kulik, & Bangert-Drowns, 1990) and the benefits accrued for student learning when teachers consistently use this model. The mastery learning model provides benefits for teachers, too: increased confidence in and satisfaction with their teaching, more equal and equitable treatment of students, and use of feedback from student learning to assess the effectiveness of their teaching are just a few.

Gentile and Lalley (2003) synthesized the literature reviews and meta-analysis on hundreds of studies. They indicated that "all reviewers agree that mastery improves performance on criterion-referenced tests," and they presented six "conservative conclusions" drawn from the summaries:

1. Student achievement using a mastery learning model is superior to traditional teaching approaches.

2. Students in mastery learning groups scored higher on retention tests after several weeks or months than did those in traditional teaching groups.

3. The higher the passing standard, the larger the gains by those students in mastery learning groups.

4. Students taught in mastery learning are significantly more likely to self-report positive attitudes toward, liking for, and confidence in their abilities in what has been taught as compared with transitional groups.

5. Teachers exposed to and using mastery learning in their own classes altered their expectations, as well as their attributions, for student achievement and what causes it (higher student expectations).

6. Regarding memory by fast and slow learners, the amount initially learned determines how much is forgotten. Fast and slow learners forget at the same rate once they have mastered material to the same level using different pacing.

There is some interesting research about reteaching we would like to present here. Dewalt and Rodwell (1988, as cited in Cotton, 1989a) and some of the mastery learning researchers have found that allocating time for reteaching is effective only if the reteaching involves materials, examples, and demonstrations that are different from those used during initial instruction. In cases where the reteaching is merely a rehash of initial instruction, additional time allocation for reteaching does not increase achievement. In general, the same instructional activities that are associated with greater amounts of time on task and higher achievement will need to be used during extra time allocations in order for that increased time to be beneficial.

Mastery learning assures teachers and administrators that students have been taught *and have learned* the essential skills, knowledge, and processes that are required to do well on the assessment in use in a district. High-performing schools want their students to experience no surprises when confronted with problems and items on any given test. "This means that students are well prepared to make maximum transfer from what they have learned in the classroom to a situation or problem on a test. *Maximum transfer* means that students have experienced similar types of problems and situations while engaged in learning activities in the classroom. Teachers must structure teaching episodes to parallel the types of learnings students will encounter on a test.

Mastery learning connects the taught curriculum to the written curriculum, which, one would hope, has embedded high-stakes tested learning (see

Standard One). It focuses the emphasis of teaching and learning on those learnings for which the student and the school system will be held accountable in a testing program. The bottom line is that when mastery learning is used, more students learn more.

STRATEGY 28: HOW

The following are some ideas on implementing Strategy 28 at the district, school, and classroom levels:

District Level

1. Have a clearly delineated expectation from the board and the administration that mastery learning is the norm of the district and that all teachers and administrators are expected to use this method in day-to-day classroom instruction.

2. Develop an administrative regulation or position paper around the expected use of the mastery learning approach by teachers in their teaching, and publish this document in staff handbooks.

3. Incorporate into the selection process of new administrators and teachers a way to ascertain their knowledge of, commitment to, and use of a mastery learning approach.

4. Establish a quality staff development approach for both input and follow-up on the mastery learning model. Traditional staff development in implementing the mastery learning model will not suffice. Such staff development does not contain the intensity, duration, or follow-up components necessary to change participant behavior. If teacher behaviors are not adequately addressed, then it is likely that the participants will do what they have always done once they are back in the classroom. Staff development in the mastery learning model must include a component requiring follow-up and on-the-job application of the skills and processes of the model. Specifically, providing professional development for administrators and teachers in the use of the mastery learning model must include the following:
   - Design a plan for the development of teachers and administrators on the mastery learning model. The plan should include a needs assessment of the existing skills, knowledge, and experiences of the staff in using the mastery learning model.
   - Establish a sequencing of staff development sessions that provides input, practice, and reflection on the stages and techniques of a mastery learning model (see Dickson & McKardle-Kulas, 2006a). Sequencing should include multiple sessions for staff development, each followed by practice time back in the classroom. In these sessions, the focus should be on the content of the approach itself, then ways to implement with ongoing coaching/mentoring, and should involve all relevant individuals (Joyce & Showers, 1995).

- Provide each participant with the instructor of the staff development program (or someone trained in the model) to come to the classroom to provide ongoing mentoring and coaching multiple times. The approach should be reflective dialogue in nature such as that used in the *Downey Walk-Through With Reflective Inquiry Approach* (Downey & Frase, 2003b).
- Provide an ongoing professional learning component as part of the school's staff development program. Teachers or administrators who need additional assistance and coaching/mentoring are provided ample opportunity to receive the assistance they need. The success of the mastery learning staff development effort will be measured in part by the degree of mastery attained by the participants in implementing the model. Principals need to be held accountable for such ongoing follow-up for teachers and the supervisor of principals for their coaching.

5. Incorporate mastery learning proficiencies into the standards of performance for staff appraisal.

School Level

6. Provide ongoing professional learning of staff on the understanding of and implementation of a mastery learning approach. Provide coaching and mentoring as part of the supervisor process. Use, as part of the supervisor process of principals, ongoing dialogue regarding the implementation of the mastery learning approach as described in Downey and Jacob's (2006) "Mentoring the Reflective Principal" seminar series.

7. Establish study teams/professional learning teams (DuFour & Eaker, 1998) to work together on sharing approaches and to plan mastery learning units of study.

8. Use data collected from assessments of student achievement to determine the effectiveness of the instructional program in general and implementation of a mastery learning model specifically.

Classroom Level

9. Draw on the following suggested sequence of tasks when applying a mastery learning approach to plan and deliver lessons (Downey et al., 2007):

   a. Determine a possible objective(s). Use a district pacing chart, if available in your area of assignment, to identify desired objective(s) to teach. This document specifies the proposed teaching order for the district objectives by grading period and lists aligned resources. It is important to remember that this sequence is the desired plan for the "typical" student, but diagnosis of pre-entry level must take place, because some students may not have the prerequisite learnings, and some students may already know the learnings. This will change the pacing of the lesson for some students. See Steps "b" and "c."

   b. Plan how to preassess/analyze readiness (prerequisite skills) for this objective and whether the student already has the learning as well as how you will assess for acquisition and mastery of the learning over time. Use the district diagnostic assessments, if available in your area of assignment, as one form of assessment as well as your informal assessments.

c. Use assessment information to go back and finalize objective(s), selecting different objectives for any given student (repeat Steps "a" and "b" until correct level of difficulty of objective is determined). This will result in differentiation of the curriculum for each student.

d. Plan the most appropriate instructional strategies to teach objective(s) and plan lesson. Here is where you can differentiate instructional strategies and approaches for each student to enhance the learning conditions of each student.

e. Identify the relevant information and examples to help students learn the objectives.

f. Plan practice experiences and opportunities for feedback. You will want several practice activities over several days to move the student to short-term memory (acquisition). Provide practices in various contexts in which the student will be asked to demonstrate the learning (e.g., real world, constructed, multiple choice).

g. Assess for initial acquisition of the learning. Use both informal and formal assessment processes. In some of the subject areas there are district acquisition assessments provided periodically (e.g., 3–6 weeks). These can be administered at this point or at the point you think each student has acquired the learning.

h. Provide enrichment and reteaching/correctives, if needed. Use the assessment data from Step "g" to determine whether any students need reteaching. If some do, design and deliver approaches different from the ones used in the original lesson for reteaching purposes. Place other students in enrichment experiences on the same concept (change the cognition, change the context, peer tutoring, etc.). If all students show acquisition of the learning in Step "g," this step may be eliminated.

i. Set up ways to maintain records of where each student is in his or her learning within the process. You will want to have, at a minimum, records on each student's objectives in terms of when taught, when acquired, when mastered. You might also want to keep track of types of differentiated instructional strategies and timeline of learnings for each student. Types of assessments used and data could also be recorded.

j. Set up distributed practice for long-term memory and assess for mastery. As you map out your teaching for a semester or a year, build in distributed-practice opportunities over several months. This can take place through warm-ups, practice of the learnings as prerequisites to new objectives, and so on. Use the district diagnostic assessments to help determine mastery.

10. Use the outline (Downey et al., 2007) in Figure 4.4 as a guide for the teacher's consideration in designing and delivery of each lesson. Note that this lesson planning outline is built around the mastery learning model (Downey, 2001); Hunter's (1982) Lesson Design; DataWorks' *Explicit Direct Instruction*

(Ybarra & Hollingsworth, 2004); Sweetwater Union High School's (San Diego) *SUHSD Lesson* (Sweetwater Union High School District, 2003); and Marzano, Gaddy, and Dean's (2000) *What Works in Classroom Instruction* practices as well as other well-researched effective teaching practices.

Figure 4.4   Curriculum Management Systems, Inc.'s Recommended Lesson Planning Outline. SpEd = special education; LEP = limited English proficient; G/T = gifted and talented

I. Design Planning

A. What do I want my students to know?	
Planning area	*Remember to . . .*
1. **Content objectives** *Estimated class time: _____ periods	• Build lessons around selected skills, knowledge, concepts, and/or processes aligned with the district curriculum. • Gauge adequate time to teach the objective or objectives* (i.e., partial to multiple class periods). • Determine actual objectives to be taught to which students based on initial assessment (see section B below).
2. **Critical attributes of the objective(s)**	• Decide what the student needs *to know* and *be able to do.* • Specify attributes in precise and measurable language. • Sequence the critical attributes in the most effective teaching order.
3. **Essential questions**	• Design at least one question to focus students for each critical attribute. • Plan for a variety of question types (e.g., open ended, higher levels of inquiry).
4. **Essential terms**	• Identify and define essential terms included in the content of the objectives using language students understand (consider second-language acquisition expectations). • Determine where in the lesson you will teach these terms most effectively.
5. **Essential prerequisites**	• Select prerequisites required to learn the objective(s), noting that some learnings require no prerequisites. • Start by reviewing prerequisites in the district curriculum. • Detail specific prerequisites for special student populations (e.g., SpEd, LEP, G/T).
B. How will I know if students have learned the content objective(s)?	
1. **Initial assessment** (diagnosis)	• Determine whether each student has the prerequisite skills and which of the new learnings he or she already knows. • Plan both formal and informal strategies to identify student readiness to learn.

Design Planning

Planning area	Remember to . . .
	• Select strategies to teach quickly essential prerequisites to students who need them. • Identify the performance target at the outset (i.e., what will provide evidence of adequate student performance?).
2. Acquisition assessments (short-term learning)	• Plan to provide periodic acquisition assessments (e.g., quizzes, labs, worksheets, discussions) throughout the lesson(s), which may also serve as practice activities. • Plan for a variety of assessment contexts (e.g., test format, real world). • Revisit the learnings continuously through ongoing assessments of the objective(s) for several weeks (e.g., in warm-up activities, homework, future test items, quizzes).
3. Mastery assessments (long-term learning)	• Specify how you will return to this objective(s) in future lessons to review and reinforce mastery. • Plan for a variety of question types, including item format of high-stakes tests. • Allow multiple ways to demonstrate mastery (including end-of-course exams, portfolios, etc.). • Plan to provide multiple opportunities to demonstrate mastery.
C. What resources and strategies will I use to teach the objectives(s)?	
1. Resources	• Select instructional resources critically, aligning with both content and context of objective(s). • Create or seek additional materials as needed to support attainment of learning objective(s).
2. Strategies	• Consider a variety of ways to present the learning (e.g., inductively, deductively, inquiry, direct instruction, concept formation, structured discovery, synectics, divergent). • Select the most appropriate strategies based on what is being taught: skills, knowledge, concepts, and/or processes. • Select research-based instructional strategies, such as those in Marzano et al.'s (2001) *Classroom Instruction That Works,* as appropriate. • Consider strategies for differentiation and special student populations (e.g., SpEd, LEP, G/T). Teach objectives using multiple modalities (e.g., visual, auditory, written, tactile, and kinesthetic).

(Continued)

Figure 4.4 (Continued)

II. Delivery Planning

How will I construct the learning experiences for each lesson?		
Monitoring and feedback ❑ Provide students with signals and reminders designed to sustain the learning activity and hold students accountable throughout the lesson(s). ❑ Monitor the quality of student participation and products throughout the lesson(s). ❑ Provide continuous targeted academic feedback that is specific to the content throughout the lesson(s).	*Part of instruction*	*Remember to . . .*
	Set/advanced organizer	❑ Furnish students with a clear vision of the learnings to come with a meaningful reason for mastering the objective(s)—include how it fits into the big picture of their education and the world around them (e.g., a problem that needs solving, a current scenario, a recurring human theme a unit of study, a link to something students want to know, etc.). ❑ Reveal the specific content objective(s) and the type of learning (e.g., skill, knowledge, concept, and/or process) to be mastered. ❑ Activate what students have already learned in life and school that relates to the new learning (i.e., scaffolds prior knowledge).
	Relevant input	❑ Teach the critical attributes and key terms of the objective(s) using a variety of research-based instructional strategies. ❑ Use high-interest, real world examples and nonexamples. ❑ Provide explicit samples of how students will demonstrate mastery—the format(s) and standards of performance. ❑ Ensure universal engagement throughout the lesson (e.g., by writing the answers, pair sharing, using whiteboards, cue checks). ❑ Use the essential questions to focus on critical attributes of the objective(s). ❑ Provide for language development activities as appropriate to meet student needs.

II. Delivery Planning

How will I construct the learning experiences for each lesson?		
	Part of instruction	*Remember to . . .*
		❑ Group students in a variety of ways (e.g., individuals, pairs, small and large groups; cooperative learning, reciprocal teaching, Socratic seminars).
		❑ Check students' initial understanding of the learnings and determine which students are ready to move to guided practice.
	Guided and independent practice	❑ Help students develop increased proficiency under close, guided supervision with corrective feedback.
		❑ Provide independent practice experience under continued teacher supervision (i.e., observe cues as students work alone).
		❑ Provide a variety of ways and multiple opportunities to move toward mastery.
		❑ Use homework carefully (i.e., to reinforce the learnings in which you are confident students can be successful without support, to gather new information for readiness for next learnings, to complete extended readings).
	Closure	❑ Provide final practice on the key concepts to clarify the objective(s) learned.
		❑ Use the information from the closure activities to diagnose next teaching steps (e.g., reteach, move on, individual review).
	Mastery acquisition and follow-up	❑ Allow multiple ways and opportunities to demonstrate acquisition of the learnings (e.g., end-of-unit exams, projects, presentations).
		❑ Return to this content objective(s) over time to review and reinforce mastery, either embedded in future lessons or as stand-alone activities.

To increase student achievement, school districts and individual schools must do something different from what they have done in the past. The mastery learning model is one tool that can be used to ensure that teachers are well prepared to teach the aligned district curriculum. If teachers teach what is tested, teach it the way it is tested, and use the mastery learning model so that student mastery is attained, higher test scores will result.

STRATEGY 29

Align Teaching With the Curriculum

Teachers and other instructional staff align their teaching with the content and cognitive type and in the context specified by the district curriculum objectives and/or other external assessments, especially if the district objectives do not have this type of precision.

STRATEGY 29: WHAT

Perhaps the most crucial delivery strategy for higher student achievement is for all instructional staff to align their teaching with the district curriculum, especially if that curriculum has been backloaded to include high-stakes assessment items. Teachers need to teach the learnings tested; teach the learnings the way they are tested, some of the time; and teach the learnings deeply (Downey & English, 2005b). Alignment of the taught curriculum with the written curriculum means that the learnings being taught are a match but does not dictate how a teacher teaches those learnings. *Alignment* is defined as the degree to which expectations (district curriculum objectives) and assessments are in agreement and serve in conjunction with one another to guide the teacher's aligned teaching toward what students are expected to know and do (Webb, 1997).

As Guskey (1997, p. 13) stated, "Although essentially neutral with regard to what is taught, how it is taught, and how the results are evaluated, mastery learning does demand consistency and alignment" of the components with the learning goals and objectives. Alignment of the teaching with the curriculum is essential to effective teaching and learning (English, 1993). Cohen (1987) indicated that "lack of excellence in American schools is not caused by ineffective teaching, but mostly by misaligning what teachers teach, what they intend to teach, and what they assess as having been taught" (p. 19).

Alignment of instruction with the desired end is not a new concept (Cohen, 1987); however, our experience is that many teachers are still allowing the textbook instead of the district curriculum to drive their teaching. In essence, the textbook becomes the surrogate curriculum (English, 1993). Unfortunately, as we discuss in other parts of this book, these textbooks and other instructional resources vary greatly in their alignment to the desired student outcomes (Kulm,

Roseman, & Treistman, 1999; Price-Baugh, 1997; see also Strategy 25). Publishers will tout that their materials are well aligned, but on further examination the alignment appears to be more topical than anything else.

Many teachers believe that the district leadership expects them to use the textbook beginning with page 1 and to move through the material with no scrutiny as to the material's alignment with the learnings. We should not be surprised that teachers are mainly resource driven, because often more time is spent on how to use a resource than how to use the resource as an instructional tool aligned with objectives.

An important consideration in raising student achievement is the extent to which the district has an aligned written, taught, and tested curriculum (English, 1993). Each component is an essential part of designing an instructional program to match the extant accountability system in place (i.e., national test, state test, district designed/adopted tests, college entrance test, etc.). A first step in this process is the design of a curriculum that embeds high-stakes tested learnings into its standards and objectives (see Strategy 1). This ensures that the written curriculum is congruent with what is being assessed on external tests while internal tests are aligned with the district's written curriculum.

Measured learning is greatly enhanced by teacher adherence to a written, aligned, and articulated curriculum that promotes continuity and cumulative acquisition of skills and knowledge from grade to grade and school to school. Strategy 29 is about curriculum delivery—teachers ensuring that the learnings to which they are teaching are the designed and written curriculum student learnings. *Taught curriculum* comprises the learnings taught when the teacher teaches. This strategy is about the non-negotiable curriculum teachers are to teach. Teachers still have the flexibility to determine the means (instructional approaches) toward students' achievement of the learnings.

The written curriculum in a school district is the statement of priorities and shows the emphasis the district has placed on various parts of the curriculum. The written curriculum, adopted by the board of education, becomes the officially sanctioned content for curriculum delivery. Implementation of the official curriculum is the responsibility of each teacher in the system.

The school district leadership has the right and responsibility to clearly state the expectation that teachers use the approved curriculum. Teachers have a right to know what those expectations are and how they will influence their teaching. Learning expectations should be clear and explicit regarding the content, context, and cognition levels teachers are to use in the classroom (see Strategy 2). Unfortunately, many state and national standards are global and duplicative in nature (Marzano, 1998), and as a result it is critical that the district curriculum bring greater precision and clarity to the standards.

The district educators are responsible for ensuring continuity and equality of access across the system in the delivery of the curriculum and for equitable delivery for each student (see Strategy 26). They do this through the consistent delivery of the curriculum by each teacher across grades and schools that provide students with the learning opportunities for which students and teachers are accountable.

The board of education, through its policy-making authority, establishes the expectation for teaching the prescribed curriculum. Policy should be clear and direct regarding the actions of teachers in the system and should be directive rather than descriptive. Board policy becomes the framework to guide and direct the professional staff in the delivery of the curriculum.

STRATEGY 29: WHY

Teaching not aligned with the written curriculum may fragment the learnings of students so that students' educational experience does not match the types of skills, knowledge, and processes they will encounter on external and internal assessments. Not teaching the aligned curriculum may skew teaching so that students are spending excessive amounts of time learning skills, knowledge, or processes deemphasized on the test and the district curriculum while not receiving the appropriate instruction on items emphasized on assessments and in district curriculum expectations.

Cohen (1987) found that when instruction and assessment are aligned during sample lessons, low- and high-aptitude students both score well. Effect sizes associated with alignment ranged from 1.91 to 21.74. According to Cohen, "The critical effect size considered educational significant had been defined as .70" (p. 17). Wishnick (1989) determined that the alignment effect was powerful for all achievers but had the greatest effect on low achievers. As English and Steffy (2001) indicated, students who come from a culture that is different from the culture of the district's curriculum and internal and external assessments are more dependent on teachers to align their teaching. Such alignment when the curriculum has embedded high-stakes tested learnings in it benefits more the low-achieving student. As Shannon and Bylsma (2007) stated,

> An aligned system increases equity and excellence for students when (1) learning standards or targets are known, (2) sufficient opportunities are provided to learn them, (3) instruction is focused on the targets, (4) assessments match the content of the learning standards, and (5) assessment formats are familiar.

English and Steffy (2001) called this the "doctrine of no surprises" (p. 88).

F. M. Mitchell (1998) revealed that when teachers aligned teaching with the curriculum, socioeconomic level, race, gender, and school size were for the most part negated: "There was no statistically significant difference in the effect of curriculum alignment after one year of treatment [alignment of the teaching to the curriculum] when analyzed by socioeconomic level, race, gender or school size" (p. 96).

One of the reasons for existing gaps between student achievement is lack of taught alignment (Blank, Porter, & Smithson, 2001). In the Second International Mathematics and Science Study, Blank et al. (2001) examined instruction in math and science in 11 states. They attributed the poor performance of U.S. students to alignment issues. The study found that there was improved student performance on standardized tests when teachers carefully aligned instruction with learning goals and assessments with a measurable impact of 31 percentile points in student achievement. Blank et al. reported that several studies show that taught alignment "cancels out" more traditional predictors of student achievement, such as socio-economic status, gender, race, and teacher effect. They also found other benefits, such as better communication and collaboration among teachers, as well as helping teachers understand how their instructional decisions contribute to students' overall learning.

High-performing schools and school districts direct teaching to the expected set of performance standards that enable students to succeed on tests. Aligning teaching with the curriculum just makes sense. It makes sense from the point of view of the student and from the point of view of the teacher and administrator. It is totally consistent with the notion of "Teach what you test, teach it the way you test it, and vary teaching methodology accordingly so that mastery is assured"— elements that lead to "no surprises" for students.

One other note on why to use Strategy 29: If the board of education has officially adopted the curriculum of the district, as we call for in this book, then teaching the prescribed district curriculum is congruent with board policy. Not teaching the board-adopted curriculum constitutes unprofessional conduct. Individuals would not intentionally do this, but unless there is a clear commitment to teaching the curriculum, this is the situation into which staff may put themselves. Board adoption of the curriculum establishes the equivalent of a law for the district. It states clearly what is expected of the teaching staff relative to the delivery of curriculum. There is good reason why we emphasize that the board should adopt the curriculum. It ensures that the adopted curriculum will be the delivered curriculum and that the written, taught, and tested curriculum is congruent.

STRATEGY 29: HOW

High-performing school systems have clearly communicated expectations for the delivery of the curriculum. Teachers and administrators are well aware of what those expectations are and what their roles in implementing the curriculum are. High-performing systems take the necessary steps to ensure that what is taught in the classroom is consistent with the written and tested curriculum.

Curriculum leaders in school districts take actions to establish procedures to monitor the delivery of curriculum at the school site level. The following steps are suggested:

District Level

1. Design and implement administrative regulations or procedures to fully implement board policy relating to the delivery of curriculum.

2. Communicate clearly expectations to administrators and teachers about the delivery of curriculum.

3. Develop and implement administrator staff development on monitoring/ coaching/mentoring the curriculum, such as CMSi's "Maximizing Student

Achievement" series (Downey, English, Poston, & Steffy, 2007, 2008). Principals in particular must be skilled in monitoring the curriculum and teaching methodology. Walk-through training for principals (Downey & Frase, 2003a, 2003b) is strongly recommended. Training for supervisors of principals, such as the "Mentoring the Reflective Principal" CMSi series, also is recommended (Downey & Jacob, 2006). The focus on these approaches is one of coaching and mentoring with reflective dialogue, not inspection and a "Gotcha!" approach. Make monitoring part of the job performance for all administrators. Central office administrators should focus on working with principals to increase their capacity to monitor curriculum and work with teachers. The persons who evaluate principals should have as part of their job description and duties the responsibility for monitoring the monitors and coaching the coaches.

4. Report periodically the status of teaching in the district—both from the point of view of pedagogy and delivery of the adopted curriculum.

School Level

5. Communicate clearly to teachers the expectation that the aligned curriculum is to be delivered in the classroom. Work with teachers who may have concerns about abandoning past practices and pet projects. Help them understand the benefits for students and the school when the aligned written curriculum is taught in the classroom.

6. Provide extensive professional development for all instructional staff on curriculum alignment and its value, such as the CMSi Principal–Teacher Series on Higher Student Achievement, including "Raising Student Test Scores: A Baker's Dozen" (Downey & English, 2005b), "Taking the Mystery Out of High Stakes Tests" (Downey, Steffy, & English, 2006), "Examining Student Work for Standards Alignment and Real World/Test Formats" (Downey & English, 2005a), and "Aligning Lesson Stakes Standards" (Dickson & McKardle-Kulas, 2006b).

7. Work with teachers on the selection of their activities and resources as part of their daily lesson planning to ensure alignment. As Shannon and Bylsma (2007) stated,

    To determine the match of textbooks and supplemental materials and activities with the learning targets, educators must systematically check instructional materials against the essential learnings. Simply following textbook suggestions does not guarantee coherent programs of curriculum and instruction. Where textbooks do not match, additional supplementary materials must be obtained.

8. Provide staff development of peer study and observation groups on the curriculum and its delivery. A protocol for peer classroom observations using the informal Downey (2008) walk-through is suggested.

9. Inform teachers that an administrator will be in their room on a frequent basis to monitor the delivery of the curriculum and to observe teaching. The practice of "managing by wandering around" will provide a solid base for principals to use in working with teachers to increase their capacity to deliver the curriculum. Use the nonevaluative approach as recommended by Downey (2008).

10. Establish the expectation with office personnel and others that the principal will be out in classrooms on a frequent basis and that only true emergencies should supersede that activity.

11. Use the SchoolView program to gather school- and districtwide data on classroom curricular alignment with the district curriculum about three times a year (Downey, 2005).

12. Manage time wisely. Administrators should use time spent in moving from one part of the building to another as an opportunity to drop in on classrooms. It takes only minutes to monitor curriculum and teaching in a classroom, and the benefits far outweigh any inconvenience. Skills in conducting classroom walk-throughs are crucial for any building administrator. More important is the training on how to conduct reflective conversations with staff as part of their ongoing coaching and mentoring. Reflective approaches are more powerful than inspection approaches for long-lasting change in behavior (Frase, 2005; Garmston, 2000; Peterson, 2000).

13. Develop a working rapport with teachers that enables them to reflect on their own teaching practices. Encourage teachers to critically analyze their own teaching behaviors to see whether there are areas for growth in pedagogy or delivery of the aligned curriculum.

14. Align site-based staff development efforts to focus on areas identified by building administrators and elicit teacher self-reflection as needed for curriculum delivery or teaching methodology.

Classroom Level

15. Increase your knowledge of curriculum alignment through readings and staff development.

16. Plan your lessons around specific district curriculum objectives if the curriculum has embedded learnings from high-stakes testing and identified them as such (see Strategy 1). If the curriculum standards are vague, duplicative, and not backloaded, work with your teaching colleagues to prioritize and sequence across grades specific learning objectives that have a high probability of being assessed. If you are working with low-performing students, teach a reduced number of objectives with plenty of time for distributed practice for mastery (see Strategies 30 and 31).

17. Sequence your lesson objectives so that the most frequently tested learnings and/or the ones with which students have the most difficulty are presented early so that you can provide multiple practice opportunities for students to master the objectives.

18. Assess where each student is on the objectives and prerequisites to ensure that you are teaching an aligned curriculum set of objectives at the right level of difficulty for each student.

19. Provide multiple practice opportunities in various assessment situations—for example, multiple-choice, completion-type tests, and authentic real world performances to enhance the transfer of learning to a variety of contexts.

20. Use the mastery learning approach of formative assessments to determine each student's acquisition and mastery of the learning objectives.

21. Ensure reteaching and enrichment activities are aligned with the curriculum objectives while varying content, context, and cognitive type.

22. Monitor and keep track of each student's progress on each objective—initial acquisition as well as mastery for long-term retention.

Teaching the aligned curriculum is an essential element in improving student achievement. High-performing schools and school districts have clear policy, clear expectations for the delivery of curriculum, and systems in place to monitor curriculum delivery and to make appropriate adjustments in curriculum or teaching.

STRATEGY 30

Provide Differentiated Curriculum and Instruction as Well as Differentiated Time to Learn

Teachers and other instructional staff modify their instruction to provide objectives at the right level of difficulty for each student based on ongoing diagnostic assessments, provide differentiated instruction based on student learning needs, and teach prerequisite knowledge as needed. Teachers and other instructional staff provide differentiated time for students to master the objectives, recognizing that students learn at different rates.

STRATEGY 30: WHAT

Differentiation is an instructional approach to teaching in which educational curriculum content, instructional process, and student products are adapted according to student readiness, interest, and diagnosis of current level of performance on specific standards/objectives. Unlike *individualized instruction*, in which teaching must be directed to the specific needs and skills of each individual student, *differentiated instruction* often addresses the needs of student clusters. Differentiation serves students' unique learning needs, backgrounds, learning styles, and interests—it is a tailoring of assignments to suit students' needs (Starr, 2004). There could be some individualization in terms of prerequisite, reteaching, enrichment, and time to learn.

In an interview, Tomlinson (quoted in Bafile, 2006) stated:

> On some level, differentiation is just a teacher acknowledging that kids learn in different ways, and responding by doing something about that through curriculum and instruction. . . . Differentiation suggests we look at "ballparks" or "zones" in which students cluster—so that on a particular day, depending on our students and their needs—we might offer two or three or four routes to a goal—not 23 or 30 [individualization]. . . . Differentiation focuses also on helping students understand ideas and apply skills so that they develop frameworks of meaning that allow them to retain and transfer what they study. . . . [A] common surprise for teachers is that many students who are restless, uninvolved, or misbehave in one-size-fits-all settings become "less problematic" in effectively differentiated classrooms. I think we often worry particularly about students who pose behavior issues in the classroom and conclude that in more flexible settings, the problems would intensify. In fact, they often lessen because the system is working better for the student.

T. Hall (2002) pointed out that our knowledge that not all students are alike is what calls for differentiated instruction. Such an approach uses a flexible instructional approach that provides diverse students "multiple options for taking in information and making sense of ideas." The curriculum and the instructional approach are adjusted in the same class for the student rather than having students adjust and modify themselves to the curriculum and instructional approach. Hall specified that the teaching is a blend of whole-class, group, and individual instruction. Differentiated instruction recognizes students' varying background knowledge; experience background; readiness; language; and preferences in learning, including their interests. "The intent of differentiating instruction is to maximize each student's growth and individual success by meeting each student where he or she is, and assisting in the learning process" (T. Hall, 2002).

Effective teachers are constantly aware of the curricular and instructional needs of their students, and they make appropriate modifications in their teaching to maximize the learning for each student. These teachers have devised many ways of assessing what students learn, encouraging individual students to strive for mastery. Effective teachers have become experts at diagnosing the needs of students by using a variety of assessments and by bringing to bear all of the resources, experience, and methods they can in the delivery of the aligned curriculum.

The first and most important aspect of differentiation is *curricular differentiation*, the selection of which district curriculum objective best fits the next learning need of each student. Effective teachers are aware of the expectations and requirements for students as they encounter the curriculum. They use the district-adopted curriculum as a tool to focus their teaching efforts in order to get the maximum benefit from the teaching/learning time. Fortunately, many students have similar readiness to learn and the teacher does not have to differentiate the teaching of a given objective for each student in the group at a different time (i.e., individualized teaching). However, in a sense the teaching is individualized if the teacher has knowledge that these groups of students are ready for the same learning and can be taught in the same group.

Some students may not have the necessary prerequisite learnings to enter the new learning, and the teacher will need to provide special instruction on the prerequisites before, or as part of, the new learning to ensure students have success. Other students may already have mastered the new learning and so may be moved to another objective in the district curriculum or, if in the group, provided enrichment activities.

The second type of differentiation is *instructional differentiation*, whereby the teacher differs the instructional approaches that might be used in teaching the same objective to a group of students. Effective teachers have developed and honed their teaching skills to the point that they have many alternative approaches from which to choose for any given teaching episode. They are continually seeking improved methods to approach teaching in the classroom and base their effectiveness on the learning accrued by their students.

Moreover, as part of instructional differentiation, effective teachers recognize that students do not acquire new learnings at the same pace. It has been said that "Time is the coin of education." It is certainly one of the critical factors in the learning cycle for students. Education today is a time-based system. We expect students to learn everything we want them to learn within the time parameters we set for them—and we usually have more learnings than students can master in the time frame provided (see Strategy 5).

Obviously, some students need more time for learning than others. How a teacher accommodates the differences in learning time will go a long way toward mastery or nonmastery of the material being learned. Each student has a unique learning rate. Teachers must be aware of these learning rates and make modifications in strategy and technique to adjust their teaching for the needs of students. The time required for each student to master the skills or concepts being presented is the time management standard for the teacher. If it is important enough to learn, it is important to provide the time needed to learn.

Berliner (2007b) indicated that the "well-established relationship between aptitude and achievement could be altered if the schools were to leave the time allocations that they had made for instruction open-ended." The mastery learning approached derived from the J. B. Carroll (1963) model

> explored the idea that the single most important variable in education was opportunity to learn, a variable that had associated with it a unique characteristic, namely, that it was in a time metric. We then noted, as well, how it was the genius of Carroll to turn aptitude into a time-based measure, an alterable variable, instead of leaving it as some mysterious genetic or familial variable that was not alterable under ordinary circumstances.

Cotton (1989a) summarized the J. B. Carroll (1963) model as "the time needed for a given student to learn a given concept" that depends on five factors:

- Aptitude—the amount of time an individual needs to learn a given task under optimal instructional conditions
- Ability—capacity to understand instruction
- Perseverance—the amount of time the individual is willing to engage actively in learning
- Opportunity to learn—the time allowed for learning
- Quality of instruction—the degree to which instruction is presented so as not to require additional time for mastery beyond that required by the aptitude of the learner

Note that understanding learners and time is a most important attribute of a teacher's differentiation of instruction.

In the field of education, we have a very important concept called *Academic Learning Time* (ALT). ALT refers to situations in which student learning needs and learning objectives, material, and objectives are well matched (Anderson, 1983). ALT emerged from a large-scale research effort called the Beginning Teacher Evaluation Study, conducted in the 1970s. ALT is the engaged time that students spend working on tasks at an appropriate level of difficulty for them and in which they experience high levels of success (Cotton, 1989a).

Berliner (2007b) made the following statements about ALT:

Academic learning time (ALT), usually defined as that part of allocated time in a subject-matter area (physical education, science, or mathematics, for example) in which a student is engaged successfully in the activities or with the materials to which he or she is exposed, and in which those activities and materials are related to educational outcomes that are valued (Berliner, 1987; Fisher et al., 1980). This is a complex concept related to or made up of a number of other concepts, such as allocated time (the upper limit of ALT); time-on-task (engagement in tasks that are related to outcome measures, or, stated differently, time spent in curriculum that is aligned with the evaluation instruments that are in use); and success rate (the percent of engaged time that a student is experiencing a high, rather than low, success experience in class). Academic learning time is often and inappropriately used as a synonym for engagement, time-on-task, or some other time-based concept. Its meaning, however, is considerably more complex than that, as will be elaborated on below.

Providing more time to learn by itself will effect higher student achievement only if the teaching is aligned with the district curriculum (see Strategy 29) and that curriculum has embedded high-stakes tested learnings (see Strategy 1).

Less effective teachers have few options when putting together lessons for the classroom. Their array of methods does not permit differentiated instructional approaches based on the individual needs of students, so they teach to the middle and hope that as many students as possible will "get it." Less effective teachers do not use a variety of assessment methods to ascertain the learning levels of student, and they tend not to make modifications in what they do even though feedback from student assessments is available. Less effective teachers treat students as if they all can learn at the same time at the same pace on the same learning.

High-performing schools and school district leadership foster a norm of teaching that includes the ability to provide differentiated curriculum and instruction for students based on individual needs. These schools and districts develop these skills through staff development and actively seek out teacher candidates to fill positions who have demonstrated differentiated teaching skills.

STRATEGY 30: WHY

Differentiating instruction on the basis of students' needs increases the likelihood that students will master the essential learnings of the curriculum and perform well on district-designed or -adopted tests and external assessments. Differentiated instruction makes maximum use of time, instructional resources, and teaching methodologies to strive for mastery learning on the part of all students. The intent of teaching should be student learning rather than content coverage. The role of the teacher is master technician and manager of the curriculum to direct student learning.

High-performing schools and school districts have adopted specific strategies to develop and nurture teachers who have the abilities to differentiate their teaching to the needs of students. Staff development programs, formal and informal reward systems, teacher appraisal criteria, and school and district effectiveness are in place to foster the abilities of teachers to differentiate their teaching to the individual needs of students.

According to Tomlinson (2007), research supports differentiation. Students are more successful in school and find it more satisfying if they are taught in ways that are responsive to their readiness levels (e.g., Vygotsky, 1962/1986), interests (e.g., Csikszentmihalyi, 1997), and learning profiles (e.g., Sternberg, Torff, & Grigorenko, 1998). Research studies such as those conducted by Banks (2000) and by Cole (1995, cited in McKinley, 2007) indicate that teachers who applied changes to classroom interactions have student achievement scores that are correlated with a weakened relationship between socioeconomic class and educational achievement.

The Staff Development for Educators Web site (http://differentiatedinstruc tion.com) presents several reasons why it is critical that teachers differentiate their instruction, including that differentiation enables teachers to open up learning opportunities for all students by offering varied learning experiences, put research-based best practices into a meaningful context for learning, and use assessment as a critical tool to drive instruction.

The research on time is very interesting. Cotton (1989a) synthesized time research and developed seven major points:

- There are large differences in instructional time allocations across schools and classrooms so that students in one classroom may experience three or more times as much instruction as another.

- The ratio of school time to instructional time and the ratio of classroom time is shocking: About half the day is spent in instructional time and the other half in noninstructional situations.
- The ratio of instructional time (in classrooms) to time on task is also discouraging. Fifty percent of the time students are actually engaged in learning activities, and the rest of the time in the classroom is spent on procedural matters, transitions, disciplinary matter, off-task behavior, and so on.
- There is a small positive relationship between allocated time and student achievement.
- There is a modest positive relationship between time on task and student achievement that is stronger than the above allocated time–student achievement relationship.
- The strongest relationship is between ALT and both student achievement and attitudes. Remember that ALT is not only about time but also about alignment to the curriculum at the right level of difficulty for a student.
- Increasing allocated or engaged time is more beneficial for lower performing students than higher performing students. This makes sense, because the lower performing students depend on us to provide the amount of time needed to learn. Such students will need greater amounts of time than students who typically perform higher.

Increasing time on task is more beneficial and enhances achievement for highly anxious students (Cotton, 1989a) and for students in more highly structured subjects, such as mathematics and foreign languages, than in less structured ones, such as language arts and social studies. Berliner (2007b) also reported this finding as part of the Beginning Teacher Evaluation Study. He pointed out that in Rossmiller's (1986, cited in Berliner, 2007b) research study, the relationship between a set of time variables and reading and mathematics achievement test performance was made for students in several elementary grades. He found that the instructional time variable could predict around 10% of the variance in student achievement for students in the highest quartile. However, he found that for the students in the bottom quartile, time accounted for about 36% of the variance.

When we look at this research on time, it becomes clear that we need to provide differentiation in time for low-performing students but that extended time must be at the right level of difficulty in terms of the task (i.e., curriculum alignment). This is why the concept of ALT is so powerful.

Meeting the individual needs of students means adapting time and strategy or technique for each student. Perhaps more important is that the quality of the time students spend overshadows the quantity of time they spend. High-performing schools and school districts provide teachers with guidelines on the use of time for learning and acknowledge the decision-making responsibility of teachers to adjust, modify, and adapt their teaching to the individual needs of students. These schools and districts provide effective staff development for teachers and administrators on how to maximize learning within time constraints.

Short- and long-term mastery requires one to address the element of time. Providing quality time for learning challenges teachers to differentiate instruction based on the individual needs of students. High-performing school systems institutionalize differential use of learning time from the policy to the operational levels. It becomes part of the expectations of performance for teachers and administrators. The first step in differentiation is curriculum alignment, which should precede any instructional differentiation. Unfortunately, most discussion of differentiation misses the key point of first identifying the objectives at the right level for student success (curriculum differentiation).

STRATEGY 30: HOW

Instituting and institutionalizing differentiated instruction require a number of steps.

District Level

1. Establish a school board policy that requires differentiated curriculum and instruction by all teachers in the district as they plan and deliver their lessons. How the district defines differentiated instructional time needs to be incorporated into policy.

2. Make sure that all special population programs are aligned with the district curriculum and that district curriculum-referenced assessments are used to assess student progress on the curriculum as instruction is delivered through the programmatic efforts. Unfortunately, many programs for special population students are not aligned with the curriculum.

3. Provide comprehensive staff development for teachers and administrators on differentiated instruction. Provide on-the-job application and follow-up components to ensure full implementation. Provide frequent refreshers that allow teachers to hone existing skills and learn new ones.

4. Use data for feedback to inform teachers, schools, and the district on the effectiveness of the instructional program. Use of data for decision making should become the standard of performance for all levels (teachers, schools, district) of the instructional program.

5. Examine the school day to determine amount of allocated time for learning and probable time frames by grade level and courses for each of the subject areas.

School Level

6. Examine the school day, passing periods, lunch periods, recess, and so on, to see how more time can be devoted to classroom instruction; maximize the learning time.

7. Look for distractions to the day and eliminate or reduce them (e.g., announcements, taking students out of classrooms). Be careful about "pull-out" programs; for example, at the elementary level, schedule instrumental music lessons before and after school.

8. Set up "jump start" efforts and ways to extend the time for students to learn who need more time to learn. For example, transition summer schools with instruction tied directly to specific learning objectives on which low-performing students are behind, providing prerequisite training for certain special population students, after-school tutoring programs, Saturday School, and homework hotlines.

9. Monitor and coach teaching methods on a frequent basis. Regular and frequent classroom walk-throughs by administrators will provide a basis for working with teachers on their skills, knowledge, and techniques of differentiated instruction. Teacher reflection on their own teaching techniques is a highly effective way for teachers to be self-motivated in modifying what they do in the classroom (Downey & Frase, 2003b).

Classroom Level

10. Recognize that differentiation begins with student assessment ("Strategies for Differentiating," 2007). Assessing prerequisite skills and current level of knowledge on the proposed teaching objectives is essential to determine the correct level of curriculum objectives to teach next, and to which students. It is important to help students understand that the concept of "fairness" is based on the recognition that each student is a unique person and has different learning needs. As a result, students might be working on different tasks much of the time, and students will be given different amounts of time to learn.

11. Determine when and how the instructional approaches are to be differentiated. For instance, "Strategies for Differentiating" (2007) proposed the following strategies:

- Have flexible grouping based on student performance, personal talents, and interests. Students should not be kept in static groups.
- Vary the complexity of the activities.
- Use reading buddies or listening to stories/instruction using a tape recorder for students whose reading levels are below grade level—especially for lower elementary grade students. Reading buddies also benefit with this reading as they gain fluency in the reading.
- Vary the cognition requirements of questioning and consequent thinking skills.
- Have different questions on written quizzes. The students can have the same number of questions, but the complexity could vary with the option of students to be challenged beyond the minimal requirements.
- Use learning centers that contain both differentiated and compulsory activities. Unfortunately, most learning center activities are not differentiated in terms of complexity, student readiness, and interest.
- Provide alternative assignments and activities for students who have already mastered curriculum content. Use independent study projects in which students learn how to develop the skills for independent learning.

Buddy studies, in which two or three students work together on the same project, could be used as well. Tomlinson (1999) suggested having "Anchoring Activities," a list of activities a student can do at any time he or she has completed the present assignments or that can be assigned for a short period at the beginning of each class as the teacher and students organize themselves. These could be enrichment opportunities, problems to solve, or journals to write. They also could be long-term projects. Teachers can use this time to provide individual and small-group instruction to other students.

- Use peer and cross-age tutoring. A student could be designated as the "resident expert" for a given concept or skill and receive valuable practice by being given the opportunity to reteach concepts to peers. Research has found cross-age tutoring to be very beneficial and one of the most cost-effective instructional methods we have for both the tutor and the tutee (Levin, Glass, & Meister, 1984, cited in Berliner, 2007).
- Use tiered assignments of varying complexity, with all activities relating to the essential objectives students need to acquire.
- Accelerate or decelerate the pace at which students move through the curriculum objectives.
- Differentiate the products by

(1) giving students options of how to express required learning (e.g., create a puppet show, write a letter, or develop a mural with labels); (2) using rubrics that match and extend students' varied skills levels; (3) allowing students to work alone or in small groups on their products; and (4) encouraging students to create their own product assignments as long as the assignments contain required elements. (Tomlinson, 2007)

- Increase your repertoire of teaching strategies through staff development and reading so that you have a variety of teaching strategies to use in a differentiated classroom. Teaching strategies would include direct instruction, inquiry-based learning, cooperative learning, and information-processing strategies ("How to Differentiate Instruction," 2007).

12. Monitor student ALT so that you have a sense of the learning rates of students in your class. Making notations about each student will help you with useful information in the design and delivery of instruction.

Differentiating instruction to the needs of students creates the norm that the individual teacher, school, and school district expect high levels of learning from all students. It makes a definitive statement about the values of the system. In addition, it establishes a work ethic in the district that the academic success of each individual student is important. Adapting learning time to the needs of students increases the likelihood that students will master the essential skills, knowledge, and processes presented in the classroom. Acknowledging and acting on differential learning time adds the ingredient that enables greater numbers of students to achieve mastery.

STRATEGY 31

Provide Practice to Master the Curriculum

Teachers and other instructional staff teach to individual student mastery of the objectives, providing ample practice opportunities over time for both short- and long-term mastery.

STRATEGY 31: WHAT

We all know about the value of practice; however, we also know that because there are too many standards and objectives to teach and learn, we often are not providing the practice needed for students to master the learning. *Mastering the learning* means long-term retention of the learning. In other sections of this book, we have addressed the topic of reducing the number of objectives. Once these are reduced, the next issue is how we plan our practice of the learnings. There are several questions we need to ask:

- What type of practice should we provide?
- How much practice is enough so that students learn the content of the objective to achieve long-term mastery—long-term memory, or retention of the learning?
- How can practice be assigned so that students obtain retention of the learning in the most efficient manner possible?
- What should be the duration of practice?
- Do the type and amount of practice differ on the basis of that which is to be learned?

First, and foremost, the practice must be aligned with the content, context, and cognition of the learning. The old axiom "Practice makes perfect" is not quite explicit enough for our purposes here. What we are striving for with students is "Perfect practice makes perfect." Practice schedules have to include assurance that the skills, knowledge, concepts, and processes students are practicing are the ones they will encounter on the district-designed or -adopted tests and external assessments as well as life situations. Practice sessions must focus on the correct practice of skills, knowledge, concepts, or processes to ensure congruence with testing situations. So, as we design our practice we have to take into consideration the various scenarios in which students will be asked to demonstrate their learning. Unfortunately, when we gather data in classrooms, we often find that the activities and materials students are working with are not aligned in content, context, or cognitive types. Teachers often think there is alignment until they have been trained to have a healthy skepticism of the resources provided to them.

To maximize student achievement it is necessary to provide ample practice and learning opportunities for students to ensure both short- and long-term mastery of the material presented. Student achievement is increased when students have multiple experiences to gain speed in and familiarity with the content, context, and cognitive requirements of the tested curriculum. Practice increases speed and familiarity, which influence student testing situations. The more familiar students are with the content and context of what is being tested, the greater the likelihood that the student will transfer learnings from the classroom to testing scenarios.

For practice to be effective, it must include short-term acquisition of skills, knowledge, and processes, and long-term mastery of the same. Students may not be tested over a given skill, knowledge, concept, or process for several months (or even years) after they first learn it. Consider the case of students learning math concepts in the first, second, and third grades but who are not subjected to the state test until the end of the fourth grade. The skills, knowledge, and processes learned during those earlier school years will be part of that fourth-grade state test. It makes sense for the educators of the system to provide intermittent reinforcement of the skills, knowledge, concepts, and processes these students will need to do well on the fourth-grade test.

However, education is more than doing well on a test, it is about learning. There is little reason to present lessons on objectives and not have students retain the learning over time. The CMSi illustration of mastery learning has incorporated the concept of practice not only for initial acquisition of learning but also for using distributed practice to move the learning to the student's long-term memory. A mastery learning approach used in the CMSi seminar "Raising Test Scores: A Baker's Dozen" (Downey & English, 2005b) is presented in Figure 4.3 (see page 145).

Notice the multiple circles on Points 5 and 8 in the figure, which denote mass and distributed-practice opportunities to be built into the mastery learning approach.

The concept of practice is one of the most well-researched principles of learning in the literature. Critical to this literature is the distinction between *massed practice* and *distributed practice*. Here is a brief description of three important terms:

- Practice: The act of rehearsing a learning over and over for the purpose of improving or mastering the learning (see http://en.wikipedia.org/wiki/Practice) or to do repeated exercises for proficiency (see http://www.m-w.com/dictionary/practice).
- Massed practice: Many practice learning episodes on the same learning in the same time period (Gentile & Lalley, 2003). This is a form of practice with relatively little or no rest between repeat performances of the learning. One source indicates that "mass practice is practice sessions in which the amount of practice time is greater than the amount of rest time between repetitions" ("Distributed Practice: The Research Base," 2007). Cramming is an example of massed practice. You learn something just long enough to get through some testlike situation, but you seldom remember much about that knowledge years or even months later. This type of practice, when used over a few days and then dropped, moves the learner to short-term memory only—eventually, in fact, the learning is forgotten. Such practices are usually longer in duration than distributed practice and often lead to rote learning rather than meaningful learning ("Distributed Practice," 2007).

- Distributed practice: Provides for the rehearsal of learning over hours, days, and many weeks. There is a little practice each day, and then the practice is spread out across days, with more rest periods in between practice, after initial acquisition. This type of practice moves the learner to long-term memory over time. Gentile and Lalley (2003) indicated that "From a cognitive constructivist point of view, distributed practice also provides experience retrieving previously sorted material, comparing new examples with those stored, reorganizing what is known, and recording it for memory storage and subsequent accessibility" (p. 4). Distributed practices are relatively short in duration and move students to meaningful learning. As it has been said, it is better to "practice a little and often" (Baddeley, 1997).

Willingham (2002) presented the following scenario to illustrate the concept of *spacing effects*:

> Suppose a student is going to spend one hour learning a group of multiplication facts. How should that hour be allocated? Should the teacher schedule a single, one-hour session? Ten minutes each day for six days? Ten minutes each week for six weeks? The straightforward answer that we can draw from research evidence is that distributing study time over several sessions generally leads to better memory of the information than conducting a single study session. This phenomenon is called the spacing effect.

Part of what determines how much practice to provide is based on prior learning. Something that was initially acquired but not learned to mastery, if currently activated, can speed up the learning when working on it at a later time. According to Gentile and Lalley (2003), "If such prior knowledge of skill is absent, then the learning task is more difficult. . . . If the pre-requisite knowledge has been mislearned or is otherwise inaccurate, acquisition of the new task is further confounded with the need to unlearn prior misconceptions" (p. 3). They went on to discuss that learning occurs in phases and that the initial acquisition phase includes readiness (prior learning), learning to initial acquisition, and forgetting. Forgetting occurs unless there is more distributed practice. When you come back and practice the learning again, that relearning is faster—it takes less time to move the learning again to short-term memory. Continuing this pattern with the intervening intervals becoming greater in length eventually moves the student to long-term memory, what we call *mastery*.

The word *mastery* is used many different ways in the U.S. educational community. In many districts, the term is misused. Often there are benchmark tests to test mastery, but they are administered within 5 to 6 weeks of when the initial learning took place. More than likely, what is really being tested is short-term memory. To us, mastery of the learning means long-term retention—"You've got it for good." Gentile and Lalley (2003) indicated that this subsequent use of distributed practice of the "relearning episode constitutes additional amounts of learning, defined as practice beyond initial learning which is inversely related to forgetting" (p. 4).

How often should one practice the learning? Usually, more practice is needed, especially when a distributed-practice approach is used. More is learned initially, and then for each subsequent practice less time is needed, yet the learning has to be practiced many times (Marzano et al., 2000). Part of what happens during the practice is that students learn how to adapt to multiple contexts and situations in which they are using the learning. Much time must be devoted to this practice. The additional time may be essential to facilitate students' conceptual under-standing. The only way we know whether a student has mastered the learning is through formative assessments. In actuality, these formative assessments can be more distributed practice. Eventually, if the student performance is accurate, with no prompting, and the student demonstrates the learning a few times every time correctly, then he or she probably has mastery.

STRATEGY 31: WHY

Practice is the way we learn. It is one of the main ways human beings learn any-thing, from playing a musical instrument to learning a skill or trade (Zemelman, Daniels, & Hyde, 1998). Most of the things we value in life are learned through repetitive practice. However, we provide students with precious little time for practice in the areas of academics where skill and knowledge acquisition is crucial to tested performance. Student mastery of content and context depends on prac-tice. The ability of teachers to create practice sessions for students will determine to a great extent the degree of mastery attained. The higher the degree of mastery, the better students will perform on tested material. Therefore, the practice that students engage in *must be* congruent in content, context, and cognitive level with the material students will encounter on the test. If any of these three elements is missing, then the practice session will be out of alignment with tested material. Remember, "Perfect practice makes perfect!"

Furthermore, that practice must be distributed. Some of the early research on the benefits of distributed practice took place in the late 1800s (Ebbinghaus, 1885/1964; Jost, 1897; Thorndike, 1912, all cited in Cepeda, Pashler, Vul, Wixted, & Rohrer, 2006). Cepeda et al. (2006) stated that

> more than 100 years of distributed practice research have demonstrated that learning is powerfully affected by the temporal distribution of study time. More specifically, spaced (vs. massed) learning of items consistently shows benefits, regardless of retention interval, and learning benefits increase with increased time lags between learning presentations. (p. 16)

Practice is necessary for any type of learning. The synthesized research on prac-tice shows effects that can be substantial (Bloom, 1976; Kumar, 1991; Ross, 1988; all cited in Marzano et al., 2000). The need for many practice sessions for high level of competence are clearly described in the research literature, with the recognition that the most significant gains come in the initial practice sessions and that future practice sessions add incrementally smaller gains (Anderson, 1995; Newell & Rosenbloom, 1981; both cited in Marzano et al., 2000). Marzano et al. (2000) indi-cated that students do not reach 80% competency until they have practiced 24 times.

Moreover, the idea of distributed practice is relevant to all types of learnings and contexts. Caple (1996, cited in "Distributed Practice: The Research Base," 2007) summarized the research as follows:

> The spacing effect is an extremely robust and powerful phenomenon, and it has been repeatedly shown with many kinds of material. Spacing effects have been demonstrated in free recall, in cued recall of paired associations, in the recall of sentences, and in the recall of text material. It is important to note that these spacing results do generalize to textbook materials, meaning that subjects such as science can be manipulated by spacing effects. Also the effect of spaced study can be very long-lasting.

STRATEGY 31: HOW

The following steps are suggested for establishing a system of student practice that will help provide for short-term acquisition and long-term mastery of skills, knowledge, and processes:

District Level

1. Define clearly the purpose of practice, and communicate to instructional staff how practice helps develop long-term mastery as a part of the mastery learning instructional approach.

2. Design practice sessions into curriculum guides as an integral part of curriculum delivery. Make sure the focus of practice is congruent with the content, context, and cognitive levels of what students will encounter in test situations.

3. Provide staff development for teachers and other instructional staff on the appropriate use of practice and how to design and create meaningful practice sessions for students.

4. Include the concept of practice in the staff development on monitoring for principals so they are able to assist teachers in appropriate practice session design and so they know the difference between effective and ineffective practice observed during classroom walk-throughs.

School Level

5. Have teachers map out their curriculum over a semester or a year showing how they will bring back initial student learnings into short multiple practice opportunities over time to move students toward retention of the learning.

6. Emphasize the importance of "Perfect practice makes perfect" (i.e., aligned practice).

7. Remind staff and provide ongoing discussion of the fact that speed of execution and familiarity with concepts and test formats are crucial for effective results on any state or norm-referenced test. It is classroom practice that increases speed and brings familiarity.

Classroom Level

8. Design lessons using a mastery learning approach building in both mass and distributed practice.

9. Map out your curriculum learnings, including where the distributed practice will take place over the semester/year.

10. Use various approaches for distributed practice, for instance, sponge and warm-up activities, review prior knowledge just before moving to a new learning, build prior knowledge into homework.

11. Discourage any cramming for tests and do not use the 3 weeks before a high-stakes tests to review; instead, teach tested learnings well in advance so students have long-term retention (mastery) of the learnings. This will decrease anxiety when students take the tests.

12. Use the distributed-practice activities as formative assessments to determine when students no longer need practice. Do not grade practice or even formative assessments. If this is done, it is not practice—there is not an opportunity to make modifications. If it is graded, it is a summative assessment and no longer has the benefits of practice.

STRATEGY 32

Use Effective Instructional Practices

Teachers have high engagement rates for all students and use a variety of effective instructional practices, such as smooth, efficient classroom routines; clear and focused instruction; brisk instructional pace and smooth transitions between activities; effective questioning techniques; feedback and reinforcement regarding their learning progress; practices that promote student success in classroom interaction; comparing, contrasting, classifying; using analogies and metaphors; using nonlinguistic representations; providing for active engagement of students; high but realistic expectations for student learning and their own instructional practices; and so on.

STRATEGY 32: WHAT

Effective teachers use a variety of well-researched practices and methods to ensure student learning. They engage students in multiple-level learnings to ensure content acquisition and mastery as well as self-development, cognitive development, and metacognitive development. Effective teachers are aware that their specific behaviors and instructional strategies can alter student behavior and learning (Marzano, 1998).

The first four strategies of this chapter have dealt with, from our perspective, the four most powerful effective teaching strategies:

- Use a mastery learning approach in the planning and delivery of lessons (see Strategy 28).
- Align the taught curriculum to the expected district/state curriculum (Cohen, 1987; English, 1993). This becomes especially true when the curriculum has embedded high-stakes tested learning and clearly denotes which learnings these are (see Strategies 1 and 29). There are numerous trainings and books about effective teaching practices, but several fail to mention that the instructional practices they are touting through the research must first be used in the context of aligned teaching.
- Use formative assessments to diagnose where students are in their learning and provide the curriculum at the right level of difficulty for students (see Strategy 30). In this approach, time is the variable and the learning is the constant. When students have learning at the right level of difficulty you are increasing the ALT for that student (Berliner, 2007b).
- Teach using distributed practice and provide multiple opportunities with increasing intervals between those opportunities to rehearse the learnings (see Strategy 31).

These four effective teaching strategies are the basic instructional practices to be used by teachers at all times. In this section, we present many other teaching strategies that researchers over the years have found to be powerful in raising student achievement. A thorough discussion of this is beyond the scope of this chapter, and because there are many other books and articles fully devoted to this topic, we will share just some of the hundreds of effective teaching practices in this strategy.

One of the finest resources for a synthesis of research on teaching practices is the continually updated work "Research You Can Use to Improve Results," compiled by Northwest Regional Educational Laboratory (2007). It updates key practices that impact districts, schools, and classrooms. The major categories and practices in their document linked to instruction and instructional improvement are presented in Figure 4.5. For each of the bulleted practices listed, the Web site lists specific instructional practices and an annotated bibliography for each of the practices.

It is important in citing "Research You Can Use to Improve Results" to understand that for each one of the areas mentioned, more specific teaching practices are listed.

A synthesis of specific effective teaching practices in classroom discipline are presented in an article by Cotton (2001) as depicted in Figure 4.6.

Coles (1992) indicated that routines are a fundamental aspect of classroom life and that the learning settings and transitions must be explained and exemplified. Evertson (cited in T. L. Cooper, 2007) has a 3 = 33 formula , which means that the first 3 weeks establish the foundation for a well-run classroom, that 3 weeks of

Figure 4.5   List of Effective Classroom Teaching Practices

1. Planning and Learning Goals

   - Emphasize the importance of learning.
   - Use preplanned curriculum to guide instruction.
   - Provide instruction that integrates traditional school subjects, as appropriate.
   - Integrate workplace readiness skills into content-area instruction.
   - Provide instruction and practice in citizenship skills.
   - Use educational technology for instructional support and workplace simulation.
   - Help students prepare to become lifelong learners.

2. Management and Organization

   - Form instructional groups that fit students' academic and affective needs.
   - Make efficient use of learning time.
   - Establish smooth, efficient classroom routines.
   - Establish clear discipline policies and apply them fairly and consistently.

3. Instruction and Instructional Improvement

   - Orient students to lessons, carefully.
   - Provide clear and focused instruction.
   - Routinely provide students feedback and reinforcement regarding their learning progress.
   - Review and reteach as necessary to help all students master learning material.
   - Use validated strategies to develop students' critical and creative thinking skills.
   - Use effective questioning techniques to build basic and higher level skills.
   - Foster the development of self-directed learning skills.

4. Social Relationships and Interactions

   - Hold high but realistic expectations for student learning and their own instructional practices.
   - Provide appropriate incentives, recognition, and rewards to promote excellence.
   - Interact with students in positive, caring ways.
   - Use instructional strategies and practices that promote student success in classroom interaction.

5. Equity

   - Give students the extra time and instruction they need to succeed.
   - Support the social and academic resiliency of students.
   - Promote respect and empathy among students of different socioeconomic and cultural backgrounds.

6. Special Programs

   - Use validated practices for preventing at-risk behaviors.

7. Assessment

   - Monitor and promote student progress.

8. Parent and Community Involvement

   - Involve parents (or other family members) and community members in supporting children's learning.

Figure 4.6   List of Effective Classroom Discipline Practices (Cotton, 2001)

1. Hold and communicate high behavioral expectations.

2. Establish clear rules and procedures and instruct students in how to follow them; give primary-level children and low-socioeconomic children, in particular, a great deal of instruction, practice, and reminding.

3. Make clear to students the consequences of misbehavior.

4. Enforce classroom rules promptly, consistently, and equitably from the very first day of school.

5. Work to instill a sense of self-discipline in students; devote time to teaching self-monitoring skills.

6. Maintain a brisk instructional pace and make smooth transitions between activities.

7. Monitor classroom activities and give students feedback and reinforcement regarding their behavior.

8. Create opportunities for students (particularly those with behavioral problems) to experience success in their learning and social behavior.

9. Identify students who seem to lack a sense of personal efficacy and work to help them achieve an internal locus of control.

10. Make use of cooperative learning groups, as appropriate.

11. Make use of humor, when suitable, to stimulate student interest or reduce classroom tensions.

12. Remove distracting materials (athletic equipment, art materials, etc.) from view when instruction is in progress.

practice on the rules and procedures for classroom management will yield 33 weeks of time for sound instruction.

Emmer, Evertson, and Worsham (2000) and Evertson, Emmer, and Worsham (2000) have identified specific effective teaching practices for teachers to focus on at the beginning of the school year. In terms of room arrangement, they suggest that effective teachers should (1) arrange the classroom so it is consistent with instructional goals and activities, (2) make sure high traffic areas are not congested, (3) set yourself up so each student can be seen by the teacher, (4) have those materials and supplies used often close by, and (5) have all instructional presentations and displays set up in such a way that each student can see them with ease.

They have indicated that in the first week of school teachers need to use whole-group instruction to review learnings that students can easily attain so that the routines of the classroom can be taught and practiced (Emmer et al., 2000; Evertson et al., 2000). Such routines would include the classroom rules and procedures, consequences of rule violations, procedures for use of materials and equipment, procedures during seatwork and teacher-led instruction, and group work.

Kounin (1970, cited in Evertson & Harris, 2007) indicated that classroom management is not so much "what teachers do to stop misbehavior that characterizes effective group management, but how they prevent problems in the first place." The start of school is crucial to effective classroom management, which in turn affects higher student achievement. There is a positive correlation between establishment of effective classroom routines and higher levels of student learning. Teachers who have established routines are also found to have "improved student task engagement, less inappropriate behavior, smoother transitions between activities, and generally higher academic performance" (Kounin, 1970, cited in Evertson & Harris, 2007).

At the beginning of the school year, effective teachers do the following (Emmer et al., 2000; Evertson et al., 2000):

- Prepare and plan classroom rules and procedures in advance
- Communicate their expectations clearly
- Establish routines and procedures and teach them along with expectations for appropriate performance
- Systematically monitor student academic work and behavior
- Provide feedback about academic performance and behavior

Resnick (2007) identified nine Principles of Learning that research indicates are powerful specific instructional practices. She indicated that these are "condensed theoretical statements summarizing decades of learning research." The principles are presented, with a brief narrative, in Figure 4.7.

Figure 4.7   Resnick's (2007) Nine Principles of Learning

1. Organizing for effort	Replace effort for aptitude in terms of how much students learn. Everything is organized to evoke this effort. High minimum standards are set, and assessments are aligned with those standards.
2. Clear expectations	Communicate explicitly what is to be learned. Descriptive criteria and models of work that meets the standards are publicly displayed, and students refer to these criteria and models as they analyze and discuss their work.
3. Fair and credible evaluations	Use assessments that students find fair and stakeholders find credible. Fair evaluations are ones for which students can prepare and ones for which the assessments test their learning efforts.
4. Recognition of accomplishment	Motivate students by regularly recognizing their accomplishments. This can be in the form of celebrations of work that meet standards or intermediate progress to those standards. Progress points should be articulated so each student can meet the criteria regardless of differing entry levels.
5. Academic rigor in a thinking curriculum	Teach knowledge while engaging students in thinking. Engage students in active reasoning about the concepts to be learned. There must be a commitment to a knowledge core, high thinking demand, and active use of knowledge.
6. Accountable Talk[SM]	Talk needs to seriously respond to and further develop what others in the group have said. It puts forth and demands knowledge that is accurate and relevant to the learning under discussion. Accountable Talk uses evidence appropriate to the discipline.

7. Socializing intelligence	Use approaches that encourage intelligence. Intelligence is a set of problem-solving and reasoning capabilities that can be learned along with the habits of mind that lead one to use these capabilities. Intelligent habits of mind are learned through daily expectations placed on learners.
8. Self-management of learning	Help students develop and regularly use an array of metacognitive self-monitoring and self-management strategies. Students need to be responsible for the quality of their thinking and learning.
9. Learning as apprenticeship	Set up the structure that allows students to acquire complex interdisciplinary knowledge, practical abilities, and appropriate forms of social behavior. Organize learning environments so that complex thinking is modeled and analyzed and by providing mentoring and coaching as students undertake extended projects.

SOURCE: The Principles of Learning © 2001–2005 is the property of the Institute for Learning at the University of Pittsburgh and may not be used, reproduced or distributed without the express written permission of the University of Pittsburgh.

Marzano, Pickering, and Pollock (2001) identified the following specific instructional practices as having the powerful effects on affecting student achievement. These are presented in Figure 4.8, with a brief narrative, in order of power in terms of size effects related to student achievement.

Figure 4.8   Marzano's Powerful Instructional Practices

1. Identifying similarities and differences	Have students identify similarities and differences by engaging them in tasks that involve comparisons, classifications, metaphors, and analogies. These can be either teacher directed or student directed.
2. Summarizing and note taking	Have students summarize their learnings throughout the lessons and take notes. Summarizing requires substituting, deleting, and keeping some things to help students understand the important aspects of the learning. Reciprocal teaching, a powerful strategy, provides for a deep level of understanding necessary for effective summarizing. When note taking, the student also needs to know what is most important and then to state it in a type of summarizing manner.
3. Reinforcing effort and providing recognition	Teach about the value of effort, and keep track of effort and achievement. Link recognition to a standard of performance. Use abstract symbolic recognition. Personalize the recognition. Use a "pause, prompt, and praise" approach in complex learnings.

(Continued)

Figure 4.8 (Continued)

4. Homework and practice	Use homework to extend the school day appropriate to the grade level. Keep parent involvement in homework to a minimum, establish purpose of a given homework assignment, and then comment on assigned work. Mastering a learning requires a fair amount of focused practice. Have students keep track of their speed and accuracy.
5. Nonlinguistic representations	Use nonlinguistic representations to help students understand content in new ways. Use a variety of approaches, from graphic organizers to physical models. Nonlinguistic representations need to elaborate on knowledge.
6. Cooperative learning	Plan various grouping strategies to affect student learning. Use ability grouping sparingly. Keep cooperative groups small in size. Of all the grouping strategies, cooperative learning may be the most flexible and powerful. It should be applied consistently and systemically, but not overused.
7. Setting objectives and providing feedback	Set learning goals so they encompass the learning desired. Have students personalize the instructional goals. Feedback provides positive results. It should be corrective in nature, timely, and specific to a criterion. Have students provide some of their own feedback.
8. Generating and testing hypotheses	Have students, in all subject areas, generate and test hypotheses in their application of knowledge. This can happen both inductively (drawing new conclusions based on information we know) and deductively (using a general rule to make a prediction about a future action or event). Research indicates that the deductive approach usually works best.
9. Cues, questions, and advanced organizers	Help students retrieve what they know about a topic by activating prior knowledge. Cues involve hints about what students are to experience. Cues and questions should focus on what is important as opposed to what is unusual. Use "higher level" questions for deeper learning. Use wait time and use questions throughout the lesson. Advanced organizers—expository, narrative, skimming, and illustrating—all produce powerful results, but expository is the most powerful.

Many of the effective practices that are now getting our educational attention have been well researched over the years. In 1987, Brophy wrote an article that was a synthesis of the research of motivation strategies. He identified 33 strategies, and only 3 of these were extrinsic motivational approaches. Often, we think that we have to use extrinsic rewards for motivating students when it is our instructional approaches that really provide the motivation. Brophy's 33 strategies are presented in Figure 4.9.

Figure 4.9   List of Brophy's (1987) 33 Effective Motivational Strategies

Essential Preconditions

1. Provide a supportive environment.
2. Have appropriate level of challenge: difficulty.
3. Provide meaningful learning objectives.
4. Use motivational attempts with moderation for optimal use.

Motivating by Maintaining Success Expectations

5. Program for success.
6. Teach goal setting, performance appraisal, and self-reinforcement.
7. Help students to recognize linkages between effort and outcome.
8. Provide remedial socialization.

Motivating by Supplying Extrinsic Incentives

9. Offer rewards for good (or improved) performance.
10. Structure appropriate competition.
11. Call attention to the instrumental value of academic activities (learning used as a means to some desirable end).

Motivating by Capitalizing on Students' Intrinsic Motivation

12. Adapt tasks to students' interests.
13. Include novelty/variety elements.
14. Allow opportunities to make choices or autonomous decisions.
15. Provide opportunities for students to respond actively.
16. Provide immediate feedback to students' responses.
17. Allow students to create finished products.
18. Include fantasy or simulation elements.
19. Incorporate gamelike features.
20. Include higher level objectives and divergent questions.
21. Provide opportunities to interact with peers.

Stimulating Student Motivation to Learn

22. Model interest in learning and motivation to learn.
23. Communicate desirable expectations and attributions about students' motivation to learn.
24. Minimize students' performance anxiety during learning activities.
25. Project intensity.
26. Project enthusiasm.
27. Induce task interest or appreciation.
28. Induce curiosity or suspense.
29. Induce dissonance or cognitive conflict.
30. Make abstract content more personal, concrete, or familiar.
31. Induce students to generate their own motivation to learn.
32. State learning objectives and provide advance organizers.
33. Model task-related thinking and problem solving.

One last synthesis of research to share in this strategy is about student expectations, and it was conducted by Cotton (1989b). She indicated that researchers have found that some teachers differentially treat students for whom they have low expectations. She identified the following:

- Giving low-expectation students fewer opportunities than high-expectation students to learn new material
- Waiting less time for low-expectation students to answer during class recitations than is given to high-expectation students
- Giving low-expectation students answers or calling on someone else rather than trying to improve their responses by giving clues or repeating or rephrasing questions, as they do with high-expectation students
- Giving low-expectation students inappropriate reinforcement, for example, giving reinforcement that is not contingent on performance
- Criticizing low-expectation students for failure more often and more severely than high-expectation students and praising them less frequently for success
- Failing to give feedback to the public responses of low-expectation students
- Paying less attention to low-expectation students than high-expectation students, including calling on low-expectation students less often during recitations
- Seating low-expectation students farther from the teacher than high-expectation students
- Interacting with low-expectation students more privately than publicly and structuring their activities much more closely
- Conducting differential administration or grading of tests or assignments, in which high-expectation students—but not low-expectation students—are given the benefit of the doubt in borderline cases
- Conducting less friendly and responsive interactions with low-expectation students than high-expectation students, including less smiling, positive head nodding, forward leaning, eye contact, and so on
- Giving briefer and less informative feedback to the questions of low-expectation students than those of high-expectation students
- Asking high-expectation students more stimulating, higher cognitive questions than low-expectation students
- Making less frequent use of effective but time consuming instructional methods with low-expectation students than with high-expectation students, especially when time is limited

Cotton (1989b) indicated that these kinds of differential treatment have been noted in some teachers' actions not only by individuals but also when we consider ability groups and tracked classrooms. Students in such groupings have been "found to get less exciting instruction, less emphasis upon meaning and conceptualization, and more rote drill and practice activities than those in high reading groups and tracks" (p. 10).

As a result of these findings, the following recommended effective teaching practices as they related to student expectations are drawn from the work of several researchers (Brophy, 1983; Cooper & Tom, 1984; Cotton, 1989; Good & Brophy, 1984; Marshall & Weinstein, 1984; Patriarca, 1986; and Woolfolk, 1985; all cited in Cotton, 1989b). These are listed in Figure 4.10.

Figure 4.10   Cotton's (1989b) List of Student Expectation Effective Teaching Practices

1. Avoid unreliable sources of information about students' learning potential, for example, social stereotypes, the biases of other teachers, and so on.

2. Set goals (for individuals, groups, classrooms, and whole schools) in terms of floors (minimally acceptable standards), not ceilings; communicate to students that they have the ability to meet those standards.

3. Use heterogeneous grouping and cooperative learning activities whenever possible; these approaches capitalize on students' strengths and take the focus off weaknesses.

4. Develop task structures in which students work on different tasks, on tasks that can be pursued in different ways, and on tasks that have no particular right answer. This will minimize harmful comparisons.

5. Emphasize that different students are good at different things, and let students see that this is true by having them observe one another's products, performances, and so on.

6. Concentrate on extending warmth, friendliness, and encouragement to all students.

7. Monitor student progress closely so as to keep expectations of individuals current.

8. Give all students generous amounts of wait time to formulate their answers during recitations; this will increase participation and improve the quality of responses.

9. In giving students feedback, stress continuous progress relative to previous levels of mastery rather than comparisons with statistical norms or other individuals.

10. In giving students feedback, focus on giving useful information, not just evaluation of success or failure.

11. When students do not understand an explanation or demonstration, diagnose the learning difficulty and follow through by breaking down the task or reteaching it in a different way, rather than merely repeating the same instruction or giving up.

12. In general, think in terms of stretching the students' minds by stimulating them and encouraging them to achieve as much as they can, not in terms of protecting them from failure or embarrassment.

STRATEGY 32: WHY

High-performing schools and school districts set high expectations for teachers. These expectations include the use of effective, researched instructional practices in the design and delivery of lessons in the classroom. Teacher knowledge and use of effective teaching strategies are powerful determinants of student success. The instructional abilities of the teaching cadre within a school or district will help determine whether test scores rise, fall, or stay the same. Effective teaching practices will lead to higher student achievement.

Effective instructional practices engage a higher percentage of students in on-task behavior, produce higher student achievement, and increase student motivation and interest in the work they are doing in the classroom (Bloom, 1999). It is important to provide students with constructive feedback about their progress in attaining learning goals (Hattie, 1992). One of the most powerful things effective teachers do is to set clear instructional goals and provide students with feedback on their success in meeting those instructional goals.

Effective teachers are clear about the purpose and intended goal of their teaching, and they design learning activities to elicit the specific behaviors and learnings they want from students. Effective teachers give each student in their classes many opportunities to respond to learning situations and know how to deal with student error in a manner that generates additional learning on the part of the individual and the entire class. They enhance the students' knowledge development, cognitive development, metacognitive development, and self-goals.

For an extensive listing of the research on these effective instructional skills, review "Research You Can Use to Improve Results" (Northwest Regional Education Laboratory, 2007).

Berliner (2007a) lamented the fact that well-researched practices have not moved into classroom practices as much as desired. He described several practices as examples. One effective teaching practice was *cross-age tutoring*. He indicated that it has advantages for both the tutor and tutee as well as being one of the most cost-effective approaches (Levin, Glass, & Meister, 1984, cited in Berliner, 2007a). Another practice he described that has not really been explored enough by teachers is *reciprocal teaching*. According to Berliner, reciprocal teaching (Palincsar & Brown, 1984, cited in Berliner, 2007a) has "evidenced consistent and large effects in remediating some problems of comprehension that were thought to be intractable" (Rosenshine, 1991, cited in Berliner, 2007a). However, this technique has not often been disseminated in preservice or in-service programs of teacher education and therefore is not used in many schools.

Another practice Berliner (2007a) described as not making its way into the classroom as well as desired are *visual conceptual learnings*. Research has demonstrated that the "unusually consistent and powerful effects on transfer" (Mayer, 1989, cited in Berliner, 2007a) are clearly effective but seldom used.

Retention is still another area Berliner (2007a) identified as clear evidence of the negative effects of leaving children back in school, yet the practice persists. He stated that "Our hard-won data concerning what happens to most children who are retained in grade appears to be without use."

Glickman (1991), in an article titled "Pretending Not to Know What We Know," identified several ineffective classroom practices:

- Tracking students
- Retaining students in a grade
- Using corporal punishment (which is illegal now in most states)
- Failure to use real life activities
- Treating well-researched teaching practices in a simplistic manner and not recognizing that decisions are context driven

- Focusing on Carnegie units (the amount of credit given in high school for a course), classroom size, and grade levels

It is important that we begin to systematically bring the more powerful effective instructional practices presented in this strategy into our classrooms in a consistent manner.

STRATEGY 32: HOW

Effective instructional practices provide a critical key to improving student achievement. The following steps are suggested for establishing a consistent use of the more powerful instructional practices in every classroom:

District Level

1. Develop a list of effective well-researched instructional practices that teachers are to consider in their planning, delivery, and assessments of their units.

2. Place this list into the job description as well as in the formal appraisal list of competencies for teachers.

3. Provide new teachers with an orientation to these expectations and establish ongoing professional development opportunities for teachers and administrators to increase their knowledge of these practices.

4. Recognize that it takes years, if not an entire teaching career, to incorporate these instructional practices into one's repertoire.

5. Provide extensive training for principals and other school-based leadership on the use of these practices and how to coach and mentor staff in their use.

6. Coach and mentor principals and other instructional administrators in the implementation of these practices as part of their supervisory process.

School Level

7. Hold high expectations for the use of effective teaching practices for all teachers and instructional staff.

8. After providing professional development on alignment, mastery learning, use of assessments, begin to deliver formal and informal professional development on effective instructional practices. A good place to start this training is with the nine most powerful effective instructional practices as identified by Marzano, Pickering, and Pollock (2001) in the book *Classroom Instruction That Works*.

9. Provide for ongoing discussion and peer study teams/professional learning community teams on effective teaching practices.

10. Provide ample opportunity for participants to practice their newly acquired skills as well as opportunities for them to see the effective teaching practices modeled with a variety of learning scenarios.

11. Coach and mentor staff on the use of these powerful instructional practices as part of your ongoing walk-throughs with reflective conversations and staff meeting opportunities.

STRATEGY 33

Use Powerful Vocabulary Development Strategies

Teachers and other instructional staff purposefully incorporate powerful vocabulary development strategies throughout their teaching.

STRATEGY 33: WHAT

Because of its power in terms of higher student achievement on high-stakes tests, we have zeroed in on one major instructional teaching practice for a focus: vocabulary development. *Vocabulary* is defined as knowledge of words and their meanings—both oral and in print. There are many persuasive reasons for helping students build vocabulary, and none is more important than the contribution to reading comprehension (Lehr, Osborn, & Hiebert, 2007). Word knowledge is particularly important in our literate society. It is essential in the achievement of students in their schooling, and it definitely influences their ability to do well on tests. Numerous studies have shown a relationship between vocabulary and reading comprehension: Messages are composed of ideas, and ideas are expressed in words (Anderson & Freebody, 1981; Baumann, Kame'enui, & Ash, 2003; Becker, 1977; Davis, 1942; and Whipple, 1925; all cited in Lehr et al., 2007; and Nagy, 1988, and Nelson-Herber, 1986, both cited in C. Smith, 1997).

Unfortunately, many vocabulary practices often found in classrooms are only fairly effective. For instance, having students learning lists of words and definitions with a quiz on Friday is of limited value (Stahl & Fairbanks, 1986, cited in "Promoting Vocabulary Development" [Texas Education Association, 2002]). Another approach is to give students a long list of words in any subject area and instruct them to look up the words in a dictionary, write the definition, and then put each word into a sentence (Ellis, 2002). This, too, is a fairly ineffective approach yet one that is still quite dominant in classrooms.

Feldman and Kinsella (2007) identified the following practices as ones that should be left in the "instructional dust bin" because they involve cognitively limited or rote interactions for students:

- Copying definitions—certainly dictionaries have their place, especially during writing and after a student knows something about the word, but the act of looking up a word and copying a definition is likely to not result in vocabulary learning of new words (especially if there are long lists of unrelated words to look up and copy definitions).

- Writing sentences—writing sentences with new vocabulary AFTER some understanding of the word is helpful; however, to assign this task before studying word meaning is of little value.
- Telling students to "use context"—there is little research to suggest that context is a very reliable source of learning word meanings. Nagy (1988) found students reading at grade level had about a one in twenty chance of learning the meaning of a word from context. This, of course, is not to say that context is unimportant, simply that students will need a broader range of instructional guidance than the exhortation, "use context."
- Memorizing lists of definitions—rote learning of word meanings is likely to, at best, result in the ability to parrot back what is not clearly understood. Of course, once students have a grasp of a new word, judicious review is very helpful!

Feldman and Kinsella (2007) indicated that learning vocabulary must be based on the students' active engagement in constructing understanding of the words/terms. Teachers need to use language, images, examples, and other representational forms familiar to students to learn new words and phrases.

Boris (2007b) in her CMSi training *Vocabulary for High Stakes Testing* indicates that there are four "big ideas" teachers need to consider in the development of student vocabulary. These are shown in Figure 4.11.

Boris (2007b) indicated that for years, educators have trusted textbook authors to structure appropriate vocabulary lessons, but they may not be providing the best direction desired. One the major components she believes is missing from most classroom instruction and programs for vocabulary development is the teaching of the foundational vocabulary concepts (standards). Teachers must know these so they can not only provide formal instruction on the concepts but

Figure 4.11   Boris's (2007b) Four Big Ideas for Vocabulary Development

1. All teachers need to know the critical vocabulary concepts presented in state standards and assessed on high-stakes tests.

2. Vocabulary concepts are critical to learning and measuring student learning in high-stakes tests. All teachers need to know how to embed key vocabulary concepts into their daily insurrection and assessments. They need to look for the teachable moment.

3. The structured, direct instruction of high-frequency academic vocabulary will enhance students' ability to access and comprehend expository text.

4. When introducing a new unit or reading passage, teachers should preteach critical words, particularly concept words.

also seize the "teachable moments" for these curriculum standards. She identified the following as the critical vocabulary concepts: antonyms, synonyms, multiple-meaning words, compound words, homophones, homographs, idioms, root words, affixes, Greek/Latin roots, figure use of words, shades of meaning, denotative meaning of words, and connotative meaning of words (Boris, 2007b).

Students gain most of their word knowledge through wide reading; however, explicit instruction of specific words and their meanings also contributes greatly to their vocabulary development. Such instruction is especially important for students whose exposure to vocabulary of literate English is limited. Instruction needs to "(1) use both definitional and contextual information about word meanings, (2) involve students active in word learning, and (3) use discussion to teach the meanings of new words and to provide meaningful information about the words" (Texas Education Association, 2002, p. 16). "Promoting Vocabulary Development" (Texas Education Association, 2002) presents several key effective vocabulary development strategies around these three instructional needs as follows:

1. Use both definitional and contextual information about word meanings. Activities could include the following:
   - Teach synonyms.
   - Teach antonyms.
   - Rewrite definitions.
   - Provide example sentences.
   - Provide non-examples.
   - Discuss the difference between the new word and related words.
   - Provide activities with contextual information.
   - Have students create sentences that contain the new word.
   - Use more than one new word in a sentence.
   - Discuss the meaning of the same word in different sentences.
   - Create a scenario.
   - Create silly questions.

2. Involve students actively in word learning.
   - Have students relate new information to known information.
   - Have students translate the information in their own words.
   - Ask students to generate examples and non-examples.
   - Request students to produce anonyms and synonyms, etc.

3. Use discussion to teach word meanings.
   - Have students construct a good idea of a word's meaning from the bits of partial knowledge contributed by classmates.
   - Clarify misunderstandings of words by making the misunderstandings public and shape them into conventional meaning.
   - Involve students through covert (silent) responses while another student is called on to respond overtly—work for many practiced responses. (pp. 16–19)

Teaching word meanings as concepts is very meaningful if one uses "a variety of techniques to help students establish connections among context, prior knowledge, and the concepts of words being taught" (Stahl, 1999, p. 47, cited in "Promoting Vocabulary Development" [Texas Education Association, 2002]). Such approaches would include word maps, semantic mapping, somatic feature mapping, possible sentences, comparing and contrasting, and teaching word parts.

New terms need to be defined using language and examples that are familiar to students. The more background knowledge a student brings to the new term, the more likely learned. There are many strategies that can be used by a teacher to help students learn new terms, names, events, places, or processes. Ellis (2002) identified five facilitating elaboration tactics, which included teaching terms in the context of the subject-matter lesson and discussion of the new term; having students paraphrase the definitions of the new terms to obtain the key essence of the idea within the term as well as any critical features; making connections of the term to student background knowledge; providing exemplars and non-examplars of the meaning of the term; and using multiple context formats in which students demonstrate knowledge of the term.

Boris (2007b) indicated that prereading is an important advanced organizer to enhance students' reading comprehension. She stated that the introduction of new vocabulary should be done through direct instruction. She also recommended that students create and maintain a vocabulary journal.

On which words should we focus for vocabulary development? There is a limit on the number of words that can be taught in a year, simply because there are so many. Most writers (Archer, 2003; Beck, McKeown, & Kucan, 2002; Feldman, 2006; Feldman & Kinsella, 2007; Lehr, Osborn, & Heibert, 2007) have discussed the following word groups:

- *Function words*—words learned orally in the early years, such as *the*, *is*, and *there*, that cue the reader to the structure of the sentence. One hundred seven words account for 50% of these words found in text (Zeno et al., 1995, cited in Lehr et al., 2007).
- *Basic words*—such as *home*, *dog*, *happy*, *see*, and *radio*. These are also known as *Tier 1* words.
- *Mortar words*—high-frequency words across disciplines (e.g., *compare*, *chronology*) that are the "glue" that hold text together. These are also known as *Tier 2 words*—general academic terms (Tutro & Moran, 2003, cited in "Academic Language," 2007).
- *Brick words*—high-frequency content words within disciplines that convey meaning in text (e.g., *plot*, *idioms*, *chromosomes*, *habitat*) and are not unique to a given article or topic. These are also known as *Tier 3 words*—content-specific, technical words specific to a discipline. They can be concrete words, to more complex and hard-to visualize and abstract words, such as *democracy*, *photosynthesis*, and *balancing equations* ("Academic Language," 2007).

As stated in "Academic Language" (2007):

> The importance of vocabulary knowledge (i.e., knowing the bricks) is obvious and well-documented (McLaughlin et al., 2000; Moats, 2000; Stahl, 1999). Yet there is a danger of over-focusing on big words. If we simply pile bricks up to make a wall—e.g., overdo vocabulary quizzes and dictionary work—the wall will fall. The bricks need mortar to stick together. "Mortar" words and phrases, as the metaphor implies, are general-utility words that hold the content-specific technical words together. Other mortar words are used to create coherent and logical sentences and paragraphs. Some of these words include connectives such as therefore, however, whereas and because; prepositions such as behind, between, and without; and pronouns such as each other, themselves, and it. A more general group of mortar words includes academic vocabulary needed for the tasks, tests, and texts of school. These are often needed to describe higher-order thinking skills (Scarcella, 2003). And mortar tends to be shared across content areas, such as differ, boils down to, contrast, outweigh, led to, ramifications, analyze, theory, estimate, filter, model, link, evidence, establish, consequences, and aspects. These are the often untaught, yet integral words that hold ideas together. Moreover, mortar can be even more abstract than many brick terms, because teachers tend to give more "explanation attention" to the bricks, giving examples, diagrams, and definitions. They might use mortar terms to define and explain the bricks.

Although this strategy has focused on vocabulary development, we decided to present to readers some quick advice about reading comprehension. Boris (2007a), in her CMSi training seminar, *Reading Comprehension for High Stakes Testing*, presents 12 "big ideas" to direct teachers in the planning of their reading strategies. These are listed in Figure 4.12.

STRATEGY 33: WHY

A student's vocabulary is highly linked to his or her academic success. Becker (1977, cited in Marzano et al., 2002) indicated that vocabulary instruction is one of the most important interventions teachers can use, especially for low-performing students. Word knowledge is crucial to reading comprehension, and it shapes students' ability to comprehend what they read (Anderson & Freebody, 1981; Baumann & Kameenui, 1991; both cited in Texas Education Association, 2002). Stahl (1999, cited in Texas Education Association, 2002) stated:

> Poor readers often lack adequate vocabulary to get meaning from what they read. Consequently, reading is difficult and tedious for them, and

Figure 4.12   Boris's (2007a) Big Ideas for Reading Comprehension for High-Stakes
Testing

1. Look for opportunities to empower students to read. Hold them accountable for their reading. We spend too much time enabling students not to read.

2. Expose students to all three types of text: literary, expository, and functional. These texts should be planned into the curriculum students' experience.

3. Use basic questions to assess reading for initial understanding or literal comprehension (specific detail, action, reason, sequence)—READ THE LINES.

4. Use interpretation questions (which are often overlooked) to have students master a more complex level of understanding (interpretation, inference, extended meaning)—READ BETWEEN THE LINES.

5. Use critical analysis and strategy questions to provide higher level comprehension requiring students to apply prior academic knowledge and skills—READ BEYOND THE LINES.

6. Use living posters to support students in the building of vocabulary and comprehension skills in critical analysis.

7. Plan reading questions and embed into each and every reading opportunity across the curriculum for deep alignment.

8. Share the responsibility of asking good reading questions with students and parents.

9. Plan text-based questions to support reading comprehension that are aligned with high-stakes assessments.

10. Use the Power Reading strategy as formative assessments to build fluency, independence, and endurance, which provide valuable feedback for next-step instructional decisions. Power Reading is just one proposed assessment approach. It involves multiple passages of unseen text in which students are given increasingly lengthy reading assessments throughout the year. An item analysis is used by teachers as a reading comprehension diagnostic.

11. Use graphic organizers, note taking, outlines, and frames in your teaching of reading.

12. Create instructional experiences that support independent reading practice, holding students accountable for reading.

they are unable (and often unwilling) to do the large amount of reading they must do if they are to encounter unknown words often enough to learn them. . . . The vocabulary problems of students who enter school with poor or limited vocabularies only worsen over time.

Feldman and Kinsella (2007) indicated that vocabulary knowledge is one of the most glaring differences between successful and less successful students. They quoted a few statistics:

- High knowledge 3rd graders had vocabularies equal to low performing 12th graders (Smith, 1941).
- Top high school seniors knew 4 times the words of lower performing class-mates (Smith, 1941).
- 1st grade students from high SES (socioeconomic status) groups knew about twice as many words as lower SES students (Graves et al., 1987).
- Very little emphasis on vocabulary teaching in school curricula (Biemiller, 2001; Watts, 1995).

They further stated:

Nagy (1988) summarizes the research on effective vocabulary teaching as coming down to three critical notions; 1) integration—connecting new vocabulary to prior knowledge, 2) repetition—encountering/using the word/concept many times, and 3) meaningful use—multiple opportuni-ties to use new words in reading/writing/discussion/etc. Beck and col-leagues (Beck et al., 2002) conceptualize effective vocabulary instruction as beginning with explanations NOT definitions. The critical distinction being that it is not the precise dictionary wording that drives instruction, rather it is assisting students by explaining word meanings using lan-guage, examples, metaphors, and images the students already know.

The document "Promoting Vocabulary Development" (Texas Education Association, 2002) makes several points (note that all references are as cited in this document):

- Typically students add 2,000 to 3,000 words to their vocabularies each year or six to eight new words each day (Anderson & Magy, 1992).
- There are great differences in the vocabulary size of low-performing students and higher performing students. Exposure to words varies greatly among the children of families from different socioeconomic classes. One study showed that children of parents who are "professional" are exposed to about 50% more words than children of "working class" parents. Further, children of "working class" parents are exposed to twice as many words as children of "welfare support" parents (Hart & Risley, 1995). This shows the dependency that low socio-economic children have on us to provide the learning in their formal schooling. It has been shown that we can make that difference (Snow et al., 1992).

- For children whose primary language is not English, it has been found that students become proficient in everyday conversational English before they become proficient in literate English. (Texas Education Association, 2002)

Andrew Biemiller (2001), in an article on teaching vocabulary, synthesized many ideas about why vocabulary development instruction is important. Some of his ideas included the following:

- Vocabulary growth has been inadequately addressed, especially in the elementary and preschool years, and more teacher-centered, planned curricula are needed. It is the "missing link" in reading/language instruction in U.S. classrooms.
- Vocabulary deficits particularly affect low-performing students and second-language students, and such deficits are fundamentally more remediable than many other school learning problems.
- There was a relative decline in reaching achievement targets experienced by working-class children who had become competent readers by third grade but whose vocabulary limitations increasingly had a negative effect on their reading comprehension as they advanced to seventh grade (Chall, 1990, cited in Biemiller, 2001).
- A relatively small number of words need to be learned to make a difference.
- Disadvantaged homes provide little support for vocabulary growth (Hart & Risely, 1995, cited in Biemiller, 2001).
- Vocabulary as assessed in Grade 1 predicts more than 30 percent of Grade 11 reading comprehension, much more than reading mechanics as assessed in Grade 1 (Cunningham & Stanovich, 1997, cited in Biemiller, 2001).
- When readers understand fewer than 95% of the words in a text, they are likely to lose the meaning of that text. They especially will be unlikely to infer meanings of unfamiliar words. We need to focus on root word growth rather than the acquisition of all inflected and derived forms of words. Biemiller suggested that approximately 600 root word meanings a year from infancy to the end of elementary school will make the difference.
- Vocabulary differences present by Grade 2 may account for most vocabulary differences in elementary school. Biemiller found that by the end of Grade 2 there is a difference of approximately 3,000 root words between high- and low-quartile students in a normative population.
- To catch up, children with a disadvantaged vocabulary have to acquire vocabulary at rates faster than other students.
- Although students differ in their opportunities to learn words and the ease with which they learn words, they can learn vocabulary at normal rates.

S. Baker, Simmons, and Kameenui (2007) conducted a synthesis of the research on vocabulary acquisition that incorporated several of the points made earlier in this chapter. A summary of their findings is presented in Figure 4.13.

Figure 4.13   S. Baker et al.'s (2001) Synthesis of Research on Vocabulary Acquisition

1. Vocabulary acquisition is crucial to academic development. Not only do students need a rich body of word knowledge to succeed in basic skill areas, but they also need a specialized vocabulary to learn content area material. A foundation of vocabulary knowledge must be in place early if children are going to perform successfully in school.

2. Students learn an amazing number of words during their early school years, as many as approximately 3,000 per year on the average, or 8 words per day. However, the number of words students learn varies greatly. As some students are learning 8 or more words per day, other students are learning only 1 or 2.

3. Even as early as kindergarten, sizable differences are found between students in the number of words known. This vocabulary gap tends to increase significantly throughout school. Thus, early differences in vocabulary knowledge have strong implications for students' long-term educational success.

4. Multiple factors may contribute to differential rates of vocabulary growth. Biological factors that may partially account for differential rates of vocabulary growth include general language deficits and memory problems. Also, a strong relation has been found between environmental indicators such as socioeconomic status and vocabulary knowledge, indicating that home factors may contribute substantially to students' vocabulary knowledge.

5. Nearly all strategies of increasing vocabulary knowledge result in greater learning than that which occurs during typical opportunities. These methods have included semantic mapping and semantic features analysis procedures, the key word method, and computer-assisted instruction.

6. Words can be known at different levels of understanding. Therefore, choice of vocabulary intervention procedure should be based on the procedure's efficiency with respect to teacher and student time and its usefulness in helping students learn the meaning of other words independently.

7. Directly teaching word meanings does not adequately reduce the gap between students with poor versus rich vocabularies because of the size of the gap. It is crucial, therefore, that students also learn strategies for learning word meanings independently.

8. The relation between reading comprehension and vocabulary knowledge is strong and unequivocal. Although the precise causal direction of the relation is not understood clearly, there is evidence that the relation is largely reciprocal.

9. The development of strong reading skills is the most effective independent word learning strategy available. However, students who are in the greatest need of vocabulary acquisition interventions tend to be the same students who read poorly and fail to engage in the amount of reading necessary to learn large numbers of words.

10. The meaning of words is learned during independent reading activities, but the effects do not appear to be very powerful. Words need to be encountered in text multiple times before their meaning becomes part of a student's vocabulary. However, although independent reading is not an efficient way to learn word meanings, the tremendous number of words typical students in the primary and middle grades encounter in written text nevertheless result in considerable vocabulary learning.

11. Improvements in beginning reading instruction are crucial if students are to develop the skills necessary to engage in significant amounts of independent reading and hence acquire a sufficiently large vocabulary.

STRATEGY 33: HOW

Effective vocabulary development is essential to improving student achievement. The following steps are suggested for establishing a consistent use of the more powerful vocabulary development practices in every classroom:

District Level

1. Develop a position paper on the teaching of vocabulary in the classroom and ensure all staff members are aware of and can implement this position.

2. Specify the following by grade level and course in the district's written curriculum:
   - A set of basic Tier I words to be taught at the elementary level
   - Specific mortar words—general academic terms that have high frequency across disciplines. These are the Tier 2 words that are to be directly taught in that grade/course.
   - The high-frequency content words within a discipline—brick words—to be taught.

School Level

3. Provide the professional development for each teacher and instructional support staff to know how to teach vocabulary and use effective vocabulary development strategies.

4. Observe for effective vocabulary development strategies as part of informal walk-throughs and provide follow-up reflective conversations as desired.

Classroom Level

5. Teach the vocabulary standards to mastery.

6. Use the following process to provide direct instruction on words that are critical to new content for the most powerful learning (Marzano et al., 2002):
   - Present a brief explanation or description of the term/phrase.
   - Present a nonlinguistic representation of the new term/phrase.

- Have students generate their own explanations/descriptions of the term/phrase.
- Have students create their own nonlinguistic representation of the term/phrase—for example, associate an image with the new term/phrase.
- Ask students every so often to review the accuracy of their explanations and representations for a term/phrase.

7. Teach new terms in context of meaningful subject matter and facilitate discussion on that term (Ellis, 2002).

8. Teach fewer vocabulary terms, but teach them to deep understanding (Ellis, 2002).

9. Teach terms central to the unit or theme under study (Ellis, 2002).

10. Teach terms that address key concepts or ideas. Pick one to five terms from a chapter that address critical concepts in the chapter (Ellis, 2002).

11. Provide instruction so that students encounter words in context more than once (Marzano et al., 2002).

12. Teach terms that will be used repeatedly through the year—that are foundational concepts upon which much information is built over time (Ellis, 2002).

13. Facilitate paraphrasing of a new term's definitions so students identify the core idea associated with the meaning of the term and its distinguishing features (Ellis, 2002).

14. Make background knowledge connections to each new vocabulary word (Ellis, 2002).

15. Identify examples and applications and nonexamples and nonapplications related to the meaning of the vocabulary term (Ellis, 2002).

16. Create multiple formats in which students can use and elaborate on the meaning of new vocabulary terms (Ellis, 2002).

STRATEGY 34

Establish Individual Learning Plans for Low-Achieving Students

Individual learning plans are developed for students who test data indicate are underachieving. Low-quartile students and/or "bubble" students are provided intensive assistance to remediate deficiencies.

STRATEGY 34: WHAT

An individual learning plan (ILP) is a specific intervention effective educators use to provide intensive assistance to special population students—especially, in this instance, low-achieving students. Low-achieving students are targeted to receive all the resources the school or district can bring to bear to prevent or remediate learning deficiencies. ILPs are similar to the individual education plans (IEPs) created for special education students. They are designed to focus instruction on learnings identified as essential for students to become productive members of society and to perform well on district-designed or -adopted tests and external assessments.

The ILP is a high-performing educator's way of providing a set of curricular learnings that will bring all students to high levels of learning. ILPs usually are used with students who typically are 2 more years below grade level and often with students who are 1 year below grade level. The district curriculum is used along with diagnostic assessments to determine pre-entry, acquisition, and mastery levels of learning for each student. ILPs are designed on the basis of these data.

Such plans are best used when they are developed for about six to eight weeks using the course/grade level standards. The goal is to reduce the number of learnings for such students and accelerate their learning around the key concepts within those learnings so that some of the learnings can be moved to on-grade level within a year. It is hoped that, within 3 years, a student who was 2 years below level can be approaching his or her traditional grade level.

First, students who would fit the profile of need for an accelerated program of learning are identified. An ILP would be designed for each student on the basis of both formal and informal assessment data. Obviously, this tool is used when one has a mastery learning philosophy regarding the delivery of the curriculum. It helps set up the differentiation needed for each student.

The ILP is a differentiated approach to planning with the recognition that "one size fits all" just does not work for student populations with normal variation or a predominant group of students who have had low performance. The ILP recognizes that the needs of each student are different from another student and must be addressed as such (see http://en.wikipedia.org/wiki/Individual_Learning_Plan).

The term *ILP* is used in the literature to mean many things—a career plan for students to graduate from high school or college, a learning plan students develop for themselves, a professional growth plan for an educator. Here we are suggesting a student instruction plan the teacher designs to help plan the delivery of the curriculum for each student at the right level of difficulty. Unlike the IEP, it does not require a study group to make the decision about it. The teacher is the designer of the plan. Students could be a part of that planning with the teacher to help motivate students in goal setting.

The ILP is a way to manage the mapping out of the curricular learnings for the day, week, and month for groups of students and to identify where each student is in that plan. The plan needs to be flexible and dynamic so that teachers can modify it as learning progresses and as informal and formal assessments provide data on learning. The ILP does, typically, call for more extensive record keeping.

Recently, many electronic versions of ILPs have been developed that could help with that record keeping. It is important to make sure when examining online and electronic versions that you make sure that the ILPs being purported are allowing you to specify specific learning objectives that a given student needs to learn and a way to incorporate appropriate resources and activities to help you in the teaching–learning act. Also, there must be a place to record ongoing formative assessments to determine acquisition and mastery of the learning.

ILPs should be kept very simple and remain free of signatures. The ILPs should include a list of the objectives to be taught and prerequisites required and a place to note assessment data on a student's progress toward the learning of the objectives. A place for determining prerequisite skills level and then acquisition of those skills as well as a way to record ongoing formative assessments to determine acquisition and mastery levels is also needed. The tool needs to be flexible to allow the teacher to move around the priority objectives as needed for each student.

STRATEGY 34: WHY

Schools and districts desiring to increase student achievement must target low-achieving students in order to get the greatest gains over time. Low-achieving students (especially those influenced by low socioeconomic status) require additional resources and time for learning. The ILP is designed to provide those resources and time. The implementation of the ILP maximizes the system's efforts to meet the student's individual needs and increases the likelihood that the student will be prepared to respond to testing content and context. When implemented correctly, the plans ensure that the instructional intervention is deeply aligned with the content, context, and cognitive levels of the test in use.

The ILP encourages focused, purposeful teaching. It guides lesson planning and gives the professional staff specific intervention strategies for each student. The teacher's ability to respond to the individual needs of the student is enhanced, because the ILP provides the road map for success. The teacher manages, directs, and coaches the students to high levels of achievement. Using effective teaching practices, the power of teaching is multiplied exponentially. The ILP is the initial planning needed to differentiate the learning and the time for learning for each student (see Strategies 30 and 33).

The earlier the planned intervention, the better. Hill and Crévola (1999) indicated that students need to quickly catch up with their peers. As a result, if the intervention is neither timely nor effective, then students who are behind continue to fall even further behind, which causes diminished self-esteem and increased alienation from learning. According to Hill and Crévola, "Schools have a narrow window of opportunity to help these students catch up, and the only real answer to narrowing the learning gap is to intervene quickly, relentlessly, and with all the resources at the school's disposal" (p. 135). Providing such individual help using a plan of action (ILP) is one of the most difficult challenges facing educators, because we often have a wide range of needs and ability within each classroom. Teachers should have detailed understanding of each student and how to manage the classroom and teach to these varying levels of student needs (Hill & Crévola, 1999).

The ILP is a management tool that is used to plan and monitor each student's progress on learning. Such plans help the teacher determine the starting points for teaching for each student and to use the diagnostic information to drive classroom instruction (Hill & Crévola, 1999). Effective teachers monitor their students' progress so that they can ensure that each student is always working within his or her level of challenge, or "zone of proximal development" (Vygotsky, 1978, cited in Hill & Crévola, 1999). Assessment provides the data to help teachers ensure that teaching is matching the learning needs of students.

In a short article ("Individual Learning Plans," 2007), the following were proposed as several ideas regarding the value of such plans. They are used to do the following:

- Tailor teaching to meet the specific needs of their students
- Build personalized programs
- Track learning progress
- Set learning targets
- Record students' development toward and achievement of targets
- Identify students' strengths, weaknesses, and learning goals
- Plan next steps

STRATEGY 34: HOW

Schools and districts are well acquainted and skilled in developing IEPs for special education students; however, these skills have never been applied to students who are not part of a special education program. The same skills and processes apply, but the process is much simpler, and fewer people are involved. The content and focus of the ILP are different from those of the IEP, but the intent is the same: to provide each student with a plan of action to increase academic learning leading to mastery.

The following steps are suggested:

District Level

1. Set up a simple structure for ILPs and describe their use in policy and administrative regulation.

2. Provide staff development and examples for teacher use.

3. Create a technology-based approach for the ILPs for ease of teacher use in monitoring and keeping record of each student's progress on the district standards.

School Level

4. Identify and specify the individual learning needs of low-achieving students. Specify those needs in each of the major content areas. Include content and context deficiencies.

5. Set up study groups for teachers to plan their ILPs for appropriate students.

Classroom Level

6. Develop, for appropriate students, an ILP every 6 to 8 weeks, keeping it fluid.

7. Identify and define instructional strategies for each standard content area in which there are deficiencies. Design instructional lessons using effective teaching practices to ensure that instructional learnings are met.

8. Include many opportunities for feedback to students on their progress in meeting instructional standards and objectives. Also include opportunities for students to assess their own progress and reflect on how they could improve their performance over time.

9. Ensure that all intervention strategies and techniques meet elements of deep alignment with the prescribed curriculum. Content, context, and cognitive levels must be congruent with those of tested situations. A goal of the instructional intervention must be "no surprises" for students when they encounter tested items.

10. Develop, write, implement, check, revise (as necessary), and assess the ILP for each student to produce high levels of performance on assessments.

The ILP is a very effective way to influence low-performing students' achievement. It is instructionally sound and equitable. It offers the school or district educators a mechanism to increase learning for those students who need the most help.

ANALYSIS OF STANDARD FOUR

Now it is time for you to evaluate the status of your school or school district on *Standard Four: Use a Mastery Learning Approach and Effective Teaching Strategies*. For each strategy, think about what the current status of your situation is regarding these strategies and what changes need to be made. Write your responses in the spaces provided.

Strategy	Current status	Changes needed
28. Implement a mastery learning model.	❏ Adequate ❏ Not adequate	
29. Align teaching with the curriculum.	❏ Adequate ❏ Not adequate	
30. Provide differentiated curriculum and instruction as well as differentiated time to learn.	❏ Adequate ❏ Not adequate	
31. Provide practice to master the curriculum.	❏ Adequate ❏ Not adequate	
32. Use effective instructional practices.	❏ Adequate ❏ Not adequate	
33. Use powerful vocabulary development strategies.	❏ Adequate ❏ Not adequate	
34. Establish individual learning plans for low-achieving students.	❏ Adequate ❏ Not adequate	

5

Standard Five

Establish Curriculum Expectations, Monitoring, and Accountability

Standard Five deals with five critical functions administrators perform as they fulfill their role as an instructional leader: (1) setting high expectations, (2) monitoring the curriculum, (3) visiting classrooms, (4) using data to inform decision making, and (5) appraising staff. Although some of these functions are also carried out by teachers, such as setting high expectations and using data, they remain the most critical part of the school leaders' job responsibilities.

Schmoker, in his 2006 book *Results Now*, takes the position that we need to confront the brutal facts about our failure to use the knowledge we have to improve instruction:

> This encounter with the brutal facts is the surest, fastest path to creating the best schools we have ever had. . . . The changes that will have the most impact on student learning require only reasonable efforts and adjustments, not more time. (p. 4)

Many educators agree that what we know works is rarely translated into action that affects instruction (Glickman, 2002). As educators, we tend to hide behind organizational design documents such as school improvement plans, curriculum guides, and long-range strategic plans as documentation that we are doing our jobs. A brief two- to three-minute walk-through of 15 classrooms in most schools quickly reveals the gap between what we know about best practice and what is really happening in our schools. These visits typically reveal the following:

- Almost all students are working on the same task.
- The primary resource being used is a worksheet linked to a textbook.
- Although objectives are often written on the board, what students are doing is not related to the objectives.
- The type of cognition required of students is at a low level.
- There is little evidence of instructional differentiation.
- When students are asked "What are you learning?" they do not know.

The five strategies presented in this chapter provide specific guidance to administrators wanting to change the present status quo.

1. **Strategy 35: Provide for High Expectations for Achievement for Each Student.** The superintendent, senior officers, school-based administrators, and instructional staff articulate strong expectations for high achievement for each student.

2. **Strategy 36: Monitor the Curriculum.** Monitoring by district-level officials, including the principal's supervisor, takes place regularly to determine the progress of the curriculum; school-based administrators work collaboratively with teachers in self-reflection.

3. **Strategy 37: Visit Classrooms and Provide Follow-up.** Principals and/or other school-based administrators visit each classroom at least twice a week to monitor curriculum design and delivery alignment.

4. **Strategy 38: Use Disaggregated Data in the Decision-Making Process.** The principal monitors teacher use of all test data and has disaggregated data appropriate for teacher use in decision making.

5. **Strategy 39: Focus Staff Appraisal on Professional Growth.** The staff appraisal/evaluation process focuses on the professional growth of staff in the accomplishment of high student achievement.

STRATEGY 35

Provide for High Expectations for Achievement for Each Student

The superintendent, senior officers, school-based administrators, and instructional staff articulate strong expectations for high achievement for each student.

STRATEGY 35: WHAT

People of all ages are strongly motivated by high and reasonable expectations. This is particularly true for public school students. Because schools and school districts are systemic in nature, leadership for articulation of high expectations must start at the top or at least be institutionalized there. A variety of studies have documented that schools with high expectations for all students and with the necessary support system to implement those expectations have high rates of student achievement (Edmonds, 1986). These successful schools share a number of characteristics, including an emphasis on academics, clear expectations, high levels of student involvement in the learning process, and access to supplementary resources (Benard, 1995). Although nearly all schools claim to hold high expectations for students, in reality this is true for some groups of students and not true for others. In 1991, Asa Hilliard took the position that our current ceiling for some students is really the floor. When pressed, most teachers and administrators admit that there is a great difference between what most students are capable of and what they actually learn in schools (Bishop, 1989). Teacher expectations have a powerful influence on how much students learn (Bamburg, 1994). We all tend to internalize the level of expectation those around us hold for what we accomplish. When the expectations are high, we tend to rise to the occasion; when they are low, we tend to perform less well (Raffini, 1993).

In schools where there are low expectations for students many students may have adopted an attitude of "I can't do it." Students in these environments tend to describe themselves with negative labels and have poor self-confidence. Teachers and students talk about limitations based on gender, ethnicity, and family status. Often in these schools there is an overall feeling that any attempt to encourage excellence is discouraged and sometimes punished (Henderson & Milstein, 1996).

Krovetz (1999) identified very specific attributes for schools with high expectations and purposeful change in the areas of school culture, curriculum, instruction, and the role of teachers and administrators (pp. 150–151):

Culture

- Reasonable, positive, public, known, and consistently enforced policies and procedures are in place.
- The campus is well maintained, with little litter and graffiti.
- A broad range of student work is on display throughout the school.
- Every student can name at least two adults who know him or her well and his or her work well.
- The parent's role in supporting student learning is valued and supported through parent workshops, a parent library, and the availability of social services support.
- Members of the community are seen supporting student learning; space and training are provided for this purpose.
- Teachers, parents, and students talk openly about the commitment of the principal and district to all students learning to use their minds and hearts well.
- Staff articulate a common mission that all agree transcends personal differences.

Curriculum

- Students are actively engaged in interdisciplinary, thematic, project-based work.
- Projects have significance to students and are based on important questions raised by students, teachers, and community members.
- Curriculum respects and acknowledges the ethnography and community of the students, using this as a departure point for curriculum that explores diversity of culture and opinion within and without the community.
- Teachers individualize and modify instruction that addresses learning styles and the special needs of students.
- Students comment (or proudly complain) that the work is challenging and takes time.

Instruction

- Classes are heterogeneously grouped for most of the day, with regrouping as appropriate.
- Students are usually working in small groups or independently.
- There is a well-defined safety net in place to accelerate students who are falling behind in their academic progress.
- Common instructional strategies are being used in most classrooms within and across grade levels.
- When teachers ask questions, students are required to use higher order thinking skills to answer, and all students have equal access to respond.
- When students ask questions, teachers usually reply with a question that requires thought by the student, rather than with the answer.

Assessment

- Student learning is assessed in a variety of ways, including the use of well-publicized rubrics, public exhibitions, and self-reflection by students.
- Individual teachers use assessment strategies on a daily basis to diagnose the learning of individual students and to adjust instruction based on this assessment.
- Teachers review student work and other assessment data together to guide school and classroom practice.
- When asked, students talk articulately about their best work.

Teacher and Administrator Roles

- The principal knows students and their work well and is often seen engaged in conversations with teachers about individual students and their work.
- The principal knows students and their work well and is often seen engaged in conversations with students about their learning.

- Teachers and school and district administrators have agreed-on best practices in a limited number of areas of focus (literacy, habits of mind), and time, resources, and professional development are supporting implementation—including expert and peer coaching and collaborative action research.
- Time is provided for teachers to discuss classroom practice.
- Time is provided for teachers to discuss the needs and successes of individual students.
- Teachers talk openly about how supportive the principal and district are regarding supporting ideas and helping to provide resources.

STRATEGY 35: WHY

Numerous research studies (R. Miller, 2001) have demonstrated that students who experience higher expectations from their teachers achieve at higher levels than do students who experience lower expectations from their teachers. "Expectations are double-edged swords, raising or lowering student and teacher outcomes according to the positive or negative nature of the expectations. For Greater Expectations and other education reform efforts to succeed, a system-wide effort to raise institutional, faculty, student, and other stakeholder expectations will be necessary" (R. Miller, 2001, p. 1). Tauber (1998, cited in R. Miller, 2001) identified four critical factors to raise expectations: (1) creating a climate conducive to learning that is conveyed both verbally and nonverbally, (2) providing both affective and cognitive feedback to students, (3) increasing the pace and amount of learning expected of students, and (4) demanding greater student involvement in the learning process.

Teacher attitudes play an important role in setting expectations. Most highly effective teachers maintain high expectations for students regardless of their socioeconomic class, race, gender, or life experience (Lumsden, 1997, cited in R. Miller, 2001). Sometimes teachers lower their expectations of students because of students' resistance (Farmer, 2002). In a 1997 survey of 1,300 high school students, three main themes were identified: a yearning for (1) order, (2) structure, and (3) moral authority (Kid Source On-Line, 2007, p. 4):

- They complained about lax instructors and un-enforced rules. "Many feel insulted at the minimal demands placed upon them. They state unequivocally that they would work harder if more were expected of them."
- They expressed a desire for "closer monitoring and watchfulness from teachers." In addition, "very significant numbers of respondents wanted after-school classes for youngsters who are failing."
- Although teens acknowledged cheating was commonplace, they indicated that they wanted schools to teach "ethical values such as honesty and hard work."

The idea of high expectations is closely associated with the concept of *resiliency*, "the ability to bounce back successfully despite exposure to severe risks" (Benard,

1993, p. 44). Benard (1993) identified four attributes of children who are considered resilient: (1) *social competence*, which is related to a student's ability to engage in positive relationships; (2) *problem-solving skills*, described as the student's ability to seek out resources and help from others; (3) *autonomy*, which refers to the student's positive sense of self; and (4) *a sense of purpose and future*, which translates to a positive sense of what the future holds and a heightened sense of what a student might be able to achieve (Benard, 1993). Krovetz (1999) identified the following characteristics of students and classrooms that would be evidence that staff held high expectations of the students' ability to use their minds (p. 25):

- Lots of student writing based on students' thinking about issues that are relevant and important to students
- Teachers using questioning strategies that require students to think more deeply
- Students at work in classrooms, rather than students listening to teachers working
- Teachers modeling critical thinking through their engagement in action research projects designed to improve their own practice
- Students working cooperatively in groups in which every student is participating and individual accountability is clear
- Students engaged in learning about and contributing to the solution of real issues of concern to students and to the community
- Teachers modeling by working together as peer coaches and reviewing student work together

Deborah Meier (1995), former principal of Central Park East Secondary School in New York City, identified five "habits of mind" that require students to challenge their minds in order to answer questions such as, "How do we know what we know?"; "Who's speaking?"; "What causes what?"; "How might things have been different?"; and "Who cares?" In her lexicon, these questions relate to evidence, viewpoint, connections, suppositions, and relevance and require higher types of cognitive thought, such as analysis, synthesis, and evaluation. Classrooms where teachers require this type of thinking are classrooms where there are high expectations for students. As Krovetz (1999) stated, "Teaching to the habits of mind requires teaching with a rigor that is both beyond that expected in most classrooms today and beyond what most adults expect of themselves" (p. 78).

STRATEGY 35: HOW

The following steps are recommended for your consideration in establishing high expectations for student achievement in your school district:

1. Develop or revise a board policy and philosophy statement regarding high expectations for students in your school or school district. This could be part of an existing board or school curriculum and instruction policy.

2. Publish the new policy in the local newspaper and in all school district and school newsletters.

3. Include the requirements for high expectations in all school handbooks.

4. Train all central office and school staff (teachers, custodians, teacher aides) on the philosophy and research behind this policy.

5. Train all central office and school staff in techniques for articulating high and reasonable achievement expectations in a nurturing, caring, and firm manner.

6. Monitor staff to ensure that all staff are articulating high achievement expectations for all students to the community, parents, and students.

7. Provide further training and direction as needed to ensure that the board policy is being properly implemented.

8. Minimize labeling and tracking.

9. Adopt a philosophy that all students can learn at high levels.

10. Train staff and students to recognize resiliency in themselves and others and openly talk about resiliency as a desired characteristic for students and adults.

11. Develop a reward system that recognizes outstanding contribution of students and adults.

12. Avoid negative assumptions.

13. Set clear, meaningful goals that are challenging and agreed on.

14. Foster a "can do" attitude.

STRATEGY 36

Monitor the Curriculum

Monitoring by district-level officials, including the principal's supervisor, takes place regularly to determine the progress of the curriculum; school-based administrators work collaboratively with teachers in self-reflection.

STRATEGY 36: WHAT

Monitoring implementation of the district curriculum is crucial to organizational effectiveness. School systems are so complex that not all functions can be monitored, but the more important functions must be monitored to ensure that the organization is on track in accomplishing its mission. For instance, Strategy 17 calls for the principal to ensure that all test data are disaggregated for the teachers' use and other purposes. This is a function that must be monitored, because we know that teaching the information required on a test is crucial to student achievement. The same is true for monitoring the curriculum. This strategy is closely related to Standard One, which focuses on the development of a district curriculum. This strategy focuses on monitoring the implementation of that curriculum.

Our position is that monitoring the implementation of the district curriculum is a form of mentoring. We believe that teachers operate from a basis of informed positive presuppositions (Downey, Steffy, et al., 2004). These presuppositions include the following:

- Teachers plan instruction, teach, and evaluate the impact of their instruction on the basis of their beliefs about what will enable students to achieve the most learning.
- Teachers think about all the possible pedagogical approaches they could use.
- Teachers have criteria they use to select the most appropriate strategies/ activities.
- Teachers consciously decide which strategies or activities might be the most effective.
- Teachers make their decisions on the basis of what they believe will produce the most student achievement.

For instance, a teacher may be planning a lesson and thinking about how she will have students respond, whether she will ask for volunteers or call on students to respond (nonvolunteers). In making the decision, she may take into consideration whether the lesson is a review of material the students should already know or whether this is the beginning of a new unit. Another consideration might be her assessment of how well the students have demonstrated their learning in previous assignments. Whether the class is basically homogeneous or more heterogeneous is another consideration. She may choose to use both techniques based on whether the class includes both students identified as needing special assistance and those who are considered academic achievers. Whatever her considerations, her decisions are based on what is best for promoting student achievement for this particular class at this particular time. It has been suggested that teachers make as many as 1,000 decisions a day in which they consciously or subconsciously apply these positive presuppositions.

We believe that one way to monitor the curriculum is through reflective dialogue with teachers. In monitoring the implementation of the curriculum, through reflective dialogue with the teacher, the administrator is trying to understand the thinking process the teacher went through to arrive at a particular decision. This dialogue is really an exercise in metacognition. Many times teachers may not be aware of why they make the decisions they make. By engaging in reflective conversations about their practices, both the teacher and the administrator come to a better understanding of the thinking involved in arriving at a decision.

We do not think of this as supervision in the traditional way it has been carried out, where the principal is all knowing and identifies what teachers are doing well and where they need to improve. Frankly, we do not believe that most administrators are that knowledgeable about all the content areas and all the instructional strategies that could be used. Instead, we view reflective mentoring as formative in nature, nonjudgmental, and a vehicle to promote growth.

Mezirow (2000) stated that "it is so important that adult learning emphasize contextual understanding, critical reflection on assumptions, and validating meaning by assessing reasons" (p. 3). When applied to the function of monitoring the implementation of the curriculum, this means asking teachers to think and talk about making decisions about such things as the selection of objectives for a given unit of study, the designation of instructional time for mastery of objectives, and the sequencing of objectives. It also speaks to how teachers incorporate anticipated changes in curricular expectations. For example, in 2009 there will be changes in the National Assessment of Educational Progress in the area of reading comprehension. Teachers need to be made aware of the changes and incorporate these expectations into their current instructional practices so that students are prepared for the assessment. This new assessment replaces the 1992 framework. Students will be required to read passages of literary or informational text and answer questions dealing with facts in the text or vocabulary. In some cases, a complete answer requires a clear analysis of a coherent argument supported by sound evidence from the text.

Some of the key features of this new test include the following:

- Vocabulary will be explicitly measured and will occur in the context of a passage.
- International reading assessments and exemplary state standards were used in the construction of the test.
- The test is consistent with standards set forth by the No Child Left Behind Act.
- The revision includes preliminary standards for 12th grade.
- The revision took into account current scientific research.

The new test will assess poetry at the 4th-grade level as well as the 8th- and 12th-grade levels. Sixty percent of the assessment time will be devoted to constructed responses (both short and extended) at the 8th- and 12th-grade levels, and 50% of the assessment time will be devoted to constructed responses at the 4th-grade level. The new framework will establish clear grade-level standards.

The type of cognition required for the new assessment at the three grade levels is depicted below.

Grade	Locate Recall	Integrate Interpret	Critique Evaluate
4	30%	50%	20%
8	20%	50%	30%
12	20%	45%	35%

As can be seen from this chart, there is less focus on the student's ability to locate and recall and a greater emphasis on the student's ability to integrate, interpret, critique, and evaluate. At the 12th grade, fully 80% of the test requires students to think at higher levels of cognition.

In recent years, a number of models for monitoring the implementation of the curriculum have been developed. Many of these take the form of frequent short visits to classrooms. The fundamental belief here is that principals who visit classrooms often are more effective and more credible in their role as mentor and coach (Frase & Streshly, 2000; Freedman, 2001; Glickman, 2002).

Lauren Resnick is credited with the development of one of the most popular forms of walk-through, called the *LearningWalk* (Goldman et al., 2004). "The LearningWalk is an organized walk through a school's halls and classrooms using the Principles of Learning to focus on the instructional core" (Goldman et al., 2004, p. 3). The basic philosophy of this model includes the following three points: (1) students are taught a rigorous curriculum; (2) assessments match standards, and standards are high; and (3) student effort is a basic expectation and the environment is organized to promote that effort. In this model, the classroom visits are conducted by a small team; the visits are short in duration (5–7 minutes) and sometimes called *snapshots*. The information from these visits is used to gather evidence that will enable the team to develop thought-provoking questions that will lead to improved instruction and student achievement.

A set of nine Principles of Learning form the basis for the collection of evidence:

- Organizing the Effort
- Clear Expectations
- Fair and Credible Evaluations
- Recognition of Accomplishment
- Academic Rigor in a Thinking Curriculum
- Accountable Talk
- Socializing Intelligence
- Self-Management of Learning
- Learning as Apprenticeship

The LearningWalk is seen as part of a sequence that includes teachers receiving professional development, time for implementation, LearningWalk, and more professional development. Through the walk the team can determine the extent to which previous professional development activities have influenced teacher behavior and what type of professional development is needed in the future to promote full implementation of the Principles of Learning throughout a building.

Other models for conducting the classroom walk-through include Downey's Classroom Walk-Through (Downey & Frase, 1999), Instructionally Focused Classroom Walk Through (Richardson, 2001), The Learning 24/7 (2002) Classroom Walk-Through, and Kim Marshall's (2003) Informally Developed Classroom Walk-Through.

"Management by walking around" was a phrase introduced by Peters and Waterman in 1982 and applied to education by Frase and Hetzel (1990). The current proliferation of walk-through models is grounded in that work.

STRATEGY 36: WHY

As a wise old saying goes, "If it is not monitored, it is optional, and if it is optional it probably won't get done." When an organization has selected its mission and identified its strategies for attaining it, the job duties inherent to those functions must be monitored to determine whether they are being performed adequately. This aspect of monitoring may seem draconian, but it is not. All organizations that are successful over time monitor their progress and internal functions. When we speak of *monitoring*, we mean monitoring that is nurturing, supportive, mentoring, and coaching in nature.

Another very important aspect of monitoring is that of ensuring that the supervisor knows the status of important functions and any problems the supervisees may be confronting in completing the functions. As suggested earlier, a problem may be due to lack of training, job overload, or a lack of definition of which functions are more important than others. After consultation with the supervisee, the supervisor must take action to correct the problem so that the supervisee can perform the job.

STRATEGY 36: HOW

The following steps are designed to help achieve this strategy and make it a successful practice in your school or school district:

1. Develop a strong policy statement about district-level administrators monitoring at all levels in the organization to demonstrate the board's commitment to the practice.

2. Prioritize job duties of all central office supervisors to ensure that monitoring is a high priority.

3. Include monitoring requirements in all central office supervisors' job descriptions.

4. Provide training to all central office supervisors on monitoring of scheduling, supervisors' job requirements, student achievement, and reflective coaching.

5. Develop an evaluation strategy for assessing the effectiveness of monitoring practices.

6. Set expectations for the amount of time principals and assistant principals should be engaged in monitoring.

7. Designate procedures for how central office administrators will engage in monitoring with building administrators.

8. Hold administrative meetings in schools, and begin each meeting by engaging in brief classroom visits.

9. Place monitoring on each administrative agenda and engage in reflective dialogue with administrators to identify trends and patterns across the district regarding the implementation of the district curriculum.

10. Provide periodic training for district administrators with current best practice relative to content areas and grade levels.

STRATEGY 37

Visit Classrooms and Provide Follow-up

Principals and/or other school-based administrators visit each classroom at least twice a week to monitor curriculum design and delivery alignment.

STRATEGY 37: WHAT

On the basis of experience and research, it is believed that teachers are the most important element in the formal education of students. It follows that principals should be in classrooms. The classroom visits we suggest here are not evaluative in nature; instead, they are facilitative. When in the classroom, the principal should be observing to determine whether the written curriculum is being delivered accurately, whether students are learning objectives to mastery, whether classroom management is proper and indicative of a high-quality learning environment, whether instructional strategies are being used properly, and whether the teacher has the resources needed for effective teaching.

After conducting a series of walk-throughs, the principal may choose to conduct a reflective conversation with a single teacher, with small groups of teachers, or with the faculty as a whole. These sessions provide valuable information to the principal about how teachers arrive at the instructional and curricular decisions they make. Many times, teachers are so busy engaging in classroom activities that they are not consciously aware of why they made the decisions they did. This opportunity for reflection enables teachers to verbalize the criteria they used.

Dexter (2005) reported on a study involving 70 principals implementing walk-throughs. From a review of the literature regarding walk-throughs, she identified four common themes that emerged:

- Implementation—the visits should be short and should not be used as an evaluation tool.
- Focus—instruction and student learning should be the focus of the classroom visits.
- Reflective feedback—this feedback should be provided in brief, informal conversations.
- Collegiality—the process supports administrators and teachers working together to promote student growth and achievement.

The process is not about judging teachers but about student learning and look-ing for ways to determine what works and what does not. Ginsberg and Murphy (2002) suggested that a common vocabulary be established that enables teachers and administrators to talk about learning. This would require everyone to work together and understand that the intent is not to criticize but to engage in conver-sations to improve practice. Richardson (2001) pointed out that all teachers may not be comfortable inviting the principal to visit their classrooms, but when the principal provides teachers with the rationale for the process and explains the intended outcome, teacher cooperation is forthcoming. DuFour (2002) suggested that when there is a shift on the part of the principal from inputs to outcomes and from intentions to results, student learning is enhanced.

The Downey Classroom Walk-Through model provides a comprehensive frame-work for classroom visits and reflective conversations (Downey & Frase, 1999; Downey, Steffy, et al., 2004, 2006). The Downey model evolved over time (Downey, Steffy, et al., 2004, p. 12). By the 1980s, it included the following:

- The supervisor acted as coach and mentor rather than judge.
- The supervisor viewed the teacher as the primary client for impacting student achievement.
- Interactions between the principal and teacher moved from extrinsic moti-vators, such as notes and positive praise, to intrinsic motivations that focused on teacher efficacy.
- Occasions for providing follow-up moved from giving feedback after every visit toward an occasional, collaborative, reflective dialogue, typically in the form of a reflective question.
- Conversations with novice/apprentice teachers who needed direct, nurtur-ing feedback took on a reflective component.
- Supervisors began to realize that it is the teacher's choice whether to answer any substantial reflective question posed by the supervisor.
- The focus toward encouraging reflective inquiry by teachers on their prac-tices and decisions moved away from direct feedback from the supervisor.
- It was recognized that it is the reflective question that has the power to change what teachers believe.
- There was a strengthening of the belief that the ultimate goal of supervision is to facilitate each teacher's ability to be self-analyzing about practice.

In the 1990s, Downey added a focus on not only how teachers were teaching but also what they were teaching. With the advent of accountability and the devel-opment of state curricular frameworks, this component of the model has become increasingly important for improving student achievement. The most recent evo-lution of the model concentrates on teacher decisions rather than teacher actions.

STRATEGY 37: WHY

Numerous research studies have shown that school principal visits to the class-room are strongly linked to important outcomes, including improved student achievement. The following are 10 important outcomes and the related research studies:

1. Improved teacher self-efficacy (Chester & Beaudin, 1996; Frase, 2001)

2. Improved teacher attitudes toward professional development (Frase, 2001)

3. Improved teacher attitudes toward teacher appraisal (Frase, 1998, 2001)

4. Improved teacher satisfaction defined as "flow" experiences (Frase, 2001)

5. Increased perceived teacher efficacy of other teachers (Frase, 1998, 2001) and of the school (Frase, 2001)

6. Improved classroom instruction (Teddlie, Kirby, & Springfield, 1989)

7. Improved teacher perception of the effectiveness of the school (Frase, 1998, 2001)

8. Improved teacher perception of principal effectiveness (Heck, Larsen, & Marcoulides, 1990; Sagor, 1992; Valentine, Clark, Nickerson, & Keefe, 1981; Wimpelberg, Teddlie, & Stringfield, 1989)

9. Improved student discipline and student acceptance of advice and criticism (Blasé, 1987; Blasé & Blasé, 1998)

10. Higher student achievement across cultural lines and socioeconomic status levels (Andrews & Soder, 1987; Andrews, Soder, & Jacoby, 1986; Hallinger & Heck, 1995; Heck, 1992; Louis & Miles, 1991)

Actual practices of principals are frequently in accordance with these findings. Numerous studies have shown that principals spend more time in meetings, in their offices, on playgrounds, and even off campus, than in classrooms.

The "why" of classroom visits is quite clear when one considers these research findings, but there is also empirical and practical evidence to support the benefit of principals being in classrooms. Many of us authors have also been superintendents and principals. As practicing administrators, we saw the effect of frequent, well-focused classroom visits. As is frequently the case in the social sciences, research has finally caught up with practice.

STRATEGY 37: HOW

We offer the following guidelines for implementing this strategy:

1. Include the philosophy and directive for frequent and well-focused classroom visits in board policy—preferably in both management and curriculum policies.

2. Include the requirement for classroom visits in principals' job descriptions.

3. Include monitoring of classroom visits in principals' supervisors' job descriptions.

4. Provide extensive training in high-quality instruction, the relationship (alignment) between instruction and the written curriculum, techniques for assessing the alignment between the taught and written curriculum, and effective methods of reflective coaching.

5. Monitor the frequency and results of classroom visits in the monthly monitoring as described in Strategy 36.

6. Develop and implement an evaluation strategy to determine the effectiveness and impact of principal classroom visits.

STRATEGY 38

Use Disaggregated Data in the Decision-Making Process

The principal monitors teacher use of all test data and has disaggregated data appropriate for teacher use in decision making.

STRATEGY 38: WHAT

Currently, there is no shortage of data about schools. The National Center for Educational Statistics and every state department of education offer basic information about schools and student performance. These data typically deal with basic demographics, student achievement, and financial information. Sometimes, these data are 2 to 3 years old. In reviewing any of these data the user must be cognizant of whether the data are accurate (Kowalski, Lasley, & Mahoney, 2008). As the saying goes, "Garbage in, garbage out." Data available on national Web sites often are not user friendly. In addition, users must be aware that the data on state sites may have the same label, such as *dropout rate*, and yet the operational definition of what that means may differ state to state. The old adage of "Let the buyer beware" is relevant here. The trick is to find and use good data. Kowalski et al. (2008) identified three essential dimensions of data-driven decision making (p. 187).

- Data—accurate, comprehensive, organized, accessible facts and related evidence stored in a data warehouse
- Technology—information technology and a database management information system allowing data to be accessed and reformulated as needed
- User competency—technology literacy, information literacy, decision skills, and assessment and evaluation skills essential to transform data into information

Some of the major uses of data include the following (Johnson, 2002):

- Improving the quality of criteria used in problem solving and decision making
- Describing institutional processes, practices, and progress in schools and districts
- Examining institutional belief systems, underlying assumptions, and behaviors
- Mobilizing the school or district community for action
- Monitoring implementation reforms
- Accountability

Before data are collected or used, goals for the use of the data should be clearly delineated.

There are also voluminous databases of internal information about individual schools and school districts. This information includes both quantitative and qualitative data. Data collection tools can include direct observation, document analysis, surveys, and testing. These data can be analyzed using statistical analysis, review of field notes, surveys, and discussions. They may be reported through statistical charts and displays, contingency tables, frequency distributions, or narrative descriptions of results (Johnson, 2002, p. 154).

Using data to make decisions at the district, school, and classroom level has been called *evidence-based decision making*: "Evidence-based decision making requires that administrators both collect data and know how to interpret what those data mean" (Johnson, 2002, p. 157). Data that are used to improve student achievement should do the following: be specific enough to determine what a student is doing that is correct and what a student is doing that is incorrect, be available in time for teachers to use it to plan instruction, and be linked to specific outcomes (Marzano, Pickering, & Pollock, 2001). Everyone using data needs to take care in both collecting and assessing data. Once it is determined that the data are reliable and good, the next step is to disaggregate the data and use them to make appropriate decisions.

One aspect of this strategy deals with test data disaggregation at the district, school, classroom, and student levels. *Disaggregation* means that the test items are isolated (identified) by skill through deconstruction and linked to curriculum objectives based on content. In the past, test data disaggregation had to be performed by school personnel, typically the principal. Today, however, most test manufacturers perform test data disaggregation for a fee. This is a service the principal or central office administration should order when the specifications for the test data returns are communicated to the testing company. When test companies or central office personnel do not perform this function, the principal must.

Linking the results with the district/school curriculum objectives is absolutely crucial in order to best inform curriculum decision making. This task should be accomplished by district personnel, the principal, or other school personnel, and it is much easier when the district's written curriculum and taught curriculum are well aligned with the tested curriculum—in other words, when the curriculum is backloaded.

Levels of Test Data Disaggregation

School level: At this level, the principal disaggregates the test data to indicate how the school, the grade levels, grade level clusters (e.g., Grades 1–3/4–6), and special programs are performing on specific objectives, clusters of objectives, and total subject areas. The key here is that the disaggregated data should be used to inform instruction and curriculum emphasis; that is, if students in a certain grade or program are not meeting the expected performance levels on a certain cluster of objectives or a total subject area, then changes in curriculum emphasis and instruction are needed. The changes are directed by the data derived from the disaggregated test data.

Classroom level: At the classroom level, the teacher is interested in knowing how well his or her class and individual students performed on each subject area, subsection, cluster of objectives, and individual objective. The disaggregated data should be used by the teacher to make changes in his or her program so that each student has a good opportunity to perform well on the next test.

This is a brief overview of test result disaggregation. It is the principal's responsibility to ensure that refined, disaggregated data are available at the school, grade, classroom, and special program levels for each area tested.

The second section of Strategy 38 involves ensuring that the disaggregated data are used to influence curriculum and instruction. Just like raw data, disaggregated data have no legitimate value unless they are used to inform curriculum and instructional decision making. Ensuring their use is one of the principal's monitoring functions. Monitoring can be accomplished by including this topic in grade-level and faculty meetings in which test results and plans for using the data are discussed, by conducting individual and group interviews with teachers to discuss their individual programs and teaching changes for groups and individual students, and by making frequent visits to classrooms (see Strategy 37). The objective is to ensure that the disaggregated data are used to inform curriculum and instruction decision making to improve student achievement (Nichols, Shidaker, Johnson, & Singer, 2006).

Olsen and Jaramillo (1999, p. 165) identified key characteristics of an effective district data system:

- Integrates or links databases: All electronic databases can communicate or interface with one another
- Allows disaggregation of all measures of achievement and participation by race/ethnicity, gender, language status, and other descriptors
- Produces reliable, credible data that are updated in a timely fashion and available at key decision points in a school year
- Is easily accessible to school sites, administrators, and teachers; such access involves providing training as needed and creating a user-friendly system with the appropriate hardware and software
- Responds to inquiries easily; new reports can be produced in a timely fashion to help school personnel find the answers to their questions about student achievement or equity issues

- Maintains student information longitudinally, so student histories can be traced K–12 without having to resort to individual cumulative files
- Links data to policies and standards set by the district and schools, so progress toward attaining those standards can be measured

STRATEGY 38: WHY

In recent times, data about student achievement have been widely publicized. A major complaint about standardized testing by its nay-sayers is that the results are used for undesirable political propaganda and that they do not inform decision making in schools. The first issue is largely out of our control, because the news media and politicians are responsible, but the second issue is fully within the control of the public schools. Another complaint is that the tests do not measure all of the, or even the most important, information and skills students must acquire. We agree, but what test does? We know of none. Furthermore, we have not observed information addressed on a standardized test that does not seem important for students to learn. On the basis of this reasoning and the fact that we do not have the option of administering or not administering the tests, and the fact that the test results will be used to judge the success of public schooling, we believe that public school administrators must use test results to ensure high student achievement.

There is another, broader reason for public schools to produce high test scores. Public confidence in the schools is at a very low ebb, and to turn the tide we must demonstrate that we can do the job. After all, public schools and the people who work in them do so at the will of the legislature and the public. Some public school personnel and university professors adamantly denounce the use of standardized tests and advocate for other forms of assessment. We believe that they may be right, but we will not have the opportunity to demonstrate the value of alternate forms of assessment unless we demonstrate we can do the job on standardized tests.

Use of disaggregated data to make decisions has become expected practice. Improving our knowledge and use of data is seen as essential to school improvement.

STRATEGY 38: HOW

Try the following steps to achieve this strategy:

1. Review the district current practices regarding data collection and analysis.

2. Ensure that data are collected and analyzed in a consistent, accurate manner.

3. As data collection strategies are designed, be sure they are linked to specific objectives and analyzed to determine whether the objectives have been met.

4. In regard to test data, determine whether the test results have been disaggregated. If they have, acquire them. If they have not, conduct the disaggregation by analyzing (deconstructing) each item to determine the objective it measures. For further information regarding deconstruction, see the "How" section of Strategy 1.

5. Match the objectives tested by the standardized test (item by item), and match each to the appropriate objective in your curriculum.

6. Create a list of the test objectives that were and were not achieved. This should be done at the school, program, grade, classroom, and individual student levels.

7. Identify the objectives that were not adequately achieved and those that may be overtaught, and make curriculum delivery (instruction) changes as needed. The areas not being adequately addressed may vary from subject area to subject area, skill cluster to skill cluster, classroom to classroom, or student to student. Lists of all data should be developed.

8. Prepare teachers to receive these data by informing them of the purpose of disaggregating data and its use in redesigning curriculum and instruction.

9. Schedule and conduct faculty, grade-level, or other meetings for distributing the data, analyzing them, and making decisions to improve curriculum design and delivery.

10. Monitor the use of disaggregated data by doing the following:
    • Making it a topic of discussion at each faculty and grade-level meeting,
    • Frequently visiting classrooms to observe the conduct of planned changes in curriculum delivery (instruction), and
    • Reviewing weekly and monthly test results.

11. Discuss your school's test scores and the curriculum delivery changes made to improve achievement with other principals and central office administrators, and present related information to the parents and community.

12. Develop and display graphs, charts, or other graphics that clearly communicate objectives targeted and students' attainment of objectives over time.

Note that curriculum design is a central district function; however, the school principal may see that objectives being tested by certain test items are not included in the written curriculum. In this case, the principal should inform central office officials. If they do not respond, or respond too slowly, in making curriculum changes, we recommend that prudent changes be made at the school level to ensure that students have a fair opportunity to learn the material on which they will be tested.

STRATEGY 39

Focus Staff Appraisal on Professional Growth

The staff appraisal/evaluation process focuses on the professional growth of staff in the accomplishment of high student achievement.

STRATEGY 39: WHAT

The purpose of teacher and principal appraisals should be to improve instruction so that student learning is maximized. Toward this end, every state legislature has enacted laws requiring yearly or biyearly appraisals of teachers and administrators. Unfortunately, numerous studies have shown that teacher and principal evaluations have either not been performed or were performed with the intent to satisfy only—that is, to meet the minimal requirements of the law but not to improve instruction. In fact, numerous surveys show that teachers and principals resoundingly say that their evaluations are a waste of time; they say that evaluations do not help them improve their instruction, the original and sole purpose.

The reasoning for the laws is clear: Teachers are the most important element in the formal education of a student. In order to do the best job possible in providing an education, teachers must be well trained in their craft. Staff appraisal is one means of diagnosing teachers' instructional strengths and weaknesses. Note that the operative word here is *instructional*. We find that many times teachers and administrators are appraised on the basis of nonclassroom or noninstructional criteria, such as committee membership, evening meeting attendance, and the like. These are important, but far less so than teaching.

The results of appraisals should be used as the basis for developing and carrying out a professional development plan for each teacher and administrator. The subsequent appraisal, specified classroom visits, and conferences with the teacher should serve as follow-ups to assess the effect of the professional development activities.

This sequence represents a movement from a traditional learning environment to what we call a *collaborative, reflective learning environment*. In this environment teachers are engaged in reflective dialogue about past practice to inform future practice. This has been referred to as *relaxed reflection*, and it incorporates the idea of developmental learning. Reiman and Thies-Sprinthall (1998) summarized Furth's (1981) concept of developmental learning into seven steps:

- First there is an awareness of a moderate discrepancy in understanding the meaning of an event or idea.
- A feeling of curiosity or uneasiness arises.

- More new information accumulates that does not fit with prior understanding.
- During periods of relaxed reflection, one tries to fit the new information into the prior perspective, talking to oneself.
- A new balance is reached. The new information moves from accommodation to assimilation.
- After sufficient time, the new information becomes "old" information and can be adapted to other situations.
- A new moderate discrepancy or "perturbation" arises and the process of equilibrium continues. (p. 77)

With the Downey Walk-Through With Reflective Dialogue model (Downey, Steffy, et al., 2004), administrators are instrumental in promoting this relaxed reflection. This process could be considered as a subset of cognitive development theory. Reiman and Thies-Sprinthall (1998) outlined five key propositions of cognitive development theory:

- All persons process experience through cognitive structures.
- Cognitive structures are organized in a hierarchical sequence of stages or plateaus from less complex to the more complex.
- Each shift in stage represents a major transformation in how the person makes meaning from his or her experience.
- Development is not automatic.
- Behaviors can be determined and predicted by a person's particular stage of development. (p. 41)

"When these propositions are applied to the adult-to-adult reflective dialogue in the Downey model, it is clear that this interchange is constructivist in nature. Teachers make meaning based on their lived experiences. Meaning changes as they reflect about experience" (Downey, Steffy, et al., 2004, p. 135). This process is supported by the work of Vygotsky (1962), who is noted for stressing the importance of dialogue and discussion as a primary component of growth. The new growth environment envisioned for the appraisal process includes the following components (Vygotsky, 1962, pp. 139–140):

- The principal and teacher work much more in unison to promote each other's growth.
- There is ongoing, informal dialogue about areas for growth, a mutual sharing of information, and frequent visits to the classroom.
- Little is written down in a formal sense, but the depth of conversation is thoughtful and focused on connecting practice to improved student learning.
- There is frequent and varied use of data to inform practice.
- Feedback is seen as a critical component in the learning process.

- Teachers feel in control of their learning environment.
- Questions about strategies and techniques are welcomed and can lead to critical problem solving.
- Educators seek solutions that change the internal functioning of schools and classrooms.

STRATEGY 39: WHY

The first and primary rationale for Strategy 39 is that student achievement, or learning, is the intended product of the public schools. Some school personnel and professors contend that instruction cannot be linked to student achievement as indicated by test results. We disagree. A very strong research base exists indicating that instructional practices yield high student learning. This information must be used to inform teachers and administrators as they attempt to improve student achievement. That is the purpose of professional development.

Today, state legislatures have defined learning as that which standardized tests measure. It is our job as public school administrators to produce learning. The second rationale for the strategy is that teachers are assigned the responsibilities of designing high-quality instruction to effectively deliver curriculum to students. Their success in doing so is greatly determined by their instructional skills.

It is as simple as that! Public schools are in the business of producing learning, and the best way to accomplish that is high-quality instruction. This statement has its nay-sayers. Some people, including some teachers and administrators, believe that schools cannot overcome the impact of home life and socioeconomic status. They say that the large majority of children from low-income families simply cannot do well on tests and certainly will not learn at nearly the same level as higher income students. The reality is that they are wrong. Numerous studies and experiences by school districts clearly show that high-quality curriculum design (deep alignment among the written, taught, and tested curriculum) and high-quality teaching can result in helping low-income children achieve high test scores. To think otherwise is to lose cause for hope and sight of purpose. If the public schools, as an institution, cannot produce learning for children from all socioeconomic status levels, they will be put out of business.

Administrators' appraisals, too, should focus on professional growth to improve student achievement. Principals are given the responsibility of ensuring that all students in their schools learn. Their appraisals should be based on their ability to analyze and diagnose curriculum and instruction, to cooperatively develop and monitor teacher professional growth plans, and to attain targeted learning levels as measured by the given test or assessment procedure.

STRATEGY 39: HOW

Try these activities for accomplishing this strategy:

1. Review the last few teacher or principal evaluations you performed. How closely focused were they on curriculum design and delivery? Give the teachers an anonymous survey asking for frank comments on the worth of the appraisal process in helping them improve student achievement. Make changes in the practice as necessary.

2. Inform teachers that instructional improvement is the goal of the teachers, the principal, and administrators at all levels. Furthermore, inform them that everyone can improve and that seeking improvement is healthy, not a sign of failure. We know of no perfect person.

3. Establish high-quality instruction and high student achievement as the number one goal for your school/district. Try the following ideas to instill the philosophy:
   - Make improved student achievement and instruction the primary purpose of all faculty meetings, training events, grade-level meetings, and individual meetings with staff.
   - Arrange for teachers to observe other teachers in the classroom and to share their observations.
   - Arrange for teachers to observe the principal teach and to give constructive feedback.

4. Focus teacher appraisals on instruction with the goal of improving student achievement.

5. Seek frequent teacher input on the effectiveness of the appraisal system on improving curriculum design, instruction, and student achievement as appropriate for the teacher's position.

6. Design the appraisal process around a professional growth plan.

ANALYSIS OF STANDARD FIVE

Now it is time for you to evaluate the status of your school or school district on *Standard Five: Establish Curriculum Expectations, Monitoring, and Accountability.* For each strategy, think about the current status of your situation and the changes you feel are needed. Write your responses in the spaces provided.

Strategy	Current status	Changes needed
35. Provide for high expectations for achievement for each student.	❐ Adequate ❐ Not adequate	
36. Monitor the curriculum.	❐ Adequate ❐ Not adequate	
37. Visit classrooms and provide follow-up.	❐ Adequate ❐ Not adequate	
38. Use disaggregated data in the decision-making process.	❐ Adequate ❐ Not adequate	
39. Focus staff appraisal on professional growth.	❐ Adequate ❐ Not adequate	

6

Standard Six

*Institute Effective District and School Planning,
Staff Development, and Resource Allocation,
and Provide a Quality Learning Environment*

Organizational planning is more than simply deciding what you are going to do next week. The overall objective of school improvement planning is the enhancement of student achievement. By the mid-1950s, the concept of *strategic planning* was gaining interest. George Steiner (1979) viewed strategic planning as inextricably interwoven into the entire fabric of management, not something separate and distinct from the management process. Accompanying this movement was a shift from planning designs focused on operations to designs that stressed strategy. In 1966, Marvin Bower described 14 processes that make up a management system. Most of these processes are included in state-mandated school improvement planning procedures:

- Setting objectives: Deciding on what the organization will focus
- Planning strategy: Developing plans, ideas, and processes to accomplish objectives
- Establishing goals: Specifying short-term targets

- Developing philosophy: Establishing beliefs, dispositions, and values that guide practices
- Establishing policies: Formalized statements that guide organizational performance
- Planning the organization's structure: Deciding functions and roles of employees
- Providing personnel: Recruiting, selecting, and developing people
- Establishing procedures: Organizing the work of the system
- Providing facilities: Providing the physical plant to accommodate the work
- Providing capital: Making sure that sufficient money is available to carry out the work
- Setting standards: Establishing measures of performance
- Establishing management programs and operational plans
- Providing control information: Supplying data
- Activating people: Motivating people to accomplish the work (pp. 17–18)

By the 1990s, most school systems engaged in some form of strategic planning (Kaufman, 1988; Kaufman & Herman, 1991; Kaufman, Herman, & Watters, 1996). Fundamental to successful strategic planning was getting people out of their comfort zone and encouraging them to venture into the unknown. By this time, there was a greater emphasis on taking into consideration what might happen in the future in developing plans (R. Marshall & Tucker, 1992). Simply waiting for tomorrow to happen without considering the trends and patterns impacting the future and actively attempting to create a "desired future" was thought to make one miss an opportunity to shape a better life.

In 1994, Henry Mintzberg's *Rise and Fall of Strategic Planning* was published. He called *strategic planning* an oxymoron. For him, planning was about analysis, and strategy was about synthesis. He proposed new roles for planners and plans to support the strategy-making process: "Thus, strategy is not the consequence of planning but the opposite: its starting point" (p. 333). Strategic programming begins with codifying the strategy, then elaborating it, and finally converting the elaborated strategy into routine operations. To be successful, this type of strategic programming requires an organization that is stable and mature.

The following are 11 highly powerful strategies regarding planning, staff development, use of resources, and the learning environment itself:

1. **Strategy 40: Develop a District Planning Process That Is Strategic in Nature and Provides Guidance for the Development of District and School Long-Range Plans.** Planning efforts within the system provide the strategic vision for where the district is headed; utilize available data projections for the future; incorporate long-term budget implications; and inform the development of district, department, and unit plans.

2. **Strategy 41: Create and Implement a Singular, Focused, Multiyear District Plan That Incorporates Change Strategies for Higher Student Achievement.** Planning is built into one comprehensive district improvement plan that consolidates all planning efforts. The plan focuses on two or

three academic goals for multiyear periods of time and incorporates effective change strategies, including professional development endeavors.

3. **Strategy 42: Align School Plans With the District Plan.** The school plan is aligned with a focused, districtwide plan for increased student achievement, taking into account local contextual requirements.

4. **Strategy 43: Implement Aligned Teacher Training to Reach District and School Goals.** Teachers receive and participate in ongoing training as part of reaching the goals in the district and school improvement plans.

5. **Strategy 44: Implement Administrative Training Aligned With the Curriculum and Its Assessment and District Plan Priorities.** Principals and other school-based administrators receive and participate in ongoing training directly related to curriculum design and delivery, curriculum monitoring, student and curriculum assessment, and district and school improvement plan implementation.

6. **Strategy 45: Provide Differentiated Staff Development.** Staff development is differentiated and built around Curriculum Management Systems, Inc.'s staff development criteria.

7. **Strategy 46: Link Resource Allocations to Goals, Objectives, Priorities, and Diagnosed Needs of the System.** The district and school budgets are built after the planning and illustrate how monies have been distributed to focus on the changes/goals of the district and school plans.

8. **Strategy 47: Provide Qualified and Adequate Personnel.** There are qualified and adequate school personnel in each position.

9. **Strategy 48: Remove Incompetent Staff or Help Them Achieve Satisfactory Functioning.** Marginal staff are coached to satisfactory performance or contracts are not renewed.

10. **Strategy 49: Provide a Quality Learning Environment.** There is a safe and productive learning environment for all students.

11. **Strategy 50: Provide Quality Facilities.** Facilities are adequate and promote creative and innovative approaches to learning.

STRATEGY 40

Develop a District Planning Process That Is Strategic in Nature and Provides Guidance for the Development of District and School Long-Range Plans

Planning efforts within the system provide the strategic vision for where the district is headed; utilize available data projections for the future; incorporate long-term budget implications; and inform the development of district, department, and unit plans.

STRATEGY 40: WHAT

> Educational planning seeks to create a learner-focused and societally relevant system which will measurably and continuously move toward success, producing, hopefully, an educational system which is deliberately designed to contribute to the kind of world we want for tomorrow's children. (Kaufman et al., 1996, p. xi)

As viewed by Kaufman et al. (1996), planning for the future is a fluid, active, dynamic process. It is not a lock-step approach that is linear in nature and authoritarian in implementation; instead, it conceptualizes a vision for what can be and provides "blueprints for results-oriented progress and renewal" (p. 8). At this level of planning there is more focus on the ends and less on the means. District long-range plans, and especially school improvement plans, typically focus on means rather than ends. *Ends* deal with results, such as all third-graders reading at grade level, or graduating 100% of all students entering ninth grade. *Means* are the mechanisms by which to achieve those results. Means include time, people, and resources and how they are configured to achieve the results. Kaufman et al. (p. 21) suggested that, when thinking about ends/results, you consider the following three questions: (1) Do you care about and commit to deliver the success of learners after they leave your educational system? (2) Do you care about and commit to deliver the quality—competence—of the completers and leavers when they leave your educational system? (3) Do you care about and commit to deliver the specific skills, knowledge, attitudes, and abilities of the learners as they move from course to course? Your vision for what your educational system should accomplish is directly related to how you answer those questions, and on the basis of your answers specific plans will be developed to specify the means for achieving that vision. When considering the means, two additional questions are posed: (1) Do you care about and commit to deliver the efficiency of your educational programs, activities, and methods? (2) Do you care about and commit to deliver the quality and availability of your educational resources, including human capital, financial, and learning?

In conducting school studies, Curriculum Management Systems, Inc. (CMSi) has developed seven characteristics that are used to analyze the district's overall planning efforts. These characteristics provide a mechanism for reviewing how a district deals with ends and means. These characteristics provide the framework for answering four questions: (1) Is there planning (Design)? (2) What is the quality of planning (Design)? (3) Is there action resulting from the planning (Delivery)? (4) Is the action getting the desired results (Delivery)? The design questions relate to whether the system has written documentation for the effort, and the delivery questions relate to the implementation of the design requirements. The reviewers look for evidence of the following:

1. The governing board has placed into policy an expectation that the superintendent and staff think collectively about the future and that thinking should take some tangible form without prescribing a particular template and allowing for flexibility as needed.

2. Leadership has an implicit and explicit vision/general direction of where the organization is going for improvement purposes, and that vision emerges from a combination of having thought about the future in the context of the present.

3. Databases inform and influence the planning.

4. Budget planning operates within the overall planning process and supports achieving the mission.

5. Leadership makes day-to-day decisions toward the implicit or explicit direction and facilitate movement toward the planning direction.

6. Leadership is able to adjust discrepancies between current status and desired status and facilitate directions toward the desired status as well as be fluid in planning (emergent in nature).

7. Staff are moving in a deliberate way, which is congruent with an articulated direction.

STRATEGY 40: WHY

Although Mintzberg (1994) was a strong critic of what was termed *strategic planning* in the mid-1990s, he was not against planning; instead, as he stated, "We have been highly critical throughout this discussion, concerned that by trying to be everything, planning has risked being dismissed as nothing. In fact, we never had any intention of so dismissing planning" (p. 323). He pointed out that strategy formation requires both analysis and intuition. Often, principals and central office planners work in an environment where there is a demand for action rather than reflection, solutions that are short term rather than long range; they use soft data rather than hard data to make decisions; operate orally; and focus on getting information rapidly rather than getting the right information. Intuition plays a large role for these planners. This is juxtaposed against the planners who want enough time to deeply analyze data but are often in roles where they have little power to implement change within the organization.

Mintzberg (1994) proposed a combination of the two approaches that he called *strategy formation*: "Effective strategy formation does depend importantly on analysis, both as an input to the process and as a means of dealing with its outputs" (p. 329). Planning should emerge as a process to program critical strategies. The process begins with strategy formation and then moves to concrete planning. The first step in the strategy formation phase is to codify the strategy: "The strategy is clarified and expressed in terms sufficiently clear to render it formally operational, so that its consequences can be worked out in detail" (Mintzberg, 1994, p. 337). The second step is elaborating the strategy so that specific action plans can be developed, and the third step is the actual conversion of the elaborated strategy. Our traditional planning procedures have often started with the third step without the benefit of strategy formation. For this reason, the whole planning process can become simply a paper exercise with little potential for changing the system.

As the old saying goes, "If we keep doing what we have been doing, we will get what we got." The whole purpose of planning is to change what we are getting, for the results public education is attaining now clearly are not satisfactory.

A study reported by Learning 24/7 (2005) indicated that, on the basis of 1,500 classroom visits, higher order thinking was going on in 3% of them, 52% were using worksheets, noninstructional activities dominated student work in 35%, and clear learning objectives were evidenced in only 4% of the classrooms. Haycock (2005) reported that it is not unusual for black and Latino 12th-grade students to perform about as well as white 8th-grade students and that by 8th grade, 43% of low-socioeconomic status students are performing below a basic level on the National Assessment of Educational Progress in math.

Mediocrity is so easy that no planning is required—but we know of no teacher or principal who wants to be known for mediocrity. Instead, all want to be high achievers. History has shown, and it is the belief of CMSi, that only those organizations, schools, and people who plan and define their destination attain high levels of success. In today's ever-changing world, future planning is not an option, it is a requirement.

STRATEGY 40: HOW

1. Develop board policy and administrative regulations that provide the structure for strategy formation and operational planning at all levels within the system: district, department, unit, and school.

2. Provide professional development to each constituency responsible for strategy formation and operational planning that details timelines and connections among all the planning efforts.

3. Design a planning review process using the CMSi planning criteria to identify problems at the formative level.

4. Evaluate the effectiveness of all plans to achieve desired results.

5. Monitor implementation of the plans.

6. Incorporate the planning process and the evaluation of plans into the job descriptions of appropriate personnel.

7. Periodically report on the progress of plans at public board meetings.

8. Incorporate a process to be used to make necessary adjustments in plans.

9. Implement administrative monitoring practices that provide information regarding how the implementation of plans is affecting classroom instruction and increasing student achievement.

STRATEGY 41

Create and Implement a Singular, Focused, Multiyear District Plan That Incorporates Change Strategies for Higher Student Achievement

Planning is built into one comprehensive district improvement plan that consolidates all planning efforts. The plan focuses on two or three academic goals for multiyear periods of time and incorporates effective change strategies, including professional development endeavors.

STRATEGY 41: WHAT

Only after strategy formation is complete should a traditional planning process take place. High-quality planning must be long range and incorporate numerous considerations and elements to ensure that the results are as accurate as possible. Successful businesses and school districts know precisely what they want to accomplish for their clients and how they are going to satisfy those client needs. There are many definitions and models of planning, and all have strengths and weaknesses. These criteria typically include the following:

Mission: General-purpose benefits and educational goals of a school organization. The mission provides a description of expectations and system requirements relative to identification of the primary client, intended results, general approaches, and personnel to carry out the mission. The mission is the foundation upon which all educational programs and services are built. It describes the reason a district exists. Highly successful organizations (both public and private) usually have a clearly defined and communicated mission expressed in planning documents.

Critical Analysis: Collection and analysis of vital data about all facets of the internal and external environments of the school organization. It defines the status of a school organization and describes its future by combining forecasting results with status-check results.

Assumptions: A prediction of the events and conditions that are likely to influence the performance of a school organization, division, or key individuals. Preparing planning assumptions is a form of forecasting. Assumptions are concerned with what the organization's future will look like, and they help bridge the gap between needs and actions in the planning process.

Components: Means of grouping goals for the purpose of communicating and management. All goals will be assigned to a component, and each component will consist of one or more goals.

Objectives: Statements of results that are measurable and have time limitations. They describe the condition(s) a school organization wants to improve. The desired improvements are then translated into goals. Objectives are written for each goal. As objectives are met, goals are accomplished.

Evaluation: Statements of conditions that show evidence that an objective is satisfactorily achieved and states procedures developed for completing the evaluation. Each objective should be evaluated, and the evaluation procedures should be developed at the time the objective is written.

Action Plans: Actions to be taken that will help achieve the objectives. Each objective will have one or more activities. Significant elements of each activity include a due date, responsible person or persons, and costs.

Plan Integration: Each unit manager's plan is integrated into the budget for consideration. There is integration of plans with respect to the mission and resources. Feasibility with budget is determined, and plans are checked against the organizational beliefs and mission statement.

Planning and Budget Timeline Relationships: Goals and action plans are in place and integrated prior to the budgeting process.

Multiyear Planning and Goal Integration: Planning extends over several years, and the number of goals and actions is feasible within the resources of the district.

Linkage Documents: All documents in a system, particularly school plans, are aligned to the district plan.

Planning needs to be focused and well thought out. The plans need to be reasonable, allow for changes, incorporate change strategies, and include a method to evaluate the effectiveness of the plan's implementation (also see Strategy 42). We see many school districts engaging in planning, but most have far too many goals, and actions are often separate and isolated from other actions. Large groups of people come together, often in forums, to identify the goals. A collective approach is used, and many goals are established, well beyond the capacity of the district to carry them out. It is time to stop this type of planning.

Many governing boards and administrators fail to clearly distinguish between *board goals* and *management goals*. Board goals should be mission oriented and focused on results: student achievement goals. Management goals need to focus on the means for accomplishing the results. It is our opinion that the direction of the management goals needs to be tightly held in low-performing districts, with a focus on just two or three management goals so that intense intervention to accomplish higher student achievement can be completed.

Although many districts have plans, most of those plans do not get implemented. Just making the plan and carrying it out in a perfunctory manner seems to be the goal for many districts—they simply want to meet a requirement rather than having it actually serve as a blueprint for change. Moreover, the strategic actions identified frequently have little chance of bringing about higher student achievement. The strategies are often not well researched, and change approaches are not incorporated. The research is replete with change strategies, but often these are ignored.

STRATEGY 41: WHY

Lewis Carroll provided us with the finest of all rationales for planning. In his famous book *Alice's Adventures in Wonderland* (1865/1965), he described the confusion of the book's main character, Alice, as she was walking down a road. She came to a fork in the road and did not know which fork to follow. She spied the wise Cheshire cat in the tree and queried, "Which path should I take?" The wise cat responded, "Where is it you wish to go?" She responded, "I don't know." At that, the Cheshire cat exclaimed, "Then either will do fine" (p. 66). So much truth and wisdom are contained in this brief conversation. If we do not know where we want to go, then any path or activity will do fine, and any destination will be acceptable. School districts, however, cannot take just any road. Today, vouchers and charter schools challenge the public school monopoly, and much proposed legislation offers more serious threats. Public schools must deliver the goods as defined by the external clients—parents, the public, and the state legislatures—or the arena of competition will be opened up and public education will lose a major part of its market share. Organizations that do the best job meeting the needs expressed by the public will stay in existence and thrive. Doing so implicitly means defining and maintaining a clear and narrow focus and strategically planning a means for attaining the goals of ever-higher student achievement.

For schools, this means focusing on two or three academic goals to be attained over a 1- to 3-year period. Individual schools must follow school district missions, but in doing so they must be certain that their students learn the basics as defined by the legislature and the school district. Gone are the days when superintendents and school principals could satisfy the community and parents by telling them that the school was teaching highly valuable skills and talents indiscernible by objective or empirical measures.

It is foolhardy to believe that people can accomplish a complicated task that they do not have the skills to achieve. Hence, long-range planning must also include professionals who are designated to deliver the specified products. The CMSi rationale for long-range planning is straightforward in its belief that teachers are the primary deliverers of learning to students. Therefore, a long-range plan must include the professional development needs of teachers simply because teachers perform the most valuable job in any school district; they directly impact student achievement. The people who supervise teachers, the school principals, also can impact their success in large part. Principals are responsible for monitoring the school curriculum and the quality of the curriculum delivery demonstrated by teachers. Research (Frase, 2001; Heck, 1992) has shown that student achievement in schools where principals actively monitor classroom instruction is higher than in other schools, and the teachers demonstrate higher respect for principals, profess higher perceived efficacy for other teachers and the administration, and hold teacher evaluation and staff development in higher regard.

Planning at the local school level must be systematic and result in specific targets and goals. Without specifying these, the school cannot know the learning, skills, attitudes, or values it wishes to deliver to its students; otherwise, activities, although well intended, will be wasted.

STRATEGY 41: HOW

The following steps are recommended for guiding the development of the district plan:

1. Determine the district's overall mission, vision, and long-range plan.

2. Establish clear student achievement goals and have these approved by the board as the board's goals.

3. Establish multiyear management goals—few in number—that have a high probability of impacting student achievement. Strategies must be researched and data driven in selection.

4. Use the criteria identified earlier to develop the district plan and keep planning streamlined and integrated.

5. Ensure that the results of planning—the goals, objectives, and action plans—are doable.

6. Carry out the plan and monitor it, and do not let day-to-day operations distract you from the aim of the plan.

STRATEGY 42

Align School Plans With the District Plan

The school plan is aligned with a focused, districtwide plan for increased student achievement, taking into account local contextual requirements.

STRATEGY 42: WHAT

This book is about what needs to be in place for school staff to raise student achievement. It is important to remember that schools do not exist in a vacuum. Even though this book focuses on each individual school's staff, we must be aware that the individual school is part of a community and a larger system known as a *school district*. School districts are systemic in nature and, as such, all subsystems within them must work together to attain a common mission or product. That product is learning, however the state legislature and local school board choose to define it. This projected product is what gives schools their direction, and each school within the system must establish plans to attain the district product.

The development of school improvement plans is now a common requirement for states, provinces, and ministries of education throughout the world. These plans serve as road maps for improving student learning, distributing resources, and the design and delivery of specific staff development. As such, they become a mechanism by which schools are held accountable for improved student achievement by central administration and the general public. These plans should be directly tied to the district's long-range plans and contain the specificity for how the larger goals of the system are to be achieved.

School improvement planning is a rational approach to dealing with problems that require attention over an extended period of time to prepare for anticipated events and for limiting the negative impact of an uncertain future. A sound school improvement plan, representing the best judgment of the stakeholders, provides the necessary blueprint for applying school and district resources to programs designed to attain or maintain high student achievement. In reviewing school improvement plans while conducting curriculum management audits, CMSi has identified five criteria to evaluate the effectiveness of those plans:

Reasonableness: The plan is reasonable in that it has a feasible number of goals and objectives with the necessary resources (financial, time, and people) available.

Emergent: The plan allows for emergent thinking, trends, and internal and external changes that impact the system.

Change Strategies: The plan incorporates and focuses on action strategies/ interventions that are built around effective change strategies (e.g., capacity building of appropriate staff).

Integration of Plans and Actions: School-based improvement plans are aligned to the district goal priorities.

Evaluation: There is a written plan to evaluate whether the objectives of the plan have been accomplished (not simply an evaluation of whether the activities have taken place).

What we generally find relative to these five criteria is that school improvement plans often contain too many objectives, and the objectives are often unrelated to the district priorities. Although plans are typically designed to cover a 3-year period, how internal and external trends and changes will be accommodated in changing the plan objectives is unclear, as is how specific change strategies will be used within the plan. Finally, we rarely see school plans that include a design to systematically evaluate the effectiveness of the activities within the plan to meet projected goals and objectives.

The school principal is a key player in the design and development of school improvement plans. In the role of instructional leader and change agent, the principal can dramatically affect whether student achievement improves and whether the school improvement plan facilitates this process. Leithwood and Jantzi (1997) identified a number of characteristics of effective school principals. The following have been excerpted from their work.

1. Develop and communicate a shared vision that builds commitment.
   - Involve staff, school council members, parents, and other community members in the development and support of the school's vision.
   - Clarify the practical implications of the school's vision for programs, instruction, etc.

2. Build consensus about school goals and priorities.
   - Ensure that the school's goals are limited to a small number of well-defined goals that apply to all children in the school.
   - Build support and commitment for the school's improvement plan.
   - Use the school's goals as the basis of discussions with individual teachers about their own professional goals and make sure that teachers understand that they are supposed to develop and pursue their own professional goals.

3. Build a productive school environment.
   - Encourage risk-taking and experimentation and support it understanding that mistakes are part of the improvement process.
   - Promote an environment that values diversity and team building and that focuses on communication and information sharing.

4. Alter school structures to enhance participation in decision making.
   - Use staff meetings as opportunities for shared decision making and for teachers' professional development.
   - Follow through on decisions made jointly with teachers.

5. Model the values promoted by the school.
   - Model problem-solving and communication strategies that staff can readily use in working with students, parents, and other teachers.

6. Provide intellectual stimulation.
   - Encourage staff to develop a philosophy of life-long learning.
   - Make staff development the focus of staff meetings.
   - Be aware of current trends and issues, as well as threats and opportunities in the school environment and in society at large (that is, "see the big picture") and communicate this information to staff and the entire school community. (pp. 312–331)

The requirement for individual schools to develop school improvement plans has been in place for several years. A review of the Web sites of various state departments of education provides ample examples of what must be included in these plans, along with examples of completed plans. Although these planning requirements have evolved over the years, it is now possible to access examples of local school district requirements for this process that go beyond state requirements. One such example is from the Boston Public Schools. They first developed

A Comprehensive Plan for the Boston Public Schools in 1996 (see http://boston .k12.ma.us/teach/foc.asp). After 5 years of implementation, they identified several lessons they had learned:

- High standards lead to improved achievement for all students.
- Schools must be accountable for results to all stakeholders and determine what is working and what is not.
- School improvement is most effective when the principal and/or Instructional Leadership Team sets and maintains goals, ensures continuity over a period of years, and communicates effectively and consistently to the entire school community.
- Every school benefits from being part of a school network.
- The most vital form of professional development takes place directly in schools where teachers and administrators support and critique one another.
- No school district can operate in isolation. External partnerships are key to bringing funds and resources into schools to accelerate improvement.

By 2004, the Boston Public Schools had identified *Six Essentials for Whole School Improvement* (see http://boston.k12.ma.us/teach/foc.asp), along with expectations for schools, evidence for what one should see and hear in classrooms and around the school, and expectations for central administration. This framework provides a high degree of specificity for the school improvement planning process. The first essential is presented here as an example of how districts are providing direction, guidelines, and high expectations for this critical school improvement process.

The Core Essential: Effective Instruction. Use effective instructional practices and create a collaborative school climate to improve student learning.

Expectations for Schools

- In every classroom, teachers use an inquiry-based approach to instruction that is organized in the following way:
  - Mini-Lesson/Objective: The teacher presents and/or models the day's learning objective—a standards-based fact, concept, strategy, or skill (approximately 20% of class time, which includes a "Do Now" task, 5-minute warm-up, or review of the previous day's work).
  - Independent Work: Individually or in small groups, students apply the learning objective to their reading, writing, or other work, while the teacher confers with some students about the learning objective (approximately 60% of class time).
  - Share/Summing Up: The teacher sums up the learning objective, and students discuss how they used it in their work (approximately 20% of the learning time).

- During class, and in every subject, students read, write, and solve problems regularly, doing work of high cognitive demand to help them reach proficiency.
- The school uses a yearlong curriculum in core subjects that delineates content and skills.
- The school develops positive relationships among staff and students that support a professional learning community for adults and an engaging, motivating learning environment for students. The school has a student behavior policy.

Evidence: What You Should See and Hear in Classrooms

- Students can explain what they are learning, and why, and how it connects to what they have already learned. They are able to talk about the quality of their own work and what they must do to improve it.
- Teachers and students engage in a high level of discourse that goes beyond right/wrong and yes/no answers to an emphasis on evidence.
- Teachers give prompt and specific feedback to students on their work, based on standards. In conferences, both the teacher and students talk about the work.
- Classroom walls display current student work and charts the teacher and students have created together about the content they are studying, standards for exemplary work, and class rules. Students refer to the charts frequently.
- Classroom space is organized so that students can get what they need—books, journals, other materials—on their own.

Evidence: What You Should See and Hear Around the School

- Every classroom has areas for students to read, write, and work on their own and in pairs, as well as a common area for the whole class to meet and talk. Current exemplary student work is posted throughout the school.
- Every teacher is able to explain what his or her students are learning, and why, and to describe how his or her instruction will get students to proficiency in core academic subjects.
- The principal–headmaster and teachers—including teachers of students with special needs and English language learners and teacher–specialists—meet regularly in teams to talk about instructional practice.
- The principal–headmaster spends time in classrooms every day observing and discussing work with teachers and students.
- The principal–headmaster models learning by observing classroom practice, leading learning walks, and discussing his or her own learning with staff.

Expectations for Central Administration

- The superintendent and his or her teams use expectations for schools when observing classrooms and evaluating principals–headmasters.
- Every employee is able to explain Whole-School Improvement and his or her role in that effort.

- Central departments base their decisions on the question "How will this decision help students become better readers, writers, and thinkers and reach proficiency?" (see http://boston.k12.ma.us/teach/foc.asp).

STRATEGY 42: WHY

The key words regarding the rationale, or the "why" of this strategy, are *alignment* and *congruency*. In reading about Strategy 1 you learned that district content standards, and thus the school content standards, must be aligned with state standards. Strategy 2 discussed how objectives must be clear and precise and aligned to the content standards in order to communicate exactly what is to be learned. Strategy 3 was about aligning objectives with external assessments to ensure congruency of objectives with the external assessment. Strategy 19 focused on ensuring that all programs in a school are aligned to the district objectives. According to Strategy 25, all instructional resources must be purchased on the basis of their alignment to the objectives and used accordingly. Finally, Strategies 26 through 34 focused on aligning teaching practices to deliver the objectives while considering differing student needs.

So, what was the purpose of reviewing these strategies? That's a good question, and the answer is crucial: All of these strategies lay the groundwork for districtwide planning and the need for schools to derive their plan from the district plan, *in order to ensure alignment*. If a school chooses to go its own way, there can be no assurance that the students will achieve common goals that the district or state has deemed most important. Following the district plan is the first step in ensuring that the school plan is congruent with or aligned to the district plan. Public schools are not in private practice. They are part of a system and, as such, must devote themselves to the district's direction.

After conducting well over 300 audits over the past twenty-five years, we have been distressed to learn the unfortunate fact that many school districts do not have long-range plans of sufficient quality to guide internal decision making. What does this mean to school staff should your district not have a quality long-range plan? Very simply, it means that you must do it yourself.

STRATEGY 42: HOW

1. Obtain a copy of the district long-range plan.

2. Read the mission statement and determine how goals and objectives and action plans are linked, or are aligned to, the mission statement.

3. Begin development of your school mission statement. Be sure to consider vital data about all facets of your school (internal environment) and the community (external) environments. What does the near future hold for them regarding enrollment changes, evolving curriculum needs, and so on? In the curriculum management audit, we call these *critical analysis* and *assumptions*.

4. Develop your school mission statement in cooperation with teachers, parents, and possibly other community representatives.

5. Seek to gain commitment to the plan from these participants.

6. Ensure that the mission statement communicates a definite direction and is not so broad as to be meaningless. Remember, the mission statement defines what your school is all about.

7. Communicate this mission widely so that all groups within your school community know what the mission is and understand it.

8. From the mission statement, develop a few goals in alignment to district goals. Each goal should contribute to the attainment of the mission statement. If you have multiple goals that are focused in a given direction, group these goals as components.

9. Develop specific, measurable objectives for each goal. The objectives should state who will do what, when, and how, and how success will be determined. Remember, objectives must be very clear so that the people assigned the job of achieving them know exactly what to do and exactly how their success will be determined.

10. For each objective or group of objectives, develop action plans designed to deliver the objectives and, ultimately, the goals and mission statement.

11. Develop this plan for use over a 3-year period.

12. Develop a subplan for each of the 3 years.

13. Throughout this process, ensure that your plan is congruent with the district plan—and last, but not least, be sure you have not bitten off too much. Is your plan doable given human resource and budget considerations? All activities must be linked and integrated into the budget to ensure proper funding: See Items 1–9.

14. If the district does not have a long-range plan, suggest that one needs to be developed; then, if necessary, develop one yourself at the school level.

STRATEGY 43

Implement Aligned Teacher Training to Reach District and School Goals

Teachers receive and participate in ongoing training as part of reaching the goals in the district and school improvement plans.

STRATEGY 43: WHAT

Teachers are the prime deliverers of the mission of the school system. They are the "firing line" officers charged with the primary responsibility to deliver the learning specified by the system. As such, they need to receive and participate in ongoing training as part of reaching the system's goals and of achieving the school's improvement plan. Teachers are the most important group in the organization in terms of the goal accomplishment.

Without training aligned with the system's goals and improvement plans, teachers have little or no direction on the procedural steps to take or the processes to implement in order to reach those goals. Where there is no understanding of goals or plans there is a rudderless administration, and it is impossible to predict the system's final destination. Training needs to be relevant; based on solid data regarding organizational performance; and focused on building competence, commitment, and effectiveness in confronting and overcoming organizational obstacles to reaching the system's mission and goals.

According to Kowalski (2003), professional development is more of a "re-educative" process (p. 231). On the basis of a review of the literature on adult learning, Butler (1992) identified a variety of descriptors of adult learners:

- Adult learning takes place throughout a lifetime.
- Adults learn in a variety of ways and require different lengths of time for the learning to take place.
- When adults learn, they bring a variety of life experiences to the learning situation. Like students, they learn best when the new learning is tied to past experiences.
- Adult learners' stage of development, whether personal, chronological, or professional, affects the learning experience.
- Adult learners make decisions about what they will take from a learning experience in both a conscious and unconscious way.
- Adults learn best when the learning is self-directed, self-motivated, and when they take responsibility for their own learning.
- New learning works best when it is followed by a period of reflection and coaching to facilitate integration and application of the new learning.
- Continued learning depends on achieving satisfaction that the new learning is enabling the teacher to achieve personal goals. (p. 3)

All new learning involves change. According to G. E. Hall and Loucks (1978), change is a highly personal process, and simply exposing teachers to the new knowledge will not ensure that they will utilize the change. In addition, growth will happen over time, and it requires different amounts of time for different people. This change can be in a product, a process, or a function (R. M. Smith, 1982). However, if the change is unaligned with the fundamental culture and values of the school, it will not be institutionalized within the system (Hoy & Miskel, 2005; Kowalski, 2006).

Research has shown that the most effective staff development is linked to school improvement rather than personal professional development. Teachers should be able to see a clear link between acquisition of the new skill and improvement in their school and effectiveness. Today, there is great interest in DuFour and Eaker's (1998) professional learning communities. DuFour (2004) described a *professional learning community* as "a place where the focus is on (a) learning rather than teaching, (b) working collaboratively, and (c) being held accountable for results" (p. 6). This model has three fundamental characteristics: (1) a relentless attention to knowing whether children are learning, (2) a culture of collaboration, and (3) a focus on results.

In 2001, the National Staff Development Council revised its standards for staff development. These standards are referenced as the bedrock for developing an effective professional improvement program. They are organized around three areas—(1) context standards, (2) process standards, and (3) content standards—and they are all designed to improve the learning of students as their ultimate goal.

Context Standards

- Organizes adults into learning communities whose goals are aligned with those of the school and district.
- Requires skillful school and district leaders who guide continuous instructional improvement.
- Requires resources to support adult learning and collaboration.

Process Standards

- Uses disaggregated student data to determine adult learning priorities, monitor progress, and help sustain continuous improvement.
- Uses multiple sources of information to guide improvement and demonstrate its impact.
- Prepares educators to apply research to decision making.
- Uses learning strategies appropriate to the intended goal.
- Applies knowledge about human learning and change.
- Provides educators with the knowledge and skills to collaborate.

Content Standards

- Prepares educators to understand and appreciate all students; create safe, orderly and supportive learning environments; and hold high expectations for their academic achievement.
- Deepens educators' content knowledge, provides them with research-based instructional strategies to assist students in meeting rigorous academic standards, and prepares them to use various types of classroom assessments appropriately.
- Provides educators with knowledge and skills to involve families and other stakeholders appropriately.

STRATEGY 43: WHY

Curriculum audits have often found that teacher training is unfocused and voluntary in its design and delivery. The connection between organizational aims and purposes is often weak; in some cases, nonexistent. Rational organizations define and develop aims and purposes, design and implement action to achieve those purposes, and monitor performance for informed decision making relative to progress and corrective action.

Once the system focuses its energies on specific goals, goals that are selected and determined by research-based information that documents real need, the system must initiate the process of *optimization*. Optimizing an organization requires keeping an "eye on the ball" and preventing fragmentation of or distraction from the goal. It also calls for aligning all activities and resources of the organization with its purposes. Planning is simply a design and schedule of actions to satisfy and fulfill *organizational needs* (identified as discrepancies between what the system wants to accomplish and what it has accomplished currently).

Key personnel are the human resources that give the organization the means to satisfy needs, meet goals, and accomplish organizational aims and purposes. It goes without question that key personnel must be included in training activities designed to prepare, reinforce, and shape behaviors congruent with the system's goals and purposes. Of course, this means teachers. If the product of the school system is learning, the teacher is the builder of that product. To build it in accordance with organizational intentions, training is needed that matches what the system intends to accomplish.

STRATEGY 43: HOW

Training needs to be goal focused, needs driven, compatible with best practice, and adequate in scope and quality. To accomplish these attributes, consider the following steps and actions:

1. Clarify and document the organizational aims, purposes, objectives, and mission. There is nothing more damaging to organizational effectiveness than confusion about what the system stands for, believes in, and is trying to accomplish. Training needs to be designed to develop comprehensive understanding of the organization's direction among teachers and to build fidelity and loyalty to the organization's mission. It is critical that personnel in the system acknowledge and internalize that individuals within an organization must support the organization's aims and purposes if the organization is to endure.

2. Conduct a needs assessment of how well the system is achieving its aims and purposes. This step is akin to taking stock to see where the organization is compared with its desired status. This assessment of standing and performance must be clearly connected to the system's expectations, goals, and purpose. The data gathered should inform teachers and others in training

conferences of where the system is falling short, where it is reaching its goals, and where the system is exceeding its goals. Training needs to be designed to acquaint teachers with where the system is in terms of effectiveness and success.

3. Develop options and alternatives to address organizational needs. Once training has been completed regarding what the organization wants to accomplish and how well it is doing in the pursuit of those intentions, teachers need to participate in training activities designed to develop and visualize meeting identified needs. Training needs to be provided in topics related to research findings, peer organization experience, theoretical approaches, documented best practice, and so on. At this point, the organization needs to decide which courses of action it will follow.

4. Train teachers in the procedures and processes needed to complete the courses of action selected. It is not enough to identify and adopt a plan to implement a promising organizational strategy. Teachers need to be trained in the following:
   - The course of action
   - How it works
   - What it takes to make it work
   - How to support it
   - How to determine whether it is working satisfactorily

5. Do not overlook the necessity of dissemination of results and progress. Once teachers have been trained to solve organizational problems, they need feedback on their progress and performance to aid in operational decision making. Operational decisions may include continuation of strategies, modification of strategies, or termination of strategies. Without training and feedback, uninterrupted progress is impossible.

6. Educational leaders need to be aware of the power and necessity of appropriate training. Given adequate and relevant training, teachers can focus their pedagogy and energy on accomplishing the goals and mission of the system.

STRATEGY 44

Implement Administrative Training Aligned With the Curriculum and Its Assessment and District Plan Priorities

Principals and other school-based administrators receive and participate in ongoing training directly related to curriculum design and delivery, curriculum monitoring, student and curriculum assessment, and district and school improvement plan implementation.

STRATEGY 44: WHAT

Administrators can make or break good school systems. The leader is the most critical person in the organization and has the strongest influence on the internal integrity and character of the organization. Without leadership skills, management savvy, and curriculum knowledge, the leader is impeded in building organizational effectiveness and success in the design and delivery of learning.

Training can make a huge difference in the skills, capabilities, and knowledge of school administrators, particularly in curriculum management. The role of the leader in curriculum management is critical to the success of the system in reaching its goals and objectives for learners. Without adequate and valuable training, the organization will not be able to accomplish its aims and purposes.

In 2005, the results of a meta-analysis conducted by the Mid-continent Research for Education and Learning were published in *School Leadership That Works: From Research to Results* (Marzano, Waters, & McNulty, 2005). From earlier analysis of more than 5,000 studies, 69 were selected for examination because they most directly related principal leadership with student achievement. These studies included more than 14,000 teacher ratings of principal leadership for 2,802 principals. We present the results here because they form the basis for the design and implementation of administrator professional development. The dependent variable in each of these studies was student achievement, and the independent variable was leadership. Both student achievement and school leadership measures were quantitative and measurable.

Affirmation: Recognizes and celebrates school accomplishments and acknowledges failures.

Change Agent: Is willing to and actively challenges the status quo.

Is comfortable leading change initiatives with uncertain outcomes.
Systematically considers new and better ways of doing things.

Communication: Establishes strong lines of communication with teachers and among students.

Is easily accessible to teachers.
Develops effective means for teachers to communicate with one another.

Contingent Rewards: Recognizes and rewards individual accomplishments.
Uses performance versus seniority as the primary criterion for reward and advancement.

Culture: Fosters shared beliefs and a sense of community and cooperation.

Promotes a sense of well-being.
Promotes cohesion among staff.
Develops an understanding of purpose.

Discipline: Protects teachers from issues and influences that would detract from their teaching time or focus.

Protects instructional time from interruptions.

Flexibility: Adapts his or her leadership behavior to the needs of the current situation and is comfortable with dissent.

Is comfortable with major changes in how things are done.
Adapts leadership style to needs of specific situation.
Can be directive or nondirective as the situation demands.

Focus: Establishes clear goals and keeps those goals in the forefront of the school's attention.

Continually keeps attention on established goals.

Ideals and Beliefs: Communicates and operates from strong ideals and beliefs about schooling.

Demonstrates behaviors that are consistent with beliefs.

Input: Involves teachers in the design and implementation of important decisions and policies.

Uses leadership team in decision making.

Intellectual Stimulation: Ensures faculty and staff are aware of the most current theories and practices and makes the discussion of these a regular aspect of the school's culture.

Keeps staff informed about current research and theory regarding effective schooling.
Continually exposes the staff to cutting-edge ideas about how to be effective.
Systematically engages staff in discussions about current research and theory.
Currently involves the staff in reading articles and books about effective practices.

Involvement in Curriculum, Instruction, and Assessment: Is directly involved in the design and implementation of curriculum, instruction, and assessment.

Is involved in helping teachers design curricular activities.
Is involved with teachers to address instructional and assessment issues.

Knowledge of Curriculum, Instruction, and Assessment: Is knowledgeable about current curriculum, instruction, and assessment practices.

Provides conceptual guidance for teachers regarding effective classroom practice.

Monitoring and Evaluating: Monitors the effectiveness of school practices and their impact on student learning.

Monitors the effectiveness of curriculum, instruction, and assessment.

Optimizer: Inspires and leads new and challenging innovations.

Inspires teachers to accomplish things that might seem beyond their grasp.
Portrays a positive attitude about the ability of the staff to accomplish substantial things.
Is a driving force behind major initiatives.

Order: Establishes a set of standard operating procedures and routines.

Provides and enforces clear structures, rules, and procedures for students and staff.
Establishes routines regarding the running of the school that staff understand and follow.

Outreach: Is an advocate and spokesperson for the school to all stakeholders.

Ensures the school is in compliance with district and state mandates.
Advocates on behalf of the school in the community.
Advocates for the school with parents.
Ensures the central office is aware of the school's accomplishments.

Relationships: Demonstrates an awareness of the personal aspects of teachers and staff.

Remains aware of personal needs of teachers.
Maintains personal relationships with teachers.
Is informed about significant personal issues within the lives of staff members.
Acknowledges significant events in the lives of staff members.

Resources: Provides teachers with materials and professional development necessary for the successful execution of their jobs.

Ensures teachers have necessary materials and equipment.
Ensures teachers have necessary staff development opportunities that directly enhance their teaching.

Situational Awareness: Is aware of the details and undercurrents in the running of the school and uses that information to address current and potential problems.

Is aware of informal groups and relationships among staff of the school.
Is aware of issues in the school that have not surfaced but could create discord.
Can predict what could go wrong from day to day.

Visibility: Has quality contact with teachers and students.

Makes systematic frequent visits to classrooms.
Maintains high visibility around the school.
Has frequent contact with students.

STRATEGY 44: WHY

Curriculum management consists of several discrete and unique factors that must be constructed and implemented successfully, and they must be crafted and woven together in a system that is functional, practicable, and sound. Administrative personnel must provide the leadership to put all of the components of a sound curriculum management system in place and to develop the relationships necessary for the components to work in concert. In 2004, the National Association of Secondary School Principals published *Breaking Ranks II: Strategies for Leading High School Reform*. This publication is a follow-up to *Breaking Ranks: Changing an American Institution*, which was first published in 1996.

The crafters of the 2004 edition clustered their recommendations around three themes: (1) Collaborative Leadership and Effective Learning Communities; (2) Personalization; and (3) Curriculum, Instruction and Assessment, with a focus on the role of principal. "The principal is the principal teacher, the first among many—part of a team of professionals. His or her job is to gather this community, to find its special genius, to press it hard, to nurture it, to depend on it" (National Association of Secondary School Principals, 2004, p. xi). The themes presented in *Breaking Ranks* are designed to lead to improved student achievement. Like the work of Mid-continent Research for Education and Learning cited earlier, it forms the basis for the design and implementation of focused administrative staff development.

The school system would find it very difficult to successfully achieve its goals and purposes without strong administrative leadership, and administrative leadership would find it very difficult to be successful in leading the organization without suitable and pertinent training. Training is the glue that pulls the components together and makes them work harmoniously toward the goals and purposes of the organization.

STRATEGY 44: HOW

Follow these steps to implement this strategy:

1. Identify relevant knowledge for principals and school administrators in curriculum management and provide training regarding the following:
   - Board policies and system expectations for schools, employees, and learners
   - System curriculum objectives (what students are to know, think, do, feel, or be like) as authorized by the governing authority
   - State, national, content area standards or testing components
   - System job descriptions for educational leaders (knowledge, skills, communication, modeling, duties, and responsibilities)

2. Diagnose school leaders' strengths and weaknesses in critical curriculum management skills. Include curriculum design and delivery, instructional efficacy, effectiveness in working with people, and data management

requirements (key data on status, progress, growth, change, etc. of measured learning).

3. Design and develop training to fill in the gaps of administrator knowledge, skills, and behaviors in curriculum management. Train administrators in the need for direction (i.e., what the curriculum is and how to know whether it is valid). Other attributes of curriculum management to be included in administrator training include the following:
   • The nature and power of curriculum quality control
   • Defined specific learner objectives that are expected to be attained
   • Scope and quality of curriculum expectations (by grade level and content area)
   • Relationships across grade levels and content areas (establishing articulation and coordination)
   • Learner objectives and their validation and measurement within the system
   • Supportive material needed to deliver the curriculum
   • Instructional materials and references for specific objectives
   • Instructional strategies recommended for effective attainment of objectives

4. Design and implement training for administrators in the measurement of learning and progress. Administrators need to know and be able to do the following:
   • Monitor achievement results as measured for students, classrooms, and schools
   • Manage a range of assessment instruments used at all grade levels and in all content areas
   • Implement methods for disaggregating data for instructional and curriculum decision making

5. Structure administrator training activities to build and ensure skills in organizational intervention and on how to use data in determining courses of action. Components to include are as follows:
   • How school-based plans and actions are best determined and what data are used to determine selections
   • How to determine and take courses of action that are congruent with best practice
   • How to design and conduct training and professional development focused on assessed needs
   • How to provide resources to schools in accordance with curriculum objectives and needs
   • How to intervene in the operations of a school, based on rational and appropriate evidence of need

Feedback from teachers in dozens of curriculum audits indicates that many administrators often avoid personal involvement in curriculum management and instruction and fail to accept accountability for learning. However, if a school system is to be effective, successful, and proficient in meeting its goals, the administrator must be an instructional leader and an exemplary curriculum manager. Anything less in terms of role expectations will preclude organizational success in design and delivery of learning.

STRATEGY 45

Provide Differentiated Staff Development

Staff development is differentiated and built around Curriculum Management Systems, Inc.'s staff development criteria.

STRATEGY 45: WHAT

Everyone understands the importance of staff development to higher student achievement. This can be done only through the development of staff capacity.

One important way to develop staff capacity is to differentiate staff development based on the needs of teachers. When this is done, teachers see more relevance in the professional development they are receiving. In the late 1990s, Steffy and Wolfe (1997) expanded a model for differentiated professional development called *The Life Cycle of the Career Teacher* (Steffy, 1989; Steffy, Wolfe, Pasch, & Enz, 2000). This model is based on the idea that teachers go through phases in their development as they progress through their careers. Three important phases include the *apprentice teacher* (newly certified and beginning his or her first year as a contracted teacher); the *professional teacher* (a teacher who has received tenure or a continuing contract and is considered a "good" teacher), and the *expert/master teacher* (one who is successful in assisting students in achieving high levels of student achievement regardless of the characteristics the students bring to the classroom). Steffy and Wolfe argued that teachers at different phases required different professional development to support their continued growth over time and that, without those opportunities, teachers would begin to distance themselves from the organization and begin to blame outside variables, such as parental support or lack of prior learning, for students' inability to meet high standards. The model suggested that if teachers are given opportunities to develop their teaching skills at the right level of difficulty, they will continue to grow and develop over time. In 2000, the model was expanded and presented as a

> means for assuring that teachers grow professionally . . . a framework for designing professional development activities to support growth . . . a process that must be nurtured and encouraged for growth to occur, and . . . a new vision of the profession as playing a powerful role in its own development. (Steffy et al., 2000, p. 106)

The authors included suggestions for addressing the unique need of teachers at various phases of the model through professional development. Needs of teachers at the apprentice, professional, and expert/master phase are presented here (pp. 120–123).

Apprentice Teacher Phase

Concern: Feeling overwhelmed by full-time responsibilities.

Recommendation: Teacher educators, mentors, and administrators must offer developmentally sequenced workshops that

- Are timely and offer sufficient information
- Are explicit and include diverse teaching models that address different learning styles
- Accommodate individual needs

Concern: Feeling a need to be competent and accepted within the school site.

Recommendation: Prepared mentors offer context specific information by

- Reviewing district curriculum guides and offering successful methods of delivering content
- Identifying and locating appropriate instructional resources and materials
- Responding to emerging apprentice need on a daily basis through a team approach

Concern: Questioning career choice.

Recommendation: Apprentice teacher cohort groups provide psychological support to one another by

- Identifying common concerns and needs
- Conducting problem-solving meetings and determining appropriate solutions
- Building a sense of community within the school and across the district
- Sharing ideas, materials, and strategies that work

Concern: Addressing school or district disregard of apprentice teachers.

Recommendation: Develop school environments that are friendly to new teachers that provide

- Optimum teaching loads for new teachers
- Realistic class/student assignments
- Comprehensive induction programs that continually support new teachers
- Time to confer with and observe other teachers under the direction of a trained mentor

Professional Teacher Phase

Concern: Addressing boredom with the profession and lack of professional growth.

Recommendation: Because professional teachers must expand and refine their instructional practices, they need professional development opportunities that

- Support personal reflection—a process enforced by the National Board for Professional Teaching Standards
- Provide colleagues time and opportunity to learn from one another
- Attain their professional goals and develop their professional interest
- Enable them to be grounded in current research and best practice

Concern: Eliminating professional isolation.

Recommendation: Administrators must recognize the ongoing contributions teachers make and deliberately design and allow time for teachers to interact, including

- Weekly/daily planning time with peers
- Time for peer observation and feedback
- Financial support to attend professional conferences and seminars
- Internet interactions with colleagues

Concern: Addressing a lack of career growth opportunities.

Recommendation: In most professions, an ascending ladder of job responsibilities recognizes experience with promotions in title and pay. Because this is not the case with the teaching profession, professional teachers need some recognition of their expanding knowledge and skills, which may be accomplished by encouraging these teachers to engage in

- Peer-coaching teams or professional learning communities within a school or district
- Leading on-site in-service workshops
- Developing units of study for school or district sharing
- Engaging in action research projects
- Coaching pre-service teachers in early internships in collaboration with a university

Expert Teacher Phase

Concern: Finding time for professional growth.

Recommendation: Expert teachers need time and district support to continue their professional growth, including

- Time to attend professional conferences during and after school
- Encouragement to present at state and national conferences
- Sabbatical leaves to continue their own education

Concern: Fulfilling a need to share professional talents.

Recommendation: Administrators and teacher educators must involve expert teachers in pre-service instruction and induction programs, including

- Support to create videos of exemplary lessons to share at seminars
- Opportunities to co-instruct methods courses and/or in-service workshops with university faculty members
- Serving as mentors to apprentice teachers in a practicum experience
- Writing for professional journals to share classroom experiences and programs

Concern: Addressing a lack of career growth opportunities.

Recommendation: Like professional teachers, expert teachers need some recognition of their expanding, exceptional knowledge and skills, which may be accomplished by encouraging these teachers to

- Coordinate peer-coaching or professional learning community teams within a school or district
- Develop and deliver district in-service workshops
- Offer input into administrative decisions as site-based team members (Steffy et al., 2000, pp. 120–123)

Unfortunately, little time has been invested in the staff to help them effect positive growth and change for the school or district. School improvement plans often budget money for things rather than growth—then we wonder why change does not take place.

Many districts spend money on additional staff, more equipment, and new programs, and still student achievement does not take place. When we examine these districts, there is always a common thread: little or no staff development. When there is staff development, the approach used usually violates the research on change. An all-day or half-day workshop is conducted and staff are told to "go forth and do." There is seldom a support system in place to fully institutionalize an intervention.

The Curriculum Management Improvement Model recommends following certain criteria when designing staff development endeavors:

1. Is based on policy that directs staff development activities and actions to be aligned to and an integral part of the district strategic and/or long-range plan and its implementation.

2. Fosters a norm of improvement and development of a learning community.

3. Provides for organizational, unit, and individual development in a systemic manner.

4. Is provided for all employees.

5. Expects each principal/supervisor to be a staff developer of those supervised.

6. Is based on a careful analysis of data and is data driven; uses disaggregated student achievement data to determine adult learning priorities; and monitors progress and helps sustain improvement of each person carrying out his or her work.

7. Focuses on research-based approaches that have proven to increase productivity.

8. Provides for the following: initiation, implementation, institutionalization, and renewal.

9. Is based on adult human learning and development theory and directs staff development efforts congruent with system priorities as reflected in the district plan.

10. Uses a variety of staff development approaches.

11. Provides the follow-up and on-the-job application necessary to ensure improvement.

12. Requires an evaluation process that includes multiple sources of information, focuses on all levels of the organization, and is based on actual changed behavior and increased student achievement.

13. Provides for systemwide management oversight of staff development efforts.

14. Is supported with the necessary funding and resources needed to deliver staff development called for in the districtwide strategic and/or long-range plan and is reflected in the system's budget allocations.

When staff development takes place, one of the greatest violations is the lack of recognition that people come to training with different experience, capabilities, and knowledge. It is essential that we provide differentiated training to move people toward the implementation of a new behavior.

STRATEGY 45: WHY

Just as we want teachers to differentiate their instruction in the classrooms so students are receiving learning opportunities at the right level of difficulty, so too must we do this for adult learners. In fact, adult learners are probably less tolerant than young people when we are not at the right level of training. Educators are a very heterogeneous group, and training situations need to take this into consideration.

The most important reason for differentiation is that if we do not address it, we decrease the likelihood of moving our staff toward the change desired. We must understand variation in learners. Often, just giving people a choice of whether to attend a staff development activity increases attendance and attention to the learning. Certainly, we can use the more experienced individuals in the setting to help mentor the others attending the sessions. We ideally should have different professional development opportunities to meet the varying needs of our staff with respect to a new intervention in the system.

There is one caution here. We note frequently that teachers are given a potpourri of fragmented staff development offerings. District officers have often used this approach in an attempt to meet the differing needs of staff, but then in the process they fail to focus on the changes mandated by the district's priorities. First, and foremost, the staff development efforts must be aligned to the district goals for change.

STRATEGY 45: HOW

We want to say "Just do it," but here are a few steps that can help you implement this strategy:

1. Educate all individuals responsible for staff development training in effective adult learning approaches, and address the need to differentiate the training.

2. Align all staff development activities to planned priority goals for change. These activities need to be included in the district and school improvement plans.

3. Differentiate staff development based on teacher career development phase and learning style.

4. Create staff development plans using the CMSi criteria presented earlier in this strategy.

5. Evaluate the effectiveness of staff development activities in addressing the differing needs of the trainees and in changing their behavior.

STRATEGY 46

Link Resource Allocations to Goals, Objectives, Priorities, and Diagnosed Needs of the System

The district and school budgets are built after the planning and illustrate how monies have been distributed to focus on the changes/goals of the district and school plans.

STRATEGY 46: WHAT

As states and provinces have looked for ways to hold school systems accountable for how they use funding, a strong interest and focus on student achievement and results has emerged (McNeil, 2007). How the funds are used has become important for policy and funding decision makers. Most research on the association between school resources and student outcomes has concentrated on finances measured in dollars; however, more recent actions have used "what the money buys" (e.g., smaller classes, better materials and environments, time adequacy, etc.) as relevant measures of a school's instructional quality (Green, 2007). It has not always been that way.

For years, school programs, services, and activities were created, planned, proposed, or terminated because of funding availability or nonavailability. Budget processes preceded and heavily influenced curriculum decisions. Curriculum initiatives often had to be modified, reduced, or reconfigured to fit limited availability of funding. In a way, it was like cutting the pattern to fit the cloth. In that metaphor, the garment may not fit the body (Poston, Stone, & Muther, 1992).

In educational institutions, if the budget drives the curriculum, instead of the other way around, as has been the case (English, 1987), the educational program in all likelihood will not meet the needs of clientele. Educational quality has historically often been compromised in the name of budget cutting, cost reduction, or retrenchment.

Something had to give. If educational leaders persisted at doing what had always been done, the result, which was not in accordance with what communities and nearly all states wanted, would never change. (Almost every state in the United States has prescribed a set of standards, exit competencies, or high-stakes testing in the past 30 years in an attempt to reform public school education. Some governance bodies have even instituted takeovers of underperforming school systems.)

Reform has been thrust on public schools, and the public is demanding three things from schools to gain economic confidence: (1) alignment with resources available, (2) prudence with funds provided, and (3) demonstration of results and value for money spent. This relationship of demands is graphically represented in Figure 6.1 (Pomeranz, 1992).

Prudence: Showing efficiency and setting the financial house in order
Alignment: Living within means, keeping budget within revenue levels
Performance: Tying priorities to results, showing gains in productivity

Figure 6.1   Components of Economic Confidence in Public Educational Institutions

Without economic confidence, public institutions may not be supported financially. In recent decades, school systems have not enjoyed substantial economic confidence from the tax-paying public. Restraints on taxes for schools and demands for improvement in results have created a pattern of precious few discretionary dollars for schools to meet the increasing needs of clientele. To gain economic confidence, schools must live within the money provided by state and local governing authorities, show wise use of those funds (including demonstrations of benefit for given costs), and exemplify educational quality and acceptable results.

Moreover, demands for cost-effectiveness have prompted school systems to modify how resources are allocated. More than 35 years ago, a leading authority pointed out the need for focusing more on results, saying "of all the ways to [evaluate modes and methods of funding], none has attracted more attention than cost–benefit analysis" (Blaug, 1970, p. 62).

The need for public confidence begs greater consideration of cost–benefit analyses, but prevailing budgeting and resource allocation systems, with traditional line-item budgeting processes, are not suitable to meet the demand. Cost–benefit or cost-effectiveness analysis requires organizing line item costs to types of activities. Activities can be evaluated for efficacy, allowing schools to get greater "bang for the buck" in educational resource allocations. In recent history, however, few studies have indicated that cost–benefit or cost-effectiveness analyses are undertaken in relation to program decision making (Hummel-Rossi & Ashdown, 2002).

With schools under such intense financial scrutiny, some changes have had to be made in budgeting processes and allocation operations. Schools have begun looking at what is expected of them and how well they are performing against those expectations, and they have proposed options and actions to address and deliver those expectations and more. Schools have come up with different budgeting processes that are characterized by the following:

Greater public and stakeholder participation in budgeting decisions, including teachers, principals, parents, students, and others.

Better conceptualizations of what program alternatives will produce in measurable results. Gains in achievement have been attached to specific initiative requests for funding. Failure to produce the intended result may mean withdrawal of those funds in future budgeting. Performance has been promised, and it has been monitored.

Program operations, measured results, and educational activities have been designed to connect to budget proposals, with clear definitions of cost and benefit. Options for delivery that may accomplish the objective at less cost have been included.

Assessment feedback balanced against costs has been used to determine whether program options and operations are continued, terminated, or modified.

In school systems, budgeting is changing, and it is placing curriculum and program planning ahead of budget allocations. Allocations then follow the priorities of the system until the resources are exhausted. These new approaches indicate greater gains in productivity if benefits can be increased and costs can be decreased.

STRATEGY 46: WHY

School leaders have a new set of demands facing them from the funding public: The schools must demonstrate what they want, why they want it, and what will happen if they are funded. Also, budget requests have to be made in programmatic increments and whole activities instead of in line items and tabulations of costs. Unless school leadership can recover the economic confidence of the public, the future of public schools may continue to be in jeopardy.

There is another key reason for changing the methods of budgeting, other than for credibility. Curriculum-driven, or performance-based, budgeting also produces greater cost–benefit relationships. When scrutinized by cost and return, program components change and improve to meet the higher standard of efficiency. Greater organizational efficacy results as program managers find different, better, and perhaps even less expensive ways to meet their mission. Moreover, once people see a tangible connection between an educational program increment (or alternative), the program component gains greater likelihood of funded support because of its clarity and definition of characteristics. Line-item proposals, which often read as "percentage" increases, do not provide that type of tangible connection among action, cost, and predicted result.

Researchers have cautioned educators that unless the issue of how money is spent (and how it is used) is resolved, simply allocating more money to education will not necessarily result in increased student achievement or the reduction of inequities and inefficiencies in the delivery of educational services (Hummel-Rossi & Ashdown, 2002).

With diminishing financial resources to meet widening educational needs, school organizations can ill afford to keep trying to operate in business-as-usual fashion. It is critical that purpose, options of delivery, and cost relationships be aggregated by program increments to demonstrate tangible connections between costs and benefits of educational activities. Without documentation of what the program delivers and tools to measure it, the program increment, or piece, would have little to justify its funding.

STRATEGY 46: HOW

Approaches to allocating resources array themselves across several types; however, it is recommended that the description of each program piece includes key attributes, including the following:

- Description of program aims and purposes and defined results
- Information about how the program outcomes will be evaluated
- Clear explication of what is abandoned, or lost, if the program is not funded
- Aggregated cost of all requirements for the program by increment or piece

Ten school-level steps are recommended to link resources to school organizational goals, planning, and results:

1. Create and develop a program list that defines the major activities within the school. At least 15 to 20 programs or activities need to be identified. Examples include kindergarten, art, music, basic instruction (core academic areas), library services, technology services, custodial services, extracurricular activities, staff development, and so on.

2. Aggregate all costs incurred by each program area for the previous year. Include all line items, such as salaries, supplies, benefits, and so on. Do not separate cost items unless they characterize a major activity of the school. The object is to change how people perceive the budget. It should be seen as a collection of program activities, not a long list of line item costs.

3. Assign a manager or coordinator (administrator, employee, patron, or community member) to lead each program area planning team. Invite the community to be involved. It is helpful to bring others in as much as possible, recognizing that more voices produce better information for consideration.

4. Each program area planning team sets it own schedule, with meetings scheduled at convenient times to facilitate parent participation. Each team develops a set of increments for their program. Each increment will represent a portion of the program that may or may not be funded (see Item 7).

5. Set a schoolwide budget planning team meeting schedule. Include two members from each program area planning team—one employee, one citizen (not employed by the school system).

6. Provide reference materials and information to each member of the schoolwide team, including budget history, budget areas by program, and so on.

7. Set increment ranges for each program area budget. It is recommended that each program area budget develop at least one increment that costs less (2%–5%) than the previous year, but only if the program would be able to function at that level (presumably at a lower level of quality). Then include at least two or more increments that, if funded, would add additional services or activities to the program. Each increment proposed needs to be considered an add-on option.

8. Each program area planning team prepares its three or more increment packages. Packages are discrete parts of a greater program that has a base package and two or more add-on packages.

9. Program area teams then submit their list of program packages. The packages are assembled by the school and then rank ordered in order of preference by the schoolwide committee (use nominal group techniques). Once the program packages are all rank ordered (some add-on packages may be a higher priority than the base package of another program) by the committee, it is possible to see where the funds run out and which program packages the school will not be able to fund and will have to abandon.

10. Publish the priority-ranked list of budget requests from highest priority descending to lowest priority, and illustrate (with a drawn line) where the current funding level ends. Disseminate this list, with ranking and cost information, to the community, the school superintendent, and others interested in the quality of education within the school.

11. (Optional) Move toward connecting information about results and effects of program activities as a part of the budget planning activity. Programs that successfully demonstrate increases in productivity or achievement naturally would be more attractive for funding. Using the paucity of resources more intelligently would be the result.

Some program components may be self-evident in terms of results, but tools are needed to measure growth or change as a result of the program component. With that insight, educational leaders can evaluate the effectiveness of school programs, policies and functions, and resource allocation (Olson, 2007).

This budget configuration will make it abundantly clear what the school activities are, what they cost, and how the school is unable to do everything it is asked to do without additional funding. It also shows clearly what may be lost given insufficient funding. Unfunded components would be clearly identified with both aims and expected outcomes, giving better understanding of what results accrue from their abandonment.

For the first time, what is at stake will also be evident—not cost items (supplies, etc.), but program activities for the school's clientele. Seeing what materials may be lost does not resonate effectively with the public—in fact, they may think the items were not needed in the first place. But if an *activity* or *service* is abandoned, then a different perception occurs.

Very often, once the community sees that money falls short of delivering quality educational services desirable for a given school, additional resources are provided. Money is not usually the problem—the will to spend it is often the problem. With the tangible connections clearly made between costs and program activities, better financial support is more likely than in the past.

STRATEGY 47

Provide Qualified and Adequate Personnel

There are qualified and adequate school personnel in each position.

STRATEGY 47: WHAT

The process of education is complex and difficult. Schools are labor-intensive service organizations that succeed or fail depending on the qualifications and competence of teachers, administrators, and support personnel—all of whom impact learning and student achievement. Successful educational enterprises require teachers who are professionals trained in the many skills needed to effectively organize curriculum and deliver it to the students. Moreover, support and administrative personnel need to provide help, assistance, and direction for teachers that are congruent with the mission of the organization and the needs of the teaching staff.

If that were not the case, schools could be staffed with anyone off the street and the schools would produce learning—but we know from experience and research that this is not the case. To say that school personnel can come from anywhere is an insult and a great disservice to the many competent people working in schools today. Substantial disorganization of curriculum, poor teaching, ineffective support, and inept classroom management have been noted in numerous school districts that employ noncertified teachers and inadequately trained administrators.

Furthermore, recent research demonstrates a strong correlation between student achievement and high-quality certification. This means that all school personnel who come into contact with students must be competent in their jobs in order for the school to be successful in producing the desired levels of learning (Berl, 2005).

The teaching force is changing, and the demand for hiring competent replacements is becoming critical. Some characteristics of interest from a national study on this topic include the following (Fiestritzer & Haar, 2005):

- *The public school teaching force in the United States is getting more female and older.* Eight out of 10 public school teachers (82%) are female. The proportion of K–12 teachers who are age 50 and older has risen from 1 in 4 (24%) in 1996 to 42% in 2005.
- *There is a slight shift toward more teachers of color.* The proportion of K–12 teachers who are white has gone from 91% in 1986, to 92% in 1990, to 89% in 1996, to 85% in 2005. The fastest growing group of non-white teachers are persons of Hispanic origin.
- *Teachers favor traditional measures to determine whether a person is qualified to teach.* Nearly 9 out of 10 (89%) teachers agree that "successful completion of a teacher preparation program" and "evaluation by an administrator that includes direct classroom observation" would be good measurements to use in determining teacher qualification.
- *The No. 1 reason teachers teach is because they want to help young people learn and develop.* This has been true in every year National Center for Education Information has asked the question (1990, 1996, and 2005), and it is also true for teachers entering teacher certification through alternate routes.
- *Teachers overwhelmingly rank "one's own teaching experience" highest when asked to rate the value of eight variables in developing competence to teach.* Ninety-one percent of teachers in 2005, compared with 92% in 1996, say their own teaching experience was "very valuable" in developing their competence to teach.
- *When they* began *teaching, only about one fourth to one third of teachers felt very competent in all eight of the areas of teaching surveyed:* ability to teach subject matter (36%), ability to motivate students (34%), dealing with fellow teachers (34%), organizing instruction (30%), managing time (26%), dealing

with the administrative hierarchy (26%), classroom management (25%), and classroom discipline (24%).

- *Teacher attrition is expected to average about 8% per year in the next 5 years, and half of current high school teachers expect to not be teaching in 5 years.* Forty percent of current public school teachers expect to not be teaching in K–12 schools 5 years from now. One third (34%) of high school teachers expect to be retired.

Given this backdrop of a "graying" teacher cadre, employing top-notch replacement personnel is essential. The challenge is whom to hire and how to do it. School governing bodies and administrators must develop and implement appropriate hiring practices to ensure that teacher attrition can be met and handled effectively. It is important to attract and keep quality teachers: One study in Texas showed that teacher attrition costs school systems at least $8,000 for each recruit who leaves in the first few years of teaching (Texas Center for Educational Research, 2000).

Decisions about whom to hire may sometimes be driven by idiosyncratic or political forces that need to be disregarded. One study found that very few hiring decisions are based on an authentic demonstration of a candidate's teaching ability (Liu, 2003). Surprisingly, another study found that principals and teachers (and sometimes, students and parents) often devise their own criteria, activities, and interview questions for evaluating candidates (Wise, Darling-Hammond, & Berry, 1987).

Better information and perspectives are essential in seeking and hiring qualified teachers, and it is crucial that school-based personnel know and know how to use effective hiring practices. Hiring the best qualified personnel objectively requires a strong vision and focus on what genuinely constitute competent and effective new hires. The necessity for this focus is supported by research. One factor is individual teacher responsibility: Teachers who take personal responsibility for student learning improve student achievement.

Specifically, children with teachers who have a greater sense of responsibility for student outcomes learn more in reading during the first grade (LoGerfo, 2006). Unfortunately, the findings presented in that same study also suggested that the teachers of economically disadvantaged students are less likely to take responsibility for student outcomes.

Factors that affect the quality of teachers are wide and varied. One study, conducted by Stanford University professor Linda Darling-Hammond (2002), concluded that the best predictor of student performance on national tests was the percentage of high-quality teachers they had—teachers who had majored in the subjects they taught and *were properly certified*. Darling-Hammond also reported that content knowledge, in combination with content pedagogical knowledge—that is, knowledge about how to teach the content, which, together with student teaching, constitute the major components of certification—appear to make contributions to student learning that exceed the contributions of either component individually. An important policy point from this and other studies of certification is the fact that teachers would not have been guided or encouraged to acquire the content knowledge and content pedagogical knowledge represented by in-field certification unless there were certification requirements.

What factors predict successful teaching? Research on teaching suggests a view of expertise that includes general knowledge and ability, verbal ability, and subject matter knowledge as foundations; abilities to plan, organize, and implement complex tasks as additional factors; knowledge of teaching, learning, and children as critical for translating ideas into useful learning experiences; and experience as a basis for aggregating and applying knowledge in nonroutine situations (Darling-Hammond, 2000).

Teaching experience matters, too. David Berliner's (1986) studies of expertise in teaching, for example, include experience along with several other traits as a critical aspect of expertise.

The stakes are high: Students who spend even 1 year with a bad teacher can score more than a grade level lower than students who had a good teacher, according to a University of Rochester study (Elizabeth, 2003).

Certification and *competence* are not synonymous. There are schools where the academic learning time is very low—where students are not engaged in the lesson. There are classrooms where no lesson is discernible. There are schools where many teachers are not engaged with the students; instead, they are out of the classroom, working at their desks, or reading a newspaper, but they are not working with the students. What is significant is that these are not a few isolated cases; in some schools, they are the majority (Frase, 2000).

Some authors have suggested that 5% to 20% of the teaching force is incompetent. We do not know if these figures are accurate, but even the most conservative estimate is too high and would produce disastrous results. Fully qualified and high-performing teachers and administrators are required for each position in every school. Anything less is unacceptable—education is jeopardized, and students suffer.

STRATEGY 47: WHY

Successful organizations, whether business, education, or athletic, employ highly competent people. A school is no different. A competent principal is needed to ensure that the curriculum is well designed, that the taught curriculum matches the written and tested curriculum (see Strategies 1 and 29), that the environment is safe (see Strategies 49 and 50), that instruction is effective, and that teachers have the resources needed to run effective classrooms. When any of these is not done well, student learning is negatively affected.

Mature teachers are colleagues over age 45 who possess significant experience in the field, but trends in teacher turnover place additional burdens on schools as costs associated with hiring and training continue to escalate. More important, the consequences of losing the knowledge and skills of mature employees may seriously impact school organizations' capabilities to achieve their mission or to maintain a competitive advantage in the educational marketplace.

Given this phenomenon, it is important for administrators to appreciate personnel experience; to encourage collegial transfer of knowledge and skills in the organization; and to value the personnel's knowledge of organizational history, culture, and change among mature employees (Berl, 2005).

"Good teachers matter and they matter a lot," said Thomas Carroll, executive director of the National Commission on Teaching and America's Future; "If students are in a school where they consistently receive quality teaching year to year and class to class, they have a significant advantage" (quoted in Lee, 2003).

Everyone who works in a successful school plays a vital role. Custodians keep the school facility clean and warm (see Strategy 50), teacher assistants contribute to the delivery of the curriculum, principals provide management and leadership services, and teachers provide the most important organizational function: They teach in a way that facilitates effective pupil learning and achievement. Competent people need to occupy all positions. Unfortunately, competence is not always the rule, even though staff may possess proper certification.

We cannot say this enough: Teachers provide the most important function—they teach. High-quality instruction is the cornerstone of any effective school, and it separates ineffective and marginal schools from effective schools. Without effective teaching, student learning is seriously at risk. The bottom line is that all school personnel need to be competent and perform up to par before a school can be effective. The board of education, through its line administration, must ensure that all employees are qualified and performing adequately.

STRATEGY 47: HOW

To begin, astute administrators need to know exactly what constitutes quality teacher performance in classrooms. Some of the key factors to look for in potential candidates include the following:

1. **Advanced degrees.** About half of all U.S. teachers hold a master's degree. Studies have shown that having a master's degree modestly improved student achievement up through Grade 7, but not in high school (Ferguson, 1991). However, the type of master's degree may make a difference, because recent studies of high school math teachers with a master's degree in mathematics performed slightly better than teachers without a master's degree.

2. **Teaching experience.** The preponderance of research has found that the benefits of experience are realized after only a couple of years in the classroom (Rivkin & Hanushek, 2003). However, a well-designed recent study found that teacher effectiveness continues to improve for closer to 4 or 5 years (Rockoff, 2004).

3. **Type of degree.** It is important to rely on the findings of more than one study and to not assume that what is true for one group of teachers is equally true for another. One study found that students did better on a math test if their teachers had taken courses in math education as opposed to courses in pure

mathematics. On the other hand, the same study found the reverse was true in science: Teachers who took pure physical science courses as opposed to science education courses were more effective (Monk, 1994).

4. **Certification.** Reviews of studies indicate that certification requirements contribute to higher student achievement (Darling-Hammond, 2002). However, few studies have compared traditionally certified teachers with alternatively certified teachers; one such study found that teachers who were all part of the same alternative certification program were just as effective as an equal number of teachers who were all traditionally trained and certified (J. Miller, McKenna, & McKenna, 1998).

5. **Teacher race.** Studies are contradictory on this attribute, and caution would be advised in its consideration. One study that used longitudinal data of 8th-, 9th-, and 10th-graders across the United States found no effect of the teacher's race on scores for white, blacks, or Hispanics (Ehrenberg, Goldhaber, & Brewer, 1994). Another study found that both black and white elementary students in Tennessee benefited significantly from being assigned a teacher of their own race (Dee, 2004).

6. **Teacher coursework.** There may be a limit to the benefit to be gained from coursework. One study found that the positive impact achieved from taking courses did not increase after four and six college-level courses were taken (Monk, 1994); however, strong preparation in mathematics and science makes high school teachers more effective (Chaney, 1995). On the other hand, there is a dearth of research on the kind or amount of subject matter preparation for elementary teachers: only one published study, which showed no relationship between elementary teachers' recent coursework (within 3 years) in mathematics and student achievement (Eberts & Stone, 1984).

7. **Teacher literacy.** This factor seems to be a very important contributor to teacher efficacy. Studies have repeatedly concluded that teachers who are more literate are more likely to produce greater student learning gains. For example, teacher literacy (measured by standardized vocabulary tests) increases student achievement more than any other measurable teacher attribute (Wayne & Youngs, 2003). Other study findings indicate that a teacher's level of literacy is a strong predictor of student achievement. One such study found that teachers who are highly literate improved student achievement 0.2 to 0.4 grade levels more than teachers who were the least literate (Rivkin & Hanushek, 2003). This was confirmed in a recent finding that indicates that teachers certified by the National Board of Professional Teaching Standards produce relatively higher student achievement gains (Goldhaber & Anthony, 2004).

8. **Personal attributes.** There are intangible attributes of teacher candidates that may have greater weight than the forgoing quantitative factors in terms of predicting teacher performance in producing student achievement gains. *Teach for America's* recruitment process focused on identifying teachers who possess

the attributes most likely to lead to higher student learning gains (Gitomer, Latham, & Ziomeck, 1999). The personal attributes common to teachers who produced the greatest student learning gains included the following:

a. High achieving: The individual has a history of success no matter what the endeavor.

b. Responsible: Instead of blaming others or circumstances, the individual takes full responsibility for achieving a positive outcome.

c. Critical thinker: The individual reflects about the linkages between cause and effect instead of simply reacting to the effect.

d. Organized: The individual is able to juggle multiple projects and tasks successfully.

e. Motivating: The individual is able to influence and motivate others to action, as evidenced by effective leadership in extracurricular activities, such as student-run organizations or athletic teams.

f. Respectful: The individual assumes the best about people, especially people in low-income communities.

g. Shares the goals of the organization: The individual wants to work toward eliminating educational inequities.

Despite a number of tools, measures, and data sets, perhaps the best factors of use in hiring qualified teachers are the intangible personal qualities. With care, a critical eye, and cautious subjective judgments, educational leaders may have to look at factors incumbent in candidates on a personal level.

Strategic Implementation

Administrators and others serious about forming an effective process for selecting highly qualified teaching personnel might try the following ideas for implementing this strategy:

1. Check system policies for personnel hiring requirements.
   a. Is the employment of only certified teachers and administrators required? If not, this topic must be addressed to the board.
   b. Does the policy require that only the most qualified candidates be hired for each position? Bold and successful districts announce that they want only the "best and the brightest" teachers and administrators.
   c. How does your district stack up?

2. Check your district's criteria for making hiring decisions. Do they include the following?
   a. For teachers:
      - Observation of actual teaching?
      - Well-designed interviews?
      - Problem-solving exercises regarding instruction and classroom management?
      - Consideration of academic and professional preparation curriculums and academic records on both?

- Compliance with state laws regarding employment and appropriate checks for criminal records?
- Hiring of only the best and brightest teachers?

These are some of the factors that must be considered. Some, like academic records, may seem strange, but they are not, because a growing research base is demonstrating that teachers' academic performance is strongly correlated to teaching quality and student achievement.

  b. For principals and principal supervisors:
  - Thorough and well-designed interviews by representatives from all affected employee groups and senior administration?
  - Observation of a teaching sample, analysis of it, and reflective counseling with the teacher?
  - Assessment of interrater reliability of the candidate's assessment of the teaching sample and predetermined ratings?
  - Assessment of curriculum design and delivery philosophy and knowledge?
  - Thorough interviews with previous employers?
  - Compliance with state laws regarding employment and appropriate checks for criminal records?

No hiring system can ensure that only competent people are hired or that those who are competent will perform up to par. In cases where an employee is performing at a marginal level or is incompetent, other action is needed. We address this topic in Strategy 48.

STRATEGY 48

Remove Incompetent Staff or Help Them Achieve Satisfactory Functioning

Marginal staff are coached and assisted to satisfactory performance or contracts are not renewed.

STRATEGY 48: WHAT

As stated in Strategy 39, appraisal systems should focus on professional growth for all school personnel. Nearly all employees are capable of achieving satisfactory performance, given professional growth opportunities, a will to succeed, and a commitment to the ethics and standards of the organization. Without that effort, some personnel will be ill suited for successfully working in the classroom endeavor. Action may be required.

The education profession seems to avoid dealing with mediocrity, in the opinion of some researchers (e.g., Dawson & Billingsley, 2000). In large measure, this is due to excellent teachers not being rewarded for their work and incompetent teachers rarely being held accountable for performance. However, there are times when employees' skills or attitudes are less than what is required, and responsibility for one's performance must be accepted.

The conduct of teaching has a large impact on students' ability to educate themselves (Joyce, Weil, & Showers, 1992, p. 1). Moreover, studies often link teacher quality directly with student learning (Corcoran & Goertz, 1995). Stakes are high, and teachers need support, instruction, and professional growth opportunities to demonstrate success. Without success, teachers' employment needs to be terminated, either voluntarily or involuntarily.

In such cases, the system and the school have a moral, ethical, and economic responsibility to provide honest and straightforward information to the employee regarding the deficiencies and specifically what resources it will make available to the employee for his or her use in improving his or her skill to fully competent levels. The resources should include training (specifically targeted to the areas of deficiency) and coaching by the principal and expert teachers. The coaching should initially be reflective in nature, but when improvement is not observed the coaching needs to be much more direct to ensure that the employee understands his or her status and the role of the coaching and resource assistance.

The scope of teacher competence was identified in a Virginia study (Tucker, 1997). Of 200 principals surveyed, the study results were as follows:

- The mean number of teachers reported by principals as being incompetent was 1.83. Compared with the average full-time equivalents for the respondents, this number reflected an incompetence rate of 5%.
- The mean percentage of tenured teachers who were identified formally as incompetent by principals in a 1-year period was 1.53%.
- The mean percentage of tenured teachers in 1 year who were identified formally as incompetent *and*
  - remediated by principals was 0.7%,
  - reassigned by principals was 0.3%,
  - encouraged to resign or retire by principals was 0.4%, and
  - recommended for dismissal by principals was 0.1%.

So much for the Lake Wobegon effect, where everyone is competent. It is important to remember that it is the employee's responsibility to attain competency. One cannot make other people improve, but one can provide resource assistance designed specifically to help them ameliorate their deficiencies. Once provided, use of the resources and improvement of skills are the work of the employee. This is why districts are continually advised not to say or write that they will help the employee improve or attain competency. Once this is said, the responsibility is off the employee and on the person making this statement. The promise implicit in the statement might never be fulfilled.

STRATEGY 48: WHY

It is unfortunate that a small minority of teachers do not, or are unable to, perform their professional duties at an acceptable level because of a variety of reasons, including a lack of motivation, burnout, and personal crises (Henderson-Sparks, 1995).

Incompetence in any position in education cannot be tolerated. The employee evaluation process and other observations of work should detect incompetence. When an employee is deemed incompetent, it is the school board's (district level) responsibility to provide resource assistance that he or she can use to ameliorate the deficiencies.

If, after a predetermined time, and provision of resource assistance, the employee does not demonstrate adequate improvement, then he or she should be dismissed. Each state and many employee contracts provide processes for this action for each employee group, for example, tenured and nontenured teachers, administrators, and classified employees. The process is never easy, and it is often unduly complicated.

The most disturbing finding of another Virginia study was the lack of any relationship between evaluation system components and the incidence of administrative response to incompetence (Staples, 1991). Principals' reluctance to address incompetence is a failure in administration responsibility. Unfortunately, detrimental evaluation results and a poor showing in the classroom do not predict administrative action (Staples, 1991). Deciding how to go about changing this perspective and preventing inaction is challenging, to say the least. Perhaps, with the emphasis on demonstrated achievement growth required in national legislation, principals may also be held accountable for results in student learning.

Taking a proactive stance with a teacher who is not performing satisfactorily requires "courage, honesty, knowledge, and hard work" by the principal (Staples, 1991). Some people will say that dismissal is cold and hard hearted, but there is little question that it is the right thing to do. Schools were never intended as halfway houses or havens for incompetent principals, teachers, or custodians. Schools have always had the responsibility of educating young people, and they cannot do that well with incompetent personnel. School boards, through the line administrative structure, must ensure that the schools are staffed with only highly competent personnel. To do otherwise endangers student learning, the product of our schools, and further lowers the school's esteem in the eyes of the public.

STRATEGY 48: HOW

Do the following to assess your district or school in relation to Strategy 48:

1. Check your board policy and employee appraisal system manuals. Do they clearly state that each employee's contribution to the education process is highly valued and that the district actively works to hire and retain only highly competent employees in all position?

2. Check your personnel evaluation systems:
   - Are they based on research-driven criteria of quality performance? We recommend 20 to 40 hours of training each year.
   - Are they developed to distinguish between competence and incompetence?
   - Is the process focused on professional development?

3. Check your training programs for employee evaluators. Have evaluators been adequately trained to reach high interrater reliability levels? Specifically, do they
   - Know what to look for in teaching and in the classroom?
   - Adequately assess and analyze teaching?
   - Reflect empirically supported instructional practices?
   - Know how to and actually follow through when deficiencies are noted?
   - Know coaching theory and demonstrate high-quality coaching practices?
   - Demonstrate competence in working with teachers (or other employees) to develop performance growth plans?
   - Monitor professional growth plans?
   - Demonstrate competence in operating in accordance with state, board policy, and due process imposed by employee contracts?

4. Check your professional growth plan requirements and practices:
   - Are they designed to bring about improved classroom instruction?
   - Do they require that the plan be based on observed findings?
   - Do they require monitoring by the supervisor?
   - Do they allow for reasonable resource assistance from the district?

We suggest that school personnel analyze the answers to these questions and take action as needed.

Another test to determine whether a district is accurately evaluating employee performance is to select a 10% random sample of results of evaluations for all employee groups for the past 3 years. What percentage was rated in each possible category for each employee group? In curriculum audits, auditors have found that more than 99% of all teachers and administrators in a random sample from thousands were assigned ratings ranging from "adequate" to "excellent." This is great news! What could be better? Obviously, the evaluations are heavily skewed to mediocrity and broadly accepted performance, regardless of quality. This is not actually the case—if it were, public education would be thriving, and student achievement would be forever increasing. Unfortunately, teaching competence is seldom held to a high standard. The issue is most likely that principals lack sufficient resolve and competence to evaluate teachers properly (Wise, Darling-Hammond, McLaughlin, & Bernstein, 1984).

Principals need to determine what percentage of employees is assigned each rating in their school. If the large majority is assigned a rating of "adequate" or higher, the ratings are suspect; the evaluators may be denying employees valuable feedback about their performance level.

The second step of the test is to analyze professional growth plans. Take a small random sample. Do professional growth plans target the employees' primary functions? In analyzing hundreds of teachers' professional growth plans, auditors found that the majority of them contained no targets or activities for growth of any kind, let alone targets that pertained to their primary function, teaching (see Strategies 39 and 40). Principals and other supervisors have an obligation to ensure that all employees have growth plans.

STRATEGY 49

Provide a Quality Learning Environment

There is a safe and productive learning environment for all students.

STRATEGY 49: WHAT

A safe and productive learning environment is a hallmark of effective schools. A *safe learning environment* is characterized as one in which students attend school without fear of harm from internal or external forces. Students know that they are expected to learn and achieve high expectations, but they do not have to fear punishment should they stumble. They know that their school is a safe place for learning and exploration.

A *productive learning environment* demonstrates a strong relationship between school environment and learning. The physical environment is important in student learning activities, and the school must possess several characteristics (Kleberg, 1992):

1. A suitable building design should facilitate constructive student activity.
   a. Classroom design should be flexible and stimulating and create a positive learning environment.
   b. Architecture influences the learning environment, including inside and outside space, corridors, and interior design.

2. Sufficient quality of maintenance and care of grounds reflect an institution's outlook on learning.

3. Learning spaces need to be considered in designing learning spaces.
   a. Nearly all learning involves use of the built environment.
   b. The built environment needs to be a teaching element.
      i. The space needs both unity and diversity and adaptability.
      ii. Exterior spaces, discipline-specific learning space, unique structures, informal learning space, individual study and meditation space, and school and learning discipline heritage, all need to be reflected in the design.

   c. New structures need to be built if existing ones cannot be maintained properly.

4. The psychological environment (the social quality of the school and classroom) reflects perceptions and feelings about social relationships among students and teachers. The terms *classroom psychological environment*, *classroom atmosphere*, *classroom social climate*, *classroom social interactions*, and *classroom social relationship* are often used interchangeably when scholars discuss the classroom learning environment. Classroom social environment may affect students' learning attitudes and behavior before it influences their academic achievement. Therefore, it may be more appropriate to use affective performance measures such as self-concept and different attitudinal measures, instead of academic achievement, as indicators in studying the direct relationship between classroom environment and students' educational performance. (Cheng, 1994, p. 221)

Learning is targeted as the No. 1 goal in a productive learning environment. It is announced on classroom bulletin boards, policies, and newsletters.* The factors reflected in the standards described in this book are needed to ensure a highly productive classroom learning environment. When students are actively engaged in their classrooms, mastery of content and cognitive development are highest (Pascarella, 1985).

STRATEGY 49: WHY

A safe learning environment is needed to free teachers and students from fears of harm and thereby allow them to focus on teaching and learning. As stated in Strategy 46, education is a complex process and learning is no less so. Of course, it is possible to learn in the presence of harm—we have all heard of such cases— but our students deserve to learn in safe environments unfettered by such concern. The first priority would be to provide a safe environment for students, with an aim to reflect the following characteristics (Dwyer, Osher, & Warger, 1998):

1. Full and adequate protection from discrimination of all types, so students may not suffer harassment or even physical harm.
   a. Treatment of students with equal respect without bias and unfair treatment of students because of ethnicity, gender, race, social class, religion, disability, nationality, sexual orientation, physical appearance, or some other factor both by staff and by peers.

---

* All 50 strategies listed in this book contribute to a productive learning environment in which the written curriculum is high quality; the written, taught, and tested curriculums are aligned; instruction is high quality and academic learning time is high; teachers are actively involved with students; and administrators are frequently present in classrooms and ensure that teachers have the proper tools and resources for maintaining high-quality education.

2. Emphasis on positive relationships among students and staff.
   a. Research shows that a characteristic of a safe school is a positive relationship with an adult who is available to provide support when needed.
   b. Implement an ambience of positive student interpersonal relations, encouraging students to help each other and to feel comfortable assisting others.

3. Open discussions about safety issues.
   a. Children come to school with many different perceptions and misconceptions about death, violence, and the use of weapons.
   b. Schools can reduce the risk of violence by teaching children about the dangers of firearms, as well as appropriate strategies for dealing with feelings and resolving conflicts.

4. Communications to students and the greater community that all children are valued and respected.
   a. Deliberate and systematic efforts to posting children's artwork and academic work.

5. Procedures for students to share their concerns.
   a. Help for children to feel safe expressing their feelings, needs, fears, and anxieties to school staff.

6. Have a system in place for referring children who are suspected of being abused or neglected, reflecting federal and state guidelines.

7. Promotion of good citizenship and character in addition to academic mission.

8. Identification of problems and assessment of progress toward solutions.
   a. Open and objective examination of circumstances that are potentially dangerous for students and staff and situations in which members of the school community feel threatened or intimidated.

9. Provide more efficient and effective services to students who need more support.
   a. Learn the early warning signs of a child who is troubled, so that effective interventions may be implemented.

A safe school is a top priority for any governing body, school administrator, or school community. A sound and appropriate climate for learning is also needed. The environment is a learning resource, beginning with the locality in which children live. Environments that offer diversity and variety are likely to be stimulating and exciting places in which to live and learn (Hammonds, 2007).

Learning activities need to incorporate children's interest in the environment and world about them. A program based on children's authentic experiences might include the following:

- A sensitivity to their immediate locality and, by this understanding, strengthen children's own sense of identity.

- Extension of areas of interest where children can gain positive growth in their self-image.
- Keeping the world around children an important element in their schooling.
- Providing authentic experience to develop the inquiry skills of learning.
- Providing many opportunities for teacher–pupil sharing.

It is the teacher's role to reveal the unknown in the familiar and to help children discover the unnoticed wealth within their environment. Most school grounds and the areas adjacent offer opportunities for the development of science and social studies skills as well as aspects of mathematics through the communication skills of language, arts and crafts, mime, movement, and song. The experiences and interests of children cover a wide field, from fact to fantasy. Most communities offer houses, bridges, streets, farms, streams, hills, valleys, swamps, ponds, weeds, animals, vehicles, wildlife, and more. School is a base from which children explore their environment.

In addition to awareness and understanding of the environs, schools need to provide other elements supportive of student learning within the school, including the following:

1. Time to think
   a. Children need to deepen their knowledge and understanding as well as be encouraged to slow their pace of work, to observe more carefully, to think about what they feel, to talk things out, and to define their problems.

2. Use of the environment as a resource. Opportunities need to be provided that allow children to
   a. Explore, research, and extend their knowledge;
   b. Develop an interest in patterns, textures, shapes, smells; and
   c. Look for forms of ideas for expressive activities.

Children need encouragement to combine these and many other ways of interpreting what they see. Most important, asking questions, establishing problems to be solved, and collecting information should be part of all learner interactions with the environment.

STRATEGY 49: HOW

We suggest the following for assessing and improving the safety aspect of schools:

1. First, is a safe learning environment a district and school priority? If it is not stated as such in policy and regulations and announced publicly, then appropriate action needs to be taken.

2. Assess the staff. Do all understand that students deserve an environment that is safe from unreasonable punishment and ensure the same?

3. Are students free from threats of abuse from other students or adults on or off campus? Is there a policy regarding this, and is it followed?

4. Are appropriate measures in place to prevent people who do not belong in the school or on the school grounds from being present?

5. Are all staff aware of, and do they follow, requirements for reporting possible student abuse to Child Protective Services personnel?

6. Is an effective and efficient communication and cooperation system in place with the local police and other authorities?

7. Are classrooms emulating appropriate environmental conditions? See checklist at the end of this section ("Classroom Environment Assessment Scale," 2007).

For the educational community, the learning environment is not only a resource; it also can be a support system for learners. Creating a quality learning environment requires a focus on how to optimize all factors effectively. Key points to remember include the following (Lemke & Coughlin, 1998):

- Learning contexts require and enable students to use contemporary tools to research issues, solve problems, and communicate results, both individually and in teams.
- Learning content (standards, curriculum, instruction, and assessment) reflects the knowledge-based, global society of today; educational practices mirror societal changes.
- School culture encourages, enables, and rewards educators individually and collectively to improve the learning and teaching processes.
- Productivity tools are provided with sufficient access to services, materials, and data in settings that enrich and extend learners' achievement.
- Learning environment includes the effective use of information and communication technology, which is modeled for and by students.

It is also very important to remember that to further create a productive learning environment, the "How" sections of the other 49 strategies in this book can be a valuable resource as well.

Classroom Environmental Check List (Check all that apply):

☐   Physical arrangement is conducive to learning and involvement.

☐   Arrangements and practices are conducive to student interaction.

☐   Accommodations for cultural communities are evident.

(Continued)

(Continued)

Classroom Environmental Check List (Check all that apply):

☐   Learning areas include written self-directing activities.

☐   Self-monitoring systems use reading and writing.

☐   Areas for reading and writing are available and frequently used.

☐   Materials such as paper, pencils, and scissors are easily accessible to students.

☐   Bulletin board displays are colorful and interesting.

☐   Bulletin boards display *all* students' work (without humiliating assessments).

☐   Print accompanies displays, objects, pictures, and so on.

☐   Labels and directions are used in the classroom.

☐   Books for students are displayed with covers visible.

☐   A variety of books is available; fiction and nonfiction are included.

☐   Multicultural books and materials are visible.

☐   Technology equipment is in the classroom and is used frequently.

☐   Students use technology equipment as a part of their work.

STRATEGY 50

Provide Quality Facilities

Facilities are adequate and promote creative and innovative approaches to learning.

STRATEGY 50: WHAT

School facilities play a major role in the effective delivery of curriculum. They provide a home where teachers create nurturing, productive, and creative learning environments and where students can explore education and learn to the best of their abilities.

Facilities that allow for this are physically safe and clean, classrooms are adequate in number to accommodate proper class sizes, the atmospheric climate is properly controlled, lighting is adequate, all mechanisms for people with disabilities are in place (e.g., wheelchair ramps, automatic door openers, etc.), trash receptacles are plentiful, and toilet areas are clean and exist in proper numbers for both sexes.

Because the total number of students in most school districts fluctuates, enrollment projections are needed to inform long-range planning for facility construction, expansion, and consolidation. Long-range planning allows the district to ensure high-quality and cost-effective learning facilities for the students.

Public school buildings can be designed, constructed or renovated, operated, and maintained using the concepts of "high-performance schools." These concepts focus on improved educational environments for learning, both in the building and on the site, and the impact of school buildings on the environment. The main components of high performance school buildings include the following: acoustic comfort; day lighting; energy analysis; energy efficiency; environmentally preferable materials and products; environmentally responsive site planning; high-performance heating, ventilation, and air conditioning; high-performance electrical lighting; life cycle cost analysis; renewable energy; safety and security; site selection; superior indoor air quality; thermal comfort; visual comfort; and water efficiency.

In addition to environmental benefits, high-performance schools can provide additional benefits that include better student performance, increased average daily attendance, increased teacher satisfaction and retention, reduced operating costs, reduced liability exposure, increased opportunities to utilize the school building itself as a teaching tool, and educating students about the importance of caring for the environment (Building Educational Success Together, 2006).

STRATEGY 50: WHY

America's schools are among the most unequal in the industrialized world in terms of both inputs and outcomes. Inequalities in spending, class sizes, textbooks, computers, facilities, curriculum offerings, and access to qualified teachers contribute to disparate achievement by race and class, which increasingly feeds the "school-to-prison pipeline"—a function of many young people's lack of adequate skills for joining the labor market. This creates an enormous drain on national resources, which in turn reduces the capacity to invest in education, social services, and employment (Darling-Hammond, 2006).

The need for adequate facilities in schools is not new to any of us. The maintenance of a proper and clean environment in our homes is important to the health and well-being of our families, and the same is true for our schools. The school is a home away from home for students; it is the place of their formal education. As noted earlier, astounding differences in student attitudes toward education have been observed when schools are clean and inviting and when they are not. Students and teachers in clean, healthy, and safe schools tend to be more enthusiastic, happier, robust, and better focused on learning than in schools that are unkempt and where danger is present.

In some schools, classes have been conducted in hallways full of noise and visual distractions, and the traffic areas were so cluttered that it was nearly impossible to move about without walking on trash and spilled food or hitting a bottle. Other schools have had bathrooms that were so filthy that students refused to enter them. Such extreme cases call attention to the need for facilities that support teaching and learning adequately and effectively. Cleaning them up may be a challenge (Enderle, 2004).

Factors of facility design or operation that make a difference in student learning have been identified as the result of studies, and selected factors include the following:

1. *Lighting.* In recent years, scores of educators and designers have been won over to the view that natural light—provided by the sun instead of bulbs or tubes—is desirable and beneficial for education facilities. Studies indicating that students perform better in classrooms that have the right kinds of daylight bear out the intuitive beliefs of many teachers that a classroom with natural light is a more appealing learning climate (Kennedy, 2006a).

2. *Sound.* Classrooms often get the short shrift when it comes to designing a space that allows for optimum hearing conditions for students and speaking conditions for teachers. Over the last few years, increasing concern from state regulators and facility designers has focused greater attention on improving acoustics. The main acoustical issues to consider are low background (heating, ventilation, air conditioning) sound, controlled room reverberation, and isolation from sounds in adjacent rooms and other exterior noise. Several studies suggest that when classrooms have a better balance of lower background sound and good distribution of a teacher's voice, test scores rise significantly (McKeon & Berry, 2007).

3. *Furniture.* Educators and school designers place a high priority on creating facilities that enhance learning. That applies not only to how a school is built but also to the materials and equipment used. Just as acoustical treatments or well-placed windows and skylights can make a classroom more conducive to learning, so too can the right furniture. Desks, tables, and chairs that improve the educational environment can help students maintain the focus they need to succeed at school, yet in many schools the desks and chairs in a classroom do not match the students who use them. The resulting discomfort and fatigue can prevent students from concentrating on their

work and, over time, can lead to eyestrain or injuries to legs, wrists, and necks. Schools and universities should factor in ergonomics when furnishing classrooms to keep students comfortable and focused (Kennedy, 2006b).

4. *Physical environment.* Students' attitudes toward school and teachers appeared to be most sensitive to variations in the classroom environment, and the physical environment of the school and classroom—facilities, spaces, lighting, ventilation, desks and chairs, and air pollution—affect the safety and comfort of students and thereby affect learning and personal development (Cheng, 1994).

5. *Management practices.* As accountability in schools becomes more crucial, educators are looking for comprehensive and innovative management practices that respond to challenges and realities of student academic achievement. To improve academic performance and the quality of instruction, school leaders need to create safe, clean, and secure school facilities and create visibility through facility management. School administrators need to focus on facilities and the resultant effect on school performance and learning (Ward & Burke, 2004).

STRATEGY 50: HOW

Consider these guidelines for diagnosing your school environment as a place for creative and innovative teaching and learning. Tour your school with a teacher, a parent, and a student. Ask all to complete this brief checklist:

1. *Classrooms:* There are enough classrooms to accommodate proper class sizes and grade configurations.

2. *Structure:* The structure of a school building (columns, beams, structural walls, floors, and roof structure) shows stability and serviceability.

3. *Space:* Hallways and student activity areas are adequate in size and traffic accommodation.

4. *Furniture:* Classroom furniture is flexible, sturdy, and functional and matches the ergonomic (physical comfort) needs of students.

5. *Trash receptacles:* There is one at the end of each hallway, in each classroom, and in every other room in the school. If people must dispose of their trash properly, they must have a proper place to put it.

6. *Toilet facilities:* They exist in proper numbers in each area of the campus and in the proper ratios for each sex.

7. *Toilet areas:* They are clean, and hand towels and soap are present. Hot water is available in all washroom areas.

8. *Heating and ventilation:* The proper temperature is maintained in all classrooms. Air quality is without bothersome airborne agents or offensive odor.

9. *General cleanliness:* The classroom and other rooms are swept clean each day. Chalk- and whiteboards are cleaned each day. Supplies and equipment are properly stored.

10. *Lighting:* Lighting is adequate for reading and the conduct of normal classroom activities.

11. *Theater/gymnasium areas:* They are adequate in size for use by all students and adequately furnished to accommodate all necessary school functions.

12. *Electrical systems:* Electrical service and wiring are in good condition and serviceable.

13. *Grounds:* Sidewalks, fields, lawns, parking areas, and other exterior elements are in good condition and well cared for.

14. *Roof:* The roof adequately protects the school building from rain, sun, and wind.

15. *General physical condition:* The building is in reasonable condition, with integrity of systems, including roof, flooring, walls, ceilings, and other areas of the structure.

16. *Safety:* The school is safe from intrusion, disruption, or hostile situations (see School Safety Checklist from Oklahoma State Department of Public Instruction, http://sde.state.ok.us/publ/publ_pdf/SafeSchlGuide.pdf, for specific criteria).

On the basis of the findings, develop and implement a plan for correcting any deficiencies. Check with your central office, if necessary, to determine whether enrollment projections are being completed and if plans are in place to ensure proper accommodation of students as enrollment fluctuates.

Studies have shown that school facilities affect learning. Spatial configurations, noise, heat, cold, light, and air quality obviously bear on students' and teachers' ability to perform (Schneider, 2002). Without clean air; good light; and a quiet, comfortable, and safe learning environment, schools will be suboptimized. The appropriate environment can be achieved with adequate funding, competent design, appropriate construction, and rigorous maintenance.

ANALYSIS OF STANDARD SIX

Now it is time for you to evaluate the status of your school or school district on *Standard Six: Institute Effective District and School Planning, Staff Development, and Resource Allocation, and Provide a Quality Learning Environment.* For each strategy, think about what the current status of your situation is, and the changes you feel are needed. Write your responses in the spaces provided.

Strategy	Current status	Changes needed
40. Develop a district planning process that is strategic in nature and provides guidance for the development of district and school long-range plans.	❐ Adequate ❐ Not adequate	
41. Create and implement a singular, focused multiyear district plan that incorporates change strategies for higher student achievement.	❐ Adequate ❐ Not adequate	
42. Align school plans with the district plan.	❐ Adequate ❐ Not adequate	
43. Implement aligned teacher training to reach district and school goals.	❐ Adequate ❐ Not adequate	
44. Implement administrative training aligned with the curriculum and its assessment and district plan priorities.	❐ Adequate ❐ Not adequate	
45. Provide differentiated staff development.	❐ Adequate ❐ Not adequate	
46. Link resource allocations to goals, objectives, priorities, and diagnosed needs of the system.	❐ Adequate ❐ Not adequate	
47. Provide qualified and adequate personnel.	❐ Adequate ❐ Not adequate	
48. Remove incompetent staff or help them achieve satisfactory functioning.	❐ Adequate ❐ Not adequate	
49. Provide a quality learning environment.	❐ Adequate ❐ Not adequate	
50. Provide quality facilities.	❐ Adequate ❐ Not adequate	

Summary

I t is important to realize that no one strategy is going to make a difference to your schools: Only the integration of the standards and the strategies over time will bring progress. This is illustrated as follows:

Summary Figure 1   Six Standards and 50 Strategies

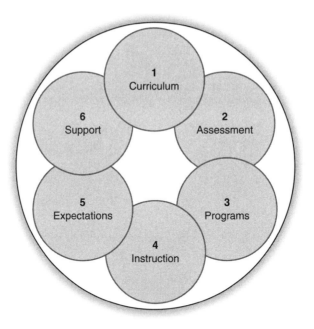

We encourage you to assess your system, whether as a district or a school, on the ideas presented in this book. You can conduct a gap analysis as to where you are and where you could be regarding the 50 strategies. Directly following this page is a comprehensive list of all six standards and their components.

We believe it is surely time for all schools to be high-performing institutions, no matter whose measures are used. Once this occurs, we can extend our curriculum further to include even more meaningful learnings so that students will not only function but also thrive in the twenty-first century.

Curriculum Management Systems, Inc.'s Six Standards and 50 Essential Strategies of High-Performing Schools
Standard One   **Establish a Well-Crafted, Focused, Valid, and Clear Curriculum to Direct Teaching**
1. **Embed External Assessment Target Objectives in the Written Content Standards and Link Them to State Standards.** There is a written set of district curriculum content standards that embed all external assessments administered to students and that are linked to state standards/expectations for every grade/instructional level and course offered.
2. **Have Clear and Precise District Curriculum Objectives—Content, Context, and Cognitive Type.** The district curriculum objectives, aligned to external assessment objectives, provide clearly specified content (skills, knowledge, concepts, processes, attitudes, etc.) to be learned; the context in which the learning must be demonstrated, including the test format; the appropriate cognitive type to be mastered; and the standard of performance—that is, the degree of mastery required.
3. **Deeply Align Objectives From External Assessments.** Objectives based on external assessments are placed (embedded) in the curriculum in a deeply aligned manner (content, context, and cognitive type).
4. **Sequence Objectives for Mastery Well Before They Are Tested.** Objectives are placed in the sequence of learning at least 6 months to 1 year before the student must first demonstrate mastery on the external test.
5. **Provide a Feasible Number of Objectives to Be Taught.** There are a feasible number of objectives to be learned so that students can master them. A time range for each is noted. District time allocations for all subject areas/courses are in place from which to compare feasibility.
6. **Identify Specific Objectives as Benchmark Standards.** Some of the objectives have been identified as district benchmark standards to be used as feedback for learning progress, program value, curriculum redesign, promotion, and so on.
7. **Place Objectives in a Teaching Sequence.** The objectives are developed in a teaching sequence rather than in the order of state standard/framework strands and are presented to teachers in the same manner.
8. **Provide Access to Written Curriculum Documents and Direct the Objectives to Be Taught.** The school-based administrators and teachers have in their possession current curriculum and instructional documents (e.g., scope and sequence charts, courses of study, guides) for all curricular areas. Policy directs teachers to teach to the objectives and administrators to monitor their implementation.
9. **Conduct Staff Development in Curriculum and Its Delivery.** School-based staff members receive quality training in the curriculum scope and sequence and in the use of curriculum documents.

(Continued)

(Continued)

Standard Two
Provide Assessments Aligned With the Curriculum
10. **Develop Aligned District Pre–Post Criterion-Referenced Assessments.** For each objective, there are criterion-referenced assessment items aligned by content, context, and type of cognition. From these items the district has secure, district-level, pre–post assessments aligned with each district objective and external assessments. Practice assessments are also available. All assessment items for each objective are equivalent/parallel. These tests will be given to students at the appropriate instructional level.
11. **Have a Pool of Unsecured Test Items by Objective.** The district staff provide multiple, equivalent (unsecured) criterion-referenced assessments for each objective. These are provided to teachers for use in diagnosing prerequisite skills acquisition and mastery of objectives.
12. **Establish Secured Performance Benchmark Assessments.** The district staff provide secured performance benchmark tests that assess some of the objectives for each grade level/course. These are administered as pre–post tests at the beginning of and near the end of the school year or at the end of each grading period.
13. **Conduct Assessment Training.** The district staff provide adequate training in classroom use of aligned assessments for directing classroom teaching.
14. **Use Assessments Diagnostically.** Teachers use the assessments to gain diagnostic data regarding student learning of the objectives (prerequisite skills acquisition and mastery), for program assessment, and to direct instruction.
15. **Teach Students to Be "Test Wise."** Teachers teach students test-taking skills that are aligned with the type of high-stakes tests being administered at the national, state, and district levels.
16. **Establish a Reasonable Testing Schedule and Environment.** The district staff and school staff provide a reasonable schedule of testing as well as a proper physical setting for all assessment situations.
17. **Disaggregate Assessment Data.** District assessments, as well as external assessments, are disaggregated by student, teacher, course/class/grade level, gender, race, socioeconomic level, and primary language and are used in making program and classroom decisions.
18. **Maintain Student Progress Reports.** Teachers maintain individual student progress reports by district objectives; students and parents are knowledgeable about the student's progress on such objectives.

Standard Three
Align Program and Instructional Resources With the Curriculum and Provide Student Equality and Equity

19. **Align Programs With the Curriculum to Ensure Congruity.** All formal and informal programs are investigated for their alignment with the district curriculum objectives, and modifications are made to ensure close alignment.

20. **Use Research and Data That Document Results to Drive Program Selection, and Validate the Implementation of Programs With Action Research.** Programs selected for use are research and data driven. Furthermore, the school staff members collect their own action research on the programs selected.

21. **Evaluate Programs to Determine Their Effectiveness in Strengthening Student Achievement of Curriculum Objectives.** Programs are evaluated to determine their effectiveness in facilitating student achievement on the curricular objectives.

22. **Align Textbooks and Instructional Resources With the District Curriculum Objectives and Assessments in Both Content and Context Dimensions.** The district staff have a process to ensure that textbooks and instructional resources are aligned with district objectives and assessments as well as other external assessments. Analysis includes deep alignment both at the content and context levels.

23. **Use Technology in Design or Selection Procedures to Ensure Strong Connections to System Learning Expectations and Feedback.** Technology software is designed or selected on the basis of strong alignment with the content, context, and cognitive type of the district objectives and assessments and its potential to enhance the quality of instruction and learning.

24. **Provide Training in the Use of Instructional Resources and Their Alignment With System Curriculum Objectives—Content, Context, and Cognitive Type.** Staff members have been provided quality training on the use of instructional resources in alignment with district objectives, with a focus on the content, context, and cognitive type of the objectives (or external assessments).

25. **Select or Modify Instructional Resources for Lessons to Ensure Full Alignment With System Objectives and Tested Learning.** Teachers select or modify instructional resources for lessons to ensure 100% alignment with the content and context of the district objectives and assessments including external assessments.

26. **Place Students in Programs and Activities in an Equitable Manner and With Equal Access to the Curriculum.** Students are placed in programs/activities in an equitable matter with equal access to the curriculum.

27. **Implement Effective Programs and Strategies With English Language Learners.** Effective programs and strategies for working with students whose primary language is not English are in place to focus on vocabulary development and reading comprehension approaches.

(Continued)

(Continued)

Standard Four
Use a Mastery Learning Approach and Effective Teaching Strategies
28. **Implement a Mastery Learning Model.** School-based administrators and all instructional staff have been trained in the mastery learning model and use it.
29. **Align Teaching With the Curriculum.** Teachers and other instructional staff align their teaching with the content and cognitive type and in the context specified by the district curriculum objectives and/or other external assessments, especially if the district objectives do not have this type of precision.
30. **Provide Differentiated Curriculum and Instruction as Well as Differentiated Time to Learn.** Teachers and other instructional staff modify their instruction to provide objectives at the right level of difficulty for each student based on ongoing diagnostic assessment, provide differentiated instruction based on student learning needs, and teach prerequisite knowledge as needed. Teachers and other instructional staff provide differentiated time for students to master the objectives, recognizing that students learn at different rates.
31. **Provide Practice to Master the Curriculum.** Teachers and other instructional staff teach to individual student mastery of the objectives, providing ample practice opportunities over time for both short- and long-term mastery.
32. **Use Effective Instructional Practices.** Teachers have high engagement rates for all students and use a variety of effective instructional practices, such as smooth, efficient classroom routines; clear and focused instruction; brisk instructional pace and smooth transitions between activities; effective questioning techniques; feedback and reinforcement regarding their learning progress; practices that promote student success in classroom interaction; comparing, contrasting, and classifying; using analogies and metaphors; using nonlinguistic representations; providing for active engagement of students; high but realistic expectations for student learning and their own instructional practices, and so on.
33. **Use Powerful Vocabulary Development Strategies.** Teachers and other instructional staff purposefully incorporate powerful vocabulary development strategies throughout their teaching.
34. **Establish Individual Learning Plans for Low-Achieving Students.** Individual learning plans are developed for students who test data indicate are underachieving. Low-quartile students and/or "bubble" students are provided intensive assistance to remediate deficiencies.

Standard Five
Establish Curriculum Expectations, Monitoring, and Accountability
35. **Provide for High Expectations for Achievement for Each Student.** The superintendent, senior officers, school-based administrators, and instructional staff articulate strong expectations for high achievement for each student.
36. **Monitor the Curriculum.** Monitoring by district-level officials, including the principal's supervisor, takes place regularly to determine the progress of the curriculum; school-based administrators work collaboratively with teachers in self-reflection.
37. **Visit Classrooms and Provide Follow-up.** Principals and/or other school-based administrators visit each classroom at least twice a week to monitor curriculum design and delivery alignment.
38. **Use Disaggregated Data in the Decision-Making Process.** The principal monitors teacher use of all test data and has disaggregated data appropriate for teacher use in decision making.
39. **Focus Staff Appraisal on Professional Growth.** The staff appraisal/evaluation process focuses on the professional growth of staff in the accomplishment of high student achievement.

(Continued)

(Continued)

Standard Six
Institute Effective District and School Planning, Staff Development, and Resource Allocation, and Provide a Quality Learning Environment
40. **Develop a District Planning Process That Is Strategic in Nature and Provides Guidance for the Development of District and School Long-Range Plans.** Planning efforts within the system provide the strategic vision for where the district is headed; utilize available data projections for the future; incorporate long-term budget implications; and inform the development of district, department, and unit plans.
41. **Create and Implement a Singular, Focused, Multiyear District Plan That Incorporates Change Strategies for Higher Student Achievement.** Planning is built into one comprehensive district improvement plan that consolidates all planning efforts. The plan focuses on two or three academic goals for multiyear periods of time. The plan incorporates effective change strategies, including professional development endeavors.
42. **Align School Plans With the District Plan.** The school plan is aligned to a focused, districtwide plan for increased student achievement, taking into account local contextual requirements.
43. **Implement Aligned Teacher Training to Reach District and School Goals.** Teachers receive and participate in ongoing training as part of reaching the goals in the district and school improvement plans.
44. **Implement Administrative Training Aligned With the Curriculum and Its Assessment and District Plan Priorities.** Principals and other school-based administrators receive and participate in ongoing training directly related to curriculum design and delivery, curriculum monitoring, student and curriculum assessment, and district and school improvement plan implementation.
45. **Provide Differentiated Staff Development.** Staff development is differentiated for staff and built around Curriculum Management System, Inc.'s staff development criteria.
46. **Link Resource Allocations to Goals, Objectives, Priorities, and Diagnosed Needs of the System.** The district and school budgets are built after the planning and illustrate how monies have been distributed to focus on the changes/goals of the district and school plans.
47. **Provide Qualified and Adequate Personnel.** There are qualified and adequate school personnel in each position.
48. **Remove Incompetent Staff or Help Them Achieve Satisfactory Functioning.** Marginal staff are coached to satisfactory performance or contracts are not renewed.
49. **Provide a Quality Learning Environment.** There is a safe and productive learning environment for all students.
50. **Provide Quality Facilities.** Facilities are adequate and promote creative and innovative approaches to learning.

References

Academic language. (2007). Retrieved October 2, 2007, from http://www.jeffzwiers.com/acalang.html

Administration for Children and Families. (2007). *The program manager's guide to evaluation.* Washington, DC: U.S. Department of Health and Human Services. Retrieved September 5, 2007, from http://www.acf.hhs.gov/programs/opre/other_resrch/pm_eval/reports/pmguide/Pmguide_toc.html

Airasian, P. (1997). *Classroom assessment* (3rd ed.). New York: McGraw-Hill.

Airasian, P. (2000). *Assessment in the classroom: A concise approach* (2nd ed.). New York: McGraw-Hill.

Alexandrowicz, V. (2000). Cultural diversity and community relations. In W. Cunningham & P. Cordeiro (Eds.), *Educational administration: A problem-based approach* (pp. 110–112). Boston: Allyn & Bacon.

Anderson, L. (1983). Policy implications of research on school time. *The School Administrator, 40*(11), 25–28.

Andrews, R., & Soder, R. (1987). Principals' instructional leadership and school achievement. *Instructional Leadership, 44,* 9–11.

Andrews, R., Soder, R., & Jacoby, D. (1986, April). *Principals' roles, other in-school variables, and academic achievement by ethnicity and SES.* Paper presented at the annual meeting of the American Educational Research Association, San Francisco.

Archer, A. (2003). *Vocabulary development.* Retrieved September 30, 2007, from http://www.fcoe.net/ela/pdf/Anita%20Archer031.pdf

Archer, J. (2007, March 7). U.S. chamber adds business viewpoint on schools' quality. *Education Week, 26*(26), 1, 15.

Armstrong, D. G. (2003). *Curriculum today.* Upper Saddle River, NJ: Merrill/Prentice Hall.

Armstrong, D. G., Henson, K. T., & Savage, T. V. (2005). *Teaching today: An introduction to education.* Upper Saddle River, NJ: Pearson Merrill/Prentice Hall.

Baddeley, A. (1997). *Human memory: Theory and practice.* London: Psychology Press.

Bafile, C. (2006). *Different strokes for little folks: Carol Tomlinson on "differentiated instruction."* Retrieved July 14, 2007, from http://www.education-world.com/a_issues/chat/chat107.shtml

Baker, K. (1998). Structured English immersion: Breakthrough in teaching limited-English-proficient students. *Phi Delta Kappan, 80,* 199–204.

Baker, S., Simmons, D., & Kameenui, E. (2007*). Vocabulary acquisition: Synthesis of the research.* Retrieved September 4, 2007, from http://idea.uoregon.edu/~ncite/documents/techrep/tech13.html

Bamburg, J. (1994). *Raising expectations to improve student learning.* Oak Brook, IL: North Central Regional Educational Laboratory.

Beck, I. L., McKeown, M. G., & Kucan, L. (2002). *Bringing words to life: Robust vocabulary instruction.* New York: Guilford Press.

Benard, B. (1993). Fostering resiliency in kids. *Educational Leadership, 51*(3), 44–48.

Benard, B. (1995). Fostering resiliency in urban schools. In B. Williams (Ed.), *Closing the achievement gap: A vision to guide change in beliefs and practice*. Oak Brook, IL: Research for Better Schools and North Central Regional Educational Laboratory.

Berl, P. (2005, September–October). Mature teachers matter. *Early Childhood Leaders' Magazine, 165,* 10–13.

Berliner, D. C. (1986). In pursuit of the expert pedagogue. *Educational Researcher, 15*(7), 5–13.

Berliner, D. C. (2007a). *Telling the stories of educational psychology*. Retrieved August 20, 2007, from http://courses.ed.asu.edu/berliner/readings/stories.htm

Berliner, D. C. (2007b). *What's all the fuss about instructional time?* Retrieved July 20, 2007, from http://courses.ed.asu.edu/berliner/readings/fuss/fuss.htm

Biemiller, A. (2001, Spring). Teaching vocabulary. *American Educator*. Retrieved September 6, 2007, from http://www.aft.org/pubs-reports/american_educator/spring2001/vocab.html

Billig, S. H., Jaime, I. I., Abrams, A., Fitzpatrick, M., & Kendrick, E. (2005). *Closing the achievement gap: Lessons from successful schools*. Jessup, MD: Educational Publications. (ERIC Document Reproduction Service No. ED491863)

Bishop, J. (1989, November). Motivating students to study—Expectations, rewards, achievement. *NASSP Bulletin,* 27–38.

Blanchard, J., & Gorin, J. (2004). *Building instructional leadership in a standards-based world: Research*. Retrieved September 10, 2007, from http://www.evansnewton.com/research/research.html

Blank, R. K., Porter, A., & Smithson, J. (2001, July). *New tools for analyzing teaching, curriculum, and standards in mathematics and science: Results from survey of Enacted Curriculum Project* (Final Report). Washington, DC: Council of Chief State School Officers. Retrieved September 15, 2007, from http://seconline.wceruw.org/Reference/sectools05.pdf

Blasé, J. (1987). Dimensions of effective school leadership: The teacher's perspective. *American Educational Research Journal, 24,* 589–510.

Blasé, J., & Blasé, J. (1998). *Handbook of instructional leadership*. Thousand Oaks, CA: Corwin Press.

Blaug, M. (1970). *An introduction to the economics of education*. London: Allen Lane.

Block, J. H., & Burns, R. B. (1976). *Mastery learning*. In L. S. Shulman (Ed.), *Review of research in education* (Vol. 4, pp. 3–49). Itasca, IL: Peacock.

Bloom, B. S. (1968). Learning for mastery. *Evaluation Comment, 1*(2), 1–12.

Bloom, B. S. (1974). An introduction to mastery learning theory. In J. H. Block (Ed.), *Schools, society and mastery learning* (pp. 3–14). New York: Holt, Rinehart and Winston.

Bloom, B. S. (1999). The search for methods of instruction. In A. C. Ornstein & L. S. Behar-Horenstein (Eds.), *Contemporary issues in curriculum*. Needham Heights, MA: Allyn & Bacon.

Bloom, B. S., Englehart, M. D., Furst, E. J., Hill, W. H., & Krathwohl, D. R. (Eds.). (1956). *Taxonomy of educational objectives: The classification of educational goals. Handbook I: Cognitive domain*. New York: David McKay.

Boris, G. (2007a). *Reading comprehension for high stakes testing: Participant's manual and trainer's kit*. Johnston, IA: Curriculum Management Systems, Inc.

Boris, G. (2007b). *Vocabulary for high stakes testing: Participant's manual and trainer's kit*. Johnston, IA: Curriculum Management Systems, Inc.

Bottery, M. (2004). *The challenges of educational leadership: Values in a globalized age*. London: Paul Chapman.

Bower, M. (1966). *The will to manage: Corporate success through programmed management*. New York: McGraw-Hill.

Bowles, S., & Gintis, H. (1976). *Schooling in capitalist America: Education reform and the contradictions of economic life*. New York: Basic Books.

Brantlinger, E. (2003). *Dividing classes: How the middle class negotiates and rationalizes school advantage*. New York: Routledge Falmer.

Brooks, J. S. (2006). *The dark side of school reform: Teaching in the space between reality and utopia*. Lanham, MD: Rowan and Littlefield.

Brophy, J. (1987, October). Synthesis of research on strategies for motivating students to learn. *Educational Leadership,* 40–48.

Budiansky, S. (2001). The trouble with textbooks. *Prism*. Retrieved September 7, 2007, from http://www.project2061.org/publications/articles/articles/asee.htm

Building Educational Success Together. (2006). *Model policies in support of high performance school buildings for all children*. Washington, DC: 21st Century Fund.

Burns, R. B. (1986). Accumulating the accumulated evidence on mastery learning. *Outcomes, 5*(2), 4–10.

Bushnell, M. (2003, May). Teachers in the schoolhouse panopticon: Complicity and resistance. *Education and Urban Society, 35,* 251–272.

Butler, J. A. (1992). *Staff development* (School Improvement Research Series, Northwest Regional Educational Laboratory). Retrieved October 31, 2007, from http://www.nwel.org/scpd/sirs/6cu12.html

Carpenter, D., Ramirez, A., & Severn, L. (2006, November). Gap or gaps: Challenging the singular definition of the achievement gap. *Education and Urban Society, 39,* 113–127.

Carroll, J. B. (1963). A model of school learning. *Teachers College Record, 64,* 723–733.

Carroll, L. (1965). *Alice's adventures in Wonderland* and *Through the looking glass.* New York: Airmont. (Original work published 1865)

Cavanagh, S. (2007). State tests, NAEP often a mismatch. *Education Week, 26*(41), 1, 23.

Cepeda, N. J., Pashler, H., Vul, E., Wixted, J. T., & Rohrer, D. (2006). Distributed practice in verbal recall tasks: A review and quantitative synthesis. *Psychological Bulletin, 132,* 354–380.

Chaika, G. (2005). Technology in the schools: It does make a difference. *Education World.* Retrieved September 12, 2007, from http://www.educationworld.com/a_admin/admin/admin122.shtml

Chaney, B. (1995). *Student outcomes and the professional preparation of 8th grade teachers.* Rockville, MD: Westat.

Cheng, Y. (1994). Classroom environment and student affective performance: An effective profile. *Journal of Experimental Education, 62,* 221.

Chester, M., & Beaudin, B. (1996). Efficacy beliefs of newly hired teachers in urban schools. *American Educational Research Journal, 33,* 233–257.

Classroom Environment Assessment Scale. (2007). Retrieved October 26, 2007, from http://www.csusb.edu/coe/sl/documents/Classroomenvironmentassessmentscale.pdf

CMSi Level I audit training. (2007). Des Moines, IA: Curriculum Management Systems, Inc.

Cohen, S. A. (1987). Instructional alignment: Searching for the magic bullet. *Educational Researcher, 16*(8), 16–20.

Coles, B. (1992). Classroom behaviour settings for science: What can pre-service teachers achieve? *Research in Science Education, 22,* 81–90.

Comprehensive School Reform Program Office. (2002). *Scientifically based research and the Comprehensive School Reform (CSR) Program.* Washington, DC: Office of Elementary and Secondary Education, U.S. Department of Education.

Cook, L. (1996). What is a "regular" English classroom? Language and cultural diversity in today's schools. *The English Journal, 85*(8), 49–51.

Cooper, T. L. (2007). Planning, organizing and managing your learning environment. Retrieved August 30, 2007, from http://teachersnetwork.org/ntny/nychelp/Professional_Development/yourenvir.htm

Corcoran, T., & Goertz, M. (1995). Instructional capacity and high performance schools. *Educational Researcher, 24*(9), 27–31.

Cotton, K. (1989a, November). *Educational time factors* (School Improvement Research Series, Close Up No. 8). Retrieved August 30, 2007, from http://www.nwrel.org/scpd/sirs/4/cu8.html-http://www.nwrel.org/scpd/sirs/4/cu8.html

Cotton, K. (1989b, November). *Expectations and student outcomes* (School Improvement Research Series, Close Up No. 7). Retrieved August 31, 2007, from http://www.nwrel.org/scpd/sirs/4/cu7.htmlhttp://www.nwrel.org/scpd/sirs/4/cu7.htm

Cotton, K. (2001). *Schoolwide and classroom discipline* (School Improvement Research Series, Close-Up No. 9). Retrieved August 30, 2007, from http://www.nwrel.org/scpd/sirs/5/cu9.html-http://www.nwrel.org/scpd/sirs/5/cu9.html

Council of Chief State School Officers. (2000). *Using data on enacted curriculum in mathematics and science: Sample results from a study of classroom practices and subject content.* Retrieved September 8, 2007, from http://www.ccsso.org/pdfs/finalsummaryreport.pdf

Csikszentmihalyi, M. (1997). *Finding flow: The psychology of engagement with everyday life*. New York: Basic Books.

Cuban, L. (2004). *The blackboard and the bottom line: Why schools can't be businesses*. Cambridge, MA: Harvard University Press.

Curriculum Management Systems, Inc. (2007). *Curriculum management audits*. Des Moines, IA: Author.

Darling-Hammond, L. (2000). Reforming teacher preparation and licensing: Debating the evidence. *Teachers College Record, 102*, 28–56.

Darling-Hammond, L. (2002). Research and rhetoric on teacher certification: A response to "Teacher Certification Reconsidered." *Education Policy Analysis Archives, 10*(36). Retrieved October 21, 2007, from http://epaa.asu.edu/epaa/v10n36.html

Darling-Hammond, L. (2006). Securing the right to learn: Policy and practice for powerful teaching and learning. *Educational Researcher, 35*(7), 13–24.

Davis, D., & Sorrell, J. (1995, December). *Mastery learning in public schools*. Retrieved June 23, 2007, from http://chiron.valdosta.edu/whuitt/files/mastlear.html

Dawson, T., & Billingsley, K. (2000). *Unsatisfactory performance: How California K–12 educational system predicts mediocrity and how teacher quality can be improved*. San Francisco: Pacific Research Institute for Public Policy.

De Corte, E. (1999). On the road to transfer. *International Journal of Educational Research, 31*, 555–559.

Dee, T. (2004). Teachers, race and student achievement in a randomized experiment. *Review of Economics and Statistics, 86*, 195–210.

Deming, W. E. (1986). *Out of crisis*. Cambridge, MA: Massachusetts Institute of Technology, Center for Advanced Educational Services.

Denham, C., & Lieberman, A. (1980). *Time to learn*. Washington, DC: National Institute of Education.

Dewey, J. (1964). Progressive education and the science of education. In R. D. Archambault (Ed.), *John Dewey on education: Selected writings* (pp. 169–181). New York: The Modern Library.

Dexter, R. (2005). Classroom walk-through with principal perceptions on implementation. *National Forum of Educational Administration and Supervision Journal, 22*(3), 24–39.

Dickson, P. (2006). *Aligning lessons*. Des Moines, IA: Curriculum Management Systems, Inc.

Dickson, P., & McArdle-Kulas, O. (2006a). *A mastery learning approach with powerful teaching strategies: Participant's manual and trainer's kit*. Johnston, IA: Curriculum Management Systems, Inc.

Dickson, P., & McArdle-Kulas, O. (2006b). *Strategic lesson planning: Aligning lessons to high stakes standards: Participant's manual and trainer's kit*. Johnston, IA: Curriculum Management Systems, Inc.

Differentiated instruction. (2007). Retrieved July 14, 2007, from http://differentiatedinstruction.com/

Distributed practice. (2007). Retrieved August 1, 2007, from http://web.ics.purdue.edu/~rallrich/learn/dist.html

Distributed practice: The research base. (2007). Retrieved August 1, 2007, from http://www.answers.com/topic/distributed-practice?cat=health_

Downey, C. J. (2001). Are your expectations clear regarding an instructional model. *Thrust for Educational Leadership, 31*, 12–20.

Downey, C. J. (2005). *School view: Gathering trend data on curricular and instructional classroom practices. Participant's manual and trainer's kit*. Johnston, IA: Curriculum Management Systems, Inc.

Downey, C. J. (2008). Classroom walk-throughs with reflective inquiry. In L. Easton (Ed.), *Powerful learning designs* (2nd ed.) Oxford, OH: National Staff Development Council.

Downey, C., & English, F. (2004). *Examining student work for standards alignment and real world test formats: Connecting resources to the curriculum*. Des Moines, IA: Curriculum Management Systems, Inc.

Downey, C. J., & English. F. W. (2005a). *Examining student work for standards alignment and real world/test formats: Connecting resources to the curriculum. Principal–teacher series for higher student achievement: Participant's manual and trainer's kit*. Johnston, IA: Curriculum Management Systems, Inc.

Downey, C. J., & English, F. W. (2005b). *Raising student test scores: A baker's dozen. Principal–teacher series for higher student achievement: Participant's manual and trainer's kit*. Huxley, IA: Curriculum Management Systems, Inc.

Downey, C. J., English, F. W., Poston, W. K., & Steffy, B. E. (2007). *Maximizing student achievement: Curriculum and assessment. Participant's manual* (6th ed.). Johnston, IA: Curriculum Management Systems, Inc.

Downey, C. J., English, F. W., Poston, W. K., & Steffy, B. E. (2008). *Maximizing student achievement: Systems factors. Participant's manual* (6th ed.). Johnston, IA: Curriculum Management Systems, Inc.

Downey, C. J., & Frase, L. E. (1999). *Conducting walk-throughs with reflective inquiry to maximize student achievement: Initial training materials.* Johnson, IA: Curriculum Management Systems, Inc.

Downey, C. J., & Frase, L. E. (2003a). *Conducting walk-throughs with reflective inquiry to maximize student achievement: Advanced seminar. Participant's manual and trainer's kit* (3rd ed.). Johnston, IA: Curriculum Management Systems, Inc.

Downey, C. J., & Frase, L. E. (2003b). *Conducting walk-throughs with reflective inquiry to maximize student achievement: Basic seminar. Participant's manual and trainer's kit* (3rd ed.). Johnston, IA: Curriculum Management Systems, Inc.

Downey, C. J., & Jacob, J. (2006). *Mentoring the reflective principal: Collaborative approaches to student achievement: Participant's manual and trainer's kit.* Johnston, IA: Curriculum Management Systems, Inc.

Downey, C. J., Steffy, B. E., & English F. W. (2006). *Taking the mystery out of high stakes tests: Examining tests and textbooks/resources. Participant's manual and trainer's kit.* Johnston, IA: Curriculum Management Systems, Inc.

Downey, C. J., Steffy, B. E., English, F. W., Frase, L. E., & Poston, W. K. (2004). *The three-minute classroom walk-through: Changing school supervisory practice one teacher at a time.* Thousand Oaks, CA: Corwin Press.

Downey, C. J., Steffy, B. E., English, F. W., Frase, L. E., & Poston, W. K. (2006). *The three-minute classroom walk-through: A multi-media kit for professional development.* Thousand Oaks, CA: Corwin Press.

DuFour, R. (2002). The learning-centered principal. *Educational Leadership, 59*(8), 12–15.

DuFour, R. (2004). What is a professional learning community? *Educational Leadership, 61*(8), 6–11.

DuFour, R., & Eaker, R. (1998). *Professional learning communities at work: Best practices for enhancing student achievement.* Bloomington, IN: National Educational Service.

Dwyer, K., Osher, D., & Warger, C. (1998). *Early warning, timely response.* Retrieved October 2007 from http://www.unl.edu/srs/pdfs/earlysigns.pdf

Eberts, R. W., & Stone, J. A. (1984). *Unions and public schools.* Lexington, MA: D.C. Heath.

Edmonds, R. (1986). Characteristics of effective schools. In U. Neisser (Ed.), *The school achievement of minority children: New perspectives* (pp. 93–104). Hillsdale, NJ: Lawrence Erlbaum.

Ehrenberg, R., Goldhaber, D., & Brewer, D. (1994). Do teacher's race, gender, and ethnicity matter? Evidence from the National Education Longitudinal Study of 1988. *Industrial and Labor Relations Review, 48,* 547–561.

Elizabeth, J. (2003, February 2). A question of quality: Examining the roots of uneven instruction quality in our schools. *Pittsburgh Post-Gazette.* Retrieved September 2007 from http://www.post-gazette.com/localnews/20030202overviewregxpl.asp

Ellis, E. (2002). *The clarifying routine: Elaborating vocabulary instruction.* Retrieved September 4, 2007, from http://www.ldonline.org/article/5759

Emery, K., & Ohanian, S. (2004). *Why is corporate America bashing our public schools?* Portsmouth, NH: Heinemann.

Emmer, E., Evertson, C., & Worsham, M. (2000). *Classroom management for secondary teachers* (5th ed.). Needham Heights, MA: Allyn & Bacon.

Enderle, J. (2004). Improving school restroom facilities. *School Planning and Management, 45*(3), 24–31.

English, F. W. (1978). *Quality control in curriculum development.* Arlington, VA: American Association of School Administrators.

English, F. (1987). *Curriculum management for schools, colleges, and businesses.* Springfield, IL: Charles C Thomas.

English, F. W. (1988). *Curriculum auditing.* Lancaster, PA: Technomic.

English, F. W. (1993). *Deciding what to teach and test.* Newbury Park, CA: Sage.

English, F. (2007). *A curriculum management audit of the Baltimore County Public School District.* Bloomington, IN: Phi Delta Kappa International.

English, F. W., & Larson, R. L. (1996). *Curriculum management for educational and social service organizations.* Springfield, IL: Charles C Thomas.

English, F. W., & Poston, W. K., Jr. (Eds.). (1999). *GAAP: Generally accepted audit principles for curriculum management.* Johnston, IA: Curriculum Management Systems, Inc.

English, F. W., & Steffy, B. E. (2000). *Deep curriculum alignment.* Lanham, MD: Scarecrow Press.

English, F. W., & Steffy, B. E. (2001). *Deep curriculum alignment: Creating a level playing field for all children on high-stakes tests of educational accountability.* Lanham, MD: Rowman & Littlefield.

Evertson, C., Emmer, E., & Worsham, M. (2000). *Classroom management for elementary teachers* (5th ed.). Needham Heights, MA: Allyn & Bacon.

Evertson, C., & Harris, A. (2007). *What we know about managing classrooms.* Retrieved August 30, 2007, from http://mailer.fsu.edu/~slynn/evertsonharris1995.html

Farmer, C. (2002). *Creating a culture of high expectations: Voices from the field.* Retrieved September 5, 2007, from http::/www.alliance.brown.edu/pubs/voices/1qtr2002/high expect.shtml

Feldman, K. (2006, June). *Developing content literacy in mixed ability secondary classrooms: Grades 4–12.* Paper presented at the Sopris West Oregon Coast Summer Institute, Keystone, CO.

Feldman, K., & Kinsella, K. (2007). *Narrowing the language gap: Strategies for vocabulary development.* Retrieved September 6, 2007, from http://www.fcoe.net/ela/pdf/Narrowing%20Vocab%20Gap%20KK%20KF%201.pdf

Ferguson, R. (1991). Paying for public education: New evidence on how and why money matters. *Harvard Journal on Legislation, 28,* 465–498.

Fiestritzer, E., & Haar, C. (2005). *Profile of teachers in the U.S. 2005.* Washington, DC: National Center for Education Information.

Frase, L. (1998, April). *An examination of the relationships among principal classroom visits, teacher flow experiences, efficacy, and student cognitive engagement in two inner city school districts.* Paper presented at the annual meeting of the American Educational Research Association, San Diego, CA. (Eric Document Reproduction Service No. ED 421 599.)

Frase, L. (2000). *Curriculum audit: School District of Philadelphia.* Des Moines, IA: Curriculum Management Systems, Inc.

Frase, L. (2001, April). *A confirming study of the predictive power of principal classroom visits on efficacy and teacher flow experiences.* Paper presented at the annual meeting of the American Educational Research Association, Seattle, WA.

Frase, L. E. (2005). Refocusing the purposes of teacher supervision. In F. English (Ed.), *The Sage handbook of educational leadership* (pp. 430–462). Thousand Oaks, CA: Sage.

Frase, L., & Hetzel, R. (1990). *School management by walking around.* Lanham, MD: Scarecrow Press.

Frase, L., & Streshly, W. (2000). *The top ten myths in educations: Fantasies Americans love to believe.* Lanham, MD: Scarecrow Press.

Freedman, B. (2001). Walking the talk of teacher supervision. *Ontario Principal's Council Register, 3*(2).

Friedman, M. (1962). *Capitalism and freedom.* Chicago: University of Chicago Press.

Fullan, M. (2001). *The new meaning of educational change.* New York: Teachers College Press.

Fuller, B., & Rasiah, A. (2005). Schooling citizens for evolving democracies. In S. Fuhrman & M. Lazerson (Eds.), *The public schools* (pp. 81–106). Oxford, England: Oxford University Press.

Furth, H. (1981). *Piaget and knowledge.* Chicago: University of Chicago Press.

Garmston, R. (2000). Why cats have clean paws. *Journal of Staff Development, 21*(3), 63–64.

Gentile, J. R., & Lalley, J. (2003). *Standards and mastery learning: Aligning teaching and assessment so all children can learn.* Thousand Oaks, CA: Corwin Press.

Gewertz, C. (2007). States mull best way to assess their students for graduation. *Education Week, 26*(37), 1, 17.

Ginsberg, M. B., & Murphy, D. (2002). How walkthroughs open doors. *Educational Leadership, 59*(8), 34–36.

Gitomer, D. H., Latham, A. S., & Ziomeck, R. (1999). *The academic quality of prospective teachers: The impact of admissions and licensure testing.* Princeton, NJ: Educational Testing Service.

Glickman, C. (1991). Pretending not to know what we know. *Educational Leadership, 48,* 4–10.

Glickman, C. (2002). *Leadership for learning: How to help teachers succeed.* Alexandria, VA: Association for Supervision and Curriculum Development.

Goldhaber, D., & Anthony, E. (2004). *Can teacher quality be effectively assessed?* Seattle: University of Washington, Center for Reinventing Public Education.

Goldman, P., Resnick, L., Bill, V., Johnston, J., Micheaux, D., & Seitz, A. (2004). *Learning walk sourcebook.* Pittsburgh, PA: Learning Research and Development Center.

Grayson, C. J., Jr. (2007). Benchmarking: What it is, how it works, and why educators desperately need it. *Education Week, 26*(21), 33, 44.

Greene, G. (2007). Getting real: A different perspective on the relationship between school resources and student outcomes. *Journal of Education Finance, 33,* 49–68.

Guskey, T. R. (1997). *Implementing mastery learning.* Belmont, CA: Wadsworth.

Guskey, T. R., & Gates, D. (1986). Synthesis of research on the effects of mastery learning to elementary and secondary classrooms. *Educational Leadership, 45*(8), 73–80.

Guskey, T. R., & Pigott, T. D. (1988). Research on group-based mastery learning programs: A meta-analysis. *Journal of Educational Research, 81,* 197–216.

Hall, G. E., & Loucks, S. (1978). Teacher concerns as a basis for facilitating and personalizing staff development. *Teachers College Record, 80,* 36–53.

Hall, T. (2002). *Differentiated instruction.* Wakefield, MA: National Center on Accessing the General Curriculum. Retrieved July 14, 2007, from http://www.cast.org/publications/ncac/ncac_diffinstruc.html

Hallinger, P., & Heck, R. (1995). Reassessing the principal's role in school effectiveness. *Educational Administration Quarterly, 32,* 5–44.

Hammonds, J. (2007). *The environment as a learning resource.* Retrieved October 26, 2007, from http://www.leading-learning.co.nz/quality-learning/environment-resource.html

Hattie, J. A. (1992). Measuring the effects of schooling. *Australian Journal of Education, 36,* 5–13.

Haycock, K. (2005, June). *Improving academic achievement and closing gaps between groups in middle schools.* Presentation given at CASE Middle Level Summit, Washington, DC.

Heck, R. (1992). Principals' instructional leadership and school performance: Implications for policy development. *Educational Evaluation and Policy Analysis, 14,* 21–34.

Heck, R., Larsen, T., & Marcoulides, G. (1990, April). *Principal leadership and school achievement: Validation of a casual model.* Paper presented at the annual meeting of the American Educational Research Association, Boston.

Henderson, N., & Milstein, M. M. (1996). *Resiliency in schools: Making it happen for students and educators.* Thousand Oaks, CA: Corwin Press.

Henderson-Sparks, J. (1995). Managing your marginal teachers. *Principal, 74*(4), 32–35.

Hill, P., & Crévola, C. (1999). *The role of standards in educational reform for the 21st century.* Alexandria, VA: Association for Supervision and Curriculum Development.

Hillard III, A. (1991). Do we have the will to educate all children? *Educational Leadership, 49,* 31–36.

Houston, P. D. (2006). The superintendent: Championing the deepest purposes of education. In P. Kelleher & R. VanDer Bogert (Eds.), *Voices for democracy: Struggles and celebrations of transformational leaders* (pp. 1–9). Malden, MA: Blackwell.

How to differentiate your instruction. (2007). Retrieved July 14, 2007, from http://www.teach-nology.com/tutorials/teaching/differentiate/planning/

Hoy, W., & Miskel, C. (2005). *Educational administration: Theory, research and practice* (7th ed.). New York: McGraw-Hill.

Hummel-Rossi, B., & Ashdown, J. (2002). The state of cost–benefit and cost-effectiveness analyses in education. *Review of Educational Research, 72,* 1–30.

Hunter, M. (1982). *Mastery teaching.* El Segundo, CA: TIP Publications.

Individual learning plans. (2007). Retrieved August 1, 2007, from http://www.studywiz.com/cgi bin/WebObjects/StudywizDEVSTUDYWIZPortal.woa/1/wa/page?pid=206

Jencks, C. (1972). *Inequality.* New York: Basic Books.

Jencks, C., & Phillips, M. (Eds.). (1998). *The Black–White test score gap.* Washington, DC: Brookings Institution Press.

Jennings, J., & Rentner, D. S. (2006). Ten big effects of the No Child Left Behind Act on public schools. *Phi Delta Kappan, 88,* 110–113.

Johnson, R. S. (2002). *Using data to close the achievement gap: How to measure equity in our schools.* Thousand Oaks, CA: Corwin Press.

Joint Committee on Testing Practices. (2004). *Code of fair teaching practices in education.* Washington, DC: Author.

Joyce, B. R., & Showers, B. (1995). *Student achievement through staff development: Fundamentals of school renewal* (2nd ed.). White Plains, NY: Longman.

Joyce, B., Weil, M., & Showers, B. (1992). *Models of teaching.* Boston: Allyn & Bacon.

Kaptain, H. (2005, June). *Effective ELL strategies and approaches.* Presentation made at the 6th annual Advanced Curriculum Auditing Conference, Big Sky, MT.

Kaptain, H. (2006). *Effective instructional delivery practices in the ESL/ELL classroom.* Johnston, IA: Curriculum Management Systems, Inc.

Katz, M. B. (1973). *Class, bureaucracy & schools.* New York: Praeger.

Kaufman, R. (1988). *Planning educational systems.* Lancaster, PA: Technomic.

Kaufman, R., & Herman, J. (1991). *Strategic planning in education.* Lancaster, PA: Technomic.

Kaufman, R., Herman, J., & Watters, K. (1996). *Educational planning: Strategic, tactical, operational.* Lancaster, PA: Technomic.

Kendall, J. S., & Marzano, R. J. (1995). *The systematic identification and articulation of content standards and benchmarks: Update.* Aurora, CO: Mid-Continent Regional Educational Laboratory.

Kennedy, M. (2006a). Seat work. *American School & University, 78*(6), 24–26.

Kennedy, M. (2006b). Smart spending. *American School & University, 79*(2), 16–23.

Kid Source On Line. (2007). Retrieved September 5, 2007, from http://www.Kidsourcr/content4/ student.expectations.html

Kleberg, J. (1992). *Quality learning environments.* Columbus: The Ohio State University Press.

Kowalski, T. J. (2003). *Contemporary school administration* (2nd ed.). Boston: Allyn & Bacon.

Kowalski, T. (2006). *The school superintendent: Theory, practice, and cases* (2nd ed.). Thousand Oaks, CA: Sage.

Kowalski, T. J., Lasley, T. J., II, & Mahoney, J. W. (2008). *Data-driven decisions and school leadership: Best practices for school improvement.* Upper Saddle River, NJ: Pearson Education.

Krovetz, M. L. (1999). *Fostering resiliency: Expecting all students to use their minds and hearts.* Thousand Oaks, CA: Corwin Press.

Kulik, C. C., Kulik, J. A., & Bangert-Drowns, R. L. (1990). Effectiveness of mastery learning programs: A meta-analysis. *Review of Educational Research, 60,* 265–299.

Kulm, G., Roseman, J., & Treistman, M. (1999). A benchmarks-based approach to textbook evaluation. *Science Books & Films, 35,* 147–153.

Labaree, D. F. (1988). *The making of an American high school: The credentials market and the Central High School of Philadelphia, 1838–1939.* New Haven, CT: Yale University Press.

Learning 24/7. (2002). *Classroom walk-through with reflective practice.* Phoenix, AZ: Author.

Learning 24/7. (2005, April). *Classroom observation study.* Paper presented at the National Conference on Standards and Assessment, Las Vegas, NV.

Lee, C. (2003, February 4). A question of quality: Do schools hire the best teachers? Probably not. *Pittsburgh Post-Gazette.* Retrieved October 2007 from http://www.post-gazette.comlocal news/20030204hiringrp2.asp-29K

Lehr, F., Osborn, J., & Heibert, E. (2007). *A focus on vocabulary.* Honolulu, HI: Pacific Resources for Education and Learning. Retrieved September 6, 2007, from http://www.prel.org/products/ re_/ES0419.htm

Leithwood, K., & Jantzi, D. (1997). Explaining variations in teachers' perception of principal's leadership: A replication. *Journal of Educational Administration, 35,* 312–331.

Lemke, C., & Coughlin, E. (1998). *Technology in American schools: Seven dimensions for gauging progress.* Santa Monica, CA: Milken Family Foundation.

Little, J. W. (2003). Looking at student work for teacher learning, teacher community, and school reform. *Phi Delta Kappan, 85,* 184–192.

Liu, E. (2003, April). *New teachers' experiences of hiring: Preliminary findings from a four-state study.* Paper presented at the annual conference of the American Educational Research Association, Chicago.

LoGerfo, L. (2006). Climb every mountain: Teachers who think they should make a difference . . . do! *Education Next, 6*(3), 68–75.

Louis, K., & Miles, M. (1991). Managing reform: Lessons from urban high schools. *School Effectiveness and School Management, 2,* 75–96.

Lucas, S. R. (1999). *Tracking inequality: Stratification and mobility in American high schools.* New York: Teachers College Press.

Mann, D., Shakeshaft, C., Becker, J., & Kottkamp, R. (1999). *Achievement gains from a statewide comprehensive instructional technology program: What impact does technology have on learning?* Charleston: West Virginia Department of Education. Retrieved September 13, 2007, from http://www.mff.org/pubs/ME155.pdf

Marino, J. (2006). *The power of alignment: Quality in education.* Retrieved September 17, 2007, from http://www4.asq.org/blogs/edu/2006/08/the_power_of_alignment.html

Marks, G., Cresswell, J., & Ainley, J. (2006). Exploring socioeconomic inequalities in student achievement: The role of the home and school factors. *Educational Research and Evaluation, 12,* 105–128.

Marshall, C., & Oliva, M. (2006). *Leadership for social justice: Making revolutions in education.* Boston: Pearson.

Marshall, K. (2003). Recovering from HSPS (Hyperactive Superficial Principal Syndrome): A progress report. *Phi Delta Kappan, 84,* 701–709.

Marshall, R., & Tucker, M. (1992). *Thinking for a living: Education and the wealth of nations.* New York: Basic Books.

Marzano, R. J. (1998). *A theory-based meta-analysis of research on instruction.* Aurora, CO: Mid-Continent Research for Education and Learning.

Marzano, R. J. (2003). *What works in schools: Translating research into action.* Alexandria, VA: Association for Supervision and Curriculum Development.

Marzano, R. J., Gaddy, B., & Dean, C. (2000). *What works in classroom instruction.* Aurora, CO: Mid-Continent Research for Education and Learning.

Marzano, R. J., & Kendall, J. S. (1998). *Awash in a sea of standards.* Aurora, CO: Mid-Continent Research for Education and Learning.

Marzano, R. J., Pickering, D. J., & Pollock, J. E. (2001). *Classroom instruction that works.* Alexandria, VA: Association for Supervision and Curriculum Development.

Marzano, R., Waters, J., & McNulty, B. (2005). *School leadership that works: From research to results.* Alexandra, VA: Association for Supervision and Curriculum Development.

McKeon, M., & Berry, L. (2007). Hear and now. *American School & University, 79,* 304–306.

McKinley, J. (2007*). Leveling the playing field and raising African American students' achievement in twenty-nine urban classrooms.* Retrieved September 20, 2007, from http://www.newhorizons .org/strategies/differentiated/mckinley.htm

McNamara, C. (2002). *Field guide to nonprofit program design, marketing, and evaluation.* Minneapolis, MN: Authenticity Consulting, Inc.

McNeil, M. (2007). Tighter link sought between spending, achievement in New York. *Education Week, 27*(2), 1.

Meier, D. (1995). *The power of their ideas: Lessons for America from a small school in Harlem.* Boston: Beacon Press.

Mezirow, J., & Associates (2000). *Learning as transformation: Critical perspectives on a theory of progress.* San Francisco: Jossey-Bass.

Miller, J., McKenna, M., & McKenna, B. (1998). A comparison of alternatively and traditionally prepared teachers. *Journal of Teacher Education, 49,* 165–176.

Miller, R. (2001). *Greater expectations to improve student achievement: Panel report.* Retrieved November 2007 from http://www.greaterexpectations.org/briefing_papers/ImproveStudentLearning

Mintzberg, H. (1994). *The rise and fall of strategic planning.* New York: Free Press.

Mitchell, F. M. (1998). *The effects of curriculum alignment on the mathematics achievement of third-grade students as measured by the Iowa Test of Basic Skills: Implications for educational administrators.* Unpublished doctoral dissertation, Clark University, Atlanta, GA.

Mitchell, J., & Poston, W. (1992). The equity audit in school reform: Three case studies of educational disparity and incongruity. *International Journal of Educational Reform, 1,* 242–247.

Monahan, T. (2005). *Globalization, technological change, and public education.* New York: Routledge.

Monk, D. (1994). Subject area preparation of secondary mathematics and science teachers and student achievement. *Economics of Education Review, 12,* 125–145.

Muther, C. (1990). Selecting and evaluating textbooks. In W. Poston, M. P. Stone, & C. Muther, *Making schools work: Practical management of support services.* Newbury Park, CA: Corwin Press.

National Academy of Sciences & National Academy of Engineering. (1995). *Reinventing schools: The technology is now!* Retrieved September 13, 2007, from http://www.ncrel.org/sdrs/areas/issues/methods/technlgy/te4refer.htm

National Association of Secondary School Principals. (1996). *Breaking ranks: Changing an American institution.* Reston, VA: Author.

National Association of Secondary School Principals. (2004). *Breaking ranks II: Strategies for leading high school reform.* Reston, VA: Author.

National Coalition for Equity in Education. (2007). *Discussion areas for equity.* Retrieved September 30, 2007, from http://ncee.education.ucsb.edu/discussion areas.htm

National Commission on Excellence in Education. (1983). *A nation at risk.* Washington, DC: U.S. Government Printing Office.

National Education Association. (2007). *Technology and education.* Retrieved September 11, 2007, from http://www.nea.org/technology/index.html

National Staff Development Council. (2001). *Standards for staff development.* Retrieved November 5, 2007, from http://www.nsdc.org

Neukrug, E. S., & Fawcett, R. C. (2006). *Essentials of testing and assessment.* Canada: Thomson Brooks/Cole.

Newmann, F. M., Smith, B. A., Allensworth, E., & Bryk, A. S. (2001). Instructional program coherence: What it is and why it should guide school improvement policy? *Educational Evaluation and Policy Analysis, 23,* 297–321.

Nichols, B., Shidaker, S., Johnson, G., & Singer, K. (2006). *Managing curriculum and assessment: A practitioner's guide.* Worthington, OH: Linworth Books.

Northwest Regional Education Laboratory. (2007). *Research you can use to improve results.* Retrieved August 29, 2007, from http://www.nwrel.org/scpd/re-engineering/rycu/ToC.asp#3

Olsen, L., & Jaramillo, A. (1999). *Turning the tides of exclusion: A guide for educators and advocates for immigrant students.* Oakland: California Tomorrow.

Olson, A. (2007). Growth measures for systematic change. *School Administrator, 64*(1), 10.

Ortiz, A. A. (1997). Learning disabilities occurring concomitantly with linguistic differences. *Journal of Learning Disabilities, 30,* 321–332.

Owings, W., & Magliaro, C. (1998). Grade retention: A history of failure. *Educational Leadership, 56,* 86–88.

Parenti, M. (1978). *Power and the powerless.* New York: St. Martin's Press.

Pascarella, E. (1985). College environmental influences on learning and cognitive development: A critical review and synthesis. In J. Smart (Ed.), *Higher education: Research* (Vol. 1, pp. 1–61). New York: Agathon Press and the American Educational Research Association.

Perna, D. M., & Davis, J. R. (2007). *Aligning standards & curriculum for classroom success.* Thousand Oaks, CA: Corwin Press.

Peters, T. J., & Waterman, R. H., Jr. (1982). *In search for excellence.* New York: Warner Books.

Peterson, K. D. (2000). *Teacher evaluation: A comprehensive guide to new directions and practices.* Thousand Oaks, CA: Corwin Press.

Pomeranz, M. (1992, November). *Gaining economic confidence: Earning greater support for public universities.* Unpublished speech presented to a meeting of the faculty, Iowa State University.

Pophan, J. W. (1995). *Classroom assessment: What teachers need to know.* Boston: Allyn & Bacon.

Poston, W. (1991a). *A curriculum management audit of Cumberland County, North Carolina.* Arlington, VA: American Association of School Administrators.

Poston, W. (1991b). The equity audit in school reform: Building a theory for institutional research. *International Journal of Educational Reform, 1,* 235–241.

Poston, W., Mitchell, J., Sweeney, J., Rice, R., & Willis, K. (1991). *Equity audit and demographic assessment*. Ames: Iowa State University, Department of Professional Studies.

Poston, W., Stone, P., & Muther, C. (1992). *Making schools work: Practical management of support services*. Newbury Park, CA: Corwin Press.

Price-Baugh, R. (1997). Correlation of textbook alignment with student achievement scores (Doctoral dissertation, Baylor University, 1997). *Dissertation Abstracts International, 58* (05A), 1529.

Raffini, J. (1993). *Winners without losers: Structures and strategies for increasing student motivation to learn*. Needham Heights, MA: Allyn & Bacon.

Ramirez, J. D., & Baker, K. (1987). *Becoming a more frequent speaker of a second language*. Paper presented at the annual meeting of the American Educational Research Association, Washington, DC.

Ream, R. K. (2003). Counterfeit social capital and Mexican-American underachievement. *Educational Evaluation and Policy Analysis, 25,* 237–262.

Reiman, A., & Thies-Sprinthall, L. (1998). *Mentoring and supervision for teacher development*. New York: Longman.

Resnick, L. (2007). *Principles of learning*. Retrieved September 2, 2007, from http://ifl.lrdc.pitt.edu/ifl/index.php?section=pol

Richardson, J. (2001, October–November). Seeing through new eyes: Walk-throughs offer new way to view schools. *Tools for Schools,* 1–7.

Rivkin, S., & Hanushek, E. (2003). How to improve the supply of high quality teachers. In D. Ravitch (Ed.), *Brookings Papers on Education Policy 2004*. Washington, DC: Brookings Institution Press. Retrieved October 21, 2007, from http://www.brookings.edu/dybdocroot/press/books/abstracts/BPEP/200401.pdf

Rockoff, J., (2004). The impact of individual teachers on student achievement: Evidence from panel data. *American Economic Review, 94,* 247–252.

Sagor, R. (1992). Three principals who make a difference. *Educational Leadership, 49*(5), 13–18.

Sanders, J., (1994). *The Program Evaluation Standards: How to assess evaluations of educational programs*. Newbury Park, CA: Sage.

Schmoker, M. (2006). *Results now*. Alexandria, VA: Association for Supervision and Curriculum Development.

Schneider, M. (2002). *Do school facilities affect academic outcomes?* Washington, DC: National Clearing House for Educational Facilities.

Secretary's Commission on Achieving Necessary Skills. (1991). *What work requires of schools: A SCANS report for America 2000*. Washington, DC: U.S. Department of Labor.

Shannon, G. S., & Bylsma, P. (2007). *Nine characteristics of high performing schools*. Olympia, WA: Office of Superintendent of Public Instruction. Retrieved July 23, 2007, from http://www.k12.wa.us/research/pubdocs/NineCharacteristics.pdf

Sleeter, C. E. (2005). How White teachers construct race. In C. McCarthy, W. Crichlow, G. Dimitriadis, & N. Dolby (Eds.), *Race, identity, and representation in education* (pp. 243–256). New York: Routledge.

Smith, C. (1997). *Vocabulary instruction and reading comprehension* (ERIC Digest D412506). Retrieved June 23, 2007, from http://www.ericdigests.org/1998–1/vocabulary.htm

Smith, R. M. (1982). *Learning how to learn: Applied theory for adults*. Chicago: Follett.

Snipes, J., Doolittle, F., & Herlihy, C. (2002). *Foundations for success: Case studies of how urban school systems improve student achievement*. Washington, DC: Council of the Great City Schools.

Staples, S. (1991). A study of tenured teacher dismissals in Virginia, 1987–1990 (Doctoral dissertation, Virginia Polytechnic Institute and State University, 1991). *Dissertation Abstracts International, 52,* 49.

Starr, L. (2004). *Differentiated instruction*. Retrieved July 14, 2007, from http://www.education-world.com/a_curr/strategy/strategy042.shtml

Steffy, B. (1989). *Career stages of classroom teachers*. Lancaster, PA: Technomic.

Steffy, B., & Wolfe, M. (1997). *The life cycle of the career teacher: Maintaining excellence for a lifetime*. West Lafayette, IN: Kappa Delta Pi.

Steffy, B., Wolfe, M., Pasch, S., & Enz, B. (2000). *Life cycle of the career teacher*. Thousand Oaks, CA: Corwin Press.

Steiner, G. (1979). *Strategic planning: What every manager must know*. New York: Free Press.

Sternberg, R. J., Torff, B., & Grigorenko, E. L. (1998). Teaching triarchically improves student achievement. *Journal of Educational Psychology, 90*, 374–384.

Stiggins, R. J. (1994). *Student-centered classroom assessment*. Upper Saddle River, New Jersey: Prentice Hall.

Strategies for differentiating. (2007). Retrieved July 14, 2007, from http://members.shaw.ca/priscil latheroux/differentiatingstrategies.html

Stripling, R. (2007). *A curriculum management audit of the Wake County Public School System*. Bloomington, IN: Phi Delta Kappa International.

Sweetwater Union High School District. (2003). *Planning for learning: The SUHSD Lesson*. Sweetwater, CA: Author.

Teddlie, C., Kirby, P., & Stringfield, S. (1989). Effective versus ineffective schools: Observable differences in the classroom. *American Journal of Education, 97*, 221–236.

Texas Center for Educational Research. (2000). *The cost of teacher turnover*. Austin: Texas State Board for Teacher Certification.

Texas Education Association. (2002). *Promoting vocabulary development: Components of effective vocabulary instruction* (online revised edition). Retrieved May 9, 2005, from http://www.tea.state.tx .us/reading/products/redbk5.pdf

Thorndike, E. L. (1924). Mental discipline in high school studies. *Journal of Educational Psychology, 15*, 83–98.

Tomlinson, C. (1999). *The differentiated classroom: Responding to the needs of all learners*. Alexandria, VA: Association for Supervision and Curriculum Development.

Tomlinson, C. (2007). *Differentiation of instruction in the elementary grades*. Retrieved July 14, 2007, from http://www.ericdigests.org/2001–2/elementary.html

Trinity Church of England School. (1996). *What counts as technology?* Retrieved September 13, 2007, from http://atschool.eduweb.co.uk/trinity/watistec.html

Tucker, P. (1997). Lake Wobegon: Where all teachers are competent (or, have we come to terms with the problem of incompetent teachers?). *Journal of Personnel Evaluation in Education, 11*, 103–126.

Tyack, D. B. (1974). *The one best system: A history of American urban education*. Cambridge, MA: Harvard University Press.

Valentine, J., Clark, D., Nickerson, N., & Keefe, J. (1981). *The middle school principal*. Reston, VA: National Association of Secondary School Principals.

Vygotsky, L. (1986). *Thought and language*. Cambridge, MA: MIT Press. (Original work published 1962)

Ward, R., & Burke, M. (2004). *Improving achievement in low-performing schools: Key results for school leaders*. Newbury Park, CA: Corwin Press.

Washington Educational Research Association. (2001). *Ethical standards in testing: Test preparation and administration*. University Place, WA: Author.

Wayne, A. J., & Youngs, P. (2003). Teacher characteristics and student achievement gains: A review. *Review of Educational Research, 3*, 89–122.

Webb, N. L. (1997, January). *Determining alignment of expectations and assessments in mathematics and science education* (NIKSE Brief, Vol. 1, No. 2). Madison: University of Wisconsin, National Institute for Science Education.

Willingham, D. T. (2002). *Allocating student study time: "Massed" versus "distributed" practice*. Retrieved August 1, 2007, from http://www.aft.org/pubs-reports/american_educator/sum mer2002/askcognitivescientist.html

Wimpelberg, R., Teddlie, C., & Stringfield, S. (1989). Sensitivity to context: The past and future of effective schools research. *Educational Administration Quarterly, 25*(1), 82–107.

Wise, A., Darling-Hammond, L., & Berry, B. (1987). *Effective teacher selection: From recruitment to selection*. Santa Monica, CA: RAND Corporation.

Wise, A., Darling-Hammond, L., McLaughlin, M., & Bernstein, H. (1984). *Teacher evaluation: A study of effective practices*. Santa Monica, CA: RAND Corporation.

Wishnick, K. T. (1989). Relative effects on achievement scores of SES, gender, teacher effect and instructional alignment: A study of alignment's power in mastery learning (Doctoral dissertation, University of San Francisco, 1989). *Dissertation Abstracts International, 51* (04A), 1107.

Wollack, J. (2001). Review of Key Math revised: A diagnostic inventory of essential mathematics. In B. S. Plake & J. C. Impara (Eds.), *The fourteenth mental measurements yearbook* (pp. 640–641). Lincoln, NE: Buros Institute of Mental Measurement.

Woolfolk, A. E. (1987). *Educational psychology.* Englewood Cliffs, NJ: Prentice Hall.

Wuersten, L. (2005). *Science: Learning community capacity building lesson alignment tool.* Seattle, WA: State Department of Public Instruction.

Ybarra, S., & Hollingsworth, J. (2004). *Explicit Direct Instruction (EDI) implementation rubric.* Fowler, CA: DataWorks Educational Research.

Yeh, S. S. (2006). Can rapid assessment moderate the consequences of high-stakes testing? *Education and Urban Society, 39,* 91–112.

Young, M. (1996). English (as a second) language arts teachers: The key to mainstreamed ESL student success. *The English Journal, 85*(8), 17–24.

Zemelman, S., Daniels, H., & Hyde, A. (1998). *Best practice: New standards for teaching and learning in America's schools.* Portsmouth, NH: Heinemann.

Index

CORWIN PRESS

The Corwin Press logo—a raven striding across an open book—represents the union of courage and learning. Corwin Press is committed to improving education for all learners by publishing books and other professional development resources for those serving the field of PreK–12 education. By providing practical, hands-on materials, Corwin Press continues to carry out the promise of its motto: **"Helping Educators Do Their Work Better."**